Macroeconomics

Michael Bradley

University of Maryland, Baltimore County

Scott, Foresman and Company

Glenview, Illinois
Dallas, Tex.   Oakland, N.J.   Palo Alto, Cal.
Tucker, Ga.   London, England

To my family,
with love and thanks

Library of Congress Cataloging in Publication Data

Bradley, Michael, 1939-
    Economics.

        Includes index.
        CONTENTS: [v. 1.] Microeconomics.—
[v. 2.] Macroeconomics.
        1. Economics. I. Title.
[HB171.5.B6946 1980b]   330   79-22967
ISBN 0-673-15335-5 (v. 1.) pbk.
ISBN 0-673-15336-3 (v. 2.) pbk.

12345678910-KPF-85848382818079

Preface

In the preface to the first edition of his *Principles of Political Economy* in 1848, John Stuart Mill wrote, "The appearance of a treatise like the present, on a subject on which so many works of merit already exist, may be thought to require some explanation." There are far more "works of merit" on economic principles available today than there were in 1848. Why, then, produce yet another?

Macroeconomics offers a much-needed alternative to the other principles texts currently on the market. It fills a gap between the massive encyclopedic texts that attempt to include every conceivable institutional detail and the shorter books that skimp on explanations and applications. The book also fills a widening gap between the increasingly simplified principles texts and the increasingly sophisticated and rigorous texts at the intermediate level.

Macroeconomics isn't a particularly easy subject to learn, but it isn't made any easier by oversimplifications or shallow explanations. *Macroeconomics* reflects my own experience in teaching principles courses and my basic optimism concerning students' motivation to learn and instructors' motivation to teach. Nothing is made unnecessarily difficult, but I haven't shied away from the fact that some important concepts are difficult and that solutions to complex problems aren't to be found in simplistic bromides. All topics are presented clearly, in terms that can be easily understood by undergraduate students and with maximum use of real-world illustrations and applications.

Controversy is a vital part of modern economics which cannot and should not be ignored. *Macroeconomics* examines several areas of current economic debate, giving fair treatment to opposing arguments and alternative solutions to problems. I have been careful throughout the book to distinguish between positive and normative questions, pointing out the limitations as well as the strengths of economic analysis in resolving issues that are partly positive and partly normative.

Organization

Macroeconomics is intended to serve as the text in a one-semester or one-quarter introductory course at the university level. The book attempts to take the principles student as close as is reasonably possible to the frontiers of modern macroeconomic thinking. Since some of that thinking can be difficult, chapters have been designed to give instructors maximum flexibility both in what they teach and in the order in which they teach it. Wherever possible, more rigorous material has been consolidated into a few specific chapters and appendices, which instructors may skip if they wish without undermining subsequent analysis.

The introductory chapters on demand, supply, markets, and equilibrium serve as a basic microeconomic foundation for subsequent chapters on the aggregate economy. The macroeconomic analysis begins by presenting a simple aggregate demand–aggregate supply model which illustrates the role of these key variables in determining aggregate output, employment, and the price level. The basic Keynesian income determination model and the chapters on money show aggregate demand in an economy with a constant price level. This sets the stage for a comprehensive treatment of contemporary unemployment and inflation, utilizing a more modern and realistic approach to aggregate demand and aggregate supply. An analysis of policy strategies to deal with unemployment and inflation through demand management and supply management policies concludes the basic macro portion of the text.

The chapters on international economics stress basic principles of trade and exchange and apply those principles to a number of current trade policy issues. The final section of the text, on economic growth and development, provides students with a sense of the kinds of important economic choices that must be made in coming years.

Special Features

Macroeconomics contains a number of special features to make it more useful to students and instructors.

Previews at the beginning of each chapter and each part provide an overview of the material that will be covered and show how it fits into the overall structure of the text. These previews give students a sense of continuity as they study.

Definitions and key points are set off from the text and highlighted. This calls students' attention to important concepts and makes subsequent review of the material much easier.

Applications are used frequently to reinforce the relevance of the analysis and enhance student interest by breaking up the analytical discussions. Two types of applications appear throughout the text. Relatively brief **Close-ups** demonstrate the real-world basis of many theoretical concepts. Longer **Applying the Tools** provide detailed applications of analytical techniques to important problems and issues of yesterday and today.

Questions and Problems at the end of every chapter require the student to apply the concepts that he or she has learned. Some of the questions are straightforward and analytical with clear-cut answers; others are more subtle "discussion" questions that point out not only the ways that analysis can be applied, but also some of its limitations. The problems at the end of nearly every chapter are designed to make students more comfortable with analytical tools and concepts by working with them.

Appendices are used to increase instructors' flexibility in teaching from *Macroeconomics*. A mathematical appendix to Chapter 1 concisely reviews virtually all of the mathematical concepts used in principles of economics courses. In addition to providing a review, it can help make students less anxious about the difficulty of the math required. Appendices at the end of other chapters treat special topics—the *IS-LM* model, for example—in more depth and more analytical detail than would be expected in most principles courses.

Supplementary materials serve as important aids to instructors and students. Accompanying *Macroeconomics* is an **Instructor's Manual** that provides helpful teaching tips and suggested answers to chapter questions and problems, as well as nearly a thousand test questions. For those who adopt the text, **Transparency Masters** of the most important figures and tables will also be available. For students, an excellent **Study Guide** by Bruce Allen of Michigan State University and Bruce Mann of the University of Puget Sound provides ample opportunity for further applying the analytical tools studied in *Macroeconomics*.

**Acknowl-
edgments**

In this book's seemingly endless gestation period, I have received a great deal of help from many colleagues and friends. I have deluged my colleagues in the economics department at UMBC with questions and manuscript pages for comments and suggestions. I would, of course, be remiss if I didn't also acknowledge the contributions of the several thousands of students who have taken principles of economics with me—their hard questions and unwillingness to accept inadequate explanations have contributed greatly to this work.

Like many authors, I consider criticism of my work a bad-tasting medicine that is good for me. My book has benefitted greatly by the comments of the following excellent (but tough) reviewers of the manuscript:

John Chizmar, Illinois State University
Ward S. Curran, Trinity College (Conn.)
Thomas Dalton, Northern Illinois University
Richard W. Douglas, Bowling Green State University
James Johannes, Michigan State University
Steven Klepper, SUNY, Buffalo
Prem Laumas, Northern Illinois University
Bruce Mann, University of Puget Sound
Jeffrey Miller, University of Delaware
W. Douglas Morgan, University of California, Santa Barbara
Richard Rosenberg, Pennsylvania State University
Michael Salemi, University of North Carolina
Richard T. Selden, University of Virginia
George Tauchen, Duke University
Barbara White, SUNY, Buffalo

My special thanks go to Professor Bruce T. Allen of Michigan State University, who remains my toughest critic and one of my closest friends. The people at Scott, Foresman have also been extremely helpful. I want to thank in particular Bruce Borland and George Lobell for signing the project and managing it to completion, and Dane Tyson, who is without peer as an editor. My appreciation goes as well to the many designers, artists, typesetters, and others who contributed so much to the book.

Finally, I must thank my wife, Ann, and my children, Sarah and Jim, for their support and understanding through an experience from which most families are spared.

Michael Bradley

Columbia, Maryland

Contents

Part Two

Understanding the Aggregate Economy 63

Part Three

Aggregate Demand: The Goods Market 99

Part Four

Aggregate Demand: The Money Market   189

Part Five

Inflation and Unemployment   271

Part Seven

The Economic Future

PART ONE
An Introduction to Economics

Throughout history, every individual and every society has been forced to choose among alternative uses of scarce resources, money, and time. In choosing to take this course, you were forced to give up the opportunity of taking a course in physics or French, or perhaps just sleeping an hour later in the morning. In buying this textbook, you were forced to give up the opportunity of treating yourself to a meal at a good restaurant or buying a new shirt. Understanding how and why such choices as these are made is what economics is all about.

In this first section, we'll look closely at how economics approaches the dual problem of scarcity and choice. The **production possibilities model**, introduced in Chapter 2, illustrates the problem graphically and suggests some ways in which it can be alleviated. The remainder of the section presents a general overview of how a market economy—an economy not unlike our own—uses free market forces to make key economic decisions.

1

The Art and Science
of Economics

Preview: In this first chapter, we'll take a general look at the subject matter and methods of economics. Since much of this text deals with economic theory, we'll focus particular attention on how economists go about building and testing their theories. We'll also explore some of the limitations of economic theory and the questions that even the best course in economics can't answer.

Most students in introductory college economics courses are being exposed to economics for the first time and don't know exactly what to expect—except that the subject must be very hard or else it would have been taught in high school. They may even have heard economics referred to as the *dismal science*—hardly a reassuring description.

In fact, economics is an exciting and vital subject. It deals with problems and issues that are critical to us as members of society. Perhaps more importantly, it deals with nearly every aspect of our individual daily lives—from buying a car to taking a vacation to getting married and having children. In fact, it could be argued without much exaggeration that there is *no* human activity which does not fall within the realm of economics.

Economics can, however, be an exasperating subject for students and professional economists alike. Dramatic economic events since the late 1960s have raised serious doubts about many things we economists thought we already understood. Economics has never been a field noted for consensus among its practitioners, but seldom has there been more economic controversy than there is today. Lay all the economists in the world end to end, goes one old saying, and they won't reach an agreement.

Perhaps the most valuable lesson of economics is that every course of action has a cost. If we spend more on income maintenance programs for the poor, we'll have to spend less on other public programs or raise taxes. If we follow the Proposition 13 approach of the late 1970s and cut taxes drastically, we may have to give up the public services our taxes paid for. If we want cleaner air, we may have to pay higher prices for some of the goods we consume and do without others altogether. The goal of economics isn't to find universal bliss, but to find the best way of allocating our scarce resources among alternative uses to achieve competing goals—to balance the costs borne by society with the benefits received.

A basic understanding of economics won't provide you with a set of "correct" answers to the unresolved questions and continuing controversies over economic problems and issues. It will, however, give you something much more valuable—the basic tools to approach problems logically and analytically. Many economic problems are so complex that recognizing the relevant questions (let alone finding answers) is difficult or impossible without a logical and analytical approach. We live in a constantly changing world, and even if we did have correct answers to all of today's economic problems, those answers might not be relevant to future problems. But the ability to deal with issues in a logical manner never becomes obsolete.

Theories, Models, and Facts

Much of what we study in economics involves the use of theories.

- **Economic theories** are logical explanations of cause-and-effect relationships among economic variables.

The goal of almost all economic theories is to explain what *has* happened and predict what *will* happen in an economy. Many students find theory the hardest part of economics to learn or accept. Economists themselves don't agree on the validity of all theories, and some even reject theorizing as an approach to understanding economic relationships and problems. Such disagreement isn't all bad: skepticism about the validity or relevance of established theories has been an important force for progress throughout the history of economic thought.

Economic theories present and analyze economic relationships in unrealistic abstract settings or *models*.

- A **model** is a simplified picture of the real world.

Economic models allow economists to present their theories in a way that is easy to see and understand. Frequently, the model itself is part of the economist's theory, and if we accept the model, we accept the theory. The lack of realism in many economic models is a necessary evil, because economic relationships may be impossible to identify or analyze in the very complicated real world. Many of the laws of the physical sciences are also stated for highly unrealistic conditions: the *law of falling bodies*, for example, is stated for a vacuum; this "vacuum model" of the real world is necessary in order to isolate the force of gravity on falling bodies from the effects of the atmosphere.

Building and Testing Economic Theories

The first step in constructing a theory is to isolate the things we're interested in from other things. If we want to analyze the effect of higher gasoline prices on the consumption of gasoline, for example, we'd have to eliminate all of the other variables that may affect gasoline consumption—population, tastes, income, housing patterns, etc. Since we can't isolate variables physically in a laboratory, we have to isolate them by making **assumptions**. To isolate the effect of changes in the price of gasoline from all of the other variables that affect sales and consumption of gasoline, we have to assume that all of those other variables remain unchanged. This particular assumption is made so frequently in economics that it even has a name.

- The **ceteris paribus** assumption states that all variables except those under investigation remain constant.

Human behavior is extremely complex, of course, so before we can make many predictions about the way households or firms will respond to economic variables, we also have to make some simplifying assumptions about the general pattern of economic behavior. Economics makes two very basic assumptions about behavior that are usually lumped together into one:

- Economics assumes that economic behavior is **rational** and aimed at **maximizing** something.

Rationality doesn't necessarily mean moral, ethical, or desirable behavior, nor does the assumption of rationality mean that people don't make mistakes.

- **Rationality** means that behavior is consistent with reaching a known goal or objective.

We don't have to assume that every single individual behaves rationally all of the time. This is an assumption of a *general* pattern of behavior, and it's more reasonable than the alternatives. **Irrational behavior** is deliberate behavior that is inconsistent with reaching a known goal, and **random behavior** is behavior that isn't directed at any goal or objective.

Economics assumes that the *goal* of rational economic behavior is to *maximize* something. We assume that households try to maximize their satisfaction or **utility.** In the theory of a private, market economy, firms are assumed to seek maximum **profits** (sales revenue minus costs of production). These simplified assumptions about behavior aren't always valid empirically, but they aren't unreasonable as simplified approximations of behavior. The crucial test of a theory isn't the empirical accuracy of its assumptions, but the ability to make general predictions that are generally supported by the evidence. Of course, in societies where these assumptions about economic behavior aren't reasonable approximations of actual motives, the predictions from the theory probably won't be supported by the facts, and theories based on other assumptions may well be needed.

In addition to these basic general assumptions, most models will contain a number of specific assumptions as well. It is important to realize how vital the assumptions of a model are, since we arrive at an economic theory by applying simple logic to the assumptions. For example, let us make the following assumptions about the shoppers at a local grocery:

1. The shoppers are *rational*.
2. The shoppers try to maximize their satisfaction from their weekly food budgets, and will buy a quantity of each good where the *last unit* bought is just worth its price.
3. Successive loaves of bread are worth less to the shoppers.
4. Everything else that might affect the amount of bread people will buy remains the same *(ceteris paribus)*.

Applying simple logic to these assumptions, we'd reach a conclusion that a reduction in the price of bread, other things equal, would cause shoppers to buy more bread per week. This *conclusion*—also called a *prediction*, a *hypothesis*, or a *theory*—follows logically from the assumptions.

Our next step is to test the predictions of our theory against the facts, or *empirical evidence*.

- **Empirical evidence** is factual data based on observation and experience and not on theory.

Empirical evidence provides the real acid test of any theory. If an empirical study showed that consumers generally bought less bread at low prices than at high prices, we'd have cause to reexamine the theory and the empirical methods used. If the logic and the empirical methods are sound, and the theory still continues to give us wrong predictions, we must reject it.

"Good in theory, wrong in practice" is one of the most commonly held views of economic theory, but it's not a valid criticism. If a theory fails to give predictions that are generally consistent with the empirical evidence, the theory is rejected—in spite of any logical or mathematical beauty and rigor it may possess. Theories that consistently give the wrong predictions are "wrong in practice," but they are not "good" theories.

To be valid, however, a theory doesn't have to give accurate predictions in every conceivable case—in fact, if it does, it's probably an *identity* (something that's always true, such as 2 = 2). A theory is a *generalization*, and there may be exceptions that don't invalidate it. For example, the general prediction that auto traffic will tend to move more slowly on dark rainy nights than on bright sunny days isn't invalidated if a normally safe and sane driver gets drunk at a party and is ticketed for driving 90 miles an hour during a midnight downpour.

Marginal Analysis

Much of the attention of economic theory focuses upon *marginal units*.

- A **marginal unit** is the change in one variable that results from a given change in another variable.

People make decisions involving marginal units all the time. Whether or not you will have one more beer (in addition to the previous six) at your local tavern, for example, is a marginal decision. In this case, you would have to decide whether the additional (marginal) enjoyment you would get out of drinking the beer outweighs the additional (marginal) costs of 75¢ and a more serious hangover tomorrow. Similarly, in deciding whether or not to hire additional police officers or fire fighters, a community must decide whether the marginal protection is worth the marginal cost.

Ex Ante and Ex Post

Economic analysis deals mainly with *ex ante* relationships. **Ex ante** simply means *intended* or *before the fact*. In analyzing demand, for example, we're interested in the *ex ante* quantities of a good that consumers are willing and able to buy at a given price. The actual measured quantities are called **ex post** (after the fact) quantities.

The distinction is important. *Ex post* data may yield important information from which theory can be forged, but that theory must focus upon *ex ante* relationships if it is to have much value. We want our analysis to make predictions and not merely to record what has happened in the past.

Why Bother with Theory at All?

It's very easy to become impatient with economic theorizing and to question the value of all of this mental effort as a means of understanding economic relationships and making economic predictions. There are some alternatives to theory but they are less satisfactory.

"Common Sense" and Logical Fallacies.   Common sense, or intuition, is a valuable gift. Many breakthroughs in economics and other fields began with an intuitive notion that something was wrong with accepted ideas. However, relying on one's common sense alone can lead to two rather common logical fallacies.

The *fallacy of composition* is perhaps the most common logical fallacy in common-sense economic arguments.

- The **fallacy of composition** asserts that something true of the part must be true of the whole.

In projecting our own common sense to broad economic relationships, we tend to generalize our own reactions and experience to the economy as a whole. For example, if I have more money to spend, this is good for me. Therefore, if everybody had more money to spend, everybody would be better off. The fallacy here is obvious. If I have more money, my increased spending won't have any effect on prices, but if everybody had more money, increased spending by all of us could raise prices enough that nobody would be better off. Something that's valid for an individual economically won't necessarily be valid for the economy as a whole. "What's good for General Motors" is not necessarily good for the country.

The *fallacy of division* isn't as common as the fallacy of composition, but it does appear from time to time.

- The **fallacy of division** asserts that something true of the whole must be true of the part.

For example, lower foreign trade barriers tend to be good for the economy as a whole in the sense that resources are used more efficiently and more goods are available at lower prices. It does not follow, however, that lower trade barriers must be good for every individual or industry—workers in industries that are forced to contract or shut down as a result of import competition, for example, will be worse off as a result of lower trade barriers.

"Let's Just Look at the Facts."   Since the facts are essential for testing the predictions of theories, why not just dispense with the theory altogether and look at the facts alone? The problem is that facts alone have no logical structure and offer no logical explanation of cause and effect—even if we use sophisticated statistical techniques to show that different facts are related. Looking at the facts alone leads to a common logical fallacy with an uncommon name—the *post hoc, ergo propter hoc,* or simply the *post hoc fallacy.*

- The **post hoc fallacy** argues that because one event follows another, there is a cause-and-effect relationship between the two events—"after this, therefore because of this."

If your neighbor's dog always barks at rush hour, you can't avoid rush hour by having your neighbor get rid of the dog. If the national unemployment rate generally rises after birth rates rise in Topeka, Kansas, a massive contraception drive in Topeka would be a questionable full-employment policy.

To identify cause and effect, and even to identify the relevant facts to look at, we have to have some form of logical theory—even if we don't recognize the theory as such. Facts are essential to knowledge, but facts alone don't tell us very much.

Prejudice and Scapegoats.   The third alternative to logical theorizing as an approach to economic problems is to blame those problems on persons or groups that we don't like or don't trust—blacks, whites, Republicans, Democrats, industrialists, labor unions, short people, or just about any group will do. If we don't like or trust more than one group, we can combine them into a conspiracy—Republicans and industrialists, Democrats and unions, Arabs and Russians, to name only a few of the infinite possibilities. This approach has a distinct advantage in that it requires virtually no mental effort, but there's generally no logical relationship between our prejudices and the roots of economic problems.

Positive and Normative Arguments

As we've seen in the preceding pages, economic analysis can be a powerful tool in understanding and dealing with a variety of complex issues. It does have some serious limitations, however. Many economists like to think of their field as a set of logical principles or arguments that are free of value judgments.

- A **positive argument** involves no value judgment and can be tested by logic or fact.

It's probably impossible for economics to be completely free of value judgments, however, because economics deals with too many issues that touch our basic social, philosophical, and ethical beliefs. Thus, nearly all controversies over economic issues and policies contain *normative* as well as positive arguments.

- A **normative argument** rests on some value judgment and thus cannot be tested by logic or facts.

Sometimes positive and normative arguments *sound* quite similar. The following, for example, is a positive statement that can be tested logically or empirically.

- Taxing high incomes at a higher rate than low incomes will redistribute income between high-income households and low-income households.

Here is a similar-sounding normative statement that *can't* be proven valid or invalid without a value judgment.

- Taxing high incomes at a higher rate than low incomes is unjust because it redistributes income between high-income households and low-income households.

One of the greatest lasting benefits of a basic understanding of economics is the ability to recognize and separate the positive aspects of economic issues and arguments from the normative aspects. Economic analysis alone can't answer normative questions, but to the extent that it *can* identify the costs and benefits, gains and losses, winners and losers, from alternative economic policies, economic theory allows us to make *informed* and *intelligent* value judgements in determining proper courses of action.

A Concluding Remark

If you like unsettled questions and controversy, you'll probably like economics. If you like simple and straightforward answers to difficult and complex problems, however, you may be disappointed. You may find that economic problems are more complex than they appear on the surface, that there is generally more than one way to deal with any given problem, and that any policy has some advantages and disadvantages compared with alternative policies. You may in the end even find yourself in agreement with the late American humorist Will Rogers, who once confessed publicly that he didn't know any more about economic problems than an economist, and ". . . Lord knows, he don't know anything."

Summary

1. **Economics** is a logical and analytical approach to economic problems and issues.
2. **Economic theory** is a set of logical explanations of cause-and-effect relationships between economic variables. These variables are typically identified analytically in an abstract, oversimplified setting or **model**. Theories are typically stated as conclusions or hypotheses that follow logically from assumptions.
3. Economic theory assumes that the general pattern of economic behavior is **rational** and **maximizing**.
4. The most important test of a theory is its ability to make predictions that are generally supported by the evidence.
5. Arguments that aren't based on theory or logical reasoning typically contain logical fallacies—the fallacies of composition and division and the post hoc fallacy are quite common.

Concepts for Review

positive argument	normative argument	theory
model	assumption	*ceteris paribus*
rational behavior	maximizing behavior	utility
empirical evidence	marginal analysis	ex ante
ex post	fallacy of composition	fallacy of division
post hoc fallacy		

Questions

1. Consider the following hypotheses:
   "Other things remaining the same, more baseball tickets will be sold at a lower price than at a higher price."
   "In a vacuum, all falling objects will fall at the same rate."
   a. Which hypothesis is stated under more realistic conditions?
   b. Why is it necessary to specify "other things equal" and "in a vacuum"?
   c. Which hypothesis would be easier to test?

2. How many times do you make the *ceteris paribus* assumption (whether you recognize it or not) in your everyday life?

3. Which of the following are examples of rational behavior? If not rational, what kind of behavior is it?
   a. Stanley Fern is 5'3" tall (in his elevator shoes), weighs 110 lbs., and wants to play center on a professional basketball team. Every day, Stanley goes to the gym to work on his hook shot and rebounding.
   b. George Sloth wants to spend his life doing nothing, so he seldom gets out of bed in the morning.
   c. Kathy Kinetic is serious and energetic. Every morning she rises at 6 A.M. and works hard all day flitting from one thing to another without finishing anything.
   d. Steve Slick wants to get from Cleveland to New York, and deliberately takes the westbound lanes on the Ohio Turnpike.
   e. Steve Slick still wants to get from Cleveland to New York, but gets lost in Newark, N.J.

4. Uncle Joe runs a candy store, and gives away a lot of candy to make children happy.
   a. Could Uncle Joe be considered rational?
   b. Does Uncle Joe's behavior invalidate the assumption that firms (sellers) generally seek to maximize their profits?

5. Suppose that you're given the following facts on the price and sales of women's slacks in 1946 and 1976.

Year	Price per pair	Pairs sold (millions)
1946	$10	10
1976	$35	30

   a. What do these facts *alone* tell you about the relationship between the price of women's slacks and the sales of women's slacks?
   b. Do you accept the relationship in part (a)? If you don't accept it, how do you explain it? What are you doing in rejecting (a)?

6. Sort out the positive and normative aspects of this argument, "Taxes on liquor are a good thing, because they discourage the consumption of demon rum."

7. Pick any economic issue or policy dispute from your daily paper or television news. What are the positive aspects and the normative aspects of the dispute?

A Brief Mathematical Review

Economics uses mathematics to state and test abstract propositions clearly and conveniently. There is no reason to be intimidated by this, since the mathematics used in the book does not go beyond the ninth or tenth grade level. This appendix will help you review the basic mathematical tools used in the book. For some students, this review may not be necessary. However, if your recollection of high-school mathematics is shaky, it would be worthwhile to review these concepts and tools. The appendix can also be used as a reference when unfamiliar mathematical techniques are used in the text.

Hypotheses, Functions, and Equations

Economic analysis consists of a number of hypotheses.

- A **hypothesis** states or predicts a relationship between variables.

Hypotheses can be expressed verbally, mathematically by function or equation, or geometrically by a graph.

Functions, equations, and graphs are not inherently more difficult to understand and interpret than verbal statements, and in most cases they make the analysis easier to follow than complicated verbal statements alone. Mathematics and graphs are a kind of shorthand to make explanations *easier*—not to make an easy explanation unnecessarily difficult.

Variables and Functions

Variables are the things we study—prices, output, consumption, cost, etc. Consider any two variables x and y. A relationship between x and y could be stated verbally as follows:

- The value of y depends on the value of x.

This simple statement tells us:

1. x and y are related;
2. x is the **independent variable** (the value of x determines the value of y); and
3. y is the **dependent variable** (the value of y is determined by the value of x).

Identifying dependent and independent variables is essential in trying to identify cause and effect.

The same relationship can be expressed by the **function**

$$y = f(x),$$

which is read as "y is a function of x," or simply "y depends on x." It says exactly the same thing as the verbal statement. When a larger number of variables is involved, shorthand functions are often more convenient than verbal statements. For example, the verbal statement "The value of y depends on the values of a, b, c, d, e, x, and z" can be expressed by the function

$$y = f(a, b, c, d, e, x, z).$$

Direct and Inverse Relationships

A simple function tells us that one variable depends on the other but does not tell us the nature of the relationship. The function $y = f(x)$, for example, does not indicate whether greater values of x will cause y to rise or fall.

- If variables are **directly related,** they will vary in the *same direction*. The larger x is, the larger y will be.

- If variables are **inversely related,** they vary in *opposite directions*. The larger x is, the smaller y will be.

Equations

One specific form of function is called an equation.

- An **equation** is a function that expresses a specific relationship between variables.

Equations can state fairly complicated relationships much more clearly than verbal statements alone. For example, consider this statement.

- The value of y is a when x is zero, and every change in x causes y to change in the same direction and by some proportion (b) of the change in x.

Exactly the same thing is said in the equation

$$y = a + bx.$$

Which is harder to understand and interpret?

Solving Equations

An equation can tell us the value of y for any given value of x, or the value of x that would determine a given or desired value of y. This involves *solving* the equation for the missing variable. There is a simple, but very important, rule to remember in solving equations:

- Anything can be done to an equation without changing it, as long as the same thing is done to both sides of the equation.

For example, if $x = y$, $x + 75 \neq y$ (the sign $\neq$ means *does not equal*), but $x + 75 = y + 75$.

Consider the equation

$$y = 20 + \tfrac{1}{2}x.$$

To solve for y when $x = 50$, substitute 50 for x, and perform the operations instructed by the equation.

$$y = 20 + \tfrac{1}{2}x = 20 + \tfrac{1}{2}(50) = 20 + 25 = 45.$$

In other words, given $x = 50$, the equation defines $y = 45$.

To find the value of x that will define a given value of y, the equation is solved for x with the given value of y. Suppose we want $y = 100$. To solve for x, substitute 100 for y in the equation.

$$y = 20 + \tfrac{1}{2}x$$
$$100 = 20 + \tfrac{1}{2}x, \text{ or}$$
$$20 + \tfrac{1}{2}x = 100.$$

Isolate the terms with x on one side of the equation by subtracting 20 from both sides, and

$$20 + \tfrac{1}{2}x - 20 = 100 - 20$$
$$\tfrac{1}{2}x = 80.$$

Multiplying both sides of this by 2,

$$x = 160.$$

To verify this, see if $y = 100$ when $x = 160$ in the equation $y = 20 + \tfrac{1}{2}x$.

Graphs

Graphs, like functions and equations, express relationships between variables. Like functions and equations, the purpose of graphs is to make the analysis *easier* than it would be without them.

Graphs of Equations

Table A–1 shows values of y determined by values of x from 0 to 100 at 10-unit intervals from the equation $y = 20 + \tfrac{1}{2}x$. In Figure A–1, values of x are represented by distances along the horizontal (x) axis, and values of y are represented by distances along the vertical (y) axis. Each of the pairs of x and y in the table is represented by a point in Figure A–1. Point A shows the value of y when $x = 0$ in the equation $y = 20 + \tfrac{1}{2}x$. It has an **x-coordinate** of 0 and a **y-coordinate** of 20. Point B has an x-coordinate of 10 and a y-coordi-

Table A–1   Paired Values of x and y

x	y
0	20
10	25
20	30
30	35
40	40
50	45
60	50
70	55
80	60
90	65
100	70

nate of 25. The other points in Figure A–1 represent other pairs of x and y from Table A–1.

Figure A–1 Graph of Table A–1

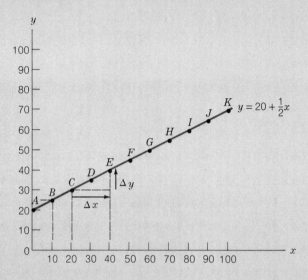

The straight line connecting the points in Figure A–1 show all possible pairs of x and y for the equation $y = 20 + \frac{1}{2}x$ for values of x between 0 and 100. This would be impossible to show with a table, because the table would be infinitely long even before $x = 1$! The straight line in Figure A–1 is a picture of the equation $y = 20 + \frac{1}{2}x$.

Figure A–2 is a graph representing an *inverse relationship* between x and y. Specifically, it is a picture of the equation $y = 100 - \frac{1}{2}x$. Like the equation, the graph makes it possible to find the value of y for a given value of x, or the value of x that would determine a given value of y.

Change and Slope

Economics frequently deals with changes in variables, and the effect of changes in one variable on changes in another.

• Change in a variable is expressed by the symbol Δ—the Greek letter *delta*.

Slope shows the degree to which one variable responds to changes in another.

• The **slope** is the ratio of the change in the dependent variable over the change in the independent variable.

Algebraically,

$$\text{slope} = \frac{\text{change in } y}{\text{change in } x} = \frac{\Delta y}{\Delta x}.$$

In an equation of the form $y = a + bx$, the slope is the term b. In the equation $y = 20 + \frac{1}{2}x$, the slope is $\frac{1}{2}$, which means that every change in x by one unit will cause y to change in the same direction by $\frac{1}{2}$ unit, or $\Delta y / \Delta x = \frac{1}{2}$. For example, let x change from $x_1 = 20$ to $x_2 = 40$. The change in x is

$$\Delta x = x_2 - x_1 = 40 - 20 = 20.$$

With $x_1 = 20$,

$$y_1 = 20 + \frac{1}{2}x_1 = 20 + \frac{1}{2}(20) = 30.$$

With $x_2 = 40$,

$$y_2 = 20 + \frac{1}{2}x_2 = 20 + \frac{1}{2}(40) = 40.$$

The change in y is

$$\Delta y = y_2 - y_1 = 40 - 30 = 10.$$

The slope is

$$\frac{\Delta y}{\Delta x} = \frac{y_2 - y_1}{x_2 - x_1} = \frac{40 - 30}{40 - 20} = \frac{10}{20} = \frac{1}{2}.$$

In Figure A–1, the slope of the line $y = 20 + \frac{1}{2}x$ is the slope of the equation. In the graph, x *runs* along the horizontal axis, and changes in x are called the **run**. Changes in y are called the **rise** since y changes vertically as x changes. If x changes from 20 to 40 in Figure A–1, the *run* is 20. Since y increases from 30 to 40 with this change in x, the *rise* is 10. The slope of the line in Figure A–1 is the same as the slope of the equation—

$$\text{slope} = \frac{\text{rise}}{\text{run}} = \frac{\Delta y}{\Delta x} = \frac{10}{20} = \frac{1}{2}.$$

In the equation $y = 20 + \frac{1}{2}x$ and in the graph of the equation in Figure A–1, there is a direct relationship between x and y, as shown by the positive (*uphill*, left to right) slope.

● **Positive slopes** indicate *direct relationships* between variables.

The equation

$$y = a - bx$$

represents an inverse relationship between x and y, and has a negative (*downhill*, left to right) slope.

● **Negative slopes** indicate *inverse relationships* between variables.

Go back to the equation $y = 100 - \frac{1}{2}x$ and the graph of the equation in Figure A–2. Let x increase from $x_1 = 20$ to $x_2 = 40$. The change in x is

$$\Delta x = x_2 - x_1 = 40 - 20 = 20.$$

With x_1, the value of y is

$$y_1 = 100 - x_1 = 100 - \frac{1}{2}(20) = 90.$$

When x increases to x_2, y falls to

$$y_2 = 100 - x_2 = 100 - \frac{1}{2}(40) = 80.$$

The change in y is

$$\Delta y = y_2 - y_1 = 80 - 90 = -10,$$

and the slope is

$$\frac{\Delta y}{\Delta x} = \frac{-10}{20} = -\frac{1}{2}.$$

In Figure A–2, y falls toward the horizontal axis as x runs out horizontally, or the *rise* is negative with inverse relationships.

Figure A–2 Inverse Relationship Between x and y

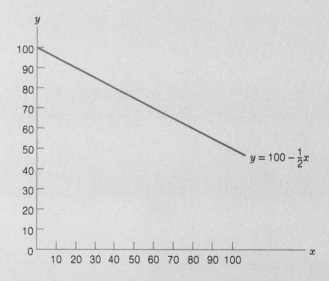

The value of the slope indicates the degree to which one variable responds to changes in the other. Compare two equations representing direct relationships,

$$y = 20 + \frac{1}{2}x$$

and

$$y = 20 + x.$$

The Value of the Slope

The equation with the greater slope indicates that y is more responsive to changes in x. Turning this around, it will take smaller changes in x to achieve a given change in y in the equation with the greater slope. Figure A–3 shows the two equations graphically. The steeper line indicates that y is more responsive to changes in x. As an exercise, draw lines representing the equations $y = 20 + \frac{1}{4}x$ and $y = 20 + 2x$.

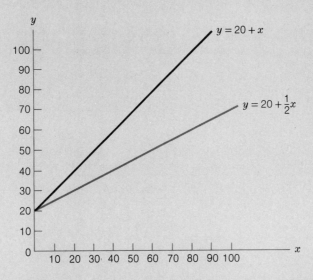

With inverse relationships, the *absolute* value of the slope (ignoring its negative sign) indicates how responsive one variable is to changes in the other. Compare the equations below representing inverse relationships between x and y.

$$y = 100 - \tfrac{1}{2}x$$

and

$$y = 100 - x.$$

The two equations are shown graphically in Figure A–4. The steeper line represents the equation with the greater absolute slope and the one in which y is more responsive to changes in x. Again, as an exercise, draw lines in Figure A–4 representing the equations $y = 100 - \tfrac{1}{4}x$ and $y = 100 - 2x$.

Linear Relationships

All of the relationships in the above examples are *linear relationships* between x and y.

- In **linear relationships**, y is equally responsive to all changes in x, and the slope is constant for all changes in x and y.

Linear relationships are shown graphically by straight lines.

Curves

Most economical relationships are *nonlinear*. Equal changes in one variable do not always produce the same change in the other. For example, food output on a 100-acre plot of land would be zero with no labor and no capital. Adding labor and capital would change output, but every additional unit of labor and capital will not add the same amount of output—if it did, the world could be fed from the single 100-acre plot of land. Eventually, the entire 100 acres would be taken up with workers and equipment, and output would be zero again. This is an example of a nonlinear relationship.

- In **nonlinear relationships,** equal changes in x will not cause equal changes in y.

Nonlinear equations involve powers of x, and will not be used in the text. However, nonlinear equations are easy to deal with graphically. Nonlinear relationships are represented graphically by *curves*.

Figure A–4 Negative Slopes

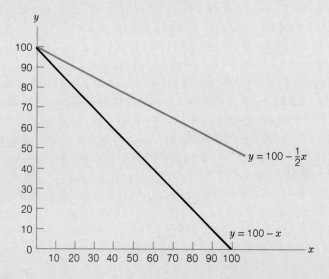

Slopes of Curves

Slopes of curves are expressed in two ways—*arc approximations* and *slopes at points* on the curve.

- The **arc approximation** of the slope of a curve is the average value of the slope of the curve between two points on the curve, or the slope of a line between the points.

Moving from point A to point B on the curve in Figure A–5 involves moving from x_1 and y_1 to x_2 and y_2. The arc approximation of the slope is

$$\frac{\Delta y}{\Delta x} = \frac{y_2 - y_1}{x_2 - x_1},$$

or the slope of the broken line between A and B. The smaller the arc—i.e., the smaller the changes in x and y—the closer the slope of the line between the points approximates the slope of the curve itself.

A straight line that touches only a single point on a curve is **tangent** to the curve at that point.

- The *slope of a curve at a point* is the slope of a straight line tangent to the curve at that point.

The slope of the curve in Figure A–5 at point A is the same as the slope of the line tangent to the curve at point A.

Figure A–5 Determining the Slope of a Curve

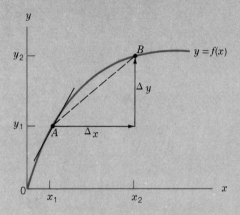

Interpreting Curves

Interpreting curves is not very difficult. As in linear relations, negatively sloped curves indicate inverse relationships and positively sloped curves indicate direct relationships.

The curve in Figure A–6a shows a direct relationship between x and y, and y moves in the same direction as changes in x along the curve. However, as x increases, the slope of the curve increases.

- The curve in Figure A–6a shows *y increasing at an increasing rate* as x increases.

The curve in Figure A–6b is positively sloped, indicating a direct relationship between x and y. However, the slope of this curve gets smaller as x increases.

- The curve in Figure A–6b shows *y increasing at a decreasing rate* as x increases.

The curve in Figure A–6c is negatively sloped, indicating an inverse relationship between x and y. As x increases, the curve gets steeper. Ignoring the minus sign of the slope, the slope increases as x increases.

- The curve in Figure A–6c shows *y decreasing at an increasing rate* as x increases.

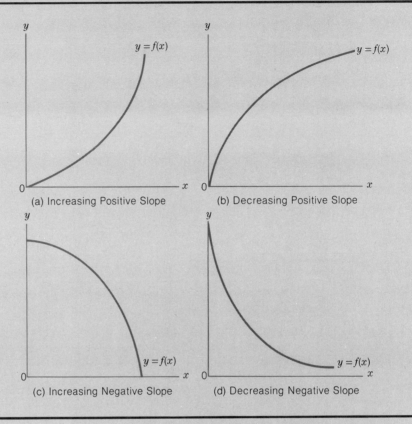

(a) Increasing Positive Slope

(b) Decreasing Positive Slope

(c) Increasing Negative Slope

(d) Decreasing Negative Slope

In Figure A–6d, the curve is negatively sloped, indicating an inverse relationship, and the slope of the curve (ignoring the minus sign) gets smaller as x increases and the curve "flattens out."

- The curve in Figure A–6d shows y *decreasing at a decreasing rate* as x increases.

In some instances, y may increase at an increasing rate for some changes in x, at a constant rate for other changes in x, and may even change from a direct relationship to an inverse relationship. Figure A–7 shows what probably would happen as labor is added to a fixed amount of land and capital. Initially, output (q) increases at an increasing rate (labor inputs between 0 and ℓ_1) and the curve resembles that in Figure A–6a. Between ℓ_1 and ℓ_2, output increases at a diminishing rate as the labor input increases and the curve resembles that in Figure A–6b. Output reaches its maximum with ℓ_2 units of labor employed—the slope of the curve is zero at this point. Beyond labor inputs of ℓ_2, increasing the labor input actually causes output to fall, and the relationship between labor input and the level of output shifts from a direct to an inverse relationship like the one shown in Figure A–6c.

Figure A–7 Productivity of Labor Curve

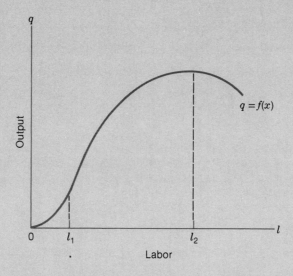

$q = f(x)$

Output

0   l_1 l_2 l

Labor

Graphic Solution of Equations

Graphs of equations make it easy to solve for one variable with a given value of the other. But what if we are dealing with more than one relationship between variables and want to find values of the variables that are consistent with both relationships? One approach is simultaneous solution of the equations representing the relationships. This is not especially difficult with two linear equations, but graphs make the solution much easier.

For example, in Figure A–8a, one positively sloped line represents one relationship—$y = 20 + \frac{1}{2}x$—and the other represents the equation $y = x$. At point A, where the two lines intersect, $y = 20 + \frac{1}{2}x$ *and* $y = x$. This is the same result we would get by simultaneous solution of the equations $y = 20 + \frac{1}{2}x$ and $y = x$.

Simultaneous solution of nonlinear equations is more difficult, but finding solutions graphically is quite easy. For example, in Figure A–8b, $y = f(x)$ and $y = x$ at the points where the curve is cut by the line $y = x$, at 0 and at A. In Figure A–8c, we have two nonlinear relationships—$y = f(x)$ and $y = g(x)$—and both are met at the point where the two curves intersect.

The Elements of Statistical Estimation

Many economic relationships can be estimated statistically from actual data with a technique called **regression analysis.** Regression analysis simply tries to find the function or equation that *fits* the data. For example, suppose that we have found statistical data for x (the independent variable) and y (the dependent variable).

Figure A–8 Graphical Solutions of Equations

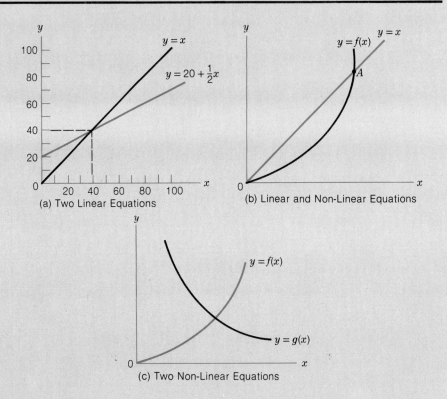

(a) Two Linear Equations

(b) Linear and Non-Linear Equations

(c) Two Non-Linear Equations

x	y
0	100
100	200
300	270
400	340
500	510
600	570
700	670
800	760
900	840
1000	920

Each of the pairs in the above table is represented by a point in Figure A–9a, which is called a *scatter diagram*. A look at the scatter diagram indicates a direct relationship between x and y.

To estimate the specific relationship between x and y, we try to find a line that comes as close as possible to all of the points in the scatter. This can be done visually by moving a line around until it apparently comes as close as possible to all of the points, or more reliably with a statistical technique called **least squares.** In Figure A–9a, the line

$$y = 82 + 0.86x$$

is the *estimated* relationship between x and y. This estimate indicates that $y = 82$ is autonomous, or can't be explained by the value of x. Every change in x by 1 unit causes y to change in the same direction by 0.86. Since the points are tightly bunched around the estimated line, we have a stable and predictable relationship between x and y.

In Figure A–9b, the scatter indicates an inverse relationship between x and y. Also, the points are more widely scattered around the estimated line, indicating a somewhat less stable and predictable relationship between x and y than in Figure A–9a.

Scatter diagrams that resemble Figure A–9c indicate that there is no relationship between x and y.

Figure A–9 Scatter Diagrams for Regression Analysis

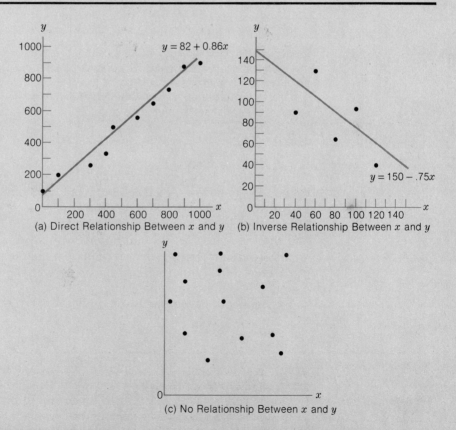

(a) Direct Relationship Between x and y

(b) Inverse Relationship Between x and y

(c) No Relationship Between x and y

2

Scarcity and Choice: The Economic Problem

Preview: Faced with limited resources and unlimited wants, society is forced to make certain economic choices. Specifically, society must decide what it will produce, how it will produce, and how it will distribute that production to its members. The **production-possibilities model** introduced in this chapter serves as a useful tool in analyzing and understanding these kinds of choices.

Although we use theory to understand many economic questions and issues, economics isn't really *about* theory. Economics is primarily concerned with a basic fact of life—**scarcity**. Since the fall of Adam, the human race has been faced with a conflict between unlimited wants and limited resources. As individuals, we have to choose among our wants to make ourselves as well off as possible with limited amounts of income, time, and stamina. As communities, we have to choose among the needs of the community to make the community as well off as possible with its limited resources.

The Limits on Production

Society's basic economic problem is to find the best combination of goods and services that can be produced with its limited capacity to produce. The capacity to produce, in turn, is limited by society's *resources*, the state of *technology*, and a number of noneconomic and institutional factors—such as religious tradition, social and economic class structures, etc.

Limited Resources

Producing goods and services is impossible without land, labor, machinery, raw materials, time, and other resources. In reality, there are millions of different resources, but for simplicity, we can classify all resources as *land*, *labor*, and *capital*.

- **Land** refers to resources that are permanently fixed in supply.
- **Labor** refers to the human strength and talent used in production.
- **Capital** refers to a class of resources that are produced by the economic system—for example, machinery and buildings.

Obviously, if the *quantities of resources* available are limited, there will be a limit on the number of possible combinations of goods and services that can be produced and consumed. The *quality of resources* also affects society's capacity to produce. Even with vast expanses of land, a country may have a very small capacity to produce agricultural crops if the land is of poor quality for agricultural production (mountains, swamps, and deserts, for example), or if the climate is too harsh for most crops. A well-fed, well-trained, and stable labor force will be more productive than a labor force made up of untrained, poorly educated, transient workers. A stock of modern machinery and equipment will be more productive than obsolete machinery and equipment.

Technology

Technology also limits the capacity to produce.

- **Technology** is the "state of the art" in production, or the known applications of scientific and technical knowledge to production.

A given state of technology defines the relationship between resource inputs and the level of output. In other words, technology tells us how much we can produce with a given quantity and quality of resources. Unfortunately, no known technology allows the production of goods and services without using scarce resources in the process.

The Economic Problem

Most societies share a common economic goal of making the members of the society as well off as possible economically. This goal, however, isn't as clearly defined as it appears, and in fact a society's definition of what is *best* economically isn't a strictly economic problem.

A given society's definition of a best economic result is affected by the dominant ideology in the society and the prevailing social and political philosophy. The definition of the best economic result may even involve religious considerations—for example, not producing or consuming goods prohibited by religious tradition or conducting business according to religious standards. The religious government of Iran, for example, attempted upon taking power to force banks to conform to Islamic laws against *usury* (charging interest on loans).

Defining the best economic outcome for society is complicated further by the fact that a result that is *best* by some generally accepted definition—for example, the *best* result for the majority of the population—usually isn't the best possible result for every person or group within society. Producing goods more efficiently by mechanization, for example, isn't best for workers who will have to be retrained or relocated or who will become unemployed as a result. In other words, the very definition of what is best economically is in part a *normative* definition resting on value judgements.

Economic analysis emphasizes *economic efficiency*, or getting the greatest possible output out of a given capacity. This emphasis simplifies reality by excluding many noneconomic considerations. For example, if making the most efficient use of productive capacity required extensive restrictions of political and economic freedom of choice, a society might well opt for more freedom, even at the expense of some efficiency.

Three Basic Economic Questions

The millions of specific economic choices that society must make boil down to three basic questions that are common to all societies and economies—*what* goods to produce, *how* to produce, and *for whom* to produce.

What?

The capacity to produce goods and services, or *productive capacity*, defines society's "menu" of possible choices of goods and services. If this capacity is fully employed, the decision to produce more of one thing requires reduced output of something else. More concisely, in economics, "there ain't no such thing as a free lunch."

Choosing *what* goods to produce requires a determination of what is best for society. In some cases, this determination is made by consumer demand as expressed in the markets for goods and services. In other instances, the decision on what goods to produce is made by a central authority. Sometimes, society's needs and priorities are determined by external considerations—for example, the demands of a major war or the real or perceived external threats to national security that dictate the output of goods for military purposes.

The *what* question also involves the choice between goods now and goods in the future. If all resources are used to produce goods for current consumption, for example, no machinery or equipment will be produced. Over time, as machines wear out and aren't replaced with new ones, our "menu" of choices shrinks. On the other hand, if we produce large outputs of machines now in order to produce more consumption goods in the future, we have to give up some current consumption.

In market economies, the decision of *what* to produce depends largely on the distribution of wealth and income. It is seldom, if ever, decided by a simple majority of the population in a one-person-one-vote election. Also the choice of *what* to produce involves normative considerations concerning the importance of various groups in determining society's economic welfare.

How?

If the object is to make society as well off as possible economically with a limited capacity, it follows that this capacity should be used as efficiently as possible. The question of *how* to produce goods and services concerns the efficient utilization of society's resources and technology.

If there are idle resources—unemployed labor, idle machines, empty factories, etc.—society loses the goods and services that could have been produced by these resources. Efficiency also involves the most efficient combinations of resources. For example, in countries where labor is very scarce relative to land and capital, it wouldn't be very efficient to produce wheat with methods that required large amounts of labor and little machinery. If a machine in a factory can be operated efficiently by one worker, it isn't efficient to put two workers on the machine.

Efficiency, or full employment of capacity, is hard to achieve for a number of reasons. Resources generally aren't sufficiently mobile among geographic areas or occupations. Lack of information, inadequate education, emotional attachments, geographical and family ties, discrimination, and other factors, for example, contribute to immobility of labor into industries, occupations, or geographic areas in which they would be most productive. Work rules to preserve individuals' jobs, managerial bureaucracies, and some governmental regulations also may contribute to inefficiency.

Deciding *how* to produce, like most economic questions, involves normative issues and value judgements as well as positive analytical questions. For example, elimination of work rules that protect individual jobs at the expense of efficiency benefits producers and possibly consumers of the affected goods and services, but a disproportionate share of the cost of such a move is borne by the affected workers. To say that elimination of the work rules is a *good* thing requires some normative argument that the benefits to producers and consumers are more important than the costs borne by the affected workers.

For Whom?

Finally, society has to decide *for whom* to produce—the distribution of output among members of the community. Should everybody get an equal share of the output? Should output and income be distributed on the basis of effort and contribution or on the basis of an individual's initial wealth? What role should tradition play in the distribution of output and income?

These questions involve many normative and positive issues. For example, rewarding persons on the basis of their individual effort and resources may be efficient but may lead to a normatively unacceptable degree of inequality of income. To say that one pattern of income distribution is *better* or *worse* than another involves normative value judgements on the importance of *equity* and *efficiency*.

Production Possibilities

To see the problem of scarcity in very simplified terms, imagine a country that produces only two goods—food (F) and clothing (C). Assume further that the country has limited resources with which to produce food and clothing, and that these resources can be used in both food and clothing production. Finally, assume a given state of *technology*—i.e., a set relationship between resource inputs and the level of output.

Table 1 Efficient Combinations of Food and Clothing

C	F
500	0
475	100
425	200
325	300
200	400
0	500

Table 1 shows some of the combinations of food and clothing that fully employ the economy's productive capacity. If all resources were used to produce food, food production would be at its maximum, $F* = 500$, and clothing production would be zero. If all resources were used to produce clothing, clothing production would be at its maximum, $C* = 500$, and food output would be zero.

The Production-Possibilities Curve

If our imaginary economy were to produce some food and some clothing, it would have to produce less than 500 units of each. This is shown clearly in Table 1. The possible combinations of goods in Table 1 define points on the economy's *production-possibilities curve* in Figure 1.

• The **production-possibilities curve** shows all the combinations of goods that can be produced with full and efficient employment of an economy's capacity to produce.

In Figure 1, the combination of 100 units of food and 475 units of clothing determines point *B* on the production-possibilities curve. The combination of 300 units of food and 325 units of clothing determines point *D* on the curve. All combinations of outputs on the production-possibilities curve require full employment of all resources, combined as efficiently as possible. At all points on the production-possibilities curve, there will be no idle or inefficiently used resources (such as two workers doing a job that requires only one).

Notice in Table 1 and Figure 1 that successive 100-unit increases in the production of food require successively larger reductions of clothing production, and that the production-possibilities curve gets steeper as we move from $C^* = 500$ toward $F^* = 500$. This is because all resources aren't equally suited for producing both goods. If the maximum clothing output were produced, clothing production would employ all of the economy's resources—even those least suitable for clothing production. Likewise, producing the maximum output of food requires the employment of all resources in food production—again including those not well-suited for this task.

To raise food output from 0 to 100 in Figure 1, we'd expect the land, labor, and capital least suited to clothing production and most suited to food production to be taken out of clothing production to produce food. In this case, little clothing would have to be given up for the first 100 units of food produced.

However, increasing food production to 200, 300, 400, and 500 would require the use of resources less and less suitable for food production.

Figure 1 Production Possibilities Curve

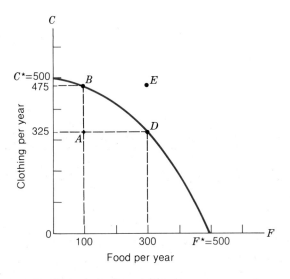

As clothing production is cut back, resources more suitable for clothing production must be removed, increasing the clothing reductions for each additional 100 units of food. Since more and more clothing must be given up for equal increases in food, clothing output falls at an increasing rate, and the production-possibilities curve *bows away* from the origin (or is *concave*).

An economy can only produce combinations of goods that lie *on* or *inside* its production-possibilities curve. Combinations of goods that define points outside the production-possibilities curve—such as 300 units of food and 475 units of clothing (point *E*) in Figure 1—cannot be produced with the economy's resources and technology.

Combinations of goods that define points inside the production-possibilities curve—such as point *A* in Figure 1—can be produced, but they don't employ the economy's capacity fully. If productive capacity isn't fully employed, the community cannot be as well off as possible economically. The unemployed capacity at point *A* could be used to increase food output from 100 to 300 without reducing clothing output, to increase clothing production from 325 to 475 without reducing food output, or to produce more of both goods along the segment *BD*. With unemployed capacity, increasing the output of a good doesn't require a reduction of output of other goods.

Opportunity Cost

In a fully employed economy, the cost of producing more of one good is the amount of other goods that must be given up. For example, suppose that the economy in Figure 1 is at point *B* and increases its food output from 100 to 300. This would require a reduction of clothing production from 475 to 325. The 150 units of clothing given up represent the *opportunity cost* of the additional 200 units of food.

- **Opportunity cost** is the cost of foregone alternatives.

Economics is about *choice*, and opportunity cost tells the cost of any choice we make. It is thus one of the most important concepts in economics. If the economy moved from point *D* to point *B* in Figure 1, the opportunity cost of the additional 150 units of clothing would be the 200 units of food that would have to be given up.

Points on the production-possibilities model answer the fundamental question of *how* goods should be produced. If the economy wishes to get the maximum output from its resources, it *must* produce a combination of goods that lies along the production-possibilities curve, since it would be impossible to produce a combination outside the curve and inefficient to produce one inside the curve.

Deciding *what* the economy should produce involves finding the combination of goods that makes the community as well off as possible. Not all combinations on the curve will make the community equally well off. Consider the points $C* = 500$ and $F* = 500$. At $C*$, the economy would produce clothing, but no food. While it's nice to be well dressed, starving to death is very painful. A well-fed, naked community producing $F* = 500$ may seem to be more interesting, but it would be uncomfortable except in tropical climates, and the undraped overfed human form has only limited appeal. The task of the economic system is to find the combination of goods on the production-possibilities curve that is best for the community, and the production-possibilities model alone can't make that judgment.

After deciding *how* and *what* goods to produce, the community must decide *for whom* the goods are to be produced, or how the goods are to be distributed among members of the community. This may be easier said than done. Deciding that one segment of the community deserves a greater share of the output than another involves a value judgment, and arguments involving value judgments are difficult to resolve with analytical tools.

Technology and Production

Technological change—change in the way that things are produced—has been a dominant theme in economic history for several centuries, and technological change is one of the main sources of modern economic growth. We can analyze one of the effects of technological change, expansion of productive capacity, by returning to a simple food-and-clothing economy.

Suppose that a technological change—say, the discovery of a new type of fertilizer—makes it possible to produce more food with the resources available. The maximum food output goes from $F*$ to $F**$ in Figure 2. Nothing happens to clothing technology, but the technological change in food production changes the production-possibilities curve to $C*F**$. The shaded area represents additional combinations

Figure 2 Technological Change in Production

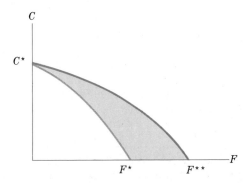

of food and clothing that can be produced as a result of the technological change in food production.

You should work out for yourself the effect of a technological change in clothing production and a technological change in both industries on the economy's production possibilities. Many other things can alter an economy's production-possibilities curve—for example, discovery of new or superior resources and depletion of resources.

Close-up

Technological Change in Agriculture

In the United States, technological change has been especially dramatic in the agricultural sector. The invention of new machinery (from the cotton gin and the reaper to modern self-propelled grain combines), the development of new strains of seed, and the application of chemistry to agriculture have created what many have termed a *Green Revolution*.

These technological advances have raised the output per worker and the output per acre of land dramatically. In the table below, notice the large increases in the production of corn and soybeans over the period 1940–1969, despite a drop in total farm population of nearly two-thirds and an even more impressive decline in the proportion of the total population involved in agriculture. One clue as to how these production increases have been possible lies in the rapid increases in the use of agricultural technology—tractors and fertilizer.

	Total Farm Population (1000's)	% of Total Population	Tractors Used (1000's)	Fertilizer Used (1000 tons)	Value of Products ($ Millions)	Corn (Millions of bushels)	Soybeans (Millions of bushels)
1940	30,547	23.2	1,597	9,360	6,682	2,457	78
1945	24,420	17.5	2,354	15,128	16,231	2,869	193
1950	23,048	15.3	3,394	18,343	22,217	3,075	299.2
1954	19,019	11.8	4,243	22,773	24,645	3,058	324.1
1959	16,592	9.4	4,673	25,313	30,493	3,697	515.6
1964	12,954	6.8	4,755	30,681	35,292	3,361	669.7
1969	10,307	5.1	4,810	38,948	45,609	4,357	1041.5

Source: U.S. Bureau of the Census, *Historical Statistics of the United States: Colonial Times to 1970, Bicentennial Edition.* Washington, D.C., 1975.

Technological change and rising productivity in agriculture freed labor from the agricultural sector for nonagricultural employment. The additional labor available in the nonagricultural sector contributed to an increased capacity of the economy to produce industrial goods.

Figure 3 Growth vs. Consumption

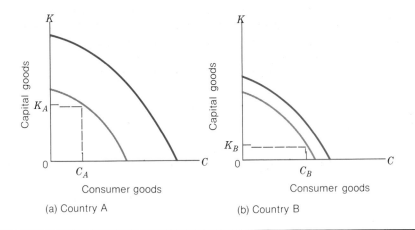

(a) Country A   (b) Country B

Growth vs. Consumption

Another major economic choice which can be analyzed using the production-possibilities model is the choice between growth and consumption. The choice of goods produced today may affect a country's productive capacity in the future. If, for example, we produced no industrial machinery this year, our productive capacity would shrink in the future as existing machines wore out. For a more general example, we can classify all goods as **consumer goods** (goods for current consumption) and **capital goods** (goods, such as industrial machinery, to be used for further production). Now, consider two imaginary economies with identical production possibilities, as shown in Figure 3.

Initially, Country B produces more consumer goods (C_B) than does Country A (C_A), but Country A produces more capital goods (K_A) than does Country B (K_B). Living standards would be higher in Country B initially, because Country B produces more consumer goods. The additional capital goods in Country A add little to the living standards of the people.

However, in the future, Country A will have a larger capacity to produce consumer goods and capital goods than will Country B because of its greater output of capital goods now. The expansion of productive capacities in the two countries is shown by the shift of their production-possibilities curves outward in Figure 3. Country A's additional capacity in the future would allow it to produce more capital goods *and* more consumer goods than Country B.

This simple example illustrates a very important and sometimes very painful choice that societies must make—the choice between current consumption and future economic growth. This is one of the basic choices facing the economically underdeveloped countries of the Third World, and the alternatives are unattractive—maintaining current living standards and allowing capacity and output to stagnate, or promoting economic growth by worsening living standards that already border on biological survival.

Close-up

The Soviet Forced Industrialization Drive

Nowhere has the choice between restricting current consumption and promoting future economic growth been more dramatic than in the Soviet Union. In 1928, the first year of the first Five Year Plan, capital goods accounted for 39.5 percent of Soviet industrial output, and consumer goods accounted for 60.5 percent. By 1940, Soviet planners had turned these proportions around—capital goods accounted for 61.2 percent of industrial output and consumer goods accounted for 38.8 percent of industrial output.

In the table below, notice the tremendous increases in the production of industrial goods in the U.S.S.R. between 1928 and 1940, compared to the much more modest increases—and, in the case of cows, decrease—in the production of consumer goods. Note also that between 1928 and 1933, production of *all* the consumer and agricultural goods in the table actually declined.

	1928	1933	1940
Industrial Goods			
Electric Power (millions of KW)	5	16	48
Coal (millions of tons)	36	76	166
Steel (millions of tons)	4	7	18
Machine Tools (1000 units)	2	21	58
Trucks (1000 units)	0.7	39	136
Consumer and Agricultural Goods			
Cotton Fabrics (billions of meters)	3	3	4
Sugar (millions of tons)	2	1	3
Grain (millions of tons)	73	69	96
Cows (millions)	29	19	28

Based on statistics from *Narodnoe khozyaystvo SSR v 1958 godu* (Moscow, 1959).

The squeezing of the consumer goods industries was an integral part of the Soviet strategy to generate rapid economic growth. The transformation of the Soviet economy from a backward, largely agricultural economy to a major industrial power owes much to the sacrifices of Soviet consumers in the 1930s, 1940s, 1950s, and 1960s.

The production-possibilities model is a very simple picture of the choices available to society. All modern economies produce thousands of goods and services, not just two. Nonetheless, the model does illustrate some important concepts—scarcity, choice, opportunity cost—and we can apply it to problems of choice in more complex economies.

Applying the Tools

The Cost and Economic Impact of World War II

The impact of World War II on the United States was much different from the impact of the war on the other belligerent nations. The opportunity cost of prosecuting the war (in terms of the kinds of other things that had to be given up) was much lower for the United States than it was for other countries. We can see why if we look at the cost and impact of the war in terms of production possibilities of three countries involved in the war—the United States, Germany, and the Soviet Union.

The productive capacity of the United States was grossly underemployed in the 1930s. During the Great Depression, 25 percent of the labor force was out of work, and many factories and machines lay idle. In contrast, by 1939 Germany had taken up much of the slack in its economy with public works projects (like the Autobahn) and military production. Between 1928 and 1939, the Soviet Union had pushed its modest production potential to the limit in a ruthless industrialization drive (see *Close-up*, p. 34). During the course of the war, the increased demand for military goods affected these countries quite differently, as shown in Figure A. In Figure A, all goods are classified as *military (M)* or *civilian (C)* goods, and productive capacity is expressed as the capacity to produce these broad categories of goods.

The high unemployment in the United States in 1939 meant that the economy was operating inside its production-possibilities curve, as shown by the outputs C_{1939} and M_{1939} in Figure A (i). Between 1939 and 1945, the United States was able to increase military production dramatically from M_{1939} to M_{1945} without a drastic reduction of the output of civilian goods. There was some reduction of output of civilian goods in the United States during the war, but the effect on most American households was more of an inconvenience than a drastic deterioration in the quality of life.

Figure A

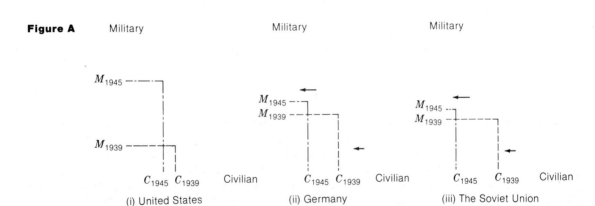

(i) United States (ii) Germany (iii) The Soviet Union

In Germany and the Soviet Union, the costs of prosecuting the war (in terms of civilian goods) was much greater than in the United States. Both countries had less slack in their economies at the outset of the war. Germany was producing very close to its production-possibilities curve, as shown by C_{1939} and M_{1939} in Figure A(ii). The Soviet Union was probably producing *on* its production-possibilities curve in 1939, as shown in Figure A(iii). In these countries, the increased military production during the war required substantial reductions of the output of civilian goods. In addition, both countries were invaded during the war, and their productive capacities were partially destroyed. This pushed the production-possibilities curves of Germany and the Soviet Union inward to the darker curves in Figures A (ii) and (iii). Civilian goods production was so low in these countries in 1945 that biological survival was a very real problem for many German and Soviet households.

This doesn't mean that World War II was *free* for the United States. Although the war required no drastic reductions in the output of civilian goods or in living standards, the resources used to produce military goods during the war could have been employed in the production of civilian goods. The prosecution of the war and the support of allied countries during the war meant that the United States had to forego the alternative of employing its capacity to produce more civilian goods.

The Economic System

Every society has a set of economic arrangements and economic institutions that make up its **economic system.** The economic system is the end product of a variety of economic and noneconomic forces in the society—prevailing social philosophy and ideology, historical experience, traditional relationships among social classes, as well as political goals and the adequacy of resources to meet those goals. Societies deal with the problem of scarcity and choice through their economic systems, and there are about as many different economic systems in the world as there are societies.

Despite their diversity, however, the economic systems of the world do have a common goal: to make the society as well off as possible. Of course, it is in the process of trying to define and achieve this goal that systems differ. The very definition of what is *best* for the society depends on who makes the decision—buyers and sellers in the market place, governmental economic policymakers, or central economic planners. The means by which economic welfare (once the term has been defined) is to be maximized also leads to important differences among the world's economic systems.

We'll take a closer look at various economic systems in Chapter 19. For the time being, however, we'll focus our attention upon economic problems and relationships in a basically private market economy, since this is the closest approximation to our own economy.

Summary

1. All human societies face the problem of **scarcity**—unlimited wants in the face of limited resources and limited capacity to produce.
2. All societies have to make three basic economic choices—**what** to produce, **how** to produce it, and **for whom** to produce.
3. A society's feasible combinations of goods—given its resources and technology—is defined by its **production-possibilities curve**, which shows combinations of goods that require full efficient employment of the economy's capacity to produce.
4. In a fully employed economy, producing more of something means that the output of something else must be reduced.
5. The cost of foregone alternatives is called **opportunity cost**.
6. The production-possibilities curve may shift as a result of technological change, changes in resource quality, or as a result of a change in the proportion of the economy's capacity devoted to the production of capital goods.

Concepts for Review

scarcity
choice
land
labor
capital
technology
efficiency

productive capacity
production-possibilities curve
opportunity cost
technological change
capital goods
consumer goods
economic system

Questions

1. Sarah and Jim's parents have told the children that they "can't get everything they want."
   a. What economic lesson are the parents teaching the children?
   b. If the parents were the world's richest couple, would their argument be valid?
2. In the early years of the Vietnam War, President Johnson assured the nation that the war wouldn't reduce our output of consumer goods, nor would it lead to cuts in government spending on nonmilitary programs. Under what circumstances would this be plausible?
3. Petroleum is an important raw material used in producing many goods in our economy. Explain the effect of the following developments on our production possibilities.
   a. The discovery of new sources of petroleum.
   b. The depletion of petroleum reserves.
   c. The discovery of a substitute for petroleum in automobile transportation.
4. Some people argue that the United States has gone "beyond the problem of scarcity," and that scarcity would not be a problem in our society if we changed the economic system and the pattern of distribution of goods and services among members of the community. Do you think that this is a valid argument?

Problems

1. The following combinations of steel and wheat outputs require full employment of Neverland's productive capacity.

Combination	Steel, million tons/yr.	Wheat, million tons/yr.
A	12	0
B	11	3
C	9	6
D	6	9
E	0	12

a. Construct Neverland's production-possibilities curve from the above information.

b. Could the economy produce 9 million tons of steel and 9 million tons of wheat per year? Explain.

c. Could the economy produce 9 million tons of steel and 3 million tons of wheat per year? Could it be maximizing the society's economic welfare if it produced this combination of goods? Explain.

d. Do all combinations of goods that employ productive capacity fully make society equally well off economically?

e. What is opportunity cost? What is the opportunity cost of moving from combination B to combination C above?

f. Does it require a value judgement to argue that combinations inside the production-possibility curve aren't the best possible combinations for the community? Does it require a value judgement to argue that moving from one point on the production-possibility curve to another point on the production-possibility curve is good or bad?

3

Demand, Supply, and Price: An Overview

Preview: In a market economy, society's necessary economic choices are made through the interaction of individual buyers and sellers behaving in their own best interests in the free market. The **partial equilibrium model of supply and demand** introduced in this chapter demonstrates how the prices generated by these market activities ensure that the quantities of goods and services supplied by producers will exactly equal the quantities demanded by consumers.

Households, Firms, and Markets

What do we mean when we speak of a market? What determines the boundaries of a market?

- A **market** is a setting in which buyers and sellers can deal with each other conveniently.

The U.S. economy is made up of many markets, and different markets have different characteristics, or **market structures**. Some markets are very small geographically, such as the markets served by neighborhood grocers. Others, such as commodities markets and markets for financial securities, are national or even worldwide markets. Some markets have many small buyers and sellers that compete vigorously with each other. Others have only a few buyers or sellers. In fact, some markets have only one buyer or one seller.

Economic analysis of the market economy assumes two basic economic units—households and firms.

- The **household** is the basic buyer of products and the basic seller of resources.

- The **firm** is the basic seller of products and the basic buyer of resources.

In a market economy, the actions of these buyers and sellers in product and resource markets are translated into economic choices for the community.

Consumer Sovereignty

Economic theory typically assumes that a market economy is directed by **consumer sovereignty** (*rule by the consumer*). Every household tries to spend its income on the combination of goods and services that it believes will give it maximum satisfaction. In economic terms, the household wants to maximize *utility* (*utility* is the economist's term for *satisfaction*) through its choice of goods and services. By purchasing the combination of goods and services that maximizes utility, the household casts *dollar votes* in the product market.

Firms in a market economy are assumed to want to produce the combination of goods and services that will maximize *profit*, and will thus try to produce the goods and services that households want. In other words, firms try to produce in direct response to the dollar votes cast by consumers. In order to do this, firms must purchase resources (land, labor, and capital) from households, and provide income to the households in return. Each household's income depends on the scarcity of the resources it sells relative to the demand for them: scarce resources in great demand will command higher prices than abundant resources that few firms want. Firms, in turn, will economize in their use of the scarcest and highest-priced sources and will try to produce any output as efficiently as possible. In this way, the market economy decides how the total number of dollar votes will be distributed to households.

In short, economic theory assumes that in a consumer-sovereignty economy, the free interaction of buyers and sellers in product and resource markets ultimately determines the answers to the three fundamental economic questions.

- **What** the economy produces is determined by the way households cast their dollar votes (i.e., spend their incomes) and the way firms respond to those votes.

- **How** the economy produces is determined by the scarcity and prices of resources and by firms' efforts to produce efficiently and at the lowest possible cost.

- **For whom** the economy produces is determined by the distribution of dollar votes (i.e., income) to households, based on the kinds and amounts of resources households own and the need for those resources in production.

Markets and Democracy

Laissez-faire is an economic philosophy that opposes government interference in the operation of the market system. Many advocates of laissez-faire argue that the market system is an efficient and democratic means of making the community's economic choices and that it provides the greatest good for the greatest number of people. But while the market system may encourage efficiency, it does not guarantee equity. Consumer sovereignty is a *one-dollar-one-vote* system, not *one-person-one-vote*. Individuals with large incomes will cast more dollar votes than individuals with smaller incomes. If a tiny minority controls the bulk of the income in an economy, markets will respond to the preferences of this minority. There is thus no assurance that the answers provided by the market system to the fundamental economic questions will be defensible on any normative grounds.

It is possible, as many critics of the market system argue, to replace markets with some other means of economic decision-making, such as a central economic authority. But simply replacing the market system with some other mechanism wouldn't resolve all potential questions of equity and fairness. Whose view of economic welfare, social justice, and equity should prevail? To whose needs would the economic authority most likely respond? These are questions you should ask yourself as we look more closely at the market system.

Prices in the Market Economy

Everybody is familiar with prices. However, not many people are aware of the economic significance of prices in the market system—what they do and what would happen if they didn't exist.

Contrary to some rather optimistic views, there simply aren't enough raw materials, labor, land, and capital to produce enough of everything for everybody. Economics is concerned with *scarce* goods and resources.

- **Scarce goods and resources** are those that don't exist in sufficient quantities that all users can have as much as they want.

Since there isn't enough of a scarce good or resource to go around, there must be some means of deciding which of the potential users will be able to get the good. In a market economy, *prices ration scarce goods and resources* by excluding users who are unwilling or unable to pay the price. A price of $10 on a bleacher seat at the World Series rations the seats to those who are willing and able to pay $10 to see the game. It excludes baseball fans who don't have the $10, as well as persons with only passing interest in the World Series who wouldn't get $10 worth of enjoyment out of attending a game.

Goods and resources that *are* so abundant that all users can have as much as they want are *free* goods and resources. Things may be free because they exist in very large quantities relative to the demand for them (e.g., sunlight) or simply because nobody wants them (e.g., garbage). There is no need to ration a free good or resource, so free goods and resources don't have prices (actually, the price is zero).

Simply setting the price of a good at zero, however, doesn't make it free in the strict economic sense. A law setting the price of World Series tickets at zero wouldn't make the tickets a free good, except in the unlikely event that the number of persons interested in seeing a game was equal to or smaller than the number of seats available. When the price of a scarce good is set so low that consumers demand more of the good than is made available by sellers, some non-price means of rationing will have to be devised. The "free" Series tickets might be rationed first-come-first-served, through a lottery, or in some other way. The long lines at gas pumps during the gasoline crunch of 1979 provided a vivid example of first-come-first-served rationing.

Common sense suggests that the prices of scarce goods are determined by demand and supply. If the supply of World Series seats were infinite, their price would be very low (zero, in fact); if only a hundred tickets were available, their price would be very high (as ticket scalpers well know). In the winter, when fresh vegetables are scarce, their prices are so high that many consumers can't afford them; in late summer, when supplies are plentiful, many grocers barely find it worthwhile to stock fresh vegetables because the prices are so low. Gasoline frequently costs more in summer, when people are taking long automobile trips and demand for gas is high, than in winter, when many people leave their cars at home and take public transportation to work. All these examples illustrate the importance of demand and supply in determining prices. A fuller understanding of price determination, however, requires a closer look at these relationships.

Demand and Price

The quantity of a good that consumers would be willing and able to buy (*ex ante*) depends upon a number of things—the price of the good, the prices of other goods, consumers' incomes, tastes, custom and tradition, and legal regulations, among others. The *law of demand* states a general relationship between the price of a good and the quantity demanded by consumers:

- The **law of demand:** Assuming everything else remains constant (*ceteris paribus*), the quantity of a good demanded by buyers tends to vary inversely with the price of the good. In other words, the quantity of a good demanded will be greater at low prices than at high prices.

Like all economic laws, the law of demand can only tell us what *usually* happens. There may be some owners of Jaguars who would no longer buy them if the price of Jaguars fell enough that members of the middle-class could afford them. But the decrease in quantity of Jaguars demanded by such snobs would be overwhelmed by the increase in quantity demanded by the middle class. Thus the law of demand holds true as a generalization, if not for every buyer of every good. One way to test the law of demand is to try to sell one of your text-books (not this one, of course) at a high price and at a low price; see how many potential customers you have at each price.

The Demand Schedule and the Demand Curve

The law of demand is illustrated in the hypothetical *demand schedule* in Table 1.

- A **demand schedule** shows the quantity of a good demanded at various prices, *ceteris paribus*.

Table 1 shows the hypothetical quantity of coffee demanded at various prices ranging from $1 to $8 a pound.

In real commodities markets, the price of coffee changes by very small amounts. What if the price fell from $4 to $3.90, $3.99, or even $3.9999 a pound? A demand schedule showing such small changes in prices would be extremely long and cumbersome. Fortunately, there is a way to avoid such long demand schedules. We can graph the quantity demanded at each price (from Table 1) on axes labeled **price** and **quantity**. Points A through I in Figure 1 are the result. Connecting these points with a line then shows all the possible combinations of price and quantity demanded, and defines the *demand curve* for coffee.

- A **demand curve**, or **demand function**, illustrates the relationship between the price of a good and the quantity demanded, *ceteris paribus*.

Table 1 Demand Schedule for Coffee

Price per pound of coffee	Quantity of coffee demanded (billions of pounds per year)
$8.00	20
7.00	40
6.00	60
5.00	80
4.00	100
3.00	120
2.00	140
1.00	160

Changes in Quantity Demanded vs. Changes in Demand

In order to isolate the relationship between the price of a good and the quantity demanded, the demand curve D in Figure 1 assumes that all other variables (e.g., taste, income, prices of other goods, numbers of buyers) that would affect the amount consumers would be willing and able to buy remain constant.

A drop in the price of coffee in Figure 1 from $6 to $5 a pound would cause a movement along D from point C to point E. The increase on

Figure 1 Demand Curve for Coffee

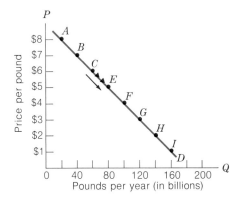

the quantity axis from 60 billion to 80 billion pounds a year is a response to a change in the price of coffee and is called an increase in
the *quantity demanded*.

- **Changes in quantity demanded** are due to changes in the price of
  the good and are shown as *movements along the demand curve*.

An increase in coffee sales from 120 million to 160 million pounds a
year at a constant price of $3.00 reflects a change in some other variable.
If consumers developed a stronger preference for coffee over other
drinks, or if their incomes rose, or if the number of coffee drinkers increased, more coffee would be demanded at any price. Changes in variables other than price alter the entire relationship between price and
quantity demanded and cause *changes in demand*, as illustrated in Figure
2. There will be a new quantity demanded at every price and a different
price that consumers would be willing and able to pay for any quantity.

Figure 2 Change in Demand

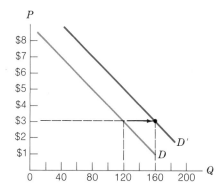

• **Changes in demand** are due to changes in variables other than the price of the good and are shown as *shifts of the demand curve*.

If more coffee is demanded at every price, the demand curve will shift to the right—as shown by the shift of the demand curve from D to D' in Figure 2.

In the demand curve graph, the variables price and quantity are called *endogenous* variables. **Endogenous** means literally *originating from within*. All other variables besides price and quantity are called **exogenous** variables. Exogenous, you won't be surprised to learn, means *originating from outside*.

Figure 3 illustrates changes in demand and changes in quantity demanded that result from changes in a number of significant variables. Study this figure carefully until you understand why each change occurs as it does.

Supply and Price

Making something as a hobby and giving it away isn't economic activity. Rational, profit-maximizing firms will produce and sell a good or service only if they can receive a price for it. In a competitive market, the quantity of a good which firms will be willing and able to produce and sell tends to vary directly with the price of the good. Higher prices encourage producers to offer larger quantities of products for sale. Unfortunately, there isn't a *law of supply* equivalent to the law of demand—the exceptions are more numerous and important than the rare exceptions to the law of demand.

The Supply Schedule and the Supply Curve

The quantity of a good supplied by sellers depends on a number of things—the price they can get for the good, the prices of resources used to produce it, and the state of production technology. To isolate the relationship between the price of a good and the quantity supplied, it is necessary to assume that all the other variables remain constant.

The **supply schedule** in Table 2 shows a hypothetical relationship

Table 2 Supply Schedule for Coffee

Price per pound of coffee	Quantity of coffee supplied (billions of pounds per year)
$8.00	170
7.00	160
6.00	150
5.00	140
4.00	130
3.00	120
2.00	110
1.00	100

Figure 3 Changes in Quantity Demanded vs. Changes in Demand

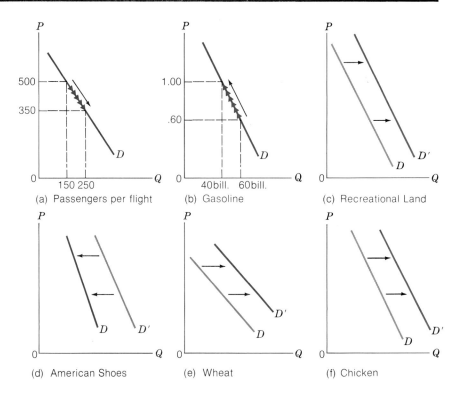

(a) Passengers per flight

(b) Gasoline

(c) Recreational Land

(d) American Shoes

(e) Wheat

(f) Chicken

Changes in Quantity Demanded
a) Airlines lower New York–Los Angeles fare from $500 to $350, increasing passengers per flight from 150 to 250.
b) Increase in price of gasoline from 60¢ to $1.00 a gallon reduces quantity demanded from 60 billion to 40 billion gallons a year.

Changes in Demand
c) Rising income increases demand for recreational land.
d) Imports of low-priced shoes reduces demand for American-made shoes.
e) Increasing population increases demand for wheat.
f) Rising beef prices increase demand for chicken.

between the price of coffee and the quantity supplied. The prices and quantities supplied in Table 2 define points on the **supply curve** S in Figure 4. Notice the general relationship between price and quantity

supplied that is suggested by the shape of the supply curve: as price
goes up, quantity supplied also goes up.

Figure 4 Supply Curve for Coffee

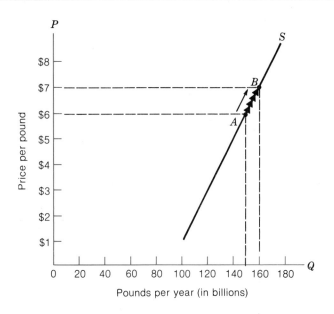

Changes in Quantity Supplied vs. Changes in Supply	Producers will adjust the quantity of a good they are willing and able to

Producers will adjust the quantity of a good they are willing and able to
produce and sell in response to a change in the price of the good. This is
called a *change in quantity supplied*. In Table 2, an increase in the
price of coffee from $6 to $7 a pound would cause the *quantity supplied* to increase from 150 billion pounds a year to 160 billion pounds
a year. In Figure 4, this change in quantity supplied would be shown as
a movement along the supply curve S from A to B.

- **Changes in quantity supplied** are due to changes in the price of
  the good and are shown as *movement along the supply curve*.

Changes in any exogenous variables that affect supply—e.g., technology, costs of labor and materials, weather—alter the relationship
between price and quantity supplied and cause *changes in supply*.

- **Changes in supply** are due to changes in variables other than the
  price of the good and are shown as *shifts of the supply curve*.

For example, the United States experienced unusually good weather
for growing corn in 1978 and harvested a record corn crop. This change
in weather was an exogenous change that increased the amount of corn

Figure 5 Change in Supply

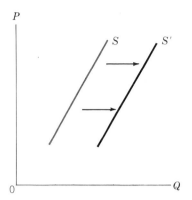

available at all prices. This *change in supply* is shown in Figure 5 as a shift of the supply curve to the right from S to S'.

Figure 6 illustrates changes in supply and changes in quantity supplied resulting from changes in various important endogenous and exogenous variables. Study the figure carefully until you understand the changes that take place.

Equilibrium Price

The interaction among buyers and sellers of a scarce good or resource determines the *equilibrium price* in the market.

- **Equilibrium price** is the price at which the quantity demanded by buyers equals the quantity supplied by sellers.

If the price is at the equilibrium level, it will tend to stay there unless something disturbs demand or supply. If the price isn't at its equilibrium level, it will tend to move toward it. The equilibrium price *clears the mar-*

Table 3 Demand and Supply Schedules

Price per pound of coffee	Quantity demanded (billions of pounds per year)	Quantity supplied (billions of pounds per year)
$8.00	20	170
7.00	40	160
6.00	60	150
5.00	80	140
4.00	100	130
3.00	120	120
2.00	140	110
1.00	160	100

ket: at this price, there will be no unsold goods or resources left in the hands of sellers and no unsatisfied buyers waiting in line.

Equilibrium price can be analyzed easily with the demand and supply schedules and curves already introduced. Table 3 combines the demand

Figure 6 Change in Quantity Supplied vs. Changes in Supply

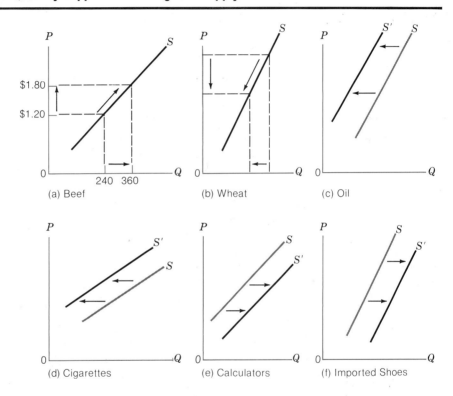

Changes in Quantity Supplied
a) Increase in price of beef from $1.20 to $1.80 a pound increases quantity supplied from 240 to 360 million pounds a week.
b) Falling wheat prices cause annual production of wheat to drop.

Changes in Supply
a) Revolutionary leaders in Iran decide to reduce oil output regardless of price.
b) A 15¢-per-pack tax on producers of cigarettes causes a reduction in supply.
c) A technological advance in the manufacture of computer chips allows production of calculators at a lower cost, increasing supply at every price.
d) Liberalization of restrictions on imported shoes leads to an increase in supply of imported shoes at every price.

Figure 7 Equilibrium Price and Quantity

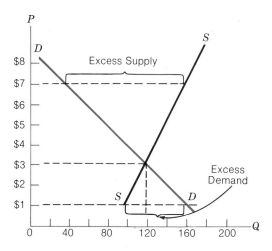

schedule from Table 1 and the supply schedule from Table 2. Figure 7 combines the demand curve (D) from Figure 1 and the supply curve (S) from Figure 4.

In Table 3 and Figure 7, the quantity of coffee demanded is **greater** than the quantity supplied at all prices below $3.00 a pound. At all of these prices, there is *excess demand* for coffee.

- **Excess demand** occurs when the quantity demanded by buyers exceeds the quantity supplied by sellers at a certain price.

With *excess demand*, competition among buyers should bid the price upward. As a result, more sellers are willing to sell more coffee at the higher price, increasing the quantity supplied and reducing the quantity demanded until price and quantity reach the equilibrium level.

At all prices *above* $3 a pound, the quantity supplied is greater than the quantity demanded, and there is *excess supply* of coffee.

- **Excess supply** occurs when the quantity supplied by sellers exceeds the quantity demanded by buyers at a certain price.

With *excess supply*, sellers will try to get rid of unsold coffee by offering it at lower prices. As the price falls, more consumers are willing to buy coffee. The quantity demanded will thus increase and the quantity supplied decrease until price and quantity reach the equilibrium level.

Shortages occur when the price of a good is below the equilibrium price because the quantity supplied isn't sufficient to clear the market of unsatisfied demand. As the price rises, the quantity supplied tends to increase and the quantity demanded falls. When the equilibrium price is reached, the "shortage" disappears. The opposite occurs if there is a **surplus** of a good on the market: the price is too high to clear the market

Figure 8 Changes in Equilibrium Price and Quantity

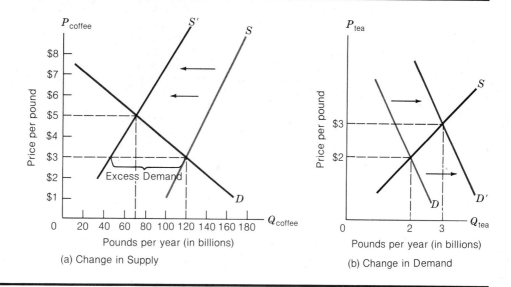

(a) Change in Supply

(b) Change in Demand

of unsold goods. As the price falls, the quantity of the good demanded increases and the quantity supplied falls until equilibrium is reached and the "surplus" disappears.

The equilibrium price, $3.00 in our example, is reached where the quantity demanded equals the quantity supplied. This price *clears the market* of unsold goods and of unsatisfied buyers. Prices above equilibrium fail to clear the market of unsold goods, and excess supply drives the price downward. Prices below equilibrium clear the market of unsold goods, but not of unsatisfied buyers, and excess demand will drive the price upward.[1]

Changes in Equilibrium Price

Equilibrium price can be disturbed by changes in demand or supply. Once the equilibrium is disturbed, the price will move toward a new equilibrium where quantity demanded again equals quantity supplied.

What would happen, for example, if the governments of some coffee-exporting countries tried to raise the price of coffee by withholding part of the crop from market? The situation is shown graphically in Figure 8a. The reduction in the supply of coffee is shown by the shift of the supply curve to the left from S to S'. At the original equilibrium price of

1. Throughout this text, equilibrium price will usually be represented by the symbol $\bar{P}$ and equilibrium quantity by the symbol $\bar{Q}$. The vertical bar over the variable letter means *equilibrium*. Also, *industry* or *market* variables will generally be represented by capital letters, *individual household* or *firm* variables by lower-case letters.

Figure 9 Changes in Equilibrium

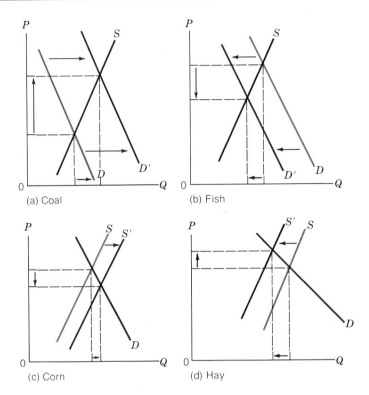

(a) Coal

(b) Fish

(c) Corn

(d) Hay

Disturbances from the Demand Side
a) Increase in demand for coal increases equilibrium price and quantity of coal.
b) Liberalization of Catholic dietary rules reduces the demand for fish, decreasing equilibrium price and quantity of fish.

Disturbances from the Supply Side
c) Favorable weather increases supply of corn, lowering equilibrium price and increasing equilibrium quantity of corn.
d) Acreage reduction lowers supply of hay, raising equilibrium price and reducing equilibrium quantity of hay.

$3.00, there is now excess demand because the quantity demanded on D is more than the quantity supplied on S'. The excess demand bids the price upward to its new equilibrium at $5.00, where the quantity demanded again equals the quantity supplied.

Equilibrium price and quantity may be disturbed by changes in other exogenous variables as well. As coffee prices rise, many people may turn to substitutes for coffee—such as cocoa and tea. This would create an increase in demand for cocoa and tea and would result in higher prices for those goods. The situation is shown graphically in Figure 8b. As more people substitute tea for coffee, the demand curve for tea shifts to the right from D to D', creating excess demand for tea at the original equilibrium price of $2. The excess demand for tea at $2 will drive the price upward until the new equilibrium price is reached at $3.

Figure 9 summarizes our discussion of equilibrium price by showing changes in equilibrium price which would result from changes in important supply and demand variables. Study this figure until you feel confident that you could predict the effect of a change in any endogenous or exogenous variable upon the equilibrium price of a good or service.

Applying the Tools

The Basic Economics of Price Controls

Even a basic understanding of prices and markets is useful in getting beyond simplistic and shallow arguments on some important economic issues. What should a community do, for example, if markets determine equilibrium prices that many of its members feel are too high or too low? The seemingly simple answer is to enact policies that keep price from rising above some desired maximum or from falling below some desired minimum. Unfortunately, as we shall see, life isn't quite so simple.

Rent Controls and Housing Shortages
In many cities, increases in the demand for rental housing have pushed equilibrium rents to levels higher than many tenants are able to pay. To deal with this problem, some city governments have enacted rent-control laws that establish maximum rents below the equilibrium level. Rent-control does keep rents from rising, but its effects go beyond this.

As Figure A illustrates, the equilibrium rent, $\overline{R}$, is reached where the quantity demanded equals the quantity supplied. The controlled rent, R^*, is an *effective maximum price*.

- An **effective maximum price** is a set maximum price which is lower than the equilibrium price.

Setting the maximum rent at R^* results in excess demand for housing at that price, or a *housing shortage*, since the rent can't rise to the level that would clear the market of potential renters. The available housing at R^* must be allocated through some non-price means—position on a waiting list, family size, income, age, need, or simply first-come-first-served. In addition, a government bureaucracy will be needed to enforce the rent controls. Unable to increase rent, many landlords will try to maintain the rate of return on their investments by reducing services to tenants, maintaining properties poorly, and ultimately abandoning the dilapidated buildings altogether when they become uninhabitable.[2] Other owners of rental properties may avoid rent controls and earn handsome returns on their investments by converting rental units to condominiums. Those renters unable to buy condos are displaced.

Figure A

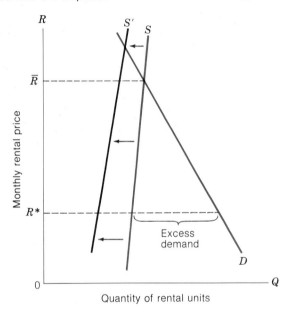

Decay and conversion have a common effect. They reduce the supply of rental housing units, as shown by the shift of the supply curve from S to S' in Figure A. This puts greater upward pressure on rents and increases the excess demand at the controlled rent (R^*). Thus, economic analysis suggests that simple rent controls are an inadequate means of providing adequate housing at reasonable costs.

Advocates of free markets argue that simply allowing rents to rise eliminates the need for enforcement machinery and will eventually increase the supply of rental housing available. Higher rents will encourage owners to maintain units and will attract resources for the construction of more units. This in turn will increase the supply of rental housing and dampen the initial rise in rents. In the short run, however, the higher rents may have a devastating effect upon those at the bottom of the income scale.

---

2. A most dramatic example of this was the rash of arsons that raged in the Bronx section of New York City in the late 1970s, as decayed units were burned by owners seeking to collect insurance or by enraged tenants who could no longer tolerate their living conditions.

Another alternative, the construction of publicly owned housing units, would increase the supply of rental housing and drive the equilibrium rent downward. But such construction is not free. With a fixed government budget, funds for public housing will have to come from reductions in other programs. If the government budget is increased to finance additional housing, members of the community will have to pay through higher taxes.

The ultimate choice among alternative plans for dealing with high rents and housing shortages depends largely upon one's values, ideology, and view of economic reality. One thing is clear from our analysis, however: rent control programs alone cannot eliminate high rents without creating a serious housing shortage.

Farm Price Supports and Minimum Wages

Sometimes price controls take the form of minimum prices set *above* the equilibrium price. In the United States, government farm price supports are a good example of **effective minimum prices**. Price supports are promoted as a way to stabilize agricultural prices and incomes and preserve the family farm. But they have had other effects as well.

Figure B

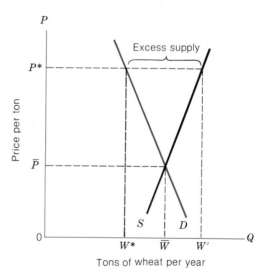

Tons of wheat per year

In Figure B, the support price of wheat, $P*$, is set above the equilibrium price, $\bar{P}$. The higher price encourages farmers to produce more wheat (W') than the amount that can be sold at that price ($W*$), resulting in excess supply. The government is forced to find some way of dealing with the excess supply. A number of alternative strategies for handling this problem will be examined in detail in a later chapter.

A *minimum wage* for employed workers is another kind of effective minimum price. In Figure C, the equilibrium market wage is $2.00 an hour. At this wage, employees are willing to supply $\bar{Q}$ hours of labor to firms, and firms in turn wish to purchase exactly $\bar{Q}$ hours. There are no workers unable to find work at the market wage, and no firms unable to find labor.

Now suppose the Congress passes legislation establishing a minimum wage of $4.00 an hour, in order to aid the lowest paid workers in the economy. At this wage,

Figure C

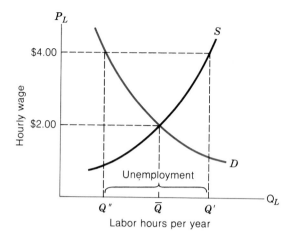

many more workers than before are willing to supply labor, so Q' hours of labor are now made available. Firms, on the other hand, are now less willing to hire labor, demanding only Q'' hours of labor. The difference between the quantity of labor supplied by households and the quantity demanded by firms represents *unemployment*.

The admirable intention behind most minimum-wage laws is to raise the wages of the lowest-paid workers in the economy; economic analysis suggests that one additional result may be a loss of employment for the very workers the laws are meant to help. Minimum wage laws and their effects on employment will be discussed in more detail in a later chapter. Our present analysis of minimum wages, like our analysis of rent controls, does demonstrate a sad truth of economics: that good intentions do not always bring about good economic results.

Interfering with markets to establish maximum or minimum prices requires some means of dealing with resulting surpluses and shortages. This doesn't necessarily mean that price controls are always bad, however. Sometimes price controls are implemented for good normative or practical reasons, and they may be fairly effective for short periods of time. Clearly, though, this seemingly simple approach to complex problems isn't sufficient by itself, and the difficulties created by price controls will be greater the longer they are maintained in the face of growing surpluses or shortages.

Partial and General Equilibrium

So far, we have looked at prices and quantities only in a single market or a couple of related markets. This approach is called **partial equilibrium analysis**. In the real world, of course, markets aren't isolated from one another and disturbances in one market may have far-reaching effects in others.

• **General equilibrium analysis** analyzes the interrelationships among all markets in the economy.

Figure 10 General Equilibrium

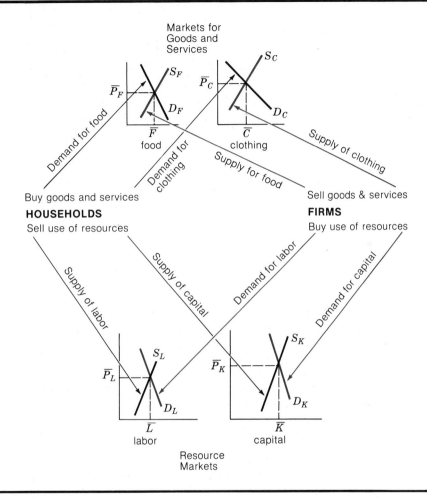

Because general equilibrium analysis is quite complex, virtually all the analysis of equilibrium in this text is partial analysis. But it is important to look for a moment at a more general picture of the market economy.

Figure 10 is a very simple sketch of a private market economy. Households own the resources (land, labor, and capital) and earn income by selling the use of their resources in resource markets. Each household decides for itself how much of its resources to sell in the resource market and how much of each good to purchase in the goods market in order to maximize utility. In other words, households exert supply pressure in resource markets and demand pressure in product markets.

Similarly, each firm chooses for itself the quantity of goods to produce in order to maximize profits. To produce the goods, the firm must purchase resources in the resource market. Thus firms exert supply pressure in product markets and demand pressure in resource markets.

Product markets will adjust to an equilibrium level of prices and

quantities where the quantity of each good demanded is equal to the
quantity supplied. Resource markets will adjust to equilibrium where
the quantity of each resource supplied is equal to the quantity demanded. Disturbance of equilibrium in one market will affect other
markets.

Suppose, for example, that households develop a stronger preference
for leisure time over income and other goods. This will reduce the
supply of labor in the labor market and cause the price of labor to rise.
As the price of labor rises, firms will try to substitute other resources
(such as capital) for labor, and the demand for capital will increase at
all prices. These resource market changes will affect the relationship
between price and quantity supplied by the firms (that is, it will shift
the firms' supply curve), which will disturb equilibrium in the product
market. In addition, since households have developed a stronger preference for leisure over other goods, the demand for goods will fall.
Goods and resource markets will continue to adjust to the initial disturbance until the economy reaches a new **general equilibrium**.

As a second example, suppose that bad weather in the Midwest
reduces the wheat harvest and the supply of wheat from S to S' in
Figure 11a. This drives the price of wheat upward from $\bar{P}_w$ to $\bar{P}'_w$.
Higher wheat prices increase the cost of producing goods that contain wheat, such as bread. In Figure 11b, this higher cost of producing
bread shifts the supply curve of bread from S_b to S'_b, and the price of
bread rises to $\bar{P}'_b$.

Higher bread prices increase the demand for goods that are substitutes for bread, such as potatoes. Thus the demand curve for potatoes in Figure 11c shifts to D'_p, and the price of potatoes rises to $\bar{P}'_p$.
The initial disturbance of equilibrium in the wheat market has now
spread to the markets for two related goods—and the story doesn't

Figure 11   Changes in General Equilibrium

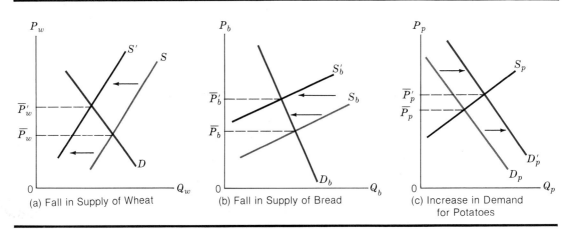

(a) Fall in Supply of Wheat   (b) Fall in Supply of Bread   (c) Increase in Demand for Potatoes

end here. Higher prices for potatoes will increase the demand for substitutes for potatoes, such as stuffing, which is made from bread, which contains wheat . . . .

Higher wheat prices also affect the allocation of resources. As the price of wheat rises, farmers are encouraged to use more of their land, labor, and capital in wheat production. This increases the supply of wheat and reduces the supplies of crops that had been produced with the reallocated resources. Thus, for example, a shortage of wheat and high wheat prices in 1973 eventually led to a popcorn shortage!

Summary

1. The basic units in economic models are **households** (which buy goods and supply the use of resources) and **firms** (which sell goods and buy the use of resources).
2. With **consumer sovereignty**, the basic decisions for the economy are made by the utility-maximizing actions of households and the profit-maximizing actions of firms in markets. Firms respond to consumer preferences as expressed by *dollar votes* in the markets for goods and services.
3. The basic function of prices is to ration and allocate scarce goods and resources among potential buyers. *Free* goods and resources are so abundant relative to the demand for them that they command no price.
4. The **demand function**, or **demand curve**, shows the relationship between price and quantity of a good demanded, other things equal. In all relevant circumstances, there is an inverse relationship between price and quantity demanded.
5. Movements along a demand curve in response to a change in the price of the good are called **changes in quantity demanded**. Changes in the quantity people are willing and able to buy due to changes other than changes in price are called **changes in demand**.
6. A **supply function**, or **supply curve**, shows the relationship between the price of a good and the quantity supplied, other things equal. Movements along a supply curve due to a change in price are called **changes in quantity supplied**, and changes in the amount supplied due to changes other than changes in price are called **changes in supply**.
7. **Equilibrium price and quantity** are reached when there is no tendency for price to change. This occurs where the quantity demanded equals the quantity supplied. Price tends to move toward or remain at its equilibrium level.
8. If the price is below equilibrium, quantity demanded exceeds quantity supplied and **excess demand** causes the price to rise. If the price is above equilibrium, the quantity supplied exceeds quantity demanded, and **excess supply** drives the price downward.
9. An **effective maximum price** set below equilibrium price keeps price from rising to its equilibrium level, and results in excess demand. An **effective minimum price** set above equilibrium price keeps price from falling to equilibrium, and results in excess supply.
10. **Partial equilibrium** analyzes equilibrium in a single market independently of other related markets. **General equilibrium** analyzes equilibrium in all markets and the interrelationships among markets.

Concepts for Review

market	law of demand	excess demand
market structure	demand schedule	excess supply
household	demand curve or	shortage
firm	function	surplus
consumer	endogenous	price controls
sovereignty	exogenous	effective maximum price
laissez-faire	supply schedule	effective minimum price
price	supply curve	partial equilibrium
scarce goods	equilibrium price	general equilibrium
free goods	cleared market	

Questions

1. Nostalgia buffs and older students may recall a popular song entitled "The Best Things in Life Are Free."
   a. How many things in your life are free, in the sense that economics defines the term *free*?
   b. Can you think of any things that were free to your parents, grandparents, or great-grandparents that aren't free to you? What happened to the things that used to be free?
2. The energy crisis has produced a controversy over whether higher gasoline prices or gasoline rationing is the more effective means of allocating gasoline.
   a. Are higher prices and rationing really different? How should the alternatives be stated to be more accurate economically?
   b. Would there be any rationing of gasoline if we simply "froze" gasoline prices?
3. Why is the law of demand stated with a *ceteris paribus* assumption?
4. Would it be correct to define *equilibrium price* as the price at which the quantity bought equals the quantity sold?
5. Does *consumer sovereignty* mean the same thing as *majority rule*?
6. In each of the following, will the effect be an increase or decrease in demand, an increase or decrease in quantity demanded, an increase or decrease in supply, or an increase or decrease in quantity supplied?
   a. Higher oil prices encourage the production of more oil.
   b. An international cartel of oil producers decides to withhold oil from the market at prevailing prices.
   c. Higher retail prices of gasoline reduce gasoline consumption.
   d. Higher gasoline prices cause more people to travel by train and bus.
   e. A massive antismoking advertising and public information program causes the sales of cigarettes to fall.
7. Suppose that all the product and resource markets in the economy are in equilibrium, and suddenly the price of coal rises. We know from the law of demand that the quantity of coal demanded will fall. Can you think of several other markets which might be affected (directly or indirectly) by the coal price increase? What would be the nature of those effects?

Problems   1. If electronic gizmos cost $300 each, consumers wouldn't be able or
willing to buy any gizmos at all, while producers would be willing and
able to supply 500 gizmos. Every $20 reduction in the price of gizmos
would increase the quantity of gizmos demanded by 10. Every $20
reduction in the price would decrease the quantity of gizmos supplied
by 40.

   a. From the above information, fill out a demand schedule showing the
   quantity of gizmos demanded at prices of 300, 280, 260, 240, 220,
   200, 180, 160, 140, 120, and 100. On a graph, construct the demand
   curve for gizmos from this information.

   b. Fill out a supply schedule showing the quantity supplied at the
   prices in part (a), and construct the supply curve for gizmos from
   this information on the same graph you used for the demand curve.

   c. Find the equilibrium price and quantity of gizmos from the
   information, and explain how you know that you have found
   equilibrium price and quantity.

   d. Suppose that the government froze the price of gizmos at P*=$100
   because it was felt that this is the fair price to pay for them. What
   would be the results of this action?

   e. Suppose that, as a result of improvements in gizmo technology,
   sellers are now willing and able to offer an additional 20 gizmos for
   sale at every price. Explain the effects of this (if any) on demand,
   supply, equilibrium price, and equilibrium quantity.

PART TWO

Understanding the Aggregate Economy

The study of economics has traditionally been broken down into two main parts. **Microeconomics** explores the interactions between buyers and sellers in the market for a *particular* good or resource, and analyzes how those interactions determine price, output, and employment in that market. **Macroeconomics** explores the interactions between *all* buyers and sellers in *all* markets and analyzes how those interactions determine a price level and a level of output and employment *for an entire economy*. In other words, macroeconomics deals with the same basic variables as microeconomics, but it does so on an **aggregate** level—for the economy as a whole.

The central problems we will explore in macroeconomics are ones we read or hear about nearly every day: inflation, unemployment, recession. This section presents a general overview of these problems and of the macroeconomist's approach to them. Since most of our attention in subsequent sections of the text will focus on how aggregate output, prices, and employment are determined, we'll also look closely in this section at how the levels of these key macroeconomic variables can be measured empirically.

4

Introduction to Macroeconomics

Preview: We now turn our attention from *microeconomics* to *macroeconomics*—the study of the economy as a whole. Instead of the market demand for a particular good, we'll look at the *aggregate demand* for *all* goods and services by *all* consumers; instead of the market supply of a particular good, we'll look at the *aggregate supply* of *all* goods and services by *all* producers and suppliers. In this first chapter, we'll focus upon some of the key theories, problems, and issues of modern macroeconomics.

Since the 1940s, economic analysis has developed two main branches —*microeconomics* and *macroeconomics*.

- **Microeconomics** deals with the parts of the economy—households, firms, and markets.
- **Macroeconomics** deals with the economy as a whole, or with economic aggregates.

It's very important that the distinction and degree of separation between microeconomics and macroeconomics not be either overstated or understated. Nearly every economic problem and issue has both a macroeconomic and a microeconomic side. For example, inflation, the hottest issue of the late 1970s, has traditionally been classified as a macroeconomic problem. If it were strictly macroeconomic, however, the problem would be very easy to solve—simply freeze all prices at current levels. The aggregate price level would stop rising and the problem of inflation would be solved. As we saw in Chapter 3, however, prices perform the critical economic functions of rationing and allocating scarce goods and resources, so freezing prices would require some nonprice means of performing this function. Excess demand and excess supply would develop in various markets, and *black markets* for goods in excess demand would become a problem.

At the other extreme, if we understate the distinction between micro-economics and macroeconomics, we are in danger of falling into either the *fallacy of composition* (what's true for the part is true for the whole) or the *fallacy of division* (what's true for the whole is true for the parts), discussed in Chapter 1. The steel industry, for example, has been faced with chronic unemployment in recent years because of competition from more efficient foreign producers. Protection of the steel industry from foreign competition—by imposing tariffs or import quotas—would increase output, employment, and profits in the American steel industry. What's good for the steel industry, however, won't necessarily be good for everybody. Consumers will have to pay higher prices for all goods that require steel in their production. If we were to restrict *all* imports, we would probably find that we had fewer goods and services available at higher prices.

Similarly, we can't turn a macroeconomic result around and conclude that what's true for the economy as a whole will necessarily be true for every part of the economy. For example, increasing the money supply and government spending can increase the demand for goods and services and lower the overall unemployment rate in the economy. However, some elements of the unemployed population won't be affected by the increase in demand: workers without necessary skills, education, and experience to perform the jobs most needed won't suddenly become employable as a result of greater demand.

In short, microeconomics and macroeconomics are related parts of the same basic subject—branches of the same tree—but they aren't identical. We can't generalize results in specific industries and markets to the economy as a whole, and we can't attribute macroeconomic results for the economy as a whole to all individual markets, firms, and households.

The Villains: Unemployment and Inflation

The main concern of macroeconomics is two fundamental economic problems that have plagued nearly all of the world's economies in recent years: unemployment and inflation. Each is bad enough alone, but the challenge in the past two decades has been to understand and deal with unemployment and inflation at the same time.

Politicians, commentators, newspapers, and economists tell us again and again that unemployment and inflation are bad for the economy and the community. Promises to deal with unemployment and inflation have become as established in campaign lexicon as defense of the flag and "Mom's apple pie." What is it about unemployment and inflation that makes them so bad economically? Why is there so much controversy over the appropriate policies to deal with them?

An old bromide asserts that "it's an ill wind that doesn't blow somebody some good." Unemployment or inflation may not be bad for everybody economically. Unemployment generally is the most serious problem for the segment of the economy that's unemployed and suffers a loss of income. Inflation is most harmful to those whose money incomes are fixed or don't rise as fast as the prices of the goods and services they buy, and for creditors (people and institutions to whom debts are owed).

The aggregate problem of unemployment generally doesn't have a very heavy impact on those who remain employed and those whose incomes aren't interrupted or reduced. Inflation doesn't harm those whose money incomes at least keep pace with the prices of the goods and services they buy, nor does it harm those firms whose profits rise more rapidly than prices. In fact, inflationary periods are actually beneficial to people and institutions that owe large debts because the debts are repaid in cheaper dollars as prices rise.

Of course, unemployment and/or inflation can reach such extreme levels that they threaten the entire social, political, and economic fabric of society. Masses of unemployed workers may form a potent revolutionary force. **Hyperinflation**—very rapid increases in prices—can lead to economic, social, and political chaos, as it did in Germany in the 1920s and more recently in Argentina. Short of these extremes, unemployment and inflation cause some potential difficulties for the community economic welfare.

Unemployment represents unused productive capacity, and the community loses the goods and services that could have been produced by this unemployed capacity. If society is to do the best it can with what it has, resources and technology must be employed fully.

Inflation doesn't always hurt everybody economically, but it "taxes" the community in the form of higher prices of goods and services, and it tends to redistribute income from those who are hurt by the inflation to those who benefit from it. The problem with inflation as a tax or a means of redistributing income is that its effects aren't always precise or predictable.

The Aggregate Demand–Aggregate Supply Model: A Sneak Preview

In order to get a very basic understanding of the sources of inflation and unemployment, we're going to take a brief look at a model of the economy that will be developed in detail in the course of this text: the **aggregate demand–aggregate supply (YD-YS) model.** Don't expect to understand it fully yet: it is only meant to provide you with a general picture of the direction we will be taking in the remainder of the text.

The YD-YS model describes the interaction between two variables that lie at the heart of modern macroeconomics:

- **Aggregate demand** (YD) is the total demand or intended expenditure for all goods and services by all buyers—private households, firms, the government, and foreign buyers.

- **Aggregate supply** (YS) is the total supply of all goods and services by all producers.

In Figure 1, the horizontal axis represents the **aggregate output** of the economy as a whole, while the vertical axis shows the average price of goods and services produced, or the **aggregate price level**, as defined by a price index. The **aggregate demand curve (*YD*)** shows the total output of goods and services the public would wish to purchase at any given price level, *ceteris paribus*. The **aggregate supply curve (*YS*)** shows the price level consistent with any given level of total output, *ceteris paribus*. The economy reaches **equilibrium aggregate output** when the aggregate demand for goods and services equals the aggregate supply—where YD intersects YS in Figure 1. Here the aggregate output of the economy depicted will be $\overline{Y}$ and the price level will be $\overline{P}$.

Inflation and Unemployment in the YD-YS Model

Inflation is defined as a sustained rise in the price level. In the aggregate demand–aggregate supply model, there are two basic causes or types of inflation.

- *Increasing aggregate demand* causes the price level and aggregate output to rise.

- *Decreasing aggregate supply* causes the price level to rise and aggregate output to fall.

Figure 1 The Aggregate Demand–Aggregate Supply Model

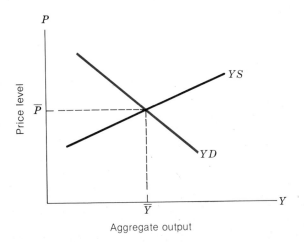

Aggregate output

Figure 2   Inflation and Unemployment

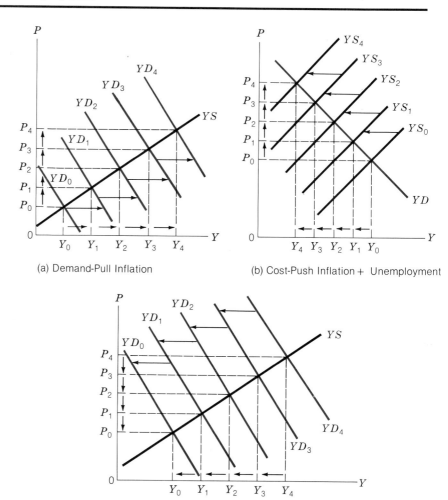

(a) Demand-Pull Inflation

(b) Cost-Push Inflation + Unemployment

(c) Demand-Deficiency Unemployment

These two types of inflation are illustrated in Figure 2. In Figure 2a, increases in aggregate demand are shown by shifts of the aggregate demand curve to the right. As aggregate demand increases from YD_0 to YD_1, YD_2, YD_3, and YD_4, aggregate output increases from Y_0 to Y_1, Y_2, Y_3, and Y_4. As aggregate output increases due to increasing aggregate demand, the price level rises as well, as shown in Figure 2a. This type of inflation is called **demand-pull inflation** because the price level is *pulled* upward by increasing aggregate demand.

In Figure 2b, the aggregate supply curve shifts upward, or to the left, indicating a higher aggregate price level at each level of aggregate output or a smaller aggregate output at every price level. As the aggregate supply curve shifts from YS_0 to YS_1, YS_2, YS_3, and YS_4, aggregate output falls and the price level rises. This type of inflation, which originates from the supply side, is called **cost-push inflation** because the price level is *pushed* upward by shifts of the aggregate supply curve to the left.

The level of employment and therefore the severity of the unemployment problem depends on the level of aggregate output. As aggregate output increases, employment increases and unemployment generally declines. As aggregate output falls, so does the level of employment, and unemployment increases.

Changes in aggregate supply and aggregate demand, then, will also affect the level of unemployment.

- A *decrease in aggregate demand* lowers aggregate output, employment, and the price level.

- A *decrease in aggregate supply* lowers aggregate output and employment, but causes the price level to rise.

The effect of a decrease in aggregate supply on the price level and aggregate output is shown in Figure 2b. As aggregate output falls, so does the level of employment, and the level of unemployment rises. In Figure 2c, aggregate demand falls from YD_4 to YD_3, YD_2, YD_1, and YD_0, causing aggregate output and the price level to fall. As aggregate output falls, the level of employment declines and unemployment increases.

But what causes these changes in aggregate demand and aggregate supply? Why are the curves in the YD-YS model shaped the way they are, and how will our predictions of inflation and unemployment be different if the shapes of the curves are different? What does it mean to say that aggregate demand *depends* on the price level? Why does the level of output vary with the price level? What can we *do* about inflation and unemployment, and how will our policies differ according to the sources of the problems?

By now, you've probably asked yourself some or all of these questions—and maybe a few more besides. Our goal in the remainder of this text will be to try to come up with some satisfactory (if not always satisfying) answers to them. In the next chapter, we'll look at how we measure the quantities on the two axes of the YD-YS model: aggregate output and the price level. After that, we'll spend a number of chapters looking closely at aggregate demand: what determines its level, what changes it, and how the government can manipulate it (through fiscal and monetary policies) in order to fight inflation and unemployment.

For many years, most orthodox economists felt that the demand side of the economy was all that really "mattered," and that *demand management* policies were the key to combating inflation and unemployment.

Unfortunately, many of the economic problems our economy has faced in recent years—oil embargoes, productivity slowdowns, stagflation— have been *supply* problems. Thus, after thoroughly reviewing the successes and failures, problems and issues surrounding the use of demand management policies, we'll return to the question of aggregate supply, rebuilding the *YD-YS* model from scratch and seeing what the model can tell us about the policy directions that must be taken in the continuing fight against inflation and unemployment.

Varieties of Macroeconomics Thinking

Modern economics, macroeconomics in particular, is hardly character- ized by universal agreement on the basic questions and analytical approaches. It probably never has been, but there have been periods in which orthodox economic ideas—what Professor John Kenneth Galbraith has called the *traditional wisdom*—have been more widely accepted by economists than is the case in modern macroeconomics.

Classical Macroeconomics: The Old Orthodoxy

The term *classical economics* has several meanings. In the history of eco- nomics, it refers to a school of economic thought that dominated eco- nomics from the late eighteenth century until the last quarter of the nineteenth. As an approach to macroeconomics, however, the term **classical macroeconomics** refers to the orthodox economic analysis that was generally accepted between the late eighteenth century and the analytical revolution started by John Maynard Keynes in the late 1930s.

A cornerstone of classical macroeconomics is a proposition known as *Say's Law*:

- **Say's Law** argues that in a competitive market economy, supply creates its own demand.

This rather puzzling little proposition has an important implication. Since producers can be assured of demand for all additional output, they will increase output until their capacities to produce are fully utilized. Aggregate output will thus reach equilibrium only when the economy is at full employment. Turning Say's Law around, the exis- tence of unemployed resources and capacity indicates *disequilibrium*, and if market forces aren't interfered with, full employment would be reached as aggregate output and prices adjusted to equilibrium.

The full-employment equilibrium in classical macroeconomics depends on flexible wages and prices. Classical economists viewed the use of labor as any other commodity that is bought and sold in the marketplace. If the price of labor is too high, there will be *excess supply* or unemployment. In the long run, however, adjustments of markets to equilibrium with flexible wages and prices would cause the wage to fall. As the wage falls, the quantity of labor demanded increases and the

Figure 3 Varieties of Macroeconomic Thinking

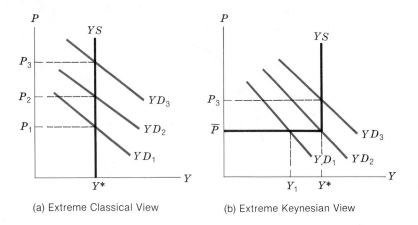

(a) Extreme Classical View   (b) Extreme Keynesian View

quantity supplied falls until the labor market is cleared at the equilibrium wage.

Similar arguments apply to other markets as well. If there is overproduction of a particular good, its price will fall relative to other prices until the excess supply is eliminated at equilibrium. Excess demand for goods or resources will drive their prices up relative to other prices, eliminating the excess demand. When all competitive markets are in equilibrium, there will be no excess demand or supply for goods or resources and no unemployed productive capacity.

In the long run, according to classical macroeconomics, equilibrium aggregate output will be reached only at full employment, so in the long run aggregate output is determined by productive capacity, not by aggregate demand. In terms of the YD-YS model, this suggests an aggregate supply curve that is vertical at the level of output consistent with full employment of productive capacity—Y^* in Figure 3a. Notice that such a curve implies that changes in aggregate demand will affect only the price level in the long run, and will have no long-run effect on the levels of aggregate output and employment. If this analysis is accurate, there is no role for the government in determining the level of output and employment, and government intervention will tend only to interfere with the adjustment of the system to full-employment equilibrium.

Keynesian Macro-economics: The "New Orthodoxy"

Much of the macroeconomic orthodoxy of the 1970s has evolved from ideas introduced by the late British economist John Maynard Keynes in his *General Theory of Employment, Interest, and Money*, published in 1936. In fact, the contemporary mainstream in macroeconomics is called **Keynesian economics.**

One of the central assertions of *The General Theory*, and a continuing source of disagreement and controversy, is that macroeconomic equilibrium *can* be reached with unemployed productive capacity or with chronic inflationary pressures, as well as at the classical full-employment level. This notion ran head-on into the classical position that in the long run private market forces would lead to equilibrium at full employment—an argument to which Keynes offered his famous reply that "in the long run, we all are dead."

In Keynesian macroeconomics, the critical variable determining equilibrium aggregate output and employment is aggregate demand. In fact, the most extreme Keynesian view implied that the aggregate supply curve was virtually horizontal, as in Figure 3b, until full employment is reached.

The classical full-employment equilibrium would be reached only if aggregate demand were YD_2 in Figure 3b. This is a possibility in the Keynesian analysis, but clearly not the only possibility. If aggregate demand falls at YD_1, the economy is underutilizing its capacity and workers are unemployed. On the other hand, if aggregate demand were at YD_3, the economy would experience rising prices or inflation because the output of goods and services can't increase beyond the full employment level (Y^*).

Keynes' major point of departure with the classical analysis was his contention that there are no automatic forces operating within the economy to drive aggregate demand to YD_2 or equilibrium aggregate output to Y^* without inflationary pressures. According to Keynes, prices are not sufficiently flexible to achieve the classical result automatically. If equilibrium is reached with unemployment, the only way to eliminate the unemployment is to increase aggregate demand. Similarly, chronic inflation as a result of excess aggregate demand can be dealt with only by policies that lower aggregate demand.

Thus the Keynesian approach provides for active government intervention in the economy to stimulate or dampen aggregate demand in order to deal with unemployment or inflation. Keynes tended to advocate the use of government spending and taxation (*fiscal policies*) over manipulation of the money supply (*monetary policies*), particularly to stimulate aggregate demand in periods of severe economic depression.

Monetarism: The Classical Resurgence

For many years Professor Milton Friedman, now retired from the University of Chicago, has been the leading spokesman for an approach to macroeconomics called **monetarism.** In fact, Friedman and the University of Chicago have been so closely identified with modern monetarism that it has been called **Chicago-school monetarism.**

Not surprisingly from its name, monetarism identifies the money supply as the critical variable in macroeconomics. There is more to monetarism than a heavy emphasis on the money supply, however. Like classical macroeconomists, monetarists usually argue that the private sector is inherently quite stable and that competitive market forces and flexible prices will generate equilibrium aggregate output at full employment of resources and capacity.

According to the monetarists, active government intervention in the economy, particularly to stimulate aggregate demand and reduce unemployment, generally does more harm than good—if it has any effect at all. In the long run, they argue, real aggregate output is determined by productive capacity, and government attempts to stimulate aggregate demand in the short run won't affect long-run equilibrium anyway. Attempts to stimulate aggregate demand in the short run by fiscal policies won't be very effective unless they are supported by appropriate changes in the money supply; this is because, in the long run, fiscal policies affect only the distribution of output between the public and private sectors of the economy, not the total aggregate output.

Monetarists have argued further that, because of incomplete information on the size or the timing of the effects of changes in the money supply, monetary authorities should do as little as possible. With incomplete information, there's a very good chance that attempting to reduce unemployment by expanding the money supply or reduce inflation by reducing the money supply will end up doing too much, too little, or the wrong thing entirely. Thus, like the classicists but in sharp contrast with the Keynesians, monetarists tend to advocate *laissez faire* as the appropriate strategy for government in the economy.

Macroeconomics in the 1980s: Sound and Fury Signifying Much

The above sketches of various schools of macroeconomic thought are hardly exhaustive descriptions or analyses, but only broad characterizations. Furthermore, most economists' ideas on macroeconomic problems fall somewhere between the extreme Keynesian and monetarist positions. However, the debates between basically monetarist and basically Keynesian economics will be one of the central themes of macroeconomics in the 1980s. Within this theme, the central issues are the following:

1. Can the economy sustain acceptably high levels of output and employment with stable prices?
2. What are the proper roles of private market forces vs. public policy in achieving price stability, full employment, and a stable trend of aggregate economic activity over time?
3. How important is money as a determinant of aggregate output, income, employment, and prices?
4. What is the proper relationship between policies dealing with government spending and taxes vs. policies dealing with the money supply in achieving economic objectives?

5. How important is aggregate supply vs. aggregate demand in causing unemployment and inflation, and what is the role of supply management vs. demand management policies in dealing with those problems?

The chapters that follow, unfortunately, won't provide answers to all of the unresolved questions in macroeconomics. They do, however, provide a basic grasp of the tools and concepts that are essential for evaluating the arguments and recognizing the relevant questions.

Summary

1. **Microeconomics** analyzes the parts of the economy—markets, firms, and households. **Macroeconomics** analyzes economic *aggregates*, or the *economy as a whole*. **Inflation** and **unemployment** are the key problems explored in the study of macroeconomics.
2. **Aggregate demand** is the total expenditure for all goods and services at any given level of **aggregate output**, or **real national income. Aggregate supply** is the total supply of goods and services by all producers. The interaction between aggregate supply and aggregate demand can result in unemployment and inflation.
3. In **classical macroeconomics,** flexible prices and **Say's Law** lead to equilibrium aggregate output only at full employment in the long run.
4. In **Keynesian macroeconomics**, the level of aggregate demand determines equilibrium aggregate output, which may or may not be at full employment. Keynes' analysis allows government a much larger role in the economy than does the classical analysis.
5. Modern **monetarism** is built on the classical foundation and represents a reaction to Keynesian macroeconomics. Monetarists tend to argue that freely operating markets and flexible prices will cause aggregate output to move toward a full-employment equilibrium in the long run. Attempts by government to regulate demand or change equilibrium will upset this adjustment.

Concepts for Review

microeconomics	aggregate supply	classical macroeconomics
macroeconomics	aggregate output	Say's Law
inflation	price level	Keynesian macroeconomics
unemployment	demand-pull inflation	monetarism
aggregate demand	cost-push inflation	

Questions

1. What is the relationship between microeconomics and macroeconomics? Are they separate subjects? Is it sufficient to understand either microeconomics or macroeconomics, but not both, to deal with current economic problems?

2. What (if anything) is wrong with the following statements?
   a. "We should limit bids for public construction projects to local contractors, since the economic health of the community is determined by the economic health of local businesses."
   b. "Since automation makes it possible to produce more goods at a lower cost, it is good for the economy and therefore good for every worker."
3. Looking at Figure 1, explain how each of the following occurrences (*ceteris paribus*) will affect the price level, aggregate output, and the level of employment:
   a. An increase in aggregate demand.
   b. An increase in aggregate supply.
   c. A decrease in aggregate demand.
   d. A decrease in aggregate supply.
4. David Ricardo (a leading classical economist of the early 19th century), John Maynard Keynes, and Milton Friedman each made one of the following statements. Match each statement with its author, and explain your choices.
   a. "(The) only effective way to stop inflation is to restrain the rate of growth of the money supply."
   b. "(There) is no limit to demand—no limit to the employment of capital while it yields any profit."
   c. "(There) will be only one level of employment consistent with equilibrium. . . . This level cannot be greater than full employment, . . . But there is no reason in general for expecting it to be equal to full employment."
5. Compare the points of similarity and disagreement among classical, Keynesian, and monetarist macroeconomics.

5

Measuring Aggregate Output, Income, and Prices

Preview: Basic to the understanding of macroeconomic problems and issues are three variables: *aggregate output, income,* and *price level.* In this chapter we'll see how aggregate output and income are defined and measured, we'll look at the meaning of price levels, and we'll examine the usefulness of measures of aggregate output as guides to a country's economic welfare.

Anybody who follows the economic news, even casually, will be bombarded with macroeconomic data. The federal government gathers, estimates, and publishes a vast array of information on output, income, prices, economic growth, and other indicators of economic performance. Economic performance and problems occupy a prominent place in political debates and issues, and most economic policy arguments are bolstered by economic data.

It's important to have a basic understanding of the meaning of the economic data to which we're exposed continually. What does it mean if somebody argues that the economy is doing poorly because Gross National Product didn't increase significantly in the last quarter? When an increase in the nation's personal income is announced, what does this mean in terms of the economic welfare of the typical family? If the Consumer Price Index increases by 10 percent in a year, how accurately does this measure any specific family's increase in cost of living?

The Flow of National Income and Output: An Overview

The first step in measuring national income and output is to recognize the distinction between *stocks* and *flows*.

- **Flows** are quantities per unit of time.
- **Stocks** are simply quantities that are not expressed with any reference to time.

For example, the *flow* of water through a pipe is measured in gallons per hour, per day, etc., while the *stock* of water in a reservoir is simply expressed in gallons.

Output and income are *flows*. As individuals, our incomes are weekly, monthly, or annual *flows*—$250 per week, $1,000 per month, or $12,000 per year—not a single lifetime figure (stock) of $500,000. One of the more depressing things to do is to look back over the past several years and add all of your annual incomes together, and wonder where all of that money went.

The answer is quite simple, if not reassuring. The weekly, monthly, and annual flows of income were accompanied by weekly, monthly, and annual *expenditure flows*—for food, housing, clothing, etc.

In its simplest representation, an economy is a circular flow of goods and services and of *productive resources* or *factors of production* between households and firms, such as the one shown in Figure 1. In the absence of coercion, we can expect households and firms to exchange goods and resources of equal value. For households, the benefits or satisfaction from the goods they receive will just equal the real costs of the resources they give up. For firms, the resource services they purchase will equal the value of the goods they offer in exchange.

- In the circular flow, the value of the goods flow equals the value of the resource flow.

Instead of exchanging resources directly for goods, households exchange their resources for money and the money for goods. Firms will

Figure 1   Simple Circular Flow in a Barter Economy

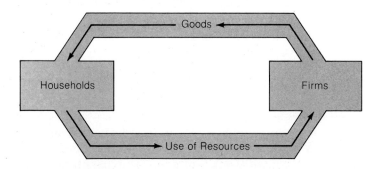

Figure 2 Simple Circular Flow in a Money Economy

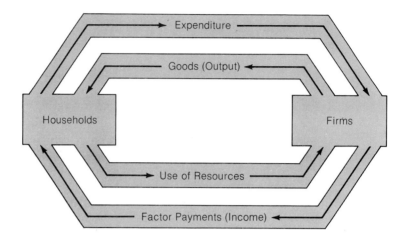

purchase resource services for money and sell goods to households for money. In Figure 2, the quantities of food and clothing in the flow and the prices of food and clothing determine the size of the expenditure (consumption) flow from households to firms. The **consumption expenditure flow** in this system represents the money value of the goods and services produced for consumption by all firms.

- **Aggregate output**, or **national product**, is the aggregate value of goods and services produced for final use in the economy per year.

In the lower loop of the circular flow, the quantities of resources in the flow and the prices of resources determine the **factor payments** or **income flow** from firms to households. This is the money value of the resource flow from households to firms.

- **National income** is the sum of the values of the factors of production or resources employed in production of goods and services.

Since households and firms exchange equal values, it follows that

$$\text{Aggregate output} = \text{National income}$$

and

$$\frac{\text{Aggregate expenditure}}{\text{for goods and services}} = \frac{\text{Aggregate}}{\text{factor payments}}$$

Measuring National Income and Output

In a single industry or market, finding the aggregate quantity supplied by all sellers and the aggregate quantity demanded by all buyers is conceptually quite simple. The quantities supplied by individual sellers or demanded by individual buyers can simply be added up.

However, adding the outputs of all firms in all industries or the quantities of all goods demanded by all buyers together to get aggregate figures for the economy as a whole isn't quite so simple. Physical units of different products can't be added together—5 billion bolts + 5 billion nuts = 5 billion bolts + 5 billion nuts. Adding outputs of different goods and services together to get a meaningful sum requires a common denominator. The only useful common denominator for this purpose is the *money value*, or the *price*.

Measuring aggregate output and income is thus basically a very large accounting problem. In a vast and complex economy, however, since it's impossible to gather all of the detailed information on economic activity from all producers, most of the measurements in the national income accounts are estimates. In addition, unavoidable errors, clerical and otherwise, inevitably affect the accuracy of the figures.

Gross National Product (GNP)

Gross National Product (GNP) is the most comprehensive measure of economic activity in the national income accounts.

- **Gross National Product** (GNP) is the value of all goods and services produced for final use in a given year, expressed in current market prices.

In 1978, the U.S. GNP was $2,106.6 billion, or $2.1 trillion. This was the value of goods and services produced for final use in 1978, expressed in 1978 prices.

The values of *intermediate goods* are not included as separate items in calculating GNP.

- **Intermediate goods** are goods that are used in the production of other goods that are ultimately sold for final use by households.

The value of intermediate goods *is* included in the values of goods produced for final use. To include the values of all intermediate goods, and the value of final goods and services, would include the values of intermediate goods more than once. This is called *double counting*.

Each stage of the production process adds value to the materials and intermediate goods produced at previous stages of the production process. Table 1 is a simplified hypothetical example of the values added at various stages of production of an automobile with a retail price of $5000.

- The **value added** at each stage of production is the value of the product at the end of that stage less the value of the materials at the beginning of that stage.

In Table 1, mining adds $100 to the value of the unmined ore used to produce one automobile, smelting adds $100 to the value of the mined ore, etc. The final value of the automobile is the sum of the values added at each stage of production. The sum of the values of all final

Table 1 Price vs. Value Added

	Sales Price	Value Added
Miner sells ore to pig-iron factory	$ 100	$ 100
Pig-iron factory sells refined iron to steel manufacturer	$ 200	$ 100
Steel manufacturer sells steel to General Motors	$ 500	$ 300
General Motors sells Chevette to dealer	$3800	$3300
Dealer sells Chevette to customer	$5000	$1200
TOTAL	$9600	$5000

goods and services, then, is the sum of the values added by all producers of raw materials, intermediate goods, and final goods.

- *GNP is the sum of the values added* by all producers at all stages of production.

If all of the items in the left-hand column of Table 1 were included as separate items in calculating GNP, the value of the iron ore would be counted five times, the value of the pig iron four times, the value of the steel three times, etc. Double counting would show the contribution of one $5000 automobile to GNP as $9500.

Close-up

The *Value Added* Tax

The tax revolt in the United States in the late 1970s made politicians very wary of raising taxes, and led to renewed interest in a **value added tax** (VAT) as a means of raising government revenue or as a substitute for some direct taxes on individuals. One politically appealing aspect of the VAT is that not many people would understand what is being taxed. Everybody understands and feels the impact of a direct tax on income, but a small percentage levy on something as obscure as value added isn't likely to generate much rebellion among taxpayers.

A value added tax is an excise tax on the value added to materials and intermediate goods by a producer, so a 10 percent VAT would levy a 10 percent excise tax on the values added by all producers at all stages of production. In other words, a 10 percent VAT would be a 10 percent excise tax on the entire GNP! A seemingly innocuous 10 percent VAT on a GNP of $2 trillion would yield $200 billion in revenue.

The VAT raises the producers' costs at each stage of production, and the producers pass the cost of the tax on to the next stage of production, until the consumers end up paying the VAT as part of the retail prices of the goods and services they buy.

There are two basic measures of GNP—the **expenditure approach** and the **factor-payments approach.** Since they are alternative measures of the same thing, both methods give the same final figure for GNP. However, the two approaches provide somewhat different information.

Measuring GNP: The Expenditure Approach

The expenditure approach to measuring GNP measures the expenditure flows for goods and services purchased by households, firms, the public sector (federal, state, and local governments), and net expenditure flow from the international sector. In other words, this approach treats GNP as a measure of aggregate output.

Personal consumption is the largest component of GNP on the expenditure side. In 1978, personal consumption amounted to $1,339.7 billion, or 63.6 percent of the 1978 GNP of $2,106.6 billion. Total consumption expenditures by households are broken down into three broad categories of expenditures, based on the types of items consumed. Expenditures on *consumer durables* are expenditures on such items as appliances, automobiles, and other durable consumer goods. In 1978, expenditures on consumer durables amounted to $197.6 billion, or 14.8 percent of total consumption expenditures by households. *Nondurable consumer goods*—such as food, utilities, etc.—are consumed in short periods of time and generally don't last from one year to the next. In 1978, *nondurables* accounted for $525.8 billion in consumption expenditure, or 39.2 percent of total consumption. The third component of consumption expenditure is for *services* (such as haircuts, repair and maintenance services, medical care, etc.), and in 1978, expenditure for services was $616.3 billion, or 46 percent of total consumption.

The other expenditure flow from the private sector is *gross private domestic investment* or *gross investment*, which includes investment expenditures by households and firms. Investment expenditures differ from consumption expenditures in that they are expenditures for goods that give firms and households future benefits, which generally extend over a period of time. For households, the major investment item is new residential construction. Investment expenditures by firms include plant, equipment, and inventory adjustments. In 1978, gross private domestic investment expenditure amounted to $344.5 billion, or 16.4 percent of GNP measured from the expenditure side.

As defined in national income accounts, investment does *not* include the purchases of financial securities (stocks and bonds) or deposits in savings accounts. These transactions simply transfer cash into other financial assets. They add nothing to the stock of housing, plant, equipment, inventories, or other forms of capital used in production.

For households, the dividing line between consumer durables and investment is somewhat arbitrary. Residential housing is a component of the investment expenditure flow because housing provides benefits for a long period of time, while the purchase of an automobile is a

Table 2   U.S. Gross National Product, 1978, Expenditure Approach (billions of $)

Personal Consumption			1,339.7
Durable goods		197.6	
Nondurable goods		525.8	
Services		616.3	
Gross Private Domestic Investment			344.5
Nonresidential structures		77.5	
Producers' durable equipment		146.2	
Residential structures		105.0	
Changes in business inventories		15.7	
Government Purchases of Goods & Services			434.2
Federal		154.0	
Defense	99.5		
Nondefense	54.5		
State and local		280.2	
Net Exports of Goods and Services			−11.8
Exports		205.2	
Imports		−217.0	
GROSS NATIONAL PRODUCT			2,106.6

Source: *Economic Report of the President, 1979.*

consumer durable expenditure. But how long is *long*? The author's new 1965 Dodge served him well until 1977, and some of the old "monitor top" refrigerators of the 1930s lasted for a generation.

The GNP also includes expenditures from the public sector for purchases of goods and services by federal, state, and local governments—payrolls, public buildings, roads, military hardware, etc. In 1978, *government purchases* amounted to $434.2 billion, or 20.6 percent of GNP from the expenditure side. This does *not* include such things as government-financed pensions or welfare payments—these are *transfer payments* for which the public sector receives no goods and services in return. Transfer payments will be treated later.

The final component of GNP from the expenditure side is *net exports*, or the *balance of trade*, from the international sector. When foreign buyers purchase U.S. exports, their payments to American sellers enter our expenditure stream, and add to our GNP. When a U.S. buyer pays a foreign seller for imported goods, these expenditures leave our income stream and diminish GNP. *Net exports*, or the *balance of trade*, is simply the difference between export expenditures and import expenditures—or exports minus imports. This shows the net effect of the international sector on the domestic GNP.

The attention given to specific issues involving imports and exports—the effect of import competition on specific industries, oil imports, "defending the dollar," etc.—tends to create the impression that the balance of trade is a much larger component of GNP than it actually is. In 1978, net exports were −$11.8 billion (we imported more than we exported), and this amounted to less than 1 percent of U.S. GNP from the expenditure side.

Adding consumption, gross investment, government purchases, and net exports together gives us GNP by the expenditure approach. This is summarized for the U.S. in 1978 in Table 2. Note that these expenditures are for goods produced in 1978. The purchase of a house built in 1958 wouldn't be included in the investment flow for 1978, because the house isn't part of the 1978 output of goods and services.

Measuring GNP: The Factor Payments Approach

In the circular flow, total expenditure for goods and services is equal to the total payment by firms for the use of resources or factors of production employed to produce those goods and services. GNP measured from the *factor payments* side represents the value of the resources used to produce goods and services, and compensation to resource owners for the use of their resources. In other words, this approach views GNP as a measure of national income.

The largest item in the factor-payments flow is *compensation of employees*—wages, salaries, and supplements paid to employees in the private and public sectors to compensate for the use of their labor. In 1978, compensation of employees amounted to $1,301.2 billion, or about 61.8 percent of GNP.

Compensation for the use of the labor and resources of self-employed persons—farmers, self-employed professionals, and self-employed proprietors—is included in the category of *proprietors' income*.

Corporate profits compensate owners of corporations. Some of this profit goes to pay *corporate profit taxes*, some is distributed to stockholders as *dividends*, and some is saved by the corporations as *undistributed corporate profits*.

Rental income compensates the owners of land and rental business and residential properties. The national income accounts also include imputed rents on owner-occupied housing—imputed rents are simply estimates of the "rent" the homeowner pays himself or herself as his or her own "landlord."

Net interest represents payments by firms for borrowed funds, and is included in the national income accounts as part of the factor payments flow. However, it should be noted that this does not include all interest payments. Interest payments on consumer loans and interest payments by the government are excluded from the definition of net interest.

The value of the capital that wears out, or is consumed, in the course of production during the year is included in the factor payments flow as *capital consumption* or *depreciation*. The size of the capital consumption component of GNP depends heavily on tax laws governing depreciation allowances, and isn't necessarily an accurate picture of the actual loss of capital equipment.

Part of the retail price or value of final goods represents *indirect taxes*

Table 3   Gross National Product, 1978, Factor Payments Approach (billions of $)

Compensation of Employees		1,301.2
Wages and salaries	1,100.7	
Wage and salary adjustments	200.5	
Proprietors' Income		112.9
Farm	25.1	
Nonfarm	87.8	
Rental Income		23.4
Corporate Profits, Adjusted		160.0
Before-tax profits	202.4	
Corporate profit taxes	84.1	
Dividends	49.3	
Undistributed corp. profit	69.1	
Capital consumption adjustment	−18.1	
Inventory valuation adjustment	−24.3	
Net Interest Payments		106.1
Indirect Business Taxes		178.2
Depreciation		216.9
Statistical Discrepancies & Misc.		7.9
GROSS NATIONAL PRODUCT		2,106.6

Source: *Economic Report of the President, 1979*

which are levied on sellers and passed on to consumers. These indirect taxes include such items as general sales taxes, special excise taxes on some goods, gasoline taxes, etc.

There are more details in the national income accounts on the factor payments side, but the additional detail isn't essential for a basic understanding of the accounts. In addition, there are clerical and estimation errors in the data. All of these items will be lumped together in a catch-all category, *statististical discrepancies and misc*. The GNP for the U.S. in 1978 measured by factor payments (or income) is summarized in Table 3.

Close-up

Are the National Income Accounts *Sexist*?

Few occupations make more demands than that of the housewife. Housewives perform many of the duties of chefs, maids, teachers, managers, purchasing agents, counselors, and paramedics. It has been estimated that a full-time housewife works 2,500 hours per year at her profession, which works out to 52 48-hour weeks. Estimates of the value of housewives' services to the household range from about $4,800 per year to over $16,000 per year.[1] It has also been estimated that the value of housewives' services is about 20 percent of the Gross National

---

1. Some of the facts in this example are based on information in Juanita M. Kreps, *Sex in the Marketplace* (Baltimore: Johns Hopkins University Press, 1971), pp. 69–73.

Product. What, then, is the value assigned to housewives' services in the GNP accounts? Zero!

Some feminists have argued that the exclusion of housewives' services from the national income accounts is "sexist," and that it reflects the low status of traditional women's roles in our society. Sexual stereotyping and sexual discrimination in education, employment, and pay are serious economic problems, but the treatment of housewives' services in the national income accounts isn't related to this.

The national income accounts exclude the value of *all* unpaid family services to the household. The value of the bachelor's housekeeping services and the household services provided by the growing number of husbands who share in household duties are excluded as well.

There are two rather simple, and non-"sexist," reasons for excluding the value of unpaid family services to the household. First of all, it would be difficult if not impossible to gather reasonably accurate data on the value of everything from the tomatoes in the backyard garden to the major do-it-yourself home improvements provided by family members. Secondly, there isn't any meaningful "market test" of the value of these services because the relationship among family members is more emotional than economic.

Although GNP is the most convenient and comprehensive summary measure of aggregate output and income of the economy, it can be misleading as the sole indicator of economic performance. Other national income aggregates that are derived from GNP are useful for a more complete picture.

Net National Product (NNP)

GNP, whether measured from the expenditure or factor payments side, includes the value of the capital that is used up in the course of production during the year as part of aggregate income. In fact, this *depreciation* or *capital consumption* represents a loss of productive resources during the year.

- **Net National Product** shows the net value of final goods and services produced during the year, after deducting the value of capital consumed.

Algebraically, if D is depreciation,

$$NNP \equiv GNP - D.$$

In 1978, for example, deducting depreciation of $216.9 billion from the GNP of $2106.6 billion gives us

$$NNP = \$2106.6 \text{ billion} - \$216.9 \text{ billion} = \$1889.7 \text{ billion}.$$

National Income (NI)

National income is often used as a general expression synonymous with GNP or NNP. However, in the national income accounts, the term *national income* (NI) has a rather precise meaning.

- **National Income** (NI) is the aggregate income earned by factors of production.

To calculate national income from the national income accounting data, simply deduct indirect business taxes (IBT) from net national product. Algebraically,

$$NI \equiv NNP - IBT.$$

To avoid confusion, all future references to "national income" in the text will be to national income in the general sense (i.e., *GNP*) and not to this specific accounting definition, unless otherwise noted.

Personal Income (PI)

We still don't know the aggregate income received by households because not all of the national income produced by factors of production actually goes to the households. In addition, households receive income that hasn't been included in the definitions of GNP, NNP, or NI.

- **Personal Income** (PI) is the aggregate income actually received by households.

The first step in calculating PI is to deduct the items included in NI that aren't received by the households. First there are *corporate profits*, which represent income to corporations. *Social insurance contributions* are paid out of the income produced, but aren't received as income by persons, so they are excluded from Personal Income. *Net interest* isn't paid to households or individuals, so it isn't included in Personal Income.

Now, we have to add income that is received by households and persons, but wasn't included in the definitions of GNP, NNP, or NI. The big item here is *transfer payments*, of which the largest portion are government transfer payments for pensions, welfare programs, and survivors' benefits. Transfer payments aren't included in the definition of factor payments because they simply transfer income, and aren't payments for the use of productive resources. However, they are included in the definition of Personal Income because they represent income received by persons.

Dividends are the portion of corporate profits that are distributed to stockholders, and therefore represent income to persons. *Personal interest income* is the interest income of persons from all sources. These items have to be added to the definition of Personal Income. Summing all of this up, then, Personal Income (PI) is

$$PI \equiv NI - \text{(corporate profit + social insurance contributions + net interest)}$$
$$+ \text{(transfer payments + dividends + personal interest income)}.$$

Disposable Personal Income (DI)

Disposable Personal Income, or *Disposable Income (DI),* is the aggregate "take-home pay" of households to allocate and spend as they wish.

- **Disposable income** (DI) is personal income (PI), minus *direct taxes.*

Direct taxes are levied directly on households. Personal income taxes, property taxes, and other taxes paid directly by households are direct taxes.

There are only two possible uses for disposable income—it must be spent for personal consumption or saved. In other words,

$$DI \equiv C + S,$$

where C is personal consumption and S is personal saving.

Table 4 summarizes the relationship between GNP and the other national income accounting aggregates for the U.S. in 1978.

Table 4 U.S. National Income Aggregates, 1978 (billions of $)

Gross National Product			2,106.6
Less: Depreciation	210.9		
Equals: *Net National Product*			1,889.7
Less: Indirect business taxes	178.2		
Misc.	7.9		
Equals: *National Income*			1,703.6
Less: Adjusted corporate profits	160.0		
Net interest	106.1		
Plus: Transfer payments		226.0	
Personal interest income		158.9	
Dividends		49.3	
Equals: *Personal Income*			1,707.4
Less: Direct personal taxes	256.2		
Equals: *Disposable Personal Income*			1,451.2
Less: Personal outlays	1,374.4		
Consumption 1,339.7			
Other 34.8			
Equals: *Personal Saving*			76.8

Source: *Economic Report of the President, 1979*

Measuring Changes in Prices and Output

Index numbers express GNP, prices, industrial production, and other variables in a given year as a percentage or proportion of their value in a base year. The index for the base year is 100 or 1.0. For example, the index of industrial production for the U.S. expresses industrial production as a proportion of industrial production in 1967 (1967 = 100). In 1978, the industrial production index stood at 145 (1967 = 100). This simply means that industrial production in 1978 was 145 percent of industrial production in 1967, or 1.45 times as large as it was in 1967.

Real and Nominal Income

The economy's *real GNP* is the circular flow of goods and resources. The flow of money expenditures for goods and services and factor payments is *money income*, or *nominal GNP*. Real GNP can't be calculated by adding up different physical quantities of different goods and resources, and money prices have to be used as a common denominator. However, changes in prices can cause the money income flow to change with no change, or even an opposite change in the real income flow.

For example, suppose that the output of food and clothing remain constant in two years (call them year 1 and year 2), while the prices of food and clothing increase by 50%. In *current prices*, or *current dollars*,

GNP in yr. 1 = (5 billion C × $20/C) + (10 billion F × $10/F)
= $200 billion.
GNP in yr. 2 = (5 billion C × $30/C) + (10 billion F × $15/F)
= $300 billion.

The 50% increase in nominal income in this case means very little in terms of living standards or economic welfare because the outputs of goods, or *real GNP* didn't change.

To measure the real output of goods and services, or real GNP over a period of years, each year's income is expressed in *constant prices*, or *constant dollars*.

- Real GNP is the value of goods and services produced per year in *constant prices*.

In the above example, if GNP is expressed in constant prices (use prices from year 1),

GNP in yr. 1 = (5 billion C × $20/C) + (10 billion F × $10/F)
= $200 billion.
GNP in yr. 2 = (5 billion C × $20/C) + (10 billion F × $10/F)
= $200 billion.

Using constant prices, there was no change in real GNP.

In practice, it's impossible to assign constant prices to the millions of goods and services produced to find real GNP in constant prices. Instead, **price indexes** are estimated which show the average price level in a given year as a percentage, or proportion of the price level in some base year.[1] For example, if we used year 1 from the previous example as the base year, the price index in year 1 would be 100 (or 1.0), indicating that prices in year 1 are 100 percent of prices in year 1. In year 2, with prices 50 percent higher than in year 1, the price index for year 2 would be 150 (or 1.5), indicating that prices in year 2 are 150 percent of prices in year 1, or 1.5 times as high as prices in year 1.

- To find real GNP in a given year in constant prices, divide the money GNP by the price index for the given year.

1. For more details on price indexes, see the appendix to this chapter.

In the previous example, real GNP in year 2, in constant prices from year 1 is

$$\text{Real GNP (in constant prices)} = \frac{\text{Money Income}}{\text{Price Index}} = \frac{\$300 \text{ b.}}{1.5} = \$200 \text{ b.}$$

Two of the more important price indexes published by the government are the **consumer price index** (CPI) and the **implicit price deflator** (IPD).

Consumer Price Index (CPI)

The *consumer price index* (*CPI*) is perhaps the most commonly used price index. It is estimated by the U.S. Bureau of Labor Statistics from data gathered in a scientifically designed statistical sample of 85 urban areas. The most commonly used version of the CPI is the index for all items in all urban areas.

- The **consumer price index** (CPI) estimates the cost of a constant *basket* of goods as a percentage of the cost of the same basket of goods in the base year.

Traditionally, the basket of goods chosen by the BLS was supposed to approximate the consumption pattern of typical urban households headed by wage earners and clerical workers. Since January 1978, an additional CPI has been estimated to show changes in cost of living for all urban households. The basket is modified at ten-year intervals to reflect changes in typical consumption patterns. The 1968 revision, for example, deleted men's pajamas and added motel rooms to the basket.

The CPI is a good indicator of inflation and changes in cost of living, but it doesn't measure the change in every household's cost of living. If you happen to live in an area where prices are rising more rapidly than the average of all urban areas, the change in the CPI will understate the change in your cost of living. If your consumption pattern differs from that of the average urban household, the CPI will give an inaccurate picture of the change in your cost of living. Table 5 shows the CPI for various classes of expenditure. If you happen to spend a larger share of your income than the average household for goods whose prices have increased most rapidly, such as medical care, the CPI for all items will understate the increase in your cost of living. The BLS also publishes CPI data for individual cities. To estimate the change in your cost of living, look at the CPI for the items that make up the largest proportion of your budget and the CPI for the nearest city for which the BLS publishes CPI data.

The CPI isn't a very accurate measure of changes in prices over very long periods of time, such as 1929–1978. The basket of goods in the CPI for 1978 is quite different than the 1929 basket, so the CPI doesn't measure the change in the cost of a constant basket of goods. Many

Table 5 Consumer Price Index for Selected Items, 1978 (1967 = 100)

ALL ITEMS	195.4
Commodities	187.1
Food	211.4
Housing	202.8
Fuel & Utilities	216.0
Household Furnishings	177.7
Apparel	159.6
Services	210.9
Medical care	219.4
Rent	164.0

Source: U.S. Department of Commerce, *Survey of Current Business*, April, 1979. Actual price indexes are compiled and published by the U.S. Department of Labor, Bureau of Labor Statistics.

products are available today that didn't even exist in the 1920s or 1930s, and there may not even be a close equivalent—for example, the 1929 equivalent to a color T.V. set. In some cases, changes in quality over long periods change the commodity dramatically. A 1980 Ford is quite different from a 1929 Model A Ford.

Implicit Price Deflator (IPD) and Real GNP

As was explained earlier, the relevant GNP comparisons over time are comparisons of *real GNP*. To find GNP in constant prices, or real GNP, current nominal GNP is deflated by a price index called the *implicit price deflator for GNP (IPD)*.

- The **Implicit Price Deflator** (*IPD*) for GNP estimates the average change in prices of all items in GNP between a base year and a given year.

The Department of Commerce publishes GNP in current dollars (or *nominal* GNP) and in "1972 dollars." To find real GNP in 1972 dollars, the nominal GNP is divided by the implicit price deflator which shows the proportional change in prices since 1972. For example, the implicit price deflator for 1978 was 152.09, or 1.5209, and GNP in current-year (1978) prices was $2106.6 billion. In 1972 prices, the real GNP in 1978 was

$$\text{GNP in 1972 prices} = \frac{\text{GNP in current prices}}{\text{implicit price deflator}} \qquad (1)$$
$$= \frac{\$2106.6 \text{ billion}}{1.5209} = \$1385.1 \text{ billion.}$$

Figure 3 shows the behavior of nominal and real GNP between 1960 and 1978. Some additional topics on index numbers are included in the appendix to this chapter.

Figure 3 Real vs. Nominal GNP

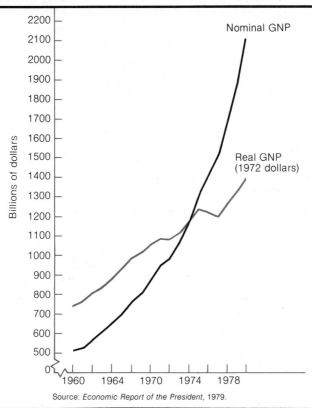

Source: *Economic Report of the President*, 1979.

GNP as a Measure of Economic Welfare

GNP is often used as an indicator of economic performance and welfare. Real GNP is a convenient and comprehensive measure of aggregate output of goods and services, and the size of the flow of goods and services produced has strong implications for economic welfare. Other things equal, the community will generally be better off economically with a large output of goods and services than with a small one. However, there isn't a one-to-one relationship between GNP and economic welfare, or between changes in GNP and changes in economic welfare. We have to look beyond the GNP figures to get a clearer picture of economic welfare.

Per Capita Income

A doubling of GNP doesn't necessarily mean a doubling of economic welfare or dramatic increases in living standards of the population. If population doubles at the same time, there is no increase in the average output of goods and services per person, or *per capita real GNP*.

- **Per capita real GNP** is the average output of final goods and services per person, or the ratio of GNP over population.

Pattern of Income Distribution

If income is very unevenly distributed among persons in a country, real GNP and even per capita real GNP doesn't tell us much about the living standards of the average person in a country. The small sheikdom of Kuwait, for example, has the highest per capita national income in the world—owing to its small population and its extensive oil reserves—but the living standard of the typical Kuwaiti citizen is more modest than the average living standards in countries with lower per capita national income but a less uneven pattern of income distribution.

Associating economic welfare with a particular pattern of income distribution requires a normative value judgement at some point. To say that greater equality or inequality of income distribution is more equitable or better requires some normative standards of equity.

Composition of GNP

The types of goods and services produced obviously affect the community's economic welfare and living standards. Suppose that two countries—A and B—have the same real GNP per capita and the same pattern of income distribution. However 70 percent of A's GNP is made up of heavy industrial machinery and military goods, while 70 percent of country B's GNP is made up of consumer goods. Obviously, households in country B will have higher living standards than those in country A.

Similarly, the relationship between growth of GNP over time and increases in community economic welfare and living standards depends heavily on the types of goods whose output is growing the fastest. For example, the Soviet Union experienced dramatic increases in GNP between 1928 and 1953, but living standards didn't grow proportionately because the growth of GNP was accomplished by squeezing the production of consumer goods to produce more heavy industrial equipment.

GNP and Gross National Cost

The value of goods and services produced, and therefore GNP, depends on costs of producing goods and services. The value added at any stage of production also reflects the cost incurred at that stage of production. In other words, we can think of GNP as a measure of the costs borne by society in producing goods and services. However, GNP is not a very accurate measure of aggregate cost because some important costs borne by society never enter the GNP calculations.

Production and consumption of goods imposes *external social costs* on the community.

- **External social costs** are costs of production and consumption of goods borne by persons not directly involved in their production or consumption.

Environmental pollution is one of the most serious forms of external social cost.

Building a nuclear power plant increases the output of electric power for consumers and provides more electrical power to be used in production of other goods, but it also contributes to thermal pollution of surrounding bodies of water as the heated water from the power plant is discharged into lakes and rivers. This accelerates the aging of bodies of water, and generally reduces the recreational value of lakes and rivers. These are external social costs borne by society, but they don't enter into the cost calculations of firms or into the final value of goods and services.

In other words, by excluding social costs, GNP and the measures of income related to it tend to understate the costs borne by society in producing its annual output of final goods and services.

Summary

1. **Real national income** or **output** is the annual circular flow of goods and services and resource services, or the annual flow of expenditures for goods and services and payments to factors of production.
2. Measuring national income and output is a large accounting problem, and the national income data are based on data gathered from producers and by statistical estimation.
3. **Gross National Product** (GNP) is the value of all *final* goods and services produced in a given year. It is the most comprehensive measure of economic activity. Other national income aggregates derived from GNP are Net National Product (NNP), National Income (NI), Personal Income (PI), and Disposable Personal Income (DI).
4. **Index numbers** express prices, output, or other variables in any given year as a percentage or proportion of their value in a base year.
5. The **Consumer Price Index** (CPI) and the **Implicit Price Deflator** (IPD) are price indexes. They express prices in a given year as a percentage of prices in a base year.
6. National income aggregates alone aren't indicators of economic welfare. Population, the composition of real GNP, the pattern of income distribution, and unmeasured social costs all must be considered in assessing the economic welfare of a country.

Concepts for Review

stock	Gross National	real GNP
flow	Product (GNP)	nominal GNP
circular flow	intermediate goods	price index
aggregate output	value added	consumer price
national product	Net National	index (CPI)
national income	Product (NNP)	implicit price
factor payments flow	National Income (NI)	deflator (IPD)
income flow	Personal Income (PI)	per capita real GNP
expenditure flow	Disposable Income (DI)	external social costs

Questions

1. The Minnow family is being visited by I. M. Sharkey, a life insurance salesman. Part of Mr. Sharkey's pitch is that the Minnows will earn $1 million in their lifetimes. Is this a very meaningful way to express a family's income? Why?

2. If Gross National Product is defined as the value of the annual output of goods and services for final use, what happens to the values of the raw materials and intermediate goods produced during the year?

3. The Soviet government defines the aggregate output of industry as the "sum of the values of the outputs of all industrial enterprises." Is this the same as defining the aggregate output of industry as the sum of the values added by all industrial enterprises? Is the distinction between the two (if any) significant?

4. Senator I. M. Phogbound has told his constituents in Temperance, Mich., that he will oppose any increases in taxes on individuals. Instead, he argues heatedly, additional revenue could be raised by a 15 percent tax on the values added by producers.
   a. What is the senator talking about?
   b. If he voted for such a tax, would he be keeping his promise to oppose additional tax burdens on individuals?
   c. About how much revenue would such a tax raise in the U.S.?

5. The Nerd and Schnook families are next-door neighbors in Drab, Pa. The Nerds have hired the Schnooks to do all of their domestic work at an annual salary of $10,000. The Schnooks have hired the Nerds to do the same thing for them at an annual salary of $10,000. What effect would this arrangement have on GNP? Explain.

6. As a full-time housewife, Ms. Jane Good worked a 40-hour week in the home, and served as a volunteer aide in a nursing home for 10 hours per week. In 1980, she took a full-time job at an annual salary of $15,000. Because of the demands of her job, she has less time to work in the home, and has to give up her volunteer activities. As GNP is defined and measured, what effect would Ms. Good's employment have on GNP? Would the change in GNP accurately reflect a change in the economy's aggregate output of goods and services? Explain.

Problems

1. The following national income data are for Lower Slobovia in 1980 (all figures are billions of dollars)

Gross Investment 250	Proprietors' Income 75
Net Interest 150	Personal Taxes 175
Indirect Business Taxes 150	Government Purchases 250
Corporate Profits 175	Exports 200
Dividends 75	Wages and Salaries 1000
Transfer Payments 275	Undistributed Corporate Profits 100
Personal Consumption 1200	Social Security Taxes 100
Imports 100	Depreciation 200

a. Calculate the following:
   GNP by the expenditure flow
   GNP by the factor-payment flow
   NNP
   National Income
   Personal Income
   Disposable Personal Income
   Personal Saving
b. The GNP of Upper Slobovia in 1980 is twice as great as Lower Slobovia's. Does this mean that the citizens of Upper Slobovia are twice as well off economically as the citizens of Lower Slobovia? Explain carefully.

How Not to Be Fooled by Growth Indexes

Index numbers are convenient and useful ways to show growth in GNP or other aggregate measures of output over time. However, the apparent clarity and convenience of index numbers hide some important subtleties that make it very easy to be misled by them. The first lesson is to be skeptical of any single index of growth of income that doesn't provide some information on the type of index it is or how it was calculated.

Real and Nominal Growth

Be sure that the index shows real grcwth, and not simply the growth in nominal or money GNP. It was explained in the chapter that the real GNP—i.e., the output of goods and services in constant prices—is more important for changes in economic welfare than the money value of this flow in current prices.

For example, the U.S. GNP in 1978 in current (1978) prices was $2106.6 billion, and the U.S. GNP in 1968 in current (1968) prices was $868.5 billion. The change in GNP over this period, expressed as an index number is

$$\frac{\text{GNP}_{78}}{\text{GNP}_{68}} \times 100 = \frac{\$2106.6\,\text{billion}}{\$868.5\,\text{billion}} \times 100 = 242.6$$

This does not mean that the ouput of goods and services in 1978 was 242.6 percent of the level of output in 1968, because prices changed over this period as well as output.

Constructing an index of GNP in constant prices—i.e., an index of *real* GNP—would be a more meaningful comparison because prices would be the same in both years. Comparing U.S. GNP in 1968 and 1978 in constant 1972 prices, for example, yields the following index of growth

$$\frac{\text{GNP}_{78}\ (\text{in }\$1972)}{\text{GNP}_{68}\ (\text{in }\$1972)} \times 100 = \frac{\$1385.1\,\text{billion}}{\$1051.8\,\text{billion}} \times 100 = 131.7$$

However, even indexes of growth in real terms can be misleading.

Look at the Base Year

Growth between a base year and a given year can be overstated or understated by the choice of the base year. Choosing an unusually bad year with an unusually low GNP as the base year will overstate growth, and an unusually good base year with an unusually high GNP will tend to understate growth.

Price Weights and the "Index Number Problem"

Index numbers can be manipulated through the choice of price weights. This is a little technical, but the following example will show how the choice of price weights affects the result.

Assume a very simple economy, producing only two goods—widgets and gadgets. We want to compare GNP in two years—a *base year* (year 0), and an *end year* (year 1). The actual number of years between 0 and 1 need not be one year, year 1 is simply to identify the end year.

Gadgets were a new item in the base year, and their output between year 0 and year 1 grew much faster than the output of widgets. By simple supply and demand reasoning, if the output of gadgets grows more rapidly than the output of widgets, gadgets become less scarce relative to widgets, and their relative price falls—as shown in Table A-1a.

Table A–1   Base-Year vs. End-Year Price Indexes

(a) Basic Data	Year 0		Year 1	
	P_0	Q_0	P_1	Q_1
Widgets	$ 1	5,000	$ 2	5,000
Gadgets	$100	100	$20	1,000

(b) Base-year Index	Year 0		Year 1	
	P_0	Q_0	P_0	Q_1
Widgets	$ 1 × 5,000 =	$ 5,000	$ 1 × 5,000 =	$ 5,000
Gadgets	$100 × 100 =	$10,000	$100 × 1,000 =	$100,000
GNP in Year 0 Prices		$15,000		$105,000

(c) End-year Index	Year 0		Year 1	
	P_1	Q_0	P_1	Q_1
Widgets	$ 2 × 5,000 =	$10,000	$ 2 × 5,000 =	$10,000
Gadgets	$ 20 × 100 =	$ 2,000	$ 20 × 1,000 =	$20,000
GNP in Year 1 Prices		$12,000		$30,000

To construct an index of growth of real GNP for this period, we have to express GNP in both years in the same prices. We have two choices—express GNP in both years in base-year prices, or express GNP in both years in end-year prices. Table A-1b shows GNP in both years in base-year prices (P_0), and Table A-1c shows GNP in both years in end-year prices (P_1).

The index of growth in *base-year prices* is called a *base-year index*, or **Laspeyere index** (I_L). It compares GNP in year 1 in base-year prices as a percentage of GNP in year 0 in base-year prices. In this case,

$$I_L = \frac{\$105,000}{\$ 15,000} \times 100 = 700.$$

An index of growth in *end-year prices* is an *end-year index*, or **Paasche Index** (I_P).

Assigning end-year prices to the same physical outputs in the two years in the example gives

$$I_P = \frac{\$30,000}{\$12,000} \times 100 = 250.$$

Both indexes are equally correct and equally truthful, but they show much different rates of growth. This illustrates the **index number problem**. Base-year indexes tend to overstate growth and end-year indexes tend to understate it. It's a "problem" because there isn't any way to eliminate it. The distortion becomes greater the greater the difference in relative prices in the two years. It would become very great if the base year were a year in the distant past.

The existence of an index number problem doesn't mean that growth indexes are useless or that they are only tools of the devious. However, the moral is clear. There are many ways to be fooled by indexes, so be wary of index numbers that don't give you any information on such things as the base year, price weights, etc.

PART THREE

Aggregate Demand: The Goods Market

We have now seen how the interaction of aggregate supply and aggregate demand determines equilibrium levels of prices and output. In the past, most activist Keynesian economists have considered aggregate demand the more important factor and have urged the use of **demand-management policies** to stabilize economic conditions. The next two sections of the text explore this notion of **aggregate demand**.

Traditionally, economists have analyzed aggregate demand by dividing the entire economy into two basic markets or sectors: the market for goods and services (the **goods market**) and the market for money and financial assets (the **money market**). In this section, we'll focus on aggregate demand in the goods market. To do this, though, we have to assume that no changes occur in the money market, that everything there remains constant. We also have to assume that prices remain constant up to full employment—in other words, that the aggregate supply curve is horizontal up to that level. Given these major assumptions, of course, aggregate demand in the goods market becomes the sole determinant of equilibrium aggregate output.

We begin our analysis by building a simple model of the economy to show how the level of aggregate demand is determined and how that level in turn determines the economy's output. We'll then look at various factors that affect the stability of aggregate demand and output over time. Finally, we'll explore the government's use of fiscal policy in its effort to stabilize aggregate demand and achieve full employment without inflation.

6

Aggregate Demand and Income Determination: The Private Sector

Preview: In order to understand the role of aggregate demand in determining the levels of aggregate output and national income, we have to construct a model of the economy. The model is usually referred to as the **simple Keynesian model**, and is used to predict changes in output and income due to changes in aggregate demand in the goods market. In this chapter, we will build a simplified version of the model, representing an economy with no public sector (and therefore no government spending or taxes) and no international sector (and therefore no import or export expenditures).

In this chapter, we examine the role of aggregate demand for goods and services in determining the level of aggregate output (or real GNP). This has implications for the level of employment, since the level of aggregate output affects the level of employment of labor to produce the goods and services. Aggregate demand also has implications for inflation. If the demand for goods and services exceeds the economy's capacity to produce, the result is *demand-pull inflation*. If aggregate demand and output aren't sufficient to generate full employment, the result is *demand-deficiency unemployment*.

This chapter focuses on the relationship between aggregate demand (AD) and aggregate output or real GNP (Y). More specifically, we're interested in aggregate demand as a determinant of *equilibrium* aggregate output or GNP. To isolate the relationship between aggregate demand and output, we have to make some simplifying assumptions. First, we'll assume that the price level is constant, so that changes in GNP represent changes in real GNP or aggregate output.

This chapter and several that follow it deal with aggregate demand and equilibrium aggregate output, or equilibrium in the goods sector of the economy. For the time being, we'll leave money and financial markets (the monetary sector) out of the analysis. The effects of money and monetary phenomena will be introduced and integrated into the analysis of income and employment in the next section of the text.

The income determination model uses the expenditure concepts introduced in national income accounting, but with an important difference. In the income determination model, consumption, saving, and investment are *desired* or *intended* expenditures—i.e., they are *ex ante* quantities. In national income accounting, expenditures are *measured*, or *ex post*, quantities. The task of the income determination model is to predict equilibrium income and changes in income, not simply to measure income after the fact. In the analysis of income determination that follows, investment and saving will refer to intended investment and intended saving unless noted otherwise.

Aggregate Demand and Output in the Circular Flow

Figure 1 illustrates the circular flow of real GNP in a simple economy composed of *private households*, *private firms*, and a *financial sector* (banks, capital markets, etc.). National income or aggregate output (Y), you will recall from the last chapter, is equal to the sum of factor payments or the sum of expenditure on final goods and services:

$$Y = \text{sum of factor payments} = \text{sum of expenditures} \qquad (1)$$

Since there is no public sector, there are no taxes on firms or households, and all factor payments accrue to households as income. The

Figure 1 The Circular Flow of Real GNP

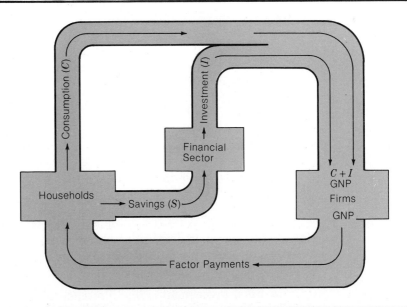

households allocate this income between *consumption* (C) and *saving* (S) which flows out of the expenditure stream to the financial sector. Investment (I) flows from the financial sector into the expenditure flow as firms and households purchase investment goods (capital equipment, new residential housing, etc.). The firms receive all expenditures for consumption and investment as receipts, so measured GNP (Y) in a closed, private economy can be expressed as

$$Y = \text{Consumption} + \text{measured Investment}. \qquad (2)$$

Now, we must look at the aggregate demand (AD) for goods and services in the closed private economy. There are only two expenditure flows, consumption (C) and investment (I), so aggregate demand (AD) at any level of aggregate output or real GNP is

$$AD = C + I. \qquad (3)$$

Apparently, from equations (2) and (3), it appears that aggregate demand is identical with GNP at any level of GNP. However, the two equations say two quite different things. The key is that *investment* in equation (2) is actual or measured investment. In equation (3), however, investment is intended investment—the amount of investment that households and firms are willing and able (or intend) to undertake at any level of aggregate output or real GNP. Thus, equation (2) says: "GNP is the sum of consumption expenditures and the measured level of investment." Equation (3), on the other hand, says: "At any level of aggregate output or real GNP, the aggregate demand for goods and services is the sum of intended consumption and intended investment expenditures."

Now, we're faced with an apparent puzzle concerning GNP and aggregate demand. Suppose that the economy had an actual GNP of $500 billion—consumption of $300 billion and measured investment expenditures of $200 billion. In other words

$$\text{Measured GNP} = C + \text{measured } I = \$300 \text{ billion} + \$200 \text{ billion}$$
$$= \$500 \text{ billion}.$$

However, at a GNP (or aggregate output) of $500 billion, suppose that aggregate demand is

$$AD = C + \text{intended } I = \$300 \text{ billion} + \$150 \text{ billion} = \$450 \text{ billion}.$$

How could aggregate demand be less than the level of real GNP? The answer is quite simple. Measured investment includes *all* investment, *unintended* as well as intended.

- **Unintended investment** is the difference between the actual or measured level of investment and intended investment.

How could investment be unintended? Is this type of investment made by accident? Most unintended investment is unintended or unexpected accumulation of inventories by firms. If *AD* isn't sufficient to purchase the entire aggregate output or real GNP, some of it remains unsold and is added to inventories of producers and sellers. To reduce their inventories to normal or desired levels, the firms will cut back on current output, and this will cause aggregate output to fall.

- If aggregate demand is less than the level of aggregate output, unintended inventory accumulation will cause aggregate output or real GNP to fall.

What would happen if aggregate demand exceeded aggregate output? Let's reverse the previous example, and suppose that at a real GNP of $450 billion, aggregate demand is $500 billion. In other words, households are willing and able to spend more than the current aggregate output. This will cause some **unintended disinvestment** as firms find their inventories falling in order to meet their customers' demands. As firms find their inventories below normal or desirable levels, they will increase inventories. To do this, they have to increase output, so aggregate output (real GNP) will rise.

- If aggregate demand exceeds aggregate output, unintended inventory depletion will encourage firms to increase output and cause aggregate output to increase.

Equilibrium Output

Aggregate output or real GNP reaches equilibrium when there is no tendency for it to change. As long as there is unintended accumulation or depletion of inventories (intended investment or unintended disinvestment), aggregate output will not be in equilibrium. Unintended inventory investment as a result of aggregate demand less than aggregate output or real GNP will encourage firms to reduce output to reduce their excessive inventories. If there is unintended inventory depletion because aggregate demand exceeds aggregate output, firms have an incentive to increase their output to satisfy customers and to replenish inventories.

Thus aggregate output or real GNP will be in equilibrium only if there is no unintended investment. This occurs only when intended expenditures (aggregate demand) equal aggregate output.

- **Equilibrium real GNP** is reached when the sum of intended expenditures equals real GNP, or GNP $(Y) = AD$.

Equilibrium can also be analyzed and understood in the context of the circular flow in Figure 1. Outflows from the income stream make the stream smaller, and inflows make it larger. Therefore, the size of the income stream will remain constant only if expenditure outflows and inflows are equal.

Figure 2 Equilibrium Real GNP: $Y = AD$

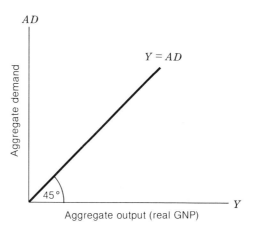

- Equilibrium GNP is reached when the sum of expenditure outflows from the income stream equals the sum of expenditure inflows into it.

In a closed, private economy, saving is the only expenditure outflow and investment is the only inflow. It follows, then, that

- Equilibrium GNP is reached in a closed private economy when the intended savings flow equals the intended investment flow, or $S = I$.

The distinction between *ex ante* (or intended) and *ex post* (or measured) saving and investment is important here. Equilibrium is reached when intended saving equals intended investment. However, if we look at measured GNP, measured saving is always equal to measured investment. With measured GNP,

$$\text{measured } Y = C + \text{measured } I.$$

The portion of GNP that isn't consumed is saved—i.e.,

$$\text{measured } S \equiv \text{measured } Y - C \equiv C + \text{measured } I - C \equiv \text{measured } I,$$

or

$$\text{measured } S \equiv \text{measured } I. \tag{4}$$

Equilibrium GNP is approached graphically in Figure 2. In Figure 2, the horizontal axis is real GNP or aggregate output and the vertical axis is intended aggregate spending, or AD—both axes would be expressed in constant dollars. We have established that equilibrium GNP requires $Y = AD$. This condition is met at all points[1] on the 45° line in Figure 2. To verify this, note that any positively sloped straight line in Figure 2 would conform to the equation

$$AD = a + bY.$$

Since the 45° starts at the origin, $a = 0$. The slope of a positively sloped 45° line is 1, so the equation for the 45° line in Figure 2 is

$$AD = 0 + (1)Y, \text{ or } AD = Y.$$

In other words, all points on the 45° line fulfill the equilibrium condition $Y = AD$.

Aggregate demand, or intended spending, is represented in Figure 3 by the aggregate demand (AD) function. This shows the level of intended spending at each level of aggregate output or real GNP. In our closed private model,

$$AD = C + I.$$

Consumption and intended saving (S) vary directly with real GNP or aggregate output. As aggregate output increases, the size of the factor payments flow—and therefore incomes received by households—increases. Some of the additional income will be consumed and some will be saved.

For the time being, to keep our analysis simple, we'll assume that intended investment is an *autonomous expenditure flow*.

Figure 3 Aggregate Demand Function

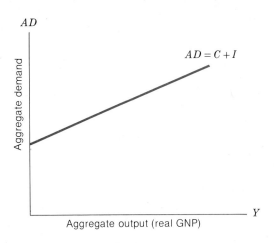

AD

Aggregate demand

$AD = C + I$

Y

Aggregate output (real GNP)

---

1. Remember, however, that it is impossible for the economy to produce more than full-employment real GNP or Y^*, regardless of the level of aggregate demand. For this reason, the equlibrium line becomes vertical at Y^*. For simplicity, this change to a vertical equilibrium line will be shown only when necessary in this text.

- **Autonomous expenditures** are determined by variables other than real GNP, and don't vary with the level of real GNP.

Some investment *is* autonomous—such as annual investment expenditures in the course of completing long-term investment projects—but some varies with income. The assumption that all investment is autonomous is made only to make the analysis simpler at this point, and more realistic cases will be analyzed later.

The sum of consumption and intended investment expenditures at each level of aggregate output or real GNP is aggregate demand (*AD*) at that level of GNP. The *AD* function in Figure 3 shows the relationship between real GNP and aggregate demand, other things constant. With all investment autonomous and consumption varying directly with real GNP, *AD* will vary directly with real GNP.

Figure 4 analyzes equilibrium real GNP by combining $Y = AD$ from Figure 2 and $AD = C + I$ from Figure 3. At equilibrium real GNP ($\overline{Y}$), intended spending must equal aggregate output, or

$$\overline{Y} = AD = C + I.$$

This is attained where the $AD = C + I$ function intersects the $Y = AD$ (or 45°) line. At this intersection, we have

$$\overline{Y} = C + I.$$

In Figure 4, then, equilibrium GNP is $\overline{Y} = AD = 600$.

Figure 4 The Simple Keynesian Model

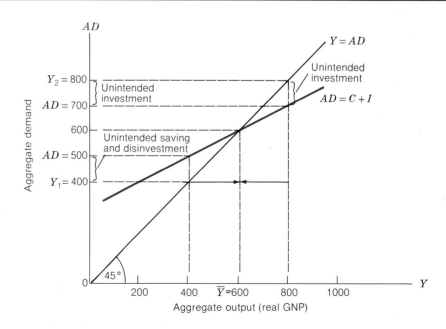

Figure 5 Saving and Investment at Equilibrium Real GNP

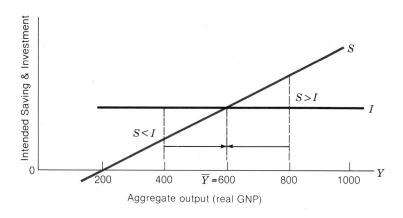

If aggregate output exceeds aggregate demand, as it does at $Y_2 = 800$ in Figure 4, aggregate demand isn't sufficient to purchase aggregate output and there is unintended investment in inventories of unsold goods. As was explained earlier, this will encourage firms to reduce their output to bring inventories back down to normal or desired levels and aggregate output will fall.

At an aggregate output of 400, where AD exceeds aggregate output, we have the opposite situation. In this case there is unintended saving because output isn't sufficient to accommodate all intended expenditure and unintended disinvestment in the form of inventory depletion. This will encourage firms to increase output to meet demand and to restore normal inventories, and aggregate output will rise.

Figure 5 looks at equilibrium GNP in terms of intended saving (S) and investment (I). It has already been explained that GNP will be in equilibrium when expenditure outflows from the income stream equal expenditure inflows into it. This occurs at $\overline{Y} = 600$ in Figure 5, where intended saving equals intended investment. At $Y = 800$, intended saving exceeds intended investment, and the income stream (GNP) will contract. At $Y = 400$, intended investment exceeds intended saving and the income stream will get larger.

The key, then, to maintaining a stable economy is the ability to predict accurately the level of aggregate demand, and then produce a level of output that will just satisfy that demand. The key to predicting the level of aggregate demand in our closed, private economy, in turn, is the ability to predict the levels of the two kinds of expenditures that make up aggregate demand, *consumption* and *intended investment*. To understand aggregate demand in more depth, then, we have to take a closer look at consumption and investment.

Consumption

Consumption is the largest component of aggregate demand, so the more we know about consumption, the better we will be able to predict aggregate demand. It should come as no surprise that, in general, the more income a household has, the more it will spend. In other words, the level of consumption (C) varies directly with the level of disposable income (Y_d). This relationship is expressed by the *consumption function*.

- The **consumption function** shows the relationship between income and consumption expenditures.

The consumption function can be written algebraically as

$$C = a + bY_d. \tag{5}$$

Note that in a private economy with no taxes, GNP and Y_d are identical, so the consumption function can be written more simply as $C = a + bY$. When taxes are introduced into the model in the next chapter, however, the relationship between consumption and disposable income will no longer be exactly the same as the relationship between consumption and GNP.

The *a* in the function represents autonomous consumption—consumption expenditure determined by variables other than aggregate output or GNP. Autonomous consumption could go on even if aggregate output and income dropped to zero through borrowing or consuming out of accumulated savings. The *b* in the consumption function is the slope, and it shows the rate at which consumption varies with income, or the fraction of additional income that is consumed; it is called the *marginal propensity to consume.*

The consumption function is shown graphically in Figure 6. When income (Y) is zero, the only consumption expenditure is autonomous

Figure 6 The Consumption Function

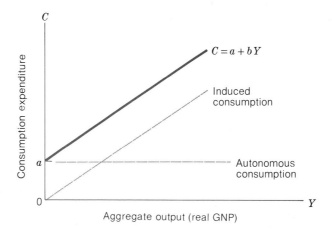

Aggregate output (real GNP)

consumption (a). This autonomous consumption is determined by variables other than current income and doesn't vary with the level of income.

A world in which all consumption is autonomous would be a very peculiar world. If the level of income dropped to zero or rose astronomically, the level of consumption wouldn't change. In reality, the largest component of the consumption expenditure flow is *induced consumption*, or consumption that varies with national income and GNP.

- **Induced expenditures** are expenditures that vary directly with aggregate output or GNP.

If we add induced consumption to autonomous consumption in Figure 6, we have the consumption function, $C = a + bY$, which shows the level of total consumption expenditure at every level of GNP.

Clearly, the values of a (autonomous consumption) and b (the slope of the consumption function, or marginal propensity to consume) are critical in determining the relationship between aggregate output, or GNP, and consumption. This warrants a closer examination of these elements of the consumption function.

Marginal Propensity to Consume

The term *propensity* literally means tendency or leaning. Keynes used the term in *The General Theory* to refer to the proportion of income consumed and the rate at which consumption changes with income. Its continuing use in macroeconomics is one of Keynes' more durable, if not enlightening, contributions to the field.

- The **marginal propensity to consume** (*mpc* or b) is the change in the level of consumption that results from a given change in income. If income increases by $1, *mpc* tells how much consumption changes as a result of that $1 increase. In other words, *mpc* is the *rate* at which consumption changes as income changes.

Graphically, *mpc* represents the slope of the consumption function. It can be written algebraically as

$$mpc = \frac{\text{change in consumption}}{\text{change in income}} = \frac{\Delta C}{\Delta Y}. \tag{6}$$

For a given consumption function, holding all of the exogenous variables that affect consumption constant, *mpc* can't be negative or greater than 1. A negative *mpc*, or an inverse relationship between consumption and the level of income, makes no sense at all if you think about it. If *mpc* = 0, this means that all consumption is autonomous and doesn't depend on income at all—this also is quite strange.

Only a society of spendthrifts would have $mpc = 1$—all changes in income matched by equal changes in consumption and no change in saving.

- For all practical possibilities, the value of the mpc lies between 0 and 1.

The mpc determines the shape of the consumption function. Both of the consumption functions in Figure 7 obey all of the rules we normally expect consumption functions to obey, but they indicate quite different relationships between consumption and the level of income. Along C_1, a *linear* consumption function, the slope or mpc is constant and consumption is equally responsive to changes in income at all levels of income. Along C_2, on the other hand, the slope or mpc diminishes as income increases. Not only is consumption lower at any level of income along C_2 than along C_1, but aggregate consumption becomes less and less responsive to changes in income as the income rises.

Many economic and noneconomic variables affect the marginal propensity to consume. Keynes' explanation of the marginal propensity to consume relied on several propositions that he presented *a priori* (as valid without proof).

> The fundamental psychological law, upon which we are entitled to depend with great confidence both *a priori* from our knowledge of human nature and from the detailed facts of experience, is that men are disposed as a rule, and on the average to increase their consumption as their income increases, but not by as much as the increase in their income.[2]

A great deal of research has been done on the consumption function since Keynes wrote, and we can identify several somewhat more precise determinants of the marginal propensity to consume. The marginal propensity to consume is affected by economic expectations. If people have optimistic expectations about future economic conditions, they will tend to consume a larger portion of additional income than they would if their economic expectations were pessimistic. The distribution of income among groups with high marginal propensities to consume and those with low marginal propensities to consume affects the aggregate mpc. The observed or estimated marginal propensity to consume tends to be higher for long periods of time than it is for short periods of time.

Autonomous Consumption

Autonomous consumption is determined by variables other than disposable income or GNP. For a given consumption function, these other variables are assumed constant; and changes in these other vari-

---

2. John Maynard Keynes, *The General Theory of Employment, Interest, and Money.* New York: Harcourt, 1936, p. 96.

Figure 7 Consumption Functions: Constant vs. Diminishing *mpc*

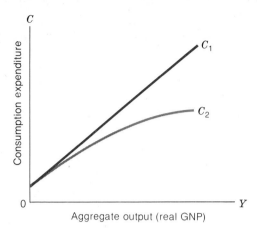

ables will change the level of autonomous consumption and cause the level of consumption expenditure to change at any level of income.

Autonomous consumption is only a small part of total consumption in the U.S. In fact, when the relationship between consumption and disposable income is estimated over a long period of years, there appears to be virtually no autonomous consumption. There may, however, be year-to-year changes in autonomous consumption, and because of the size of the consumption flow even small percentage variations in consumption involve large absolute changes in aggregate spending.

Economic expectations of consumers are important determinants of autonomous consumption and short-term shifts of the consumption function. Economic pessimism and uncertainty tend to discourage current consumption and encourage saving to meet possible future needs due to unemployment or reduced income. Economic optimism has just the opposite effect: if households are confident of future employment and income, they tend to save less and consume more at every level of income.

Expectations of future prices also affect consumption behavior, particularly expenditures for consumer durables. Expectations of rapid price increases encourage current consumption and discourage current saving. Expectations of falling prices tend to encourage current saving and to discourage current consumption in the hope of being able to make purchases at lower prices in the future.

The *availability and terms of consumer credit* affect the level of consumption. For many people, readily available credit encourages greater consumption expenditures because it allows more consumption at every level of income. Many "large ticket" consumer durables (such as automobiles) are purchased on credit, and expenditures for these items may be sensitive to the interest rates or cost of borrowing.

Expected living standards affect the level of autonomous consumption. If current disposable income falls below the level necessary to maintain a *normal* or *expected* standard of living, consumers may make up the difference between desired consumption expenditures and current income by *dissaving*—i.e., consuming out of accumulated savings and/or borrowing.

Consumption is affected by the *distribution of income* among households or groups of households with different consumption patterns. Suppose for example, that $800 billion of a total aggregate disposable income of $1000 billion is received by the upper half of households ranked by income, and that these households consume 50% of their aggregate disposable income. The remaining $200 billion is received by the lowest half of the households ranked by income, and they consume 90% of their aggregate disposable income. With this distribution of disposable income, total consumption would be

consumption by upper half = $800 billion × .50 = $400 billion

+

consumption by lower half = $200 billion × .90 = $180 billion

total consumption $580 billion

Now, suppose that the same aggregate disposable income of $1000 billion is redistributed so that all households get an equal share, and that with their new levels of disposable income all households consume 70 percent of their aggregate disposable income. As a result of the change in income distribution, total consumption changes to

total consumption = $1000 billion × .70 = $700 billion

This list of determinants of autonomous consumption is illustrative, and not exhaustive. Other variables that determine autonomous consumption include population, changes in the price level, sudden or *windfall* gains or losses of income, etc. Detailed statistical estimates of consumption functions typically contain dozens of variables in addition to the current level of disposable income or GNP. Some of the determinants of consumption other than current income are more rooted in the psychology and perception of consumers than in strictly economic motives—in fact, Keynes devoted an entire chapter of *The General Theory* to psychological or subjective determinants of consumption.

Estimates of the Consumption Function, 1929–1978

It is possible to estimate the consumption function over the last half century using statistical techniques and historical data.[3] Each of the points in Figure 8 represents disposable income (Y_d) and consumption (C) for one of the years between 1929 and 1978 in 1972 dollars.

3. Statistical estimation is explained briefly in the appendix to Chapter 1.

Figure 8 Consumption Function, 1929–1978

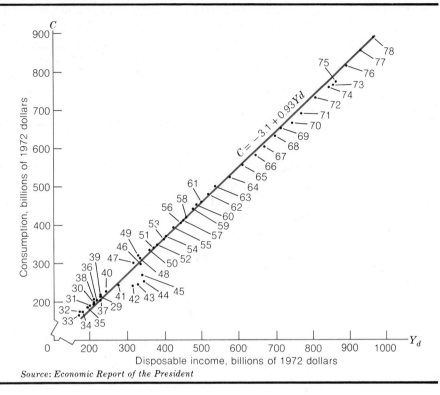

Source: *Economic Report of the President*

The estimated consumption function, C_{29-78}, is the line that *fits* these points best. The equation for the estimated consumption function for this period is

$$C_{29-78} = -3.1 + 0.93\ Y_d.$$

For the entire period 1929–78, the estimated consumption function in 1972 dollars shows virtually no autonomous consumption ($a = -3.1$ can be interpreted as $a = 0$) and a very high *mpc* ($b = .93$). However, estimated consumption functions for shorter periods of time show a somewhat different picture.

The estimated consumption function for 1930–39 in 1972 dollars is

$$C_{30-39} = 36.1 + 0.78\ Y_d.$$

The 1940s can be excluded here because of the dramatic effects of World War II on income and the restrictions on consumption during the war. For 1950–59, the estimated consumption function is

$$C_{50-59} = 12.4 + 0.89\ Y_d.$$

For the 1960s,

$$C_{60-69} = 28.2 + 0.87\ Y_d.$$

Finally, for the period 1970–75,

$$C_{70-75} = 12.6 + 0.89\ Y_d.$$

These short-run consumption functions suggest that the determinants of consumption other than disposable income are more important in the short run than in the long run. The most dramatic period, of course, is the decade between 1930 and 1939. This was a period of rapidly changing economic conditions, and most of the changes were for the worse. In constant (1972) dollars, per capita disposable income fell by about 28 percent between 1929 and 1933. In nominal terms, the decline was even greater (46 percent). For many people, the most important determinant of consumption spending during this period was the level of consumption to maintain an acceptable standard of living, hence the high level of autonomous consumption (36.1 billion 1972 dollars).

Consumption and Saving

A **saving function** shows the relationship between disposable income and intended saving. It can be derived easily from the consumption function. Since all income in a private economy must be saved or consumed,

$$S = Y - C. \tag{7}$$

Substituting the consumption function $C = a + bY$ for C,

$$S = Y - (a + bY) = Y - a - bY$$
$$= -a + (1 - b)Y. \tag{8}$$

For example, if $C = 100 + 0.6\ Y$,

$$S = -100 + (1 - 0.6)Y = -100 + 0.4\ Y.$$

These consumption and saving functions are shown in Figure 9. Any shift in the consumption function will cause the saving function to shift in the opposite direction.

The slope of the saving function is the **marginal propensity to save** (*mps*). It shows the response of intended saving to changes in income. Like the *mpc*, the *mps* will lie between 0 and 1. Also, since every $1 in additional income must be consumed or saved, the portion that isn't consumed will be saved,[4] or

$$mpc + mps = 1;\ \text{and}\ mps = 1 - mpc. \tag{9}$$

---

4. A simple proof for the wary skeptics:

$$C + S = Y$$

$$\frac{\Delta(C + S)}{\Delta Y} = \frac{\Delta Y}{\Delta Y}\ ;\ \frac{\Delta C}{\Delta Y} + \frac{\Delta S}{\Delta Y} = \frac{\Delta Y}{\Delta Y}\ ;\ \text{or}\ mpc + mps = 1.$$

Figure 9 Consumption and Saving Functions

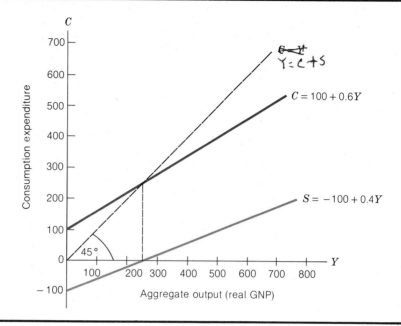

Intended saving may be positive, negative, or zero, depending on the consumption function and the level of income. At any point on the 45° line in Figure 9, $C = Y$. At $Y = \$250$ billion, where the consumption function intersects the 45° line, $C = Y$, and $S = 0$. At all levels of Y greater than $\$250$ billion, Y is greater than C, and the difference is positive saving. If Y is less than $\$250$ billion, saving is negative, and this **dissaving** represents consumption out of accumulated savings or borrowing.

Investment

The second major component of aggregate demand is *investment*. Some investment—called *induced investment*—is determined by the level of GNP; we'll look closely at induced investment in a later chapter. For now, we'll simply assume that all investment is *autonomous*—determined by variables other than GNP. In order to predict the level of autonomous investment, we will have to discover what those variables are and how they affect investment.

As defined in the national income accounts, **investment** includes three broad categories of expenditures—new capital equipment or producer durables purchased by firms, new residential and nonresidential construction, and inventory adjustments. These seemingly different types of expenditures have several things in common.

1. Investment expenditures increase the economy's capital stock—i.e., the stock of productive equipment, buildings, and finished goods.
2. Investments have current costs, and require current expenditures.
3. Investments yield their returns (if any) in the future.

In a complex economy, there are hundreds of thousands of alternative investment projects with different expected future returns, different initial costs, and different productive lifetimes. Investments will be undertaken until the productivity, or return, from the last investment made just equals the cost of undertaking it.

- The **marginal efficiency of investment** (*MEI*) is the productivity of the last investment made, expressed as an annual expected rate of return.

If alternative investment projects are ranked by expected annual rates of return, the most productive investment projects would be undertaken first. As investment increases, the rates of return on successive investment projects made will be lower, or the expected rate of return on additional investment will fall as the level of investment increases. Put another way,

- The marginal efficiency of investment varies inversely with the level of investment, other things held constant.

Potential investors consider the benefits from alternative uses of their funds—either making an investment or depositing the funds in a savings account to earn *interest*. A rational investor will only invest if the return he expects on his investment is greater than the interest rate—his opportunity cost. A firm will only invest in a project if the return from the project is greater than the interest rate on funds borrowed to finance the project. Clearly, then, the interest rate is of major importance in determining the level of investment.

Suppose that an investor is considering an investment project with a current cost (*V*) of $10,000, an expected return (*R*) of ten percent after one year. The interest rate (*r*) reflects preference for current income over future income. If the interest rate is 5% per year, should the investment be undertaken?

If the investment were made, the investor would realize

$$V(1 + R) = \$10{,}000\,(1.10) = \$11{,}000.$$

Depositing the money in a savings account at the going rate of interest would yield

$$V(1 + r) = \$10{,}000\,(1.05) = \$10{,}500.$$

Since *R* is greater than *r*, the investment should be undertaken because the return from the investment is greater than the return by depositing the money in a savings account.

If the interest rate were 15%, the investment project should not be undertaken because R is less than the interest rate. With an interest rate of 15%, depositing the funds in a savings account would realize a return of

$$V(1 + r) = \$10,000\ (1.15) = \$11,500.$$

The marginal efficiency of investment shows the return from the last (and least profitable) investment in the economy. Thus, the relationship between MEI and the interest rate will determine the level of investment in the economy.

- If MEI is greater than r, investment will tend to increase.
- If MEI is less than r, investment will tend to fall.
- The equilibrium level of investment will be reached when $MEI = r$.

The relationship between the interest rate and the level of investment is shown graphically in Figure 10. Since the interest rate and MEI are expressed as % per year, they can be shown on the same axis. Given the interest rate $r = 10\%$, investment will stabilize at I where $MEI = r = 10\%$. At I_1, MEI is greater than r, and investment will tend to rise. At I_2, MEI is less than r, and investment will tend to fall.

Changes in the interest rate will alter the level of investment. In Figure 10, for example, if the interest rate rose from r to r', the level

Figure 10 The Marginal Efficiency of Investment

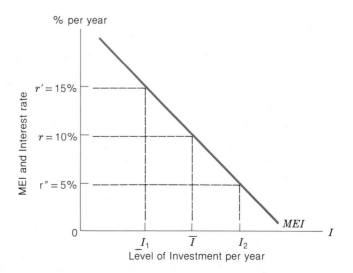

of investment would fall to I_1 where $MEI = r'$. If the interest rate fell from r to r'', the level of investment would increase to I_2 where $MEI = r''$.

Other things equal, the level of autonomous investment and aggregate demand will vary inversely with the interest rate. We can plot investment demand graphically against GNP much as we plotted the consumption function. In Figure 11, the horizontal function I_r represents investment demand at interest rate r. The line is horizontal because we are looking only at autonomous investment, which doesn't change with GNP. A decline in the interest rate will cause investment demand to rise to I_r''. A rise in the interest rate will cause investment demand to fall to I_r'.

The Simple Keynesian Model

With a basic grasp of the relationship between aggregate output or real GNP and the components of aggregate demand (consumption and intended investment), the pieces can be put together into an income determination model. First of all, we can write the *aggregate demand equation* to express the relationship between aggregate output or real GNP (Y) and intended spending ($C + I$). At any level of Y, AD is

$$AD = C + I,$$

as was shown at the beginning of the chapter.

Now, we'll simply fill in some more specific information on consumption and investment. The relationship between consumption and GNP is shown by the consumption function, $C = a + bY$. So far, we have assumed that investment is autonomous, and we will express

Figure 11   Interest Rate and the Level of Autonomous Investment

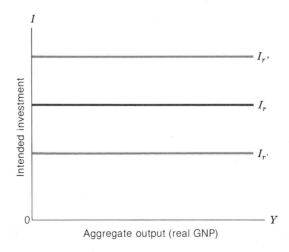

autonomous investment as I_a. Substituting this information for C and I, we now have

$$AD = C + I_a = a + bY + I_a$$
$$= a + I_a + bY. \tag{10}$$

To estimate AD at any level of Y, we need to know the values of a, I_a, and b in the AD equation. If the known or estimated values of a and b are $a = \$100$ billion and $b = 0.6$, then the consumption function becomes

$$C = a + bY = 100 + 0.6 \ Y.$$

To predict the level of consumption expenditure at any level of GNP (Y), simply plug the value of Y into the equation. For example, at $Y = \$600$ billion, consumption expenditure will be

$$C = 100 + 0.6 \ (600) = 100 + 360 = \$460 \text{ billion.}$$

If the level of autonomous investment is known or estimated to be $I_a = 100$ billion, this is substituted for I_a in the AD equation. With the given consumption function and the given level of autonomous investment, aggregate demand or intended aggregate spending at any level of GNP is

$$AD = a + I_a + bY = 100 + 100 + 0.6 \ Y = 200 + 0.6 \ Y.$$

This aggregate demand function (AD) and its components are shown graphically in Figure 12.

Figure 12 Aggregate Demand = Consumption + Investment

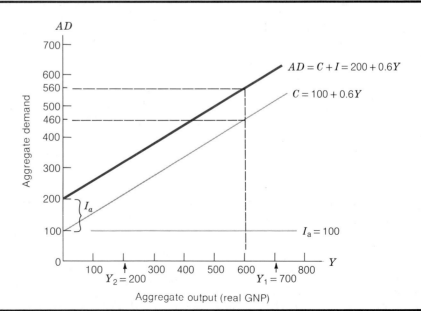

To predict aggregate demand at any given level of income ($Y =$ $600 billion, for example), simply find the expenditure coordinate of $Y =$ $600 billion in Figure 12, or plug the given value of Y into the aggregate demand equation and solve for aggregate demand as follows:

$$AD = 200 + 0.6\,Y = 200 + 0.6\,(600) = \$560 \text{ billion.}$$

Equilibrium in the Simple Keynesian Model

Whenever the economy is *not* at equilibrium, that is, when aggregate demand is greater or smaller than aggregate output (GNP), real GNP will tend to change to move the economy toward equilibrium. At a GNP of $Y_1 =$ $700 billion in Figure 12, we can see from the aggregate demand function that *ex ante* aggregate demand is only $625 billion. This means that $75 billion worth of goods won't be sold. As inventories rise above normal or desired levels, firms will reduce their output to reduce inventories to normal, and real GNP will fall, moving the economy toward equilibrium.

At a GNP of $Y_2 =$ $200 billion in Figure 12, the aggregate demand (AD) exceeds aggregate output by $120 billion. Put another way, buyers will purchase more goods and services than are being produced. This causes inventories of goods to fall—the only way one can sell more than he or she produces is to reduce inventories. As inventories fall below normal or desired levels, output must increase to restore inventories to their normal levels.

At $\overline{Y} =$ $500 billion, the aggregate demand for goods and services produced (AD) is equal to the aggregate output of goods and services or real GNP. At this point, there will be no tendency for inventories, output, or real GNP to change, and therefore $\overline{Y}$ is the equilibrium GNP.

• *Equilibrium real GNP* is reached when the aggregate demand for goods and services is equal to real GNP.

This is not a different equilibrium condition than we saw in the circular flow. Common sense suggests that if GNP is at its equilibrium level, the expenditure inflows into the income stream must equal the expenditure flows out of the income stream.[5]

Calculating Equilibrium GNP in the Simple Model

In reality, economists don't estimate or predict equilibrium GNP by drawing graphs. Instead, they derive empirical estimates of the various expenditure flows that make up aggregate demand, and express

---

5. A more formal verification is easy for those skeptics for whom common sense isn't enough. Since there are no taxes in the closed private economy, all factor payments (GNP) represent disposable income (Y_d), or $Y = Y_d$. All disposable income, and GNP in this case, must be consumed or saved by households—$C + S = Y$. At $\overline{Y}$, then $S = \overline{Y} - C$. At $\overline{Y}$, $\overline{Y} = AD = C + I$. Thus, at $\overline{Y}$, we have

$$S = Y - C = I, \text{ or } S = I.$$

Remember that S and I are *ex ante* saving and investment. If $Y \neq AD$, intended $S \neq$ intended I.

these flows as equations. The equations are then solved to estimate equilibrium GNP. To get an idea of how this works, we can solve our known AD equation to find equilibrium GNP.

We know that at any level of aggregate output or GNP, intended spending (AD) is

$$AD = 200 + 0.6 \ Y.$$

We also know that equilibrium GNP (Y) requires that intended spending equal aggregate output, or

$$\overline{Y} = AD.$$

Substituting the AD equation in the equilibrium condition, and substituting Y for $\overline{Y}$ in the AD equation, equilibrium GNP will be reached when

$$\overline{Y} = 200 + 0.6 \ Y.$$

Equilibrium GNP is found by solving this equation for Y, and this involves only simple algebra and arithmetic. First, subtract $0.6 \ \overline{Y}$ from both sides, giving us

$$\overline{Y} - 0.6 \ Y = 200$$

or

$$0.4 \ \overline{Y} = 200.$$

Dividing both sides of this expression by 0.4,

$$\overline{Y} = 200/0.4 = 500.$$

Figure 13 Equilibrium Real GNP in the Simple Keynesian Model

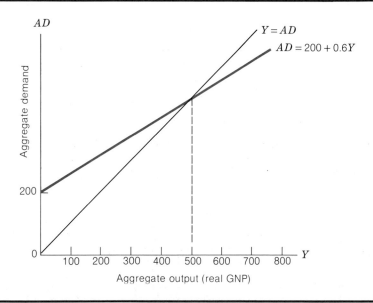

Aggregate output (real GNP)

Not surprisingly, this is the same result that is shown graphically in Figure 13 which combines the equilibrium condition $Y = AD$ (the 45° line) and the AD function $AD = 200 + 0.6\, Y$.

Aggregate Demand, Unemployment, and Inflation

We now have the tools to identify possible sources of unemployment and inflationary pressure that are related to the level of aggregate demand. In Figure 14a, equilibrium GNP ($\bar{Y}$) is less than the real GNP that would generate full employment (Y^*). In this case, the economy would experience *demand-deficiency unemployment*.

- **Demand-deficiency unemployment** of resources and capacity results from inadequate aggregate demand to generate equilibrium GNP at full employment.

In Figure 14a, the aggregate demand (AD) and the expenditure inflows and outflows determine equilibrium GNP at Y, which is less than the full employment GNP, Y^*. At the full-employment GNP, Y^*, there is a *demand deficiency* or *deflationary gap*.

- The **deflationary gap** is the amount that aggregate demand would have to increase to achieve equilibrium at full employment GNP.

In Figure 14a, equilibrium GNP will remain at Y unless the aggregate demand curve shifts. To achieve equilibrium at full employment, the aggregate demand curve would have to shift upward to AD' to close the deflationary gap.

If equilibrium GNP is greater than the full-employment GNP, this will generate inflationary pressures. In Figure 14b, the high level of aggregate demand would (if it could) generate an equilibrium GNP, Y, greater than full-employment GNP (Y^*). In this case, there is excess demand or an *inflationary gap* at the full employment GNP.

Figure 14 Unemployment and Inflation in the Simple Keynesian Model

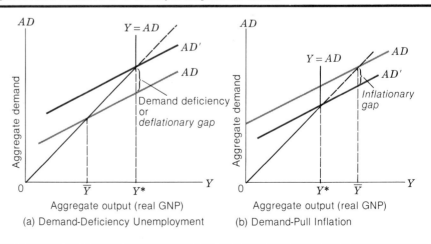

(a) Demand-Deficiency Unemployment

(b) Demand-Pull Inflation

- The **inflationary gap** is the amount that aggregate demand would have to be reduced to eliminate demand-related inflationary pressure.

To eliminate the demand-related inflation in Figure 14b, aggregate demand would have to be shifted downward to AD'.

This has been a rather long journey through an unrealistically simple economy, but this trip *was* necessary. We now have the basic tools we need to understand, analyze, and predict equilibrium aggregate output. This offers some insight into the aspects of unemployment and inflation that are related to the level of aggregate demand. The chapters that follow simply add the public sector to this simple model to analyze the impact of government on aggregate demand and equilibrium aggregate output.

It is worthwhile, however, to recall what we're doing in the analysis of income determination so far. First of all, we're looking only at the aggregate demand side, so we don't have all of the tools we need to analyze unemployment and inflation that are caused on the aggregate supply side. Also, we haven't included the impact of the monetary sector. Be patient—we can't do everything at once, and the rest follows.

Summary

1. The theory of income determination and income determination models are concerned with the variables that determine equilibrium national income or GNP, and with predicting equilibrium GNP and changes in equilibrium GNP. The variables in income determination models are *ex ante*, or intended, quantities.

2. In a closed private economy, there is no public sector and no international sector. The only expenditure flows in this simple economy are consumption, investment, and saving.

3. The **consumption function** shows the relationship between GNP or disposable income and the level of consumption. In the short run, some consumption may be autonomous, but in the long run, virtually all consumption is explained by the level of income.

4. The **marginal propensity to consume** (*mpc*) is the rate at which consumption changes as disposable income or GNP change. It is the slope of the consumption function.

5. Since disposable income equals saving plus consumption, the consumption function also determines the relationship between disposable income and saving, or the **saving function**. The **marginal propensity to save** (*mps*) is the rate at which intended saving varies with GNP.

6. The **marginal efficiency of investment** is the expected annual percentage rate of return on the last investment made. Since the most productive investments are made first, the *MEI* falls as the level of investment increases. Investments will be made for which the *MEI* is greater than the interest rate.

7. **Equilibrium GNP** is reached when the expenditure outflows from the income stream equal the expenditure inflows into it, and when the aggregate demand for goods and services equals the aggregate output of goods and services.

8. According to the Keynesian income determination model, equilibrium GNP may be reached with unemployment or with inflationary pressure.

Concepts for Review

unintended investment
unintended disinvestment
equilibrium real GNP
autonomous expenditure
induced expenditure
consumption function
marginal propensity to consume
autonomous consumption
dissaving

saving function
marginal propensity to save
investment
marginal efficiency of investment
simple Keynesian model
demand-deficiency unemployment
deflationary gap
inflationary gap

Questions

1. Explain the distinction between intended saving and investment, and measured saving and investment. Why is this distinction significant?

2. Economic forecasters and policymakers pay a lot of attention to business inventories as an indicator of future aggregate output and employment. What predictions of future real GNP and employment follow from rising inventories? What predictions follow from falling business inventories? Explain in the context of the income determination model.

3. During an economic recession in 1958, the automobile companies launched a large advertising campaign telling consumers that they "auto buy now." Apart from the obvious effect of increased demand for automobiles on the automobile industry, how would increases in automobile sales affect aggregate demand, equilibrium GNP, and the level of employment?

4. What are autonomous expenditures? Can you think of any examples of autonomous consumption and autonomous investment?

5. In 1933, disposable personal income in the United States was $45.5 billion, while personal consumption expenditures amounted to $45.8 billion. How could you explain this?

6. In constant (1972) dollars, U.S. disposable personal income increased from $859.7 billion to $890.1 billion between 1975 and 1976. In the same period, personal consumption in constant (1972) dollars increased from $774.6 billion to $819.4 billion.
   a. How could consumption expenditures rise by a greater amount than disposable income?
   b. In the context of the theory of the consumption function what could explain the behavior of consumption between 1975 and 1976?

7. It has been argued that expectations of future economic recessions (falling real GNP) or future inflationary pressure are *self-fulfilling prophecies* —i.e., things that happen by virtue of the fact that we expected them to happen. Evaluate and explain this argument in the context of the income determination model.

Problems

1. You are given the following information on consumption (C) and disposable income (Y_d) for the small peanut republic of Cartermania.

Y_d	C	mpc	S	mps
0	50			
100	140			
200	230			
300	320			
400	410			
500	500			
600	590			
700	680			
800	770			
900	860			
1,000	950			

a. Fill in the figures for intended saving (S). How did you get the figures?

b. Explain the marginal propensity to consume (mpc). Calculate mpc for all levels of disposable income in the table.

c. Explain the marginal propensity to save (mps). Calculate mps for all levels of income in the table.

d. Write the equations for the consumption and saving functions. On graph paper, draw the consumption and saving functions from the data in the table.

e. Suppose that all intended investment is autonomous, and that $I_a = 50$. Write the equation for the aggregate demand function, and draw the aggregate demand function in the graph you drew for part d.

f. Find equilibrium GNP algebraically and graphically from the above information.

2. The Adam & Eve Loose-Leaf Binder Co. is considering the purchase of a machine that would produce an expected $100,000 worth of binders over its productive lifetime of 2 years.

a. The machine has a purchase price of $85,000. Should Adam & Eve purchase the machine if the interest rate is 10% per year? Should they purchase the machine if the interest rate fell to 5% per year?

b. What variables other than the interest rate could affect Adam & Eve's decision to purchase the machine?

7

Aggregate Demand and Income Determination: Completing the Model

PREVIEW: The simple model introduced in the last chapter has taken us a long way in understanding the basic effects of aggregate demand in the goods markets on real GNP. In this chapter, we will complete the model by adding in the government and international sectors to it. We'll then look closely at how changes in the variables that comprise aggregate demand cause changes in the level of real GNP.

The Public Sector

The public sector includes all levels of government—local, state, and federal. All levels of government affect aggregate demand and income by spending and taxing, but macroeconomic policy is the nearly exclusive domain of the federal government. Adding the public sector adds three basic types of expenditures to the circular flow—government spending for goods and services, government transfer payments (pensions, income maintenance payments, etc.), and taxes. In the Keynesian model, these are reduced to two—*government spending* and *net taxes*.

Government Spending

When the government purchases a piece of equipment or hires an employee, this has the same effect on the spending flow as if a private employer had purchased the same equipment or hired the same employee. However, not all outlays by the government are included in the government spending flow in the expanded model. **Transfer payments** don't represent government purchases of productive services or of goods and aren't included as government spending in the model.

- **Government spending** includes all purchases of goods and services by local, state, and federal governments from the private sector.

Government spending is an inflow into the income stream. When the government increases its purchases from the private sector this increases the size of the aggregate spending flow.

- Other things equal, aggregate demand and equilibrium income will change in the same direction as changes in government spending.

Net Taxes

Income taxes, property taxes, sales taxes, excise taxes, and other taxes all represent expenditure outflows from the income stream to the government. Taxes reduce disposable income and thus reduce the level of consumption. Taxes on firms' profits reduce the funds that firms can distribute as dividends or reinvest in production.

The transfer payments that were excluded from the definition of GNP and from the definition of government spending in the Keynesian model do affect aggregate demand. Transfer payments are income to the households that receive them, so transfer payments tend to increase total disposable income. In the analysis of income determination that follows, the tax flow will be the **net tax flow,** which shows the net effect of taxes and transfer payments on the income stream. Specifically,

Net taxes (T) = total taxes − transfer payments.

Since transfer payments are smaller than total tax payments, the net tax flow in the model is an expenditure outflow.

- Other things equal, aggregate demand and equilibrium income will change in the opposite direction of changes in net taxes.

The International Sector

When a domestic buyer purchases an imported good, the expenditure to pay for the import represents an outflow from the domestic economy's income stream. On the other hand, when a domestic seller exports goods to foreign buyers, the expenditures to pay for the exports represent an expenditure inflow into the domestic economy's income stream. The *net effect* of the international sector is the difference between exports and imports, or **net exports.**

net exports = export expenditures (X) − import expenditures (M).

The net export flow may be positive (inflow) or negative (outflow), depending on the size of the export and import expenditures.

Equilibrium in the Complete Model

The circular flow of income in an economy with a public sector and an international sector is shown in Figure 1. The basic condition for equilibrium income in the complete model is the same as it was for the closed, private economy.

Figure 1   The Complete Circular Flow

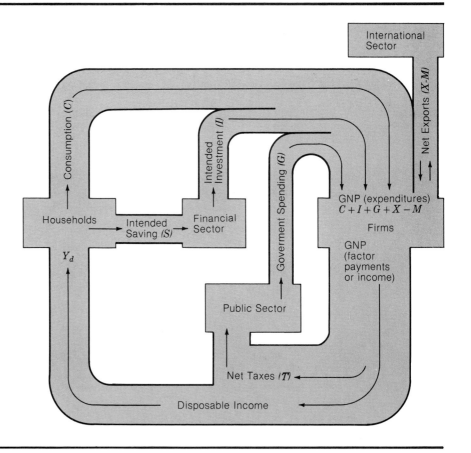

- **Equilibrium GNP** will be reached when *total expenditure inflows* into the income stream equal *total expenditure outflows* out of the income stream, and when the *aggregate demand* for goods and services is equal to the *aggregate output* of goods and services.

The only difference between this and equilibrium in the closed private economy is the additional inflows and outflows and the additional components of aggregate demand as a result of adding the public and international sectors.

The expenditure inflows and outflows in the complete model are summarized below.

	Inflow	Outflow
Private Sector	Investment (I)	Saving (S)
Public Sector	Government Spending (G)	Net Taxes (T)
International Sector	Net Exports ($X - M$)	
Entire System	$I + G + (X - M)$	$S + T$

The condition for equilibrium income in this model, then, is

$$I + G + (X - M) = S + T. \tag{1}$$

This can also be expressed as

$$\overline{Y} = C + I + G + (X - M). \tag{2}$$

Aggregate Demand in the Complete Model

At any level of GNP (Y), aggregate demand will be the sum of expenditures from the private sector (consumption and investment), the public sector (government spending), and the international sector (net exports).

$$AD = C + I + G + (X - M). \tag{3}$$

To keep the following analysis simple, two assumptions will be made in analyzing aggregate demand.

- All expenditure flows except consumption and saving will be considered *autonomous* expenditures.

- Until the international sector is analyzed in detail later in the text, we will assume that $(X - M) = 0$, and thus disregard the international sector.

Given these assumptions, the equation for aggregate demand can be rewritten as

$$AD = C + I + G. \tag{4}$$

Since we already know the relationship between the components of aggregate demand and the level of real GNP, it is possible to determine the level of aggregate demand at *any* level of real GNP.

The first step is to substitute the consumption function for C in the aggregate demand equation, giving us

$$AD = a + bY_d + I + G.$$

In the model, we'll use a simplified definition of disposable income—GNP (Y) less net taxes (T), or

$$Y_d = Y - T. \tag{5}$$

Assuming investment, government spending, and net taxes to be autonomous, the aggregate demand equation becomes

$$AD = a + b(Y - T_a) + I_a + G_a = a + bY - bT_a + I_a + G_a.$$

Grouping all of the autonomous expenditures together,

$$AD = (a + I_a + G_a - bT_a) + bY. \tag{6}$$

In Figure 2, the consumption function (C) shows the level of consumption expenditure at any level of GNP (Y). Since intended investment and government spending are assumed autonomous ($I = I_a$ and $G = G_a$), we simply add the sum of these expenditures to consumption at every

Figure 2 Aggregate Demand in the Complete Model

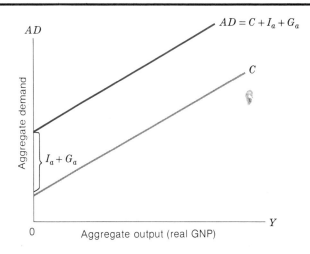

level of GNP to get the aggregate demand function (AD) in Figure 2.

Not surprisingly, if all of the components of AD are autonomous except consumption, the slope of the AD curve is the *mpc* (*b* in the consumption function and AD equation).

The aggregate demand function tells us what information to look for to predict aggregate spending. If the expenditure flows in aggregate demand are known or estimated, we can predict the level of aggregate expenditure at all levels of GNP. Suppose, for example, that the following information is known—or at least that it's the best estimate we have.

$$\text{Consumption: } C = 100 + 0.6\,Y_d$$
$$\text{Intended Investment: } I = I_a = 110$$
$$\text{Govt. Spending: } G = G_a = 100$$
$$\text{Net Taxes: } T = T_a = 50.$$

All of the numbers represent billions of dollars per year. From this information, the economy's aggregate demand function is

$$AD = a + bY - bT_a + I_a + G_a$$
$$= 100 + 0.6\,Y - 0.6(50) + 110 + 100$$
$$= 280 + 0.6Y.$$

This aggregate demand function is shown graphically in Figure 3.

To predict aggregate demand at any given level of GNP, substitute the value of GNP for Y in the aggregate demand equation and solve for AD. For example, at a GNP of $Y_1 = \$400$ billion per year,

$$AD_1 = 280 + 0.6Y_1 = 280 + 0.6(400) = \$520 \text{ billion per year.}$$

This same solution can be arrived at graphically. Simply find the aggregate demand coordinate of $Y_1 = 400$ in Figure 3. Notice that we get the same answer by this method: $AD_1 = \$520$ billion per year.

If GNP increased from $Y_1 = \$400$ billion to $Y_2 = \$600$ billion per year, aggregate spending would increase to

$$AD_2 = 280 + 0.6\,Y_2 = 280 + 0.6(600) = \$640 \text{ billion per year.}$$

The change in aggregate demand per dollar change in GNP is the slope of the aggregate demand function. When GNP increased from $Y_1 = 500$ to $Y_2 = 600$, aggregate demand increased from $AD = 520$ to $AD' = 640$, and the slope of AD is

$$\frac{\Delta AD}{\Delta Y} = \frac{AD_2 - AD_1}{Y_2 - Y_1} = \frac{640 - 520}{600 - 400} = \frac{120}{200} = 0.6.$$

Aggregate Demand and Equilibrium GNP

The condition for equilibrium in the economy with a public sector is the same as the condition for equilibrium in the closed, private economy.

$$\overline{Y} = AD.$$

The addition of autonomous government spending (G_a) and autonomous net taxes (T_a) to the aggregate demand function simply adds two more terms to the equilibrium condition.

Figure 3   Aggregate Demand and Equilibrium GNP

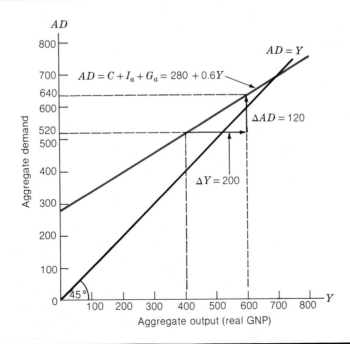

$$\overline{Y} = (a + I_a + G_a - bT_a) + b\overline{Y}.$$

To find equilibrium GNP, we simply have to solve the above equation for $\overline{Y}$, as we did in the last chapter. Subtracting $\overline{Y}$ from both sides,

$$\overline{Y} - b\overline{Y} = (a + I_a + G_a - bT_a)$$
$$(1 - b)\,\overline{Y} = (a + I_a + G_a - bT_a).$$

Finally, equilibrium GNP $(\overline{Y})$ becomes

$$\overline{Y} = \frac{1}{(1 - b)}\,(a + I_a + G_a - bT_a). \tag{7}$$

This equation has a lot of terms to remember, but this will be easier if you simply note that the parentheses contain all autonomous expenditures. So equilibrium in this model is found simply by dividing the sum of the autonomous expenditures by $(1 - b)$ or the *mps*.

To predict a specific equilibrium GNP from a known or estimated aggregate demand function—$AD = 280 + 0.6Y$, for example—simply plug the known or estimated values for autonomous spending and the *mpc* into the expression for $\overline{Y}$ that was derived above, and solve for $\overline{Y}$.

$$\overline{Y} = \frac{1}{(1 - 0.6)}\,(280) = \frac{280}{0.4} = 700.$$

This equilibrium is shown graphically in Figure 3, where the aggregate demand function $(AD = 280 + 0.6Y)$ intersects the equilibrium (45°) line labeled $Y = AD$.

Changes in Equilibrium Income

National income or GNP will remain in equilibrium unless something happens that alters the expenditure flows and aggregate demand.

- Equilibrium GNP will change in the same direction as shifts of the aggregate demand function.

If aggregate spending increases at every level of GNP, the aggregate demand function shifts upward, increasing equilibrium GNP, as shown by the shift of AD to AD' and GNP from $\overline{Y}$ to $\overline{Y}'$ in Figure 4. If the level of aggregate spending falls at every level of GNP, the aggregate demand function shifts downward and reduces equilibrium GNP, as shown by the shift of aggregate demand from AD to AD'' and equilibrium GNP from $\overline{Y}$ to $\overline{Y}''$ in Figure 4.

The list of exogenous changes that disturb aggregate demand and equilibrium GNP is nearly endless. The outbreak of a war generates large increases in government spending that raise aggregate demand and equilibrium income, and sudden reductions of government spending at the end of a war can lower aggregate demand and equilibrium income. Increases in taxes reduce disposable income, consumption,

Figure 4 Changes in Aggregate Demand and Equilibrium GNP

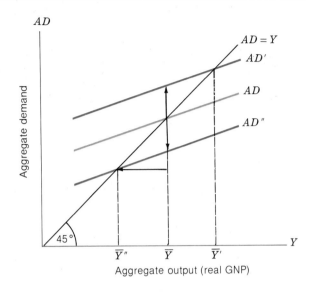

and aggregate demand at any level of GNP and tend to reduce equilibrium GNP. Optimism or pessimism about future economic conditions affect the behavior of consumption, saving, and investment and shift aggregate demand.

We can make two broad generalizations about the effects of changes in expenditure flows on equilibrium GNP.

- Aggregate demand and equilibrium GNP will change in the same direction as the expenditure flows with positive signs in the aggregate demand equation—i.e., consumption, investment, government spending, and net exports—and in the opposite direction of changes in expenditure flows with negative signs (saving and net taxes).

Applying the Tools

Aggregate Demand and World War II

Although there had been several halting recoveries and improvements in economic conditions in the 1930s, the recovery from the Great Depression was in fact brought about by the dramatic increases in government spending during World War II. In constant (1972) dollars, federal purchases of goods and services from the private sector increased about 8.4 times between 1940 and 1945, from 26.3 billion

Figure A

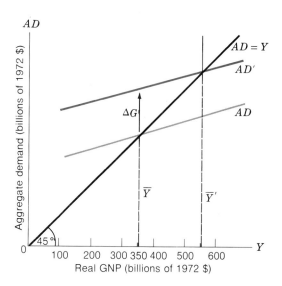

1972 dollars to 264.3 billion 1972 dollars. The effect of this increase in aggregate demand from the public sector is shown in Figure A.

Increased government spending to prosecute a war is an increase in autonomous government spending—the war wasn't related to our GNP. Increasing government spending from G to G' per year increases the expenditure inflow from $I + G$ per year to $I + G'$ per year, and the aggregate demand from $AD = C + I + G$ at every level of income to $AD' = C + I + G'$. This dramatic increase in aggregate demand increases equilibrium income from $\overline{Y}$ to $\overline{Y}'$. In fact, the general prediction that the increased aggregate demand would raise equilibrium GNP was borne out by the behavior of U.S. GNP during this period. In constant prices, U.S. GNP increased from $344 billion 1972 dollars in 1940 to $559 billion 1972 dollars in 1945.

Toward the end of the War, there was considerable disagreement among economists over how the economy would respond to peace. Many economists felt that the end of the War would bring back Depression levels of unemployment. They argued that the dramatic increases in government spending during the War had reduced unemployment, but if government spending fell dramatically after the War, aggregate demand, GNP, and unemployment would return to prewar levels.

Other economists predicted that the most serious problem after the end of the War would be inflation, and not depression. Although government spending would fall after the War, they predicted that a dramatic upward shift of the consumption function would offset the effect of reduced government spending on aggregate demand. Because of the unusually high rates of unemployment during the Depression, many households had to postpone purchases of automobiles and appliances. During the War, these goods were in very short supply because of the allocation of resources to producing military goods, and this forced households to save during the War. As the forced savings from the War years were unloaded to buy the goods that many couldn't find during the War, the consumption function would shift upward.

Both predictions were theoretically correct, but the facts clearly support the inflationary prediction. The unemployment rate did rise after the war (to 3.9 percent in 1948), but didn't even come close to the unemployment rates of the 1930s. Consumption expenditures increased in constant dollars between 1945 and 1948, despite the fact that disposable income declined during this period in constant prices. Finally, the inflationary prediction was confirmed by an increase in the Consumer Price Index by about 38% between 1945 and 1948.

Changes in Savings and the *Paradox of Thrift*

The **paradox of thrift** refers to a conflict between individual motives for saving and the macroeconomic consequences of changes in saving. If an individual has pessimistic or uncertain economic expectations, this tends to encourage him or her to save more and consume less at any given level of disposable income. It should be noted here that "saving more" could take the form of "dissaving less" by reducing consumer borrowing. What the individual is trying to do by saving more is to "hedge" against future unemployment or reduction of income.

If the uncertainty or pessimism that encourages individuals to save more at every level of income is widespread, aggregate saving (S) will increase at every level of income, as shown in 5a. If more is saved at every level of income, consumption and aggregate demand will fall at every level of income, so the increase in aggregate saving to S' and the increase in expenditure outflows to S' + T causes consumption to fall to C' and aggregate demand to fall to AD' = C' + I + G. The paradox, of course, is that at this new level of aggregate demand there will actually be *less* saving than there was before the upward shift in

Figure 5 The Paradox of Thrift

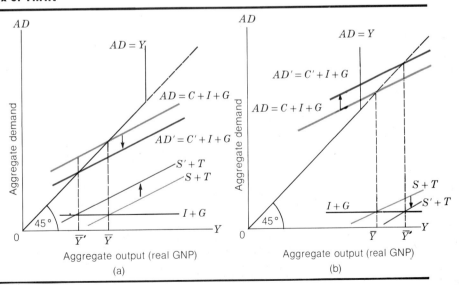

Aggregate output (real GNP)

(a)   (b)

the saving function. Also, the likelihood of unemployment and loss of income that prompted the increased saving by individuals is greater as a result of the lower level of aggregate output and real GNP.

In periods of inflation, the paradox of thrift tends to contribute to the inflationary pressure. Inflationary expectations tend to discourage current saving and encourage greater consumption. The future purchasing power of current saving is eroded by rising prices, and consumers may even find it worthwhile to borrow in order to purchase some consumer durables (such as autos) to avoid future price increases. If the economy is already in an inflationary equilibrium, as in Figure 5b, the inflationary pressures are made worse as a result of the reduction of saving and increase in consumption and aggregate demand.

The Multiplier Effect

If GNP reaches equilibrium $100 billion short of the full-employment GNP, will aggregate demand have to be increased by $100 billion to get GNP to the full employment level? If the government spends an additional $100 million per year, how much will this increase equilibrium GNP? If households decide to reduce consumption by $10 billion at every level of aggregate income, what effect will this have on equilibrium GNP? All of these questions involve an important but rather tricky concept called the *multiplier*, or to be more specific, the *autonomous expenditure multiplier*.

- The **autonomous expenditure multiplier** shows the change in equilibrium GNP as a result of a given change in autonomous spending.

Changes in autonomous spending shift the aggregate demand function, and this will cause equilibrium GNP to change by some multiple of the change in autonomous spending. The *multiplier* (k) is the ratio

$$k = \frac{\text{change in equilibrium GNP}}{\text{change in autonomous spending}} = \frac{\Delta \overline{Y}}{\Delta AD} . \qquad (8)$$

How It Works

The basic concept and mechanics of the multiplier effect aren't hard to master. Suppose that government spending increases by $20 billion per year, and that the higher level of government spending is maintained over an extended period of time.

Raising government spending by $\Delta G = \$20$ billion per year obviously adds $20 billion to the spending stream and increases aggregate spending by $20 billion per year. However, the increase in spending doesn't stop here. The additional government spending and GNP increases disposable income, and part of the additional disposable income will re-enter the income stream as additional consumption—in addition to the initial increase of government spending.

For example, if the marginal propensity to consume is $mpc = 0.6$, and all expenditures except consumption and saving are autonomous, increasing government spending by $\Delta G = \$20$ billion per year increases disposable income by $Y_d = \Delta G = \$20$ billion. This increase in disposable income will cause consumption to increase by

$$\Delta C = mpc\,\Delta Y_d = mpc\,\Delta G = 0.6 \times \$20 \text{ billion} = \$12 \text{ billion}.$$

Adding the additional consumption to the additional government spending, the income stream has increased by

$$
\begin{array}{ll}
+\;\Delta G & \$20 \text{ billion per year} \\
+\;\Delta C = mpc\,\Delta G = & \underline{12 \text{ billion per year}} \\
& \$32 \text{ billion per year}
\end{array}
$$

The increased consumption in the first "round" of spending represents an increase in disposable income in the second "round." Thus, for the second round there is additional disposable income of $\Delta Y_d = mpc\,\Delta G$, or $\$12$ billion per year. Part of this additional disposable income will re-enter the spending stream as additional consumption. The additional consumption in the second "round" of spending is

$$\Delta C = mpc\,\Delta Y_d = mpc\,(mpc\,\Delta G) = mpc^2\,\Delta G =$$
$$0.6 \times 0.6 \times \$20 \text{ billion} = \$7.2 \text{ billion per year.}$$

The increase in aggregate spending after two "rounds" of spending is thus

$$
\begin{array}{ll}
+\;\Delta G & \$20 \text{ billion per year} \\
+\;mpc\,\Delta G & 12 \text{ billion per year} \\
\;\;mpc\,(mpc\,\Delta G) = mpc^2\,\Delta G & \underline{7.2 \text{ billion per year}} \\
& \$39.2 \text{ billion per year}
\end{array}
$$

The increase in spending through four "rounds" is shown in Figure 6.

At each "round" of spending, some of the additional disposable income re-enters the income stream as additional consumption, and some leaks out of the income stream as saving. The income stream will continue to increase until all of the additional spending has leaked out. From an initial change in government spending of ΔG per year for a period of years, the increase in equilibrium GNP will be

$$\Delta \overline{Y} = \Delta G + mpc\,\Delta G + mpc^2\,\Delta G + mpc^3\,\Delta G + \ldots$$
$$= \Delta G\,(1 + mpc + mpc^2 + mpc^3 + \ldots).$$

If the rounds of spending approach infinity, and additions to disposable income and consumption approach zero, the sum in the parentheses becomes an *infinite series*, which can be written as $1/(1 - mpc)$. Thus, as the number of rounds approaches infinity, the increase in GNP as a result of an increase in government spending (or other autonomous expenditure) over an extended period approaches

Figure 6 The Multiplier Effect

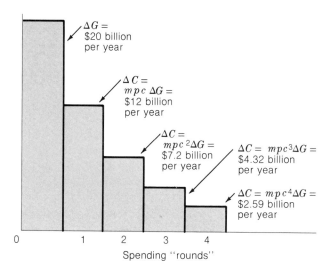

$$\Delta \overline{Y} = \frac{1}{(1 - mpc)} \times \Delta G.$$

The multiplier, then, is

$$k = \frac{\Delta \overline{Y}}{\Delta G} = \frac{1}{(1 - mpc)}. \qquad (9)$$

In our example, if $mpc = 0.6$ and all expenditures are autonomous except consumption and saving, the maximum increase in equilibrium GNP as a result of additional government spending of $\Delta G = \$20$ billion per year over an extended period is

$$\Delta \overline{Y} = k \Delta G = \frac{1}{(1 - 0.6)} \times 20 = \frac{1}{0.4} \times 20 = \$50 \text{ billion/year.}$$

The Multiplier in the Keynesian Model

The multiplier is easily shown in the context of the aggregate demand function and equilibrium GNP. With all components of aggregate demand autonomous except consumption, the aggregate demand function is

$$AD = (a + I_a + G_a - bT_a) + bY,$$

and equilibrium GNP is reached when

$$\overline{Y} = \frac{1}{(1 - b)} (a + I_a + G_a - bT_a).$$

Changing any of the autonomous expenditure flows in the parentheses will cause equilibrium to change by

$$\Delta \overline{Y} = \frac{1}{(1 - b)} \text{ (change in autonomous spending).}$$

The multiplier in the model is

$$k = \frac{1}{(1 - b)} \, .$$

. In Figure 7, with an aggregate demand function of

$$AD = 280 + 0.6\,Y,$$

equilibrium GNP was

$$\overline{Y} = \frac{1}{(1 - 0.6)} \times 280 = \frac{1}{0.4} \times 280 = \$700 \text{ billion per year.}$$

Increasing government spending by $\Delta G = \$20$ billion per year shifts the aggregate demand function to

$$AD' = 300 + 0.6\,Y$$

in Figure 7. The new equilibrium income is

$$\overline{Y}' = \frac{1}{(1 - 0.6)} \times 300 = \frac{1}{0.4} \times 300 = \$750 \text{ billion per year.}$$

The change in GNP (ΔY) is the change in autonomous spending ($\Delta G = \$20$ billion per year), multiplied by the multiplier $1/(1 - b)$.

$$\Delta \overline{Y} = \frac{1}{(1 - 0.6)} (300 - 280) = \frac{1}{0.4} (20) = \$50 \text{ billion per year.}$$

The multiplier works in both directions. If autonomous spending falls, the multiplier determines the decline in equilibrium GNP.

The Size of the Multiplier

The value of the multiplier and the strength of the multiplier effect are determined by the proportion of additional income that is consumed and the proportion of additional income saved at each "round" of spending. The higher the mpc, the greater the value of the multiplier coefficient. Since we normally expect the mpc to lie between 0 and 1, the multiplier will be finite and greater than 1 for all practical possibilities.

For example, with $mpc = 0.6$ in the previous examples, the multiplier was

$$k = \frac{1}{(1 - mpc)} = \frac{1}{(1 - 0.6)} = \frac{1}{0.4} = 2.5.$$

Figure 7 The Multiplier in the Keynesian Model

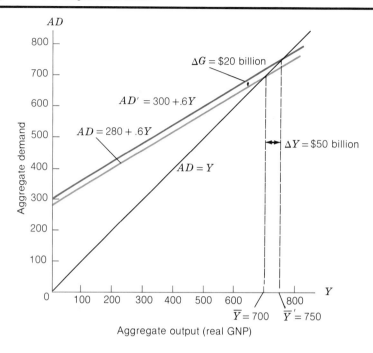

If the *mpc* were 0.8 instead of 0.6, the multiplier would be

$$k' = \frac{1}{(1 - 0.8)} = \frac{1}{0.2} = 5.$$

Obviously, the accuracy of our estimate of the aggregate demand function and the value of the *mpc* are crucial for the accuracy of predicted changes in income.

The Keynesian Model: Some Precautions

Predicting equilibrium GNP and the effects of changes in autonomous spending on equilibrium GNP in the real world isn't as simple, mechanical, or precise as in the model. Very few expenditure flows are in fact completely autonomous. We don't have completely accurate information, and in any given year short-term changes in expenditures make longer-term statistical estimates less reliable. The multiplier effect takes considerable time to work itself out completely—most empirical estimates of the multiplier effect estimate it for a period of 2 to 3 years—and while the multiplier effects are operating on one disturbance in the expenditure flows, other disturbances may come along. Again, keep in mind that we're still looking only at the aggregate demand side of income determination, and that our analysis still doesn't include the impact of the monetary sector. This makes the model a highly imperfect tool for predicting exact levels of GNP or exact changes in GNP. However, it doesn't mean that the model is practically useless. It shows important economic relationships and gives us an analytical approach to macroeconomic problems.

Summary

1. The complete Keynesian model includes expenditure flows from the private, public, and international sectors. Adding the public sector to the closed private model adds expenditure inflow (government spending) and an expenditure outflow (taxes). The impact of the international sector on aggregate demand is through net exports (exports − imports), which may be positive, zero, or negative.
2. Expanding the model doesn't change the conditions for equilibrium GNP—where inflows = outflows, and where $AD = Y$—but simply adds more components to inflows, outflows, and AD.
3. Aggregate demand and equilibrium GNP change in the same direction as changes in consumption, investment, and government spending; and in the opposite direction of changes in saving and taxes.
4. The multiplier effect shows the change in equilibrium GNP as a result of a given change in autonomous spending. The size of the multiplier effect depends on the proportion of the increased spending that re-enters the expenditure flow and the proportion that leaks out.

Concepts for Review

government spending   net exports
transfer payments   *paradox of thrift*
net taxes   autonomous expenditure multiplier

Questions

1. Explain how each of the following would affect aggregate demand and equilibrium income.
   a. Adding a 10 percent surcharge to all federal income tax liabilities.
   b. Increasing and extending public assistance programs to low-income families.
   c. Purchasing a new weapons system.
   d. Reducing federal employment.
2. What are autonomous government purchases and autonomous taxes? List some examples of each and explain.
3. What is the distinction between taxes and net taxes in the income determination model? Why is the distinction important in defining the tax flow in the model?
4. Some critics of the Keynesian income determination theory argue that World War II, and not policies based on Keynesian notions of aggregate demand, explain the end of the Great Depression. Is this a valid criticism? Explain.
5. What is the *paradox of thrift*, and why is is a paradox?

Problems

1. Adding a public sector to the closed private economy in Problem 1 from the previous chapter adds the following autonomous expenditures:

Government purchases:	$ 90 billion per year
Taxes:	$110 billion per year
Government transfer payments:	$ 30 billion per year

   a. Calculate the size of the net tax flow.
   b. Combining this information and the information on consumption and saving from Problem 1 from the last chapter, write the equation for the economy's aggregate demand, expenditure inflow, and expenditure outflow functions. Show these relationships graphically.
   c. Find the level of aggregate demand at a real GNP of $1000 billion per year. Could this be equilibrium GNP? Explain.
   d. Find equilibrium GNP. If the economy requires a real GNP of $1100 billion per year for full employment, would you predict that the economy will experience unemployment, demand-pull inflation, or neither? Explain.

2. As a result of the end of the Great War between Cartermania and Reagania, government purchases of goods and services are reduced by $20 billion per year.
   a. Find the maximum change in equilibrium GNP as a result of this change in government spending, using information from the previous question.
   b. What factors would determine the actual change in equilibrium GNP as a result of this change in government purchases?

8

Fluctuations of Aggregate Demand and GNP

Preview: Aggregate demand and output change constantly over time. Because such changes have such a major impact upon society's welfare, economists and others have been trying for many years to understand and predict fluctuations in economic activity. In this chapter, we'll look closely at how the components of aggregate demand in the goods market— consumption, investment, government spending, and taxes—contribute to the volatility of demand and output over time.

Although GNP may continually be seeking equilibrium, equilibrium GNP is probably the exception rather than the rule. Figure 1 shows the path of real GNP, consumption, investment, and government purchases in 1972 dollars for the period 1929 through 1978. For the two decades between 1958 and 1978, real GNP follows a relatively smooth path, but for the other years, the path of real GNP —like that of true love—is rough.

Fluctuations of economic activity over time have important implications for economic welfare. Drastic swings from prosperity to depression mean wide swings in living standards, and create an unstable and uncertain environment for economic decision making. Stabilization of real GNP around a long-term trend will tend to stabilize employment and inflationary pressures, and minimizing fluctuations is one of the central goals of macroeconomic policy.

There is considerable disagreement over the nature and cause of fluctuations of output and income, and this disagreement leads to disagreements over the proper policy approach to minimize instability. Controversies over stabilization policies center around several basic questions.

Figure 1 Gross National Product, Consumption, Investment, and Government Purchases 1929–1978

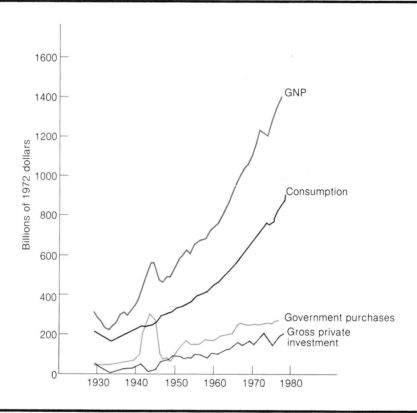

1. What causes fluctuations in economic activity and real GNP over time?
2. Can fluctuations be predicted and timed relatively accurately?
3. Is active intervention by the government to stabilize real GNP over time likely to increase, decrease, or not affect the degree of instability?

Business Cycles

Fluctuations of economic activity have been common for as long as economic data have been recorded. Over the years, economists have advanced a number of alternative explanations of fluctuations. In the classical analysis of the nineteenth century, fluctuations of economic activity were viewed as short-term adjustments to sudden economic shocks. Karl Marx saw cycles as the result of "fits and starts" in investment and the accumulation of capital, and a symptom of the internal contradictions of the capitalist system. Some economists, such as the great nineteenth century British economist William

Stanley Jevons, even explained fluctuations in terms of the cyclical pattern of sunspot activity and its effects on crops.

For many years students of business fluctuations treated them as cyclical fluctuations, or *business cycles*.

- **Business cycles** are self-reversing fluctuations in economic activity.

A very simple sketch of the phases of the business cycle is shown in Figure 2. Once an economic expansion begins, forces are set in motion that cause the expansion to continue. Rising personal income causes the demand and orders for consumer goods to increase. Sellers of consumer goods increase their orders, and producers increase output and employment. The increased output of consumer goods increases the demand for investment goods. Rising profits generate optimism that encourages further investment. Employment and income rise, keeping the expansion going.

Expansion can't go on indefinitely because the capacity to produce is limited, and some sectors of the economy reach full employment of capacity sooner than others. At high levels of output and employment, bottlenecks and shortages of basic industrial goods and resources increase the firms' costs. Higher costs lead to disappointed profit expectations and cause some firms to cut back. This reduction in demand spreads to other industries and to resource markets. Investment falls off, employment falls off, incomes fall, and the forces of contraction or **recession** spread. The point at which the expansion ends and the contraction begins is called the **upper turning point,** or **peak,** of the cycle.

Figure 2 Phases of the Business Cycle

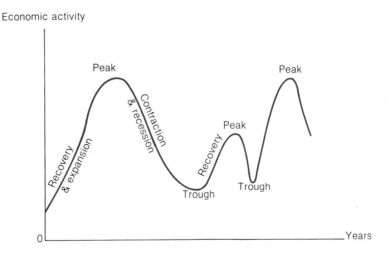

Eventually, however, the contraction will stop and another expansion will begin. Inventories eventually become depleted, capital equipment and consumer durables (automobiles and appliances, for example) wear out and must be replaced. If prices fall during the contraction, the purchasing power of accumulated savings increases, and this may encourage higher levels of consumption. These forces cause the contraction or recession to reach a **lower turning point**, or **trough**, and a new expansion begins.

Cycles don't have to be symmetrical. There may be long or short periods of expansion or contraction. A deep trough may be followed by a weak recovery and a low peak. Long periods of expansion and a high or prolonged peak may be followed by a mild recession and a shallow trough.

Measuring and Defining Business Cycles

The National Bureau of Economic Research (NBER) is a private research organization, and much of its research activity is directed at fluctuations and cycles. It was founded by the late Wesley Clair Mitchell, a major figure in the study of business cycles.

One of the most important functions of the NBER is to measure and define cyclical fluctuations.

- A **reference cycle** is defined by the NBER as an expansion and a contraction, or a cycle from trough to peak to trough.

The NBER dates the peaks and troughs of each reference cycle. Table 1 is a summary of the NBER's postwar reference cycles. Although there is a repeating pattern of expansion followed by contraction, the reference cycles aren't symmetrical.

Table 1   Postwar Recessions

Peak	Trough	Length of recession (months)
Oct. 1948	Oct. 1949	12 months
July 1953	May 1954	10 months
Mar. 1957	April 1958	13 months
April 1960	Feb. 1961	10 months
Oct. 1969	Nov. 1970	13 months
Nov. 1973	Mar. 1975	16 months

Source: U.S. Department of Commerce, *Handbook of Cyclical Indicators* (Washington: May, 1977). Also, *Business Conditions Digest*, vol. 19, No. 3 (March, 1979).

Some research on business cycles seeks to predict fluctuations, or at least turning points. This is important information. For example, if the government is following a policy of stimulating demand to minimize unemployment during a recession, it's important to know when to stop. If the stimulation of demand stops too soon, the recovery could halt before unemployment reaches an acceptably low level. If it continues too long, it could intensify inflationary pressures during an expansion.

Leading indicators reach their turning points before real GNP and can predict future peaks or troughs. For example, new orders for capital goods generally peak before real GNP, and a downturn in orders for capital goods generally suggests a future contraction or recession.

Are There Business Cycles?

Although the pattern of fluctuations shows a steady pattern of expansion, peak, recession, trough, expansion, etc.—and although most economists use the term *business cycles* loosely to refer to fluctuations—there is not widespread agreement on the causes of these fluctuations. Most business cycle theories give the heaviest weight to cyclical variations as the main cause of fluctuations. There are, however, other events that can affect the size and duration of expansions or contractions.

The economy is constantly bombarded by exogenous shocks that could cause instability in aggregate demand. Looking back over the historical record, many of the fluctuations in economic activity could be explained as the response to dramatic shifts in aggregate demand due to some important exogenous shocks—World War I, postwar demobilization, the Stock Market crash followed by drastic tightening of the money supply that discouraged investment and brought on the Depression, World War II, demobilization and reconversion after the war, the Korean War and demobilization, a large increase in demand for capital goods (explained in part by the shortages during World War II and the Korean War), and finally, the Vietnam War and its aftermath in the 1970s.

The instability or stability of real GNP over time is ultimately determined by the instability or stability of the determinants of aggregate demand over time—consumption, investment, government spending, etc. Figure 3 shows year-to-year percentage changes in real GNP, consumption, gross private domestic investment, and government purchases for the period 1950 to 1978. Even a casual look at these figures shows that consumption is the most stable component of aggregate demand over time, and investment is the least stable. Government purchases are relatively unstable over time, but this reflects the effects of exogenous events (wars and demobilizations, for example).

Figure 3 Changes in GNP and Components of GNP, 1950–1978

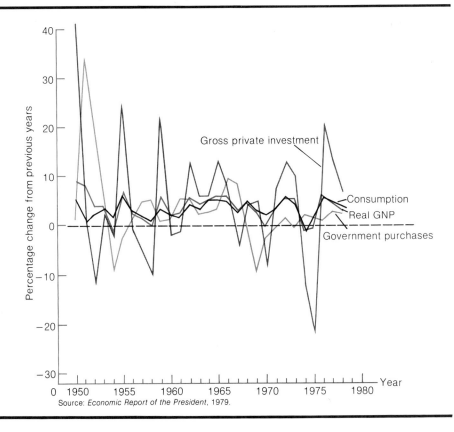

Source: *Economic Report of the President*, 1979.

**Consump-
tion
and
Instability**

Consumption is the largest component of aggregate demand and GNP. Dramatic changes in employment, incomes, and expectations can cause the consumption function to shift. General optimism, pessimism, or uncertainty about future economic conditions, employment, and income particularly affect *consumer durables* spending— purchases of "big ticket" items like cars, furniture, and appliances. If households are generally optimistic about their future economic condition, they will be more likely to make purchases of large consumer durables than if they are pessimistic or uncertain about the future economic prospects. Expenditures for consumer durables accounted for only about 16 percent of total consumption expenditures in 1978, however. The other basic types of consumer expenditure—purchases of *nondurables* (like food and clothing) and *services*— tend to be much less volatile. In fact, the most notable characteristic of consumption over time is its stability around its long-term trend, and the relatively small percentage changes in consumption from year to year—smaller even than the changes in GNP.

**The Relative
Income
Hypothesis**

One of the earliest explanations of the stability of household consumption behavior over time was the **relative income hypothesis**, formulated by Professor James Duesenberry of Harvard in 1952. Briefly, the hypothesis asserts that people gear their current consumption expenditures to their peak income achieved so far.

Figure 4 illustrates the relative income hypothesis by looking at a hypothetical household. In 1970, the household earned its highest disposable income to date ($15,000), and its 1970 consumption was 90 percent (.9) of its 1970 income, or $13,500. Now, suppose that the household's income falls from $15,000 in 1970 to $12,000 in 1974. If the household adjusted its consumption to 90 percent of its current income, its consumption spending would drop to $10,800 in 1974. However, according to the relative income hypothesis, the household wouldn't reduce consumption proportionally to a decline in disposable income below a previous peak. In Figure 4, then, the household reduces its consumption from $13,500 to $12,000 in 1974. This suggests that the household's consumption function for the period 1970-74 is C_{70-74}.

In 1975, the household's disposable income reaches a new historic high—$18,000. Consistent with the relative income hypothesis, the household adjusts its consumption in 1975 to 90 percent of its peak income, or $18,000 \times 0.9 = \$16,200$. If the household's income declined again from $18,000 in 1975 to $15,000 in 1980, the household would reduce its consumption spending less than proportionally because income in these years is below the historic peak.

Figure 4 Relative Income Hypothesis

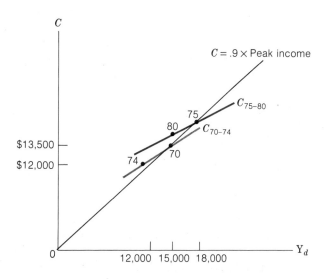

In short, as income moves to higher and higher peaks over time, households adjust consumption to the peak income. However, if it falls below the peak, consumption is reduced less than proportionally. This suggests a **rachet effect** that moves the household's short-run consumption function upward over time, but not downward.

If households' consumption behavior were consistent with the relative income hypothesis, we should expect that consumption will be more stable than disposable income over time, that the relationship between consumption and income over long periods of time will likewise be quite stable, and that the *mpc* will be lower in the short run than in the long run. All of these predictions are generally consistent with the empirical evidence on consumption presented in an earlier chapter. However, there is a serious analytical flaw in the relative income hypothesis: the implicit assumption that households never expect their long-term income trend to be below a historic peak.

The Permanent Income Hypothesis

In 1957, Professor Milton Friedman introduced the **permanent income hypothesis** according to which households gear their current consumption expenditures to their **permanent income**, or their expected average income over a period of years. As a result, there will be a more stable relationship between consumption and permanent income than between consumption and current income.

To explain permanent income in simple terms, imagine a person who receives a monthly salary of $1000 on the first day of each month. On the first of the month, the person's *measured* (or actual) daily income is $1,000. If the person geared his or her daily consumption to measured daily income—say, daily consumption = 90 percent of measured daily income—consumption expenditures would be $900 on the first of the month and zero for the rest of the month. To avoid this feast on the first and famine on the other days of the month, the typical household spreads its consumption expenditures more evenly over the month. In Friedman's terminology, the paycheck on the first of the month would be the person's *permanent income* for the entire month.

Having established that households will tend to smooth out their consumption expenditures over time, Friedman argues that there is no reason to believe that households will necessarily gear their annual consumption in any given year to their measured income in that year. Rather, he argues, households will gear their annual consumption to their *permanent income*, which Friedman defines as the expected average income over a three-year period. To illustrate, suppose that a household expects to earn an average income of $20,000 per year for the period 1980–1982—its permanent income is $20,000 per year. If it consumed 90 percent of its permanent income in each year, then, its consumption expenditures would be $18,000 in each of the years in the period. The household's actual measured income isn't constant, but varies from $18,000 in 1980 to $22,000 in 1981 and $20,000 in 1982. Thus, even though measured income fluctuates, consumption expenditure (which is geared to permanent income) is stable.

	1980	1981	1982
Measured Income	$18,000	$22,000	$20,000
Permanent income	$20,000	$20,000	$20,000
$C = .9 \times$ Permanent Income	$18,000	$18,000	$18,000

The permanent income hypothesis predicts that the ratio of consumption to disposable income may vary from year to year, but that C/Y_d will be stable over long periods of time. It also predicts that C/Y_d will be higher if measured over long periods of time than if measured over shorter periods. This prediction is consistent with the empirical relationship between consumption and disposable income. The permanent income hypothesis places a heavy emphasis on the stability of expectations over time on stabilizing consumption. Unlike the relative income hypothesis, the permanent income hypothesis doesn't preclude households' expecting permanent income to fall.

The Life-Cycle Hypothesis

A third explanation of the greater stability of consumption than GNP over time is the **life-cycle hypothesis** of consumer behavior formulated by Professor Franco Modigliani of MIT. According to this hypothesis, the household gears its annual consumption behavior to its expected average income for its earning lifetime. Suppose a household expects an annual average income of $20,000 for its earning lifetime. Typically, a household's income is below average in the early years of its life cycle, at a peak in the middle years, and below average again after retirement. Our hypothetical household's earnings behavior is represented in Figure 5.

In the early years, the household can maintain relatively high levels of consumption by borrowing against future income. During its peak earning years, it can pay off debts incurred in the early years and save for the years of low income after retirement. After retirement, the household can maintain its normal consumption and standard of living by spending the savings accumulated during the peak earning period. If the household geared consumption to its average annual income for its lifetime, year-to year changes in income would have relatively little effect on its consumption. However, over a long period of time, there will be little consumption that can't be explained by disposable income, a high *mpc*, and a very tight relationship between consumption and disposable income.

Figure 5 Life-Cycle Hypothesis

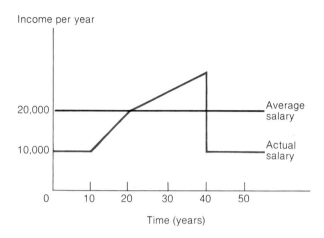

Investment and Instability

Although investment is a smaller expenditure flow and a smaller component of aggregate demand and GNP than consumption, it contributes more instability. Figure 3b shows that gross investment (*I*) was the least stable component of GNP during the period 1950–1978.

There are three basic reasons for the instability of investment—the existence of *induced investment* that varies with GNP, the so-called *accelerator effect*, and the effects of uncertainty and shifts in investors' *expectations*.

Induced Investment

Up to this point, all investment has been assumed to be autonomous. In fact, some investment depends on the level of output and real GNP.

- **Induced investment** is investment that varies with GNP.

Some investment is financed out of firms' profits, and some is financed by loans. The source of loanable funds to finance investment loans is the saving by households. Since profits and savings vary with GNP, it's reasonable to expect at least some investment expenditures to vary directly with GNP.

The rate at which investment varies with GNP is the **marginal propensity to invest** (*mpi*). Algebraically, *mpi* is the ratio

$$mpi = \frac{\Delta I}{\Delta Y}.\qquad(1)$$

Other things equal, the *mpi* will lie between its extreme values of 0 (all investment autonomous) and 1 (all additional GNP invested).

With the addition of induced investment, the relationship between investment (*I*) and GNP (*Y*) can be expressed by an investment function

Figure 6   Aggregate Demand and Induced Investment

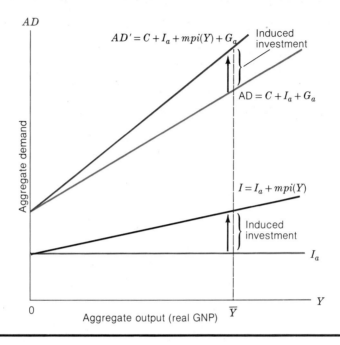

$$I = I_a + mpi\ (Y). \tag{2}$$

This investment function is shown graphically in Figure 6. At any level of GNP, total investment is composed of autonomous investment (I_a) and induced investment.

The addition of induced investment also affects the aggregate demand function. If we assume government spending and net taxes to be autonomous $(G = G_a$ and $T = T_a)$, and substitute the consumption and investment functions for C and I, aggregate demand is

$$
\begin{aligned}
AD &= C + I + G \\
&= (a + bY_a) + (I_a + mpiY) + G_a \\
&= (a + bY - bT_a) + (I_a + mpiY) + G_a \\
&= (a + I_a + G_a - bT_a) + (b + mpi)Y. \tag{3}
\end{aligned}
$$

Recall that with only autonomous investment, the slope of the aggregate demand function was b, the same as the slope of the consumption function. The addition of induced investment has increased this slope to $(b + mpi)$, as illustrated in Figure 6.

The addition of induced investment contributes to instability by strengthening the multiplier effect. With consumption the only non-autonomous expenditure, the multiplier is

$$k = \frac{1}{(1 - mpc)}.$$

If consumption and investment both vary with GNP, the multiplier becomes[1]

$$k = \frac{1}{1 - (b + mpi)} . \qquad (4)$$

This difference may look small at first glance, but its effects are really quite large. If $mpc = 0.6$, $mpi = 0.2$, and all other expenditures are autonomous, the multiplier with no induced investment is

$$k = \frac{1}{(1 - mpc)} = \frac{1}{0.4} = 2.5.$$

With induced investment added, the multiplier becomes

$$k = \frac{1}{1 - (mpc + mpi)} = \frac{1}{1 - (0.6 + 0.2)} = \frac{1}{0.2} = 5.$$

The addition of induced investment in this particular case actually *doubles* the multiplier effect.

Figure 7 Induced Investment and the Multiplier

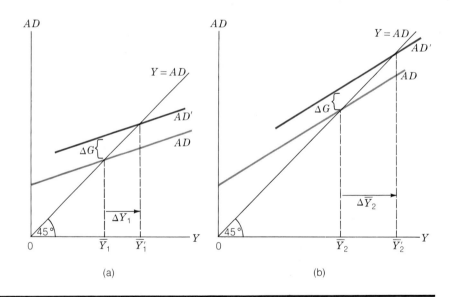

(a)   (b)

---

1. This multiplier can be derived algebraically by setting $AD = \bar{Y}$ and then solving equation 3 for $\bar{Y}$:

$$\bar{Y} = (a + I + G_a + bT_a) + (b + mpi)\bar{Y} \qquad (3)$$

$$\bar{Y} - (b + mpi)\bar{Y} = (a + I_a + G_a - bT_a)$$
$$(1 - b - mpi)\bar{Y} = (a + I_a + G_a - bT_a)$$
$$\bar{Y} = \frac{1}{(1 - b - mpi)}(a + I_a + G_a - bT_a)$$

The multiplier with induced investment is thus

$$k = \frac{1}{(1 - b - mpi)} = \frac{1}{1 - (b + mpi)} .$$

The effect of this change can be seen graphically in Figure 7. In part a (no induced investment), an increase in autonomous government spending from G_a to G_a' shifts the aggregate demand function upward by that amount and causes equilibrium GNP to rise from $\overline{Y}_1$ to $\overline{Y}_1'$. In part b (induced investment added), the slope of the aggregate demand function is now greater ($b + mpi$ instead of just b). As a result, though the increase in government spending shifts the function upward by the same amount as before, equilibrium GNP this time rises from $\overline{Y}_2$ to $\overline{Y}_2'$—about twice as much as before.

This stronger multiplier effect of shifts in autonomous spending will strengthen the destabilizing effects of economic shocks (sudden changes in expectations, wars, embargoes, etc.). It will also amplify the effects of changes in government spending and mistakes in economic policies.

The Accelerator and the Stability of Investment

Another cause of the instability of investment over time is a phenomenon known as the *accelerator effect*.

- The **accelerator effect** is the tendency of the capital stock and investment to change by greater proportions than changes in real GNP or real output.

Imagine an economy that always invests just enough to keep its stock of capital fully employed. Assume that 5 percent of the capital stock wears out every year and has to be replaced. Assume also that every $1 worth of output requires $5 worth of capital stock—i.e., that the **capital-output ratio** or ratio of required capital stock to real GNP is 5:1.

Initially, in year 0, real GNP is $500 billion, and the capital stock (KS) is $5 \times \$500$ billion = $2,500 billion. In year 1, GNP remains at $500 billion. The only investment in year 1 is the 5 percent of year 0's capital stock ($125 billion) that wore out and had to be replaced —i.e., all investment in year 1 is *replacement investment*. In Table 2, *gross investment* = replacement investment + net investment = $125 billion + 0 = $125 billion.

In year 2, real GNP increases by 10 percent to $550 billion. This will require $5 \times \$50$ billion = $250 billion in *net investment* to produce

Table 2 The Accelerator Effect

Yr.	Real GNP	Capital Stock	Replacement Investment	Net Investment	Gross Investment
0	500	2500	—	—	—
1	500	2500	125	0	125
2	550	2750	125	250	375
3	550	2750	137.5	0	137.5

the additional output. This net investment is in addition to the replacement investment of $125 billion (5 percent of the capital stock in year 1). So the 10 percent increase in real GNP causes gross investment to increase from $125 billion to $375 billion—an increase of 300 percent!

In year 3, real GNP stabilizes at $550 billion. Will this stabilize investment? No! Net investment falls to zero, because no additions to the capital stock are required to produce the same level of output. The only investment is the replacement investment to replace the capital stock from year 2 that wore out—in this case replacement investment is $5\% \times \$2,750$ billion = $137.5 billion. So, when real GNP stabilized after an increase, gross investment fell from $375 billion to $137.5 billion—a decline of about 63 percent.

This is a very simple example of the accelerator effect. In reality, the size of the accelerator may be smaller if there is unemployed capital in the economy. The example does, however, make some important points about the stability of the investment flow over time.

1. A stable investment flow over time will require steady growth of real GNP.
2. If GNP stabilizes after a period of growth, the level of investment will fall.
3. Fluctuations in investment will be greater than fluctuations in real GNP over time.

Expectations, Uncertainty, and Investment

A third force behind the instability of investment is something everyone has heard a good deal about in recent years: investor uncertainty. Investments are made on the basis of *expected* future returns. Nobody knows for sure what's going to happen in the future—not even self-styled mystics, prophets, astrologers, and wizards. In periods of particular uncertainty, investors tend to wait and see before tying their resources up in investment projects. This makes sense. A 90 percent chance that an investment would yield a return of 10 percent per year is more attractive than a 40 percent chance that it would yield the same annual rate of return.

If such "chances" were *objective*, investor uncertainty would contribute little to investment instability. Expectations about the future are *subjective*, however, and the state of investors' economic expectations can thus have a strong influence on the level of stability of investment. Suppose that with normal economic expectations, an investment project would be expected to return $1000 on a $10,000 outlay after one year—a 10 percent return. However, with more *optimistic* expectations, suppose that the same project would be expected to return $2000 after a year, or 20 percent. Suppose that the *pessimistic* expected return from the same project is $500 or 5 percent after one year. If the interest rate (r) were 10% per year, this would

Figure 8 Expectations, Investment, and Aggregate Demand

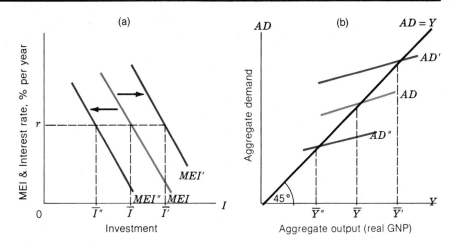

be a marginal project with normal expectations. It would definitely be undertaken if investors were more optimistic and definitely would not be undertaken if investors were pessimistic.

Expectations of all investors affect the *MEI* and the level of investment for the entire economy. Optimistic expectations of future returns tend to raise the *MEI* at all levels of investment and increase the level of investment at any interest rate. In Figure 8a, the *MEI* curve reflects "normal" expectations, *MEI'* reflects more optimistic expectations, and *MEI"* reflects more pessimistic expectations. At a given interest rate (*r*), investment would be $\bar{I}$ with normal expectations where *MEI* = *r*. Optimism would drive the level of investment to $\bar{I}'$ at the same interest rate. Pessimism would drive the level of investment to $\bar{I}''$.

The role of expectations in the stability of investment and GNP is important. Unstable expectations lead to unstable investment, aggregate demand, and equilibrium GNP. If optimism raises investment to $\bar{I}'$ in Figure 8a, aggregate demand increases to *AD'* in Figure 8b and GNP rises by $\Delta Y = k \Delta \bar{I}$. Pessimism drives investment to $\bar{I}''$ and equilibrium GNP to $\bar{Y}''$. Unstable GNP, in turn, makes expectations and investment even more unstable.

Government Spending and Instability

One of the recurring controversies in the debate over the proper role and scope of government intervention in the economy is the ability of government policies to stabilize aggregate demand and GNP over time through government spending and tax policies that stimulate aggregate demand during recessions and dampen demand-related inflationary pressures during economic expansions. This question is taken up in the analysis of fiscal policy in the next chapter.

The question of the effect of government purchases on the stability of income isn't the same as the question of the possibility of stabilizing income through government spending policies. Government purchases fluctuate for a variety of reasons other than attempts to stabilize income—wars and their aftermaths being the most obvious examples. Even since 1950, the Korean War and the Vietnam War had dramatic effects on government purchases of goods and services. In nonwar years since 1950, government purchases haven't fluctuated wildly. Furthermore, as shown in Figure 3b, fluctuations in government spending tend to run against the direction in fluctuations in investment, and may have a stabilizing effect on income.

Built-in Stabilizers

Even when economic problems are the most puzzling and disturbing, very few economists seriously expect a repeat of the economic disaster of the 1930s. In fact, many economists feel that the economy is "depression-proof," because of a number of **built-in stabilizers** that dampen expansions and contractions even in the absence of changes in economic policies.

Figure 9 Aggregate Demand and Induced Taxes

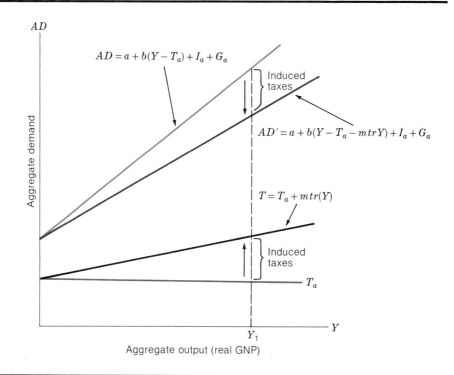

Induced Taxes

Up to this point, taxes have been treated as an autonomous flow. In fact, while some taxes (such as real estate taxes) *are* autonomous, most of the taxes that we pay vary with GNP. When GNP rises, personal income and the revenue from personal income taxes also rise. Since not all of the additional GNP and personal income is taxed away, disposable income also rises, and some of the additional disposable income is spent for consumption, increasing the revenue from sales taxes. Thus, the total tax flow contains *induced taxes* as well as autonomous taxes.

• **Induced taxes** are taxes that vary with income and GNP.

In periods of expansion and rising GNP, the induced tax flow increases, dampening the increase in aggregate demand and GNP. In recessions, falling GNP causes the induced tax flow to fall, dampening the decline in disposable income and aggregate demand.

The rate at which induced taxes vary as GNP varies is called the **marginal tax rate** (*mtr*). Algebraically, the marginal tax rate is

$$mtr = \frac{\Delta T}{\Delta Y}. \tag{5}$$

If induced taxes are *proportional taxes*, all income is taxed at the same rate, and the *mtr* is constant. A **tax function** showing the relationship between GNP (Y) and the level of tax payments could be expressed by the equation

$$T = T_a + mtr\ (Y). \tag{6}$$

This tax function is shown graphically in Figure 9. The distance between the autonomous tax flow (T_a) and total taxes (T) at any level of income represents the induced tax flow.

Adding induced taxes changes the aggregate demand function. If we assume for simplicity that investment and government spending are again autonomous $(G = G_a$ and $I = I_a)$, we can substitute the consumption and tax functions for C and T in the aggregate demand equation.

$$
\begin{aligned}
AD &= C + I + G \\
&= (a + bY_d) + I_a + G_a \\
&= [a + bY - b(T_a + mtr\ Y)] + I_a + G_a \\
&= a + bY - bT_a - b \cdot mtr\ Y + I_a + G_a \\
&= (a - bT_a + I_a + G_a) + (b - b \cdot mtr)\ Y. \tag{7}
\end{aligned}
$$

Just as the addition of induced investment *increased* the slope of the aggregate demand function from b to $(b + mpi)$, so the addition of induced taxes *reduces* the slope from b to $(b - b \cdot mtr)$ in Figure 9.

Induced taxes likewise change the multiplier effect, reducing its strength and thus making equilibrium GNP less responsive to changes in autonomous spending. With induced taxes and consumption the only non-autonomous expenditures, the multiplier becomes[2]

$$k = \frac{1}{1 - b + b \cdot mtr}.$$ (8)

Suppose that the mpc is $b = 0.8$, and that induced taxes are 25 percent of GNP ($mtr = .25$); the multiplier is

$$k = \frac{1}{1 - 0.8 + 0.8(.25)} = \frac{1}{0.4} = 2.5.$$

With the same mpc, but no induced taxes ($mtr = 0$), the multiplier would be

$$k = \frac{1}{1 - 0.8 + 0.8(0)} = \frac{1}{0.2} = 5.$$

Thus, the addition of induced taxes in this case has cut the multiplier in half.

Figure 10 Induced Taxes and the Multiplier

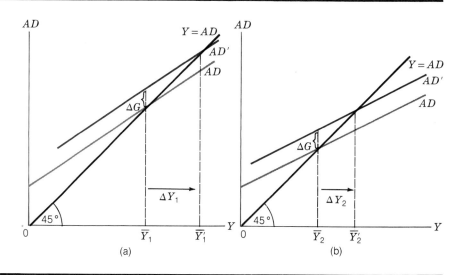

(a)   (b)

2. As with induced investment, the multiplier can be derived algebraically by setting $\overline{Y} = AD$ and then solving Equation 7 for $\overline{Y}$:

$$\overline{Y} = (a + I_a + G_a - bT_a) + (b - b \cdot mtr)\overline{Y}$$
$$\overline{Y} - (b - b \cdot mtr)\overline{Y} = (a + I_a + G_a - bT_a)$$
$$1 - b + b(mtr)\overline{Y} = (a + I_a + G_a + bT_a).$$
$$\overline{Y} = \frac{1}{1 - b + b(mtr)}(a + I_a + G_a - bT_a)$$

The multiplier with induced taxes is thus

$$k = \frac{1}{1 - b + b(mtr)}.$$

This difference is illustrated graphically in Figure 10. In part a (no induced taxes), the increase in autonomous government spending raises equilibrium GNP to $\overline{Y}_1'$. In part b (induced taxes added), the same increase in government spending raises GNP only to $\overline{Y}_2'$—about half as far. Thus, adding induced taxes has the opposite effect of adding induced investment, as a quick comparison of Figures 7 and 10 will clearly show.

Progressive taxes, such as the Federal Income Tax and some state and local income taxes, tax higher incomes at higher rates than lower incomes. As a result, progressive taxes have a stronger dampening effect on changes in aggregate demand than do proportional taxes. During expansions, the rising marginal rate of progressive taxes causes disposable income to rise more slowly relative to GNP than would be the case with proportional taxes. During recessions, the drop in the marginal tax rate causes disposable income to fall more slowly than with proportional taxes.

Unemployment Insurance

Most workers are covered by some form of **unemployment insurance** which subsidizes their income if they become unemployed. Some unemployment programs are public programs financed by payroll taxes paid by employers. In some industries, there are private programs which supplement or expand the benefits from the public programs.

Unemployment insurance dampens fluctuations in personal and disposable income, consumption, and aggregate demand. This has a stabilizing effect on GNP over time. In periods of falling aggregate demand and rising unemployment, more and more people qualify for benefits from unemployment insurance. This dampens the decline in personal income, disposable income, and consumption expenditures during recessions. When aggregate demand and GNP are rising and unemployment is falling, fewer and fewer people receive unemployment insurance benefits. Employers' payrolls increase during periods of expansion, and so do payroll taxes. So, the benefits that bolster income and aggregate demand during recessions don't continue to stimulate aggregate demand in periods of economic expansion.

Economic Fluctuations: What Can the Government Do?

One of the central goals of government *demand management* policies is to stabilize aggregate demand, employment, and output over time. Although an active economic role for the government is widely accepted, the controversy over the necessity, effectiveness, and desirability of government policies to regulate aggregate demand continues to divide economists and politicians.

The government has basically two bags of tools to regulate aggregate demand—monetary policies and fiscal policies. Since we have been analyzing the role of aggregate demand in determining aggregate output and equilibrium in the goods sector, we'll examine the fiscal tools (government spending and taxes) in the next chapter. Monetary policies will be analyzed after the monetary sector has been introduced into the analysis.

Summary

1. As long as economic data have been gathered and recorded, economic activity has shown a pattern of fluctuations over time.
2. Fluctuations are commonly referred to as **business cycles**, but strictly defined, business cycles are self-reversing fluctuations. Most modern theories of economic fluctuations try to explain fluctuations in terms of the stability or instability of the components of aggregate demand.
3. **Consumption** is the largest component of aggregate demand, but (except for consumer durables) contributes little to instability because of the stability of consumption around its long-term trend.
4. The **relative income hypothesis**, the **permanent income hypothesis**, and the **life-cycle hypothesis** are all economic theories which attempt to explain the long-term stability of consumption.
5. **Investment** is the least stable component of aggregate demand, and contributes the most to instability. The instability of investment reflects the importance of expectations in investment decisions.
6. **Induced investment** varies with GNP and makes GNP less stable by strengthening the multiplier effect.
7. Except for war years, **government spending** doesn't appear to be a major source of instability in aggregate demand or GNP.
8. **Built-in stabilizers** tend to dampen expansions and recessions automatically. **Induced taxes** and **unemployment insurance** are two important built-in stabilizers in the economy.

Concepts for Review

business cycle	ratchet effect	capital-output ratio
recession	permanent income	investor expectations
peak	hypothesis	built-in
trough	life-cycle hypothesis	stabilizers
reference cycle	induced investment	induced taxes
leading indicator	marginal propensity	marginal tax rate
relative income	to invest	unemployment
hypothesis	accelerator effect	insurance

Questions

1. What are the *phases* of the business cycle? What are the implications of the predictability of fluctuations and turning points?
2. To what extent has each of the components of aggregate demand—consumption, investment, and government spending—contributed to the stability or instability of GNP over time?
3. How do business and consumer attitudes and expectations affect the stability of aggregate demand and GNP?
4. Evaluate the following statement by the President's Council of Economic Advisers: "As inflation abates . . . , consumer confidence in the economy should improve and thus strengthen consumer markets. . . . The saving

rate is consequently expected to decline. . . ." (*Economic Report of the President,* 1979).

5. If the level of consumer debt and the stock of consumer durables are unusually high, what does this imply about the future behavior of consumption?

6. How would each of the following affect equilibrium GNP and the stability of GNP? Explain your answers.
   a. A 10% value-added tax is levied.
   b. A 10% tax is levied on personal property.
   c. The marginal propensity to invest increases.
   d. A progressive tax is levied on personal income.

Problems

1. The following expenditure flows are given for the economy of Macroland:

$$\text{Consumption: } C = 50 + 0.6Y_d$$
$$\text{Investment: } I = 50 + 0.2Y$$
$$\text{Govt. Purchases: } G_a = 75$$
$$\text{Net Taxes: } T_a = 50$$

   a. Calculate the equilibrium GNP ($\bar{Y}$) from the above data.
   b. Find the levels of consumption, autonomous investment, induced investment, government purchases, and saving at equilibrium GNP.
   c. If full-employment is reached at a real GNP of $Y^* = 1175$, does Macroland face an inflationary gap, a deflationary gap, or neither? Explain.
   d. Is equilibrium GNP in this economy more or less responsive to disturbances of aggregate demand than it would be without induced investment? Explain.

2. You are given the following expenditure flows for the small totalitarian country of Akademiia:

$$\text{Consumption: } C = 50 + 0.75Y_d \qquad \text{Investment: } I_a = 55$$
$$\text{Govt. Purchases: } G_a = 75 \qquad \text{Net Taxes: } T = 20 + 0.4Y$$

   a. Calculate equilibrium GNP ($\bar{Y}$) from the above information.
   b. What is the level of induced taxes at the equilibrium GNP?
   c. If full-employment GNP is $Y^* = 500$, does the economy face an inflationary gap, a deflationary gap, or neither?
   d. How do induced taxes affect the degree to which equilibrium GNP responds to disturbances of aggregate demand?

3. In addition to the expenditure flows for Akademiia in Problem 2, suppose that induced investment is 20 percent of GNP—i.e., induced investment = 0.20Y.
   a. Write the equation for Akademiia's aggregate demand function.
   b. What is the value of the multiplier in Akademiia with the addition of induced investment? Why is it different from the value of the multiplier in problem 2?
   c. Find equilibrium GNP ($\bar{Y}$) and the levels of induced investment and induced taxes at equilibrium GNP.
   d. If full-employment GNP is $Y^* = 500$ as before, does the economy face an inflationary gap, deflationary gap, or neither? Does it face the same problem it did in problem 2?

9

Fiscal Policy: Mechanics, Problems, and Issues

Preview: The government has at its command two basic tools for controlling or offsetting disturbances in aggregate demand. **Discretionary fiscal policies** involve manipulation of *government spending* and *taxes*. **Discretionary monetary policies** involve manipulation of the *money supply* and *interest rates*. In this chapter, we'll look closely at some of the problems and issues surrounding the use of fiscal policies, delaying our analysis of monetary policies until we have had a chance to set up a framework in the next section of the text. Keep in mind, though, that the effectiveness of any particular fiscal policy will depend heavily on the monetary policies that accompany it.

Fiscal policies are enacted to provide and pay for government programs and to regulate the level of aggregate demand. These two goals aren't mutually exclusive. Some people who advocate increased government spending to stimulate aggregate demand and reduce unemployment may object to particular spending programs. Others who think that government spending should be reduced may support maintaining or expanding spending on specific programs (often the ones from which they benefit).

In analyzing the role of the government in the determination of aggregate demand, unemployment, and inflation, we're primarily concerned with the issue of *discretionary fiscal policy*.

- **Discretionary fiscal policies** are government spending and tax policies whose *main aim* is regulation of aggregate demand in order to minimize demand-related unemployment, inflationary pressure, and instability.[1]

---

1. Since the primary interest here is the effect of fiscal policy on aggregate demand and equilibrium GNP, the analysis will be almost exclusively on federal fiscal policies. State and local governments also spend and tax, of course, but these fiscal policies are directed primarily at providing and paying for specific programs and services and not regulating aggregate demand.

In the Keynesian model, equilibrium GNP ($\overline{Y}$) may fall short of full-employment GNP (Y^*), as in Figure 1a. The resulting *deflationary gap* causes underutilization of resources and unemployment. To achieve full employment, aggregate demand would have to shift to AD' in order to raise equilibrium GNP to Y^*. If the private sector's intended consumption and investment spending is insufficient, *expansionary fiscal policies* by the government may be necessary to raise aggregate demand and close the deflationary gap.

- **Expansionary fiscal policies** are increases in government spending and cuts in taxes meant to stimulate aggregate demand and relieve unemployment.

It is also possible in the Keynesian model that equilibrium GNP ($\overline{Y}$) may fall *above* full-employment GNP (Y^*), as in Figure 1b. The resulting *inflationary gap* and excess demand mean that individuals in the private sector will bid against each other for scarce goods and resources, raising the price level. In such cases, the government may be forced to use *restrictive fiscal policies* to lower aggregate demand to AD' and close the inflationary gap.

- **Restrictive fiscal policies** are cuts in government spending and increases in taxes meant to dampen aggregate demand and relieve inflationary pressures.

Whether the real world will actually behave the way the Keynesian model suggests is, of course, another question entirely. The necessity or desirability of discretionary fiscal policy is a long-standing

Figure 1 Effects of Discretionary Fiscal Policy

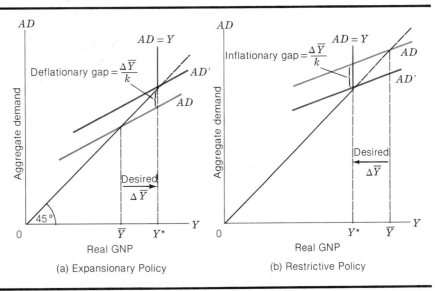

(a) Expansionary Policy   (b) Restrictive Policy

source of dispute among economists, and the experiences of the past decade have convinced a small but significant contingent of the economics profession that fiscal (and, for that matter, monetary) policies are ineffective in controlling aggregate demand, inflation, and unemployment. The possibility of achieving equilibrium GNP with less than full employment or with chronic inflationary pressure is perhaps the most important question that divided Keynes from the economic orthodoxy of the 1930s, and it is at least one of the most important questions that divide modern Keynesians and monetarists.

Government Spending vs. Taxes

It takes more than a flip of a coin to choose between fiscal policies that regulate aggregate demand through government spending and those that regulate aggregate demand through taxes. A number of important considerations are involved in making the choice between government spending and taxes.

Taxes, Government Spending, and Ideology

Modern political liberals tend to accept or advocate a broader range of services provided through the public sector and a more active role for the government in the economy than do modern conservatives. The "tax revolt" that gained widespread attention in the late 1970s had the strongest support from political conservatives and the strongest opposition from political liberals. Different political ideologies dictate different fiscal policies for raising or lowering the level of aggregate demand.

During periods of high unemployment, liberals tend to favor increased government spending through the undertaking of new public programs and expansion of existing programs. To reduce inflationary pressures, liberals tend to advocate tax increases over spending reductions, so as to avoid reducing the size and role of the public sector.

Close-up

The Democrats' Free Lunch: The Humphrey-Hawkins Bill

The famous economic saying, "There's no such thing as a free lunch," means that every benefit carries an associated cost. At election time, however, many politicians seem to disbelieve this notion, supporting bills that promise a free lunch to the voters. One such bill of major importance was the Full Employment & Balanced Growth Act of 1976, sponsored by the late Senator Hubert Humphrey (D-Minn.) and Representative Augustus Hawkins (D-Calif.) and thus known as the *Humphrey-Hawkins Bill*. The bill would establish "the right of all adult Americans able, willing, and seeking work to opportunities for useful paid employment at fair rates of compensation." In its original form, the bill required the government to pursue policies which would bring unemployment down to 3 percent by 1980; if traditional monetary and fiscal policies were insufficient to achieve this goal through the private sector, the government would act as employer of last resort, using public service job programs.

Supporters of the bill claimed that the huge expenditures necessary to hire millions of workers would not require a tax increase. Why? Because the growth in GNP and the tax base resulting from the much larger work force would mean an increase in tax revenues sufficient to pay for the new jobs. Most economists, however, including such prestigious liberals as Arthur Okun, James Tobin, and Franco Modigliani, didn't buy that logic, contending that the bill would be hugely inflationary and could not possibly achieve its objectives. By the time Jimmy Carter came to support the bill in 1978, it had been thoroughly watered down: the 3 percent goal had risen to 4 percent, no specific measures of money figures were spelled out for achieving that goal, and the President was even permitted to suggest changes in the goal after two years if he felt the economic situation required such changes.[1]

1. See "What Humphrey-Hawkins Would Mean," *Business Week*, May 31, 1976, pp. 66–67.

Political conservatives that accept *any* role for fiscal policy in stimulating aggregate demand tend to favor tax cuts over increased government spending. Tax cuts stimulate aggregate demand and at the same time achieve the conservatives' objectives of reducing the impact of the public sector. In inflationary times, conservatives tend to favor cuts in government spending, which both dampen inflationary pressures and reduce the size and role of the public sector.

Close-up

The Republicans' Free Lunch: The Kemp-Roth Bill

If our examination of the Humphrey-Hawkins Bill made you want to rush out and vote Republican, wait a moment. The "Kemp-Roth" Bill, introduced in 1978 by Representative Jack Kemp (R.-N.Y.) and Senator William V. Roth, Jr. (R-Del.), is the Republican version of the "free lunch." The bill would cut all personal taxes by one-third over a three-year period, at a cost of roughly $125 billion in lost tax revenues. Unlike more typical conservative tax-cutters, however, supporters of Kemp-Roth claim that this huge cut would require *no* cut in government spending. The reason: the tax cut would provide incentive for firms and households to work harder and spend and invest more, thus increasing national income and the tax base and entirely offsetting the original deficit. In other words, the government would be getting a proportionately smaller piece of a much larger pie.

Like the Humphrey-Hawkins Bill, the Kemp-Roth Bill rests on a kind of "fly now-pay later" theory of economic policy-making. Also like Humphrey-Hawkins, Kemp-Roth was rejected as unfeasible and highly inflationary by most economists, including such major conservative economists as George Stigler, Martin Feldstein, and Herbert Stein, who estimated that it would take "about 30 years to regain the revenue level that would have been achieved without the tax cut." Many of those Republican candidates who embraced the bill in the 1978 elections found that even in the midst of "Proposition 13 Fever," most voters agreed with the economists and demanded that any tax cuts be tied to equivalent cuts in government spending.[1]

---

1. See Seymour Zucker, "The Fallacy of Slashing Taxes Without Cutting Spending," *Business Week,* August 7, 1978, pp. 62, 64.

These generalizations don't mean that liberals will approve every proposed increase in spending or that conservatives will approve every proposed decrease. Political liberals, for example, tend to be critical of increased military spending, and every elected official or candidate for office (liberal or conservative) has to be sensitive to the spending and tax programs that are most important to his or her constituents. Also, since Congress is made up of representatives with diverse ideologies, the process of debate and compromise generally results in policies that combine some of the liberal and conservative fiscal strategies.

The Multiplier Effect of Government Spending and Taxes

Political considerations aside, does the choice of manipulating government spending or taxes *really* make any difference in regulating aggregate demand? Figure 1a is the familiar picture of an economy with equilibrium GNP ($\overline{Y}$) below the full employment GNP (Y^*). Suppose that the government has an either-or choice between taxes and government spending to close the deflationary gap. How much additional government spending (ΔG) would get equilibrium GNP ($\overline{Y}$) up to Y^*? The change in government spending will generate a greater change in equilibrium GNP ($\Delta \overline{Y}$) because of the multiplier effect. If k is the multiplier, then

$$k\,\Delta G = \Delta \overline{Y}. \tag{1}$$

Given $\overline{Y}$ and Y^*, the desired change in GNP is $\Delta \overline{Y} = Y^* - \overline{Y}$. This value can be substituted for $\Delta \overline{Y}$ in equation 1:

$$k\,\Delta G = (Y^* - \overline{Y}). \tag{2}$$

The change in government spending that yields this change in GNP will thus be

$$\Delta G = \frac{(Y^* - \overline{Y})}{k} \, . \tag{3}$$

The deflationary gap could also be closed by cutting taxes. For simplicity, assume a change in autonomous taxes—for example, a change in property taxes. The autonomous tax term in the consumption and aggregate demand functions, you will recall, is $(-bT_a)$, so changing autonomous taxes by ΔT_a will cause GNP to change by

$$- k \, b \, \Delta T_a = \Delta \overline{Y} \tag{4}$$

Again, the desired change in GNP is $(Y^* - \overline{Y})$, so we can substitute that term for $\Delta \overline{Y}$ in equation 4:

$$- k \, b \, \Delta T_a = (Y^* - \overline{Y}). \tag{5}$$

The change in taxes (ΔT) which would yield the desired change in GNP $(\Delta \overline{Y})$, then, is

$$\Delta T = - \frac{(Y^* - \overline{Y})}{kb} \, . \tag{6}$$

The negative sign in this result shows that a desired change in GNP will require a change in taxes in the opposite direction. Notice that unless $b = 1$, kb will be less than k, and it will thus take a larger reduction in taxes to raise GNP by a given amount than the increase in government that gives the same result.

This result can be reinforced with a numerical example. Suppose that full-employment GNP $(Y^*) = \$500$ billion, equilibrium GNP $(\overline{Y}) = \$400$ billion, *mpc* $(b) = 0.8$, and $k = 5$. The desired change in GNP is $Y^* - \overline{Y} = \$500$ billion $- \$400$ billion $= \$100$ billion.

The change in government spending that would yield full-employment GNP is

$$\Delta G = \frac{\$500 \text{b.} - \$400 \text{b.}}{5} = \frac{\$100 \text{b.}}{5} = \$20 \text{ billion.}$$

The change in taxes (ΔT) that would give the same result is

$$\Delta T = - \frac{\$500 \text{b.} - \$400 \text{b.}}{5 \times 0.8} = - \frac{\$100 \text{b.}}{4} = -\$25 \text{ billion.}$$

Increasing equilibrium GNP by $100 billion, then, would require a *$20 billion* increase in government spending or a *$25 billion* cut in taxes.

- A given change in GNP will require a larger change in autonomous taxes than the change in government spending that would yield the same result.

If full-employment real GNP is $Y^* = \$500$ billion and equilibrium real GNP is $\overline{Y} = \$600$ billion, the economy faces an *inflationary gap* and demand-pull inflation, as shown in Figure 1b. In this case, the desired change in GNP $(\Delta\overline{Y})$ is negative—$Y^* - \overline{Y} = \$500$ billion – $\$600$ billion = – $\$100$ billion.

To reduce equilibrium GNP by reducing government spending only,

$$\Delta G = \frac{\$500\,\text{b.} - \$600\,\text{b.}}{5} = \frac{-\$100\,\text{b.}}{5} = -\$20\,\text{billion.}$$

To achieve the same result by increasing taxes,

$$\Delta T = -\frac{\$500\,\text{b.} - \$600\,\text{b.}}{5 \times 0.8} = -\frac{-\$100\,\text{b.}}{4} = \$25\,\text{billion.}$$

In this case the tax increase is greater than the reduction of government spending that would achieve the same result.

Discre-tionary Fiscal Policy and Balanced Budgets

The *balanced budget* (government tax revenues equal to government spending) is one of the most durable of economic issues. Some people revere the balanced budget with a fervor usually accorded only to religious relics. Balanced budgets are typically identified with fiscal responsibility and *surpluses* with unusual restraint and self-discipline by public officials.

The disdain for government budget *deficits* (government spending exceeding tax revenues) seems to be nonpartisan. Republicans associate budgets deficits with Democratic administrations, and Democrats seldom miss a chance to point to budget deficits under Republican administrations.

Close-up

Should an Unbalanced Budget Be Unconstitutional?

One of the ways in which the public sentiment against "Big Government" and taxation in the late 1970s made itself felt was in the drive for a constitutional amendment to ban deficit federal spending. By mid-1979, 26 of the required 34 state legislatures had passed resolutions calling for a constitutional convention to draft such an amendment. Amendment proposals ranged from those which would ban deficit spending altogether to those that would limit spending to a set percentage of the previous year's growth in real GNP. Supporters claimed that only through the external pressure of an amendment could the Federal government be forced to limit its spending. Opponents, on the other hand, argued that such a ban would straitjacket the government in times of economic "emergency" and would be impractical or impossible to enforce.

Although the drive for a convention began as a nonpartisan, grass-roots movement, the issue was taken up by candidates for the presidential nomination in both major political parties. Former Governor John B. Connally of Texas made the balanced budget amendment part of his platform in his drive for the 1980 Republican nomination. On the Democratic side, Governor Edmund G. ("Jerry") Brown—who had been unsuccessful in his fight against "Proposition 13" in California in 1978—jumped on the amendment bandwagon to gain support in his drive for the 1980 Democratic party nomination for the presidency. Brown declared that "the time has come for this nation to balance what it produces with what it spends."[1]

---

1. "A Constitutional Ban on Red Ink?" *U.S. News and World Report*, January 29, 1979, p. 27.

One way to balance the budget is to separate government spending and taxes from the issue of full employment. In fact, some monetarists argue that government spending should be determined only by the merits of specific spending programs, and tax revenue should be sufficient to balance the budget. Full-employment and price stability would be achieved in the long run through the adjustments of prices and outputs in freely operating markets.

Unless the economy generated full employment and price stability on its own, however, we shouldn't expect discretionary fiscal policy to give us *annually balanced budgets*—i.e., government spending equal to taxes every year. Of course, if the economy generated full employment and price stability on its own, there would be no need for discretionary fiscal policies to regulate aggregate demand in the first place.

A more flexible version of the balanced budget arguments calls for *cyclically balanced budgets*, or total government spending equal to total taxes over the course of a business cycle. The argument here is that deficits will shorten and reduce the seriousness of recessions, and surpluses will dampen inflationary pressures in periods of excess demand. A major problem with this approach is that instability is not caused by cyclical changes alone, and random economic shocks appear to explain much more instability than cyclical forces. Moreover, the cyclically balanced budget would be achieved only if fluctuations were symmetrical—which they aren't. We don't find recessions and troughs offset by expansions of equal duration and peaks of equal height to the depth of the trough.

The Full-Employment Budget

When the President presents his proposed budget in January of each year, reference is often made to the *full-employment* budget. It is most commonly invoked to minimize the significance of a projected deficit in the proposed budget.

- The **full-employment budget** estimates government spending and tax revenue for the economy operating at full employment or at an acceptably low rate of unemployment.

Budgets show a *full-employment balance* if tax revenues would equal government spending if the economy were operating at full employment. Figure 2a illustrates a full-employment balanced budget graphically. Real GNP (GNP in constant prices) is shown on the horizontal axis, and government spending and taxes ($) are on the vertical axis. In the diagram, government spending (G) is autonomous, and taxes (T) vary directly with GNP. The predicted GNP (Y_p) is less than full-employment GNP (Y^*), and predicted tax revenue (T_p) is less than tax revenue at full employment (T^*), and less than government spending. The budget shows a deficit in the projected budget, but a *full-employment balance* ($T^* = G$).

If tax revenues exceed government spending at full-employment (T^* greater than G), as in Figure 2b, the budget shows a *full-employment surplus*, even though the actual budget would show a deficit. In Figure 2c, the budget shows a *full-employment deficit* (T^* less than G) as well as an actual deficit.

Figure 2 The Full-Employment Budget

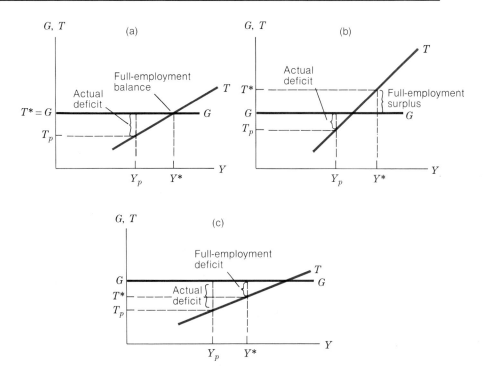

At first glance, the full-employment budget looks like nonsense. To say that we have a deficit, but would have a balanced budget at full employment seems to make about as much sense as the assertion that if my grandmother had had wheels she'd have been a car. On closer examination, however, the full-employment budget is a useful device in the design and evaluation of fiscal policy. The full-employment budget indicates whether or not a projected budget would be expansionary or restrictive at high levels of employment. Changes in the actual budget surplus or deficit may or may not indicate expansionary or restrictive changes in fiscal policy. For example, in Figure 2b, tax revenues vary with income along T as income changes. With no change in spending, tax rates, or types of taxes—i.e., no change in the direction of fiscal policy—the actual deficit will increase as GNP (Y) falls and will shrink as Y rises. However, the full-employment deficit or surplus will change only if the tax (T) or government spending (G) curves shift due to changes in fiscal policy.

A balanced full-employment budget suggests that an actual deficit is adequate to generate full-employment GNP without contributing to excess demand and inflationary pressure at high levels of employment—*if* the estimates are correct.

The full-employment budget, although a handy device for political deception (by calling nearly everything a *balanced budget*), *is* useful for fiscal policy. If the goal is to stimulate aggregate demand to reduce high unemployment, it indicates whether or not actual deficits are adequate to reduce unemployment to an acceptably low level without intensifying inflationary pressures as unemployment falls.

The Balanced-Budget Multiplier

Could discretionary fiscal policy be used to alter aggregate demand if the proposed balanced-budget amendment to the Constitution were ratified? The first impression is that it couldn't because the possibility of stimulating aggregate demand with deficits and dampening it with surpluses would be removed. However, it *is* possible to change aggregate demand and equilibrium GNP via equal changes in government spending and taxes.

Suppose that the government increases government spending and taxes by an equal amount ($\Delta G = \Delta T$) to maintain a balanced budget. For simplicity, assume that the entire ΔG enters the income stream and stimulates aggregate demand. However, increasing taxes lowers disposable income, and a reduction in disposable income (ΔY_d) reduces consumption only by a proportion of the change in disposable income ($\Delta C = mpc\, \Delta Y_d$). In other words, the change in government spending would have a greater effect on aggregate demand and equilibrium GNP than would the equal change in taxes.

The effect of an equal change in government spending and taxes on equilibrium GNP is called the *balanced-budget multiplier effect*.

- The **balanced-budget multiplier** is the change in equilibrium GNP resulting from equal changes in government spending and taxes.

The value of the balanced-budget multiplier can be derived formally using a little simple algebra. Given an autonomous expenditure multiplier k, and $mpc = b$, the effect of a change in government spending is

$$\Delta \overline{Y}_G = k \Delta G. \tag{7}$$

The effect of an equal change in taxes is

$$\Delta \overline{Y}_T = - k \, b \, \Delta T. \tag{8}$$

The net effect of these changes on equilibrium GNP is

$$\Delta \overline{Y} = \Delta \overline{Y}_G + \Delta \overline{Y}_T = k \Delta G - k \, b \, \Delta T. \tag{9}$$

Since $\Delta G = \Delta T$ in this example, they can be substituted for each other in equation 9, giving us

$$\Delta \overline{Y} = k \Delta G - k \, b \, \Delta G = (1 - b) \, k \, \Delta G. \tag{10}$$

Recall, however, that the autonomous expenditure multiplier k is equal to $1/(1 - b)$. Substituting this ratio into equation 10, we get

$$\Delta \overline{Y} = (1 - b) \cdot \frac{1}{(1 - b)} \Delta G = \frac{(1 - b)}{(1 - b)} \Delta G = \Delta G. \tag{11}$$

The balanced-budget multiplier, k_B, in this simple case then will be

$$k_B = \frac{(1 - b)}{(1 - b)} = 1. \tag{12}$$

The fact that the balanced-budget multiplier is 1 means that the change in GNP will be equal and in the same direction as the equal changes in government spending and taxes. If government spending increases by $10 billion, and taxes increase by $10 billion, equilibrium GNP will increase by $10 billion. Conversely, if taxes and government spending are both cut by $10 billion, equilibrium GNP will fall by $10 billion.

Whether the balanced-budget multiplier in any *particular* equal change in government spending and taxes will actually equal 1 depends on the proportion of the additional government spending that represents a *net* increase in aggregate spending. The increase in taxes to cover an increase in government spending reduces disposable income. This reduction in turn reduces consumption, so a portion of the increased government spending simply replaces private spending.

In reality, the balanced-budget multiplier is probably quite small, and there is even some disagreement concerning its very existence. This suggests that, while not quite impossible, the continued use of discretionary fiscal policies while maintaining a balanced budget would be difficult at best. The kinds of massive changes in government spending and taxes that would be needed to offset even relatively minor disturbances in aggregate demand would be politically unacceptable to most elected officials. As a result, an unbending requirement (through legislation or constitutional amendment) that Congress balance the budget would virtually eliminate the role of discretionary fiscal policy in regulating aggregate demand.

Close-up

The Vietnam Tax Surcharge

In 1968, President Johnson proposed, and Congress enacted, a 10 percent surcharge on individual and corporate income taxes. The object was to dampen the inflationary pressures generated by the increasing expenditures of the Vietnam War without cutting back spending on the *Great Society* programs.

The tax surcharge was supported and opposed by rather strange ideological alliances. The supporters of the surcharge included political liberals who were concerned with maintaining civilian programs, as well as political liberals and conservatives who were hawkish on the war. The opposition included, predictably, many political conservatives who advocated reduced nonmilitary spending to dampen inflationary pressure and support the war effort without extending the scope of the government in the economy, and a strange alliance of political conservatives, liberals, and radicals who were dovish on the war and saw the tax surcharge primarily as a means of supporting the war.

Inflationary pressures worsened after 1968, even with the tax surcharge. The Consumer Price Index rose by 4.2 percent in 1968, 5.4 percent in 1969, and 5.9 percent in 1970—leading many to argue that the economists were wrong again (or "wrong, as usual"). What the worsening inflation showed, however, wasn't that the prediction that rising taxes would dampen inflationary pressure was wrong, but that the tax increase wasn't sufficient to offset the inflationary impact of the war, the Great Society, and the economic expansion that had been going on since 1964.

Fiscal Policy and the National Debt

When government spending exceeds tax revenues, the government has to borrow, and this increases the *national debt*. The national debt, or the debt owed by the federal government, has been a source of controversy since the days of Hamilton and Jefferson. The great orator Daniel Webster is alleged, in the heat of debate and slightly in his cups, to have offered to pay off the national debt to eliminate it as an issue. However, Webster never made good on his offer, and the debt survives as the issue for which the shakiest economic arguments have attracted the largest popular following.

Government deficits and surpluses affect the size of the national debt. Budget surpluses can be used to repay or *retire* part of the debt. Deficits require government borrowing, and this increases the debt. Since deficits have been much more common than surpluses, as shown in Figure 3, the federal debt has been increasing, a cause of some concern but frequently for the wrong reasons.

"The National Debt Will Bankrupt the Country"

One of the most common concerns about the public debt is that it represents reckless government spending and that it will lead to national bankruptcy. The argument typically goes something like this: "As individuals we can't spend more than we make for very long without going bankrupt. Therefore, if the government continues to go in debt to finance deficits, the country will go bankrupt."

The argument seems to make sense, but there are a couple of things wrong with it. It obviously commits the fallacy of composition, as do many arguments that appeal to common sense alone. An increase

Figure 3 Surpluses (+) and Deficits (−) in Federal Budgets, 1920–1980

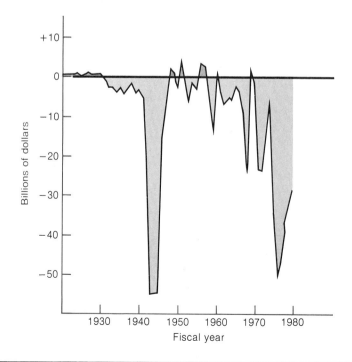

in the national debt may be undesirable economically, but the principles of household budgeting have little to do with the merits of running a deficit in the federal budget. For one thing, the government could simply print up money or raise taxes and pay off the debt—a course not open to households in financial trouble.

Bankruptcy of the federal government doesn't mean that creditors will descend on Washington to attach the Capitol and other government buildings and office equipment. Bankruptcy in this context would consist of the inability of the government to sell bonds and other government securities, or a general lack of acceptance of money issued by the government. This situation isn't impossible, but it *is* highly unlikely. If we ever reach this point, the national debt will be the least of our worries.

How "reckless" has federal spending been? How large is the debt? In absolute terms, the federal debt is an impressive figure. In fiscal 1979, the estimated federal debt was $839.2 billion, and the debt has been increasing over time. However, this isn't the entire picture. The federal debt jumped about 500 percent during World War II. Between 1946 and 1976, the net federal debt increased at an average annual rate of about 2.7 percent per year. In the same period, net private debt increased at an annual average rate of 9.78 percent per year. In this context the rise in the federal debt doesn't appear so alarming.

"The National Debt Is a Burden on the Community and on Future Generations."

This argument is more subtle than the bankruptcy arguments and is even valid under certain circumstances. It usually begins with an assertion that every baby born in the country is in debt at the moment of birth. The amount of this debt is the total outstanding federal debt divided by the total population—in 1978, about $3,840 per person. However, the validity of the argument depends on two things—to whom the debt is owed and the kinds of expenditures financed by the debt.

An *externally held* public debt is owed by the government to creditors in another country. Principal and interest payments on an externally held debt are leakages out of the domestic income stream. Since these payments are made out of the tax revenues of the debtor country, they are a real burden on the citizens of the country. The funds used to pay interest and principal on the external debt have uses in the domestic economy—they could have been used for consumption, for investments to increase productive capacity, or for other government programs that convey benefits to the citizens.

- An **externally held public debt** places a net burden on the citizens of the debtor country because the debt payments leave the country's income stream.

An *internally held public debt* is owed by the government to its own citizens. Every person or institution that owns bonds or other government securities holds a portion of the public debt. Interest and principal payments on an internally held debt stay within the country, and represent income to the holders of the debt.

• An **internally held public debt** doesn't impose a net burden on the country.

The federal debt of the U.S. government is an internally held debt. In fiscal year 1979, 78 percent of the outstanding federal debt was held by the public and 22 percent was held by government agencies.

An internally held debt does impose a *distributional burden* on some elements of society—those that don't hold any of the debt. It distributes income from the community as a whole to the holders of the debt, but because the gains and losses of benefits or satisfaction for different groups can't be added up or compared meaningfully, it's impossible to say that the internally held public debt imposes a net burden on the country.

Even an internally held debt *can* impose a net burden on future generations, however, if the debt finances *current expenditures*—i.e., goods and services that are used up in the current time period. Current expenditures don't confer benefits on future generations, who may be saddled with the debt.

Capital expenditures are on projects that last and provide benefits beyond the current time period. Future generations may bear the burden of a public debt that financed capital expenditures, but they also enjoy important benefits from the capital projects—highways, parks, schools, hospitals, and mass transit systems. The long-term U.S. debt represents almost exclusively debt incurred for capital projects. Most current expenditure projects are financed by current tax revenues or short-term borrowing, and therefore impose no burden on future generations.

Some Normative Aspects of Fiscal Policy

Fiscal policy requires choices—concerning private vs. public spending, the allocation of government spending among alternative programs, and the distribution of the tax burden. Most of these choices involve normative questions that can't be answered by analysis alone.

Spending Priorities

If you ask ten people on the street whether or not the level of government spending should be raised, the majority probably will answer no and may even suggest that it is already too high. However, the majority of your sample probably will feel that at least *some* public services are inadequate. This brings us to the messy question of priorities. With a fixed level of spending, spending more on some programs will require reductions in others.

In the late 1970s, fiscal austerity (at least in the abstract) became very popular politically. This was reflected in the federal budget for fiscal year 1980, which reduced real spending in some areas (mostly social services) and increased real spending for defense. The President was under pressure internationally and domestically to increase defense spending, but he was also under great political pressure to hold down the level of government spending.

Suppose that government spending is either for defense or "arms" (A) or for civilian programs or "butter" (B). The budget sets the level of spending. In Figure 4, the budget of $500 billion can be spent entirely on defense, entirely on civilian programs, or can be allocated between defense and civilian spending along the *budget line A*B**.

Figure 4 Spending Priorities

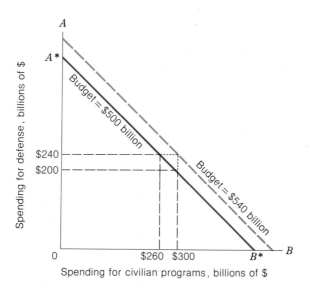

If the government initially spends $200 billion on arms and $300 billion on civilian programs, military spending can be increased to $240 billion only if civilian programs are cut to $260 billion, or the level of government spending increases to $540 billion. If there is additional pressure to hold down budget deficits, increasing government spending will require tax increases, reducing disposable income which households are free to spend as they wish. Dodging the tax increase and running up the deficit may be inflationary, and inflation taxes all members of the community whose money incomes don't keep up with price increases. There are no free lunches.

Eventually, deciding on priorities involves value judgments. Politicians advocating higher spending for specific programs at the expense of others generally make arguments that imply that the gains from expansion of the programs they advocate are greater than the losses from the programs that have to be cut or the evils of higher taxes. To say that the interests of the community are served best by spending more on defense and less on social programs, more on education and less on space research, or more on highways and less on mass transit involves value judgments on the importance of those who would benefit vs. those who would suffer.

Distributing the Tax Burden: Who Pays?

Having decided on the level of government spending and taxes, there is the question of the types of taxes that will be enacted, and how the tax burden will be distributed among members of the community. Obviously, to argue that some group should bear a larger or smaller share of the total tax burden requires value judgments.

A 10 percent tax on all income from all sources would take the same proportion of every person's income.

- **Proportional taxes** tax all levels of income at the same rate.

Most of the taxes we actually pay are nonproportional taxes that shift the tax burden among members of the community. Some taxes, called *regressive taxes*, shift the tax burden from high to low income groups.

- **Regressive taxes** tax lower incomes at a higher rate than higher incomes are taxed.

Retail sales taxes tend to be regressive. A person with an income of $5000 per year who consumed all of it would pay total sales taxes of 5 percent × $5000 = $250, which represents a full 5 percent of annual income. A person who earned $20,000 per year but consumed only $10,000 per year would pay a total sales tax of 5 percent × $10,000 = $500—only 2.5 percent of the higher total income.

Many local taxes are regressive. Per capita, *head* taxes are the most regressive because they tax every person the same *amount*, regardless of income. *Wage taxes*, or *earned income taxes* are regressive because they tax only wages and salaries and not nonwage income—and higher income households are more likely to earn rent, dividend, and interest income. *Real estate taxes* tend to be regressive, especially in areas where assessments and tax rates rise more rapidly than income.

The Federal Income Tax was a controversial issue when it was enacted in 1912, and has remained so in part because it is a *progressive tax*.

- **Progressive taxes** tax higher incomes at higher rates than lower incomes.

With a progressive tax, the marginal tax rate (the proportion of additional income taxed) increases as income increases. In the federal income tax schedules, single persons are taxed at 14 percent of the first $1000 of taxable income, 16 percent of the next $1000, 18 percent of the next $2000, and so on up to the highest marginal tax rate of 70 percent on all taxable income over $180,000 per year.

Arguments for and against progressive taxes are both positive and normative. One of the positive questions is the effect of rising marginal tax rates on the incentive to work harder to earn more income. Critics of progressive taxes argue that the higher marginal tax rate reduces the incentive to earn higher income because an increasing share or the additional income will be taxed.

The evidence on the effect of progressive taxes on incentives is mixed and inconclusive. Persons have turned down opportunities to earn income that involve more demanding work, but the effect of the marginal tax rate on such decisions is hard to identify and isolate. Many highly paid occupations and positions carry great prestige and satisfaction, and the marginal tax rate probably has little effect on decisions to enter these occupations or accept these positions.

The normative aspect of progressive taxes is the question of the fairness of taxing higher incomes at a higher marginal rate than lower incomes. Some people argue that progressive taxes are unfair because they tax the effort and sacrifice to earn higher incomes at an increasing rate. To the extent that income differentials do reflect differences in effort and sacrifice, progressive taxes tax effort at an increasing rate. However, income differences reflect more than differences in effort and sacrifice. Incomes reflect inherited wealth, talents, access to education, social status, and other factors (including simple luck) that don't involve effort or sacrifice.

Close-up

The 101 Percent Tax

Sweden is well known as a nation of high taxes, but early in 1976, the Swedish government carried the idea of high progressive taxes to new levels of absurdity. In a preelection move to attract working-class voters, Prime Minister Olof Palme shifted the burden of Sweden's cradle-to-grave social programs from individual wage-earners to companies and self-employed individuals. As a result, self-employed taxpayers were forced to pay 101.2 percent of all income above $35,000. In other words, disposable income would steadily *decrease* as pretax income rose above $35,000.

The results of the Swedish tax were hardly surprising. Film director Ingmar Bergman canceled all projects in Sweden. Numerous businesses were forced to shut their doors because the owners could not afford to earn a profit. Many singers, writers, and artists simply refused to produce (or to collect royalties on earlier work), because the royalties they might receive would be less than the tax they would have to pay on those royalties.[1]

---

1. See "The 101.2% Solution," *Time*, April 5, 1976.

Is the burden of a progressive tax greater for high-income households than for low-income households? This one isn't as easy as it looks. In terms of percentage of income taxed, of course, a progressive tax obviously places a heavier burden on high-income households. However, there is also a question of the kinds of goods that have to be given up to pay the tax.

Consider two hypothetical households—a subsistence household whose income just allows it to buy basic necessities, and a higher income household whose income is substantially above the subsistence level. *Any* tax paid by the subsistence household will force it to reduce its consumption of necessities. However, the high-income household's disposable income after paying its tax will still be well above the subsistence level, and the higher marginal tax rate won't force the high-income household to reduce its consumption of basic necessities.

Loopholes and Tax Reform

A number of wealthy persons and large corporations pay very low percentages of their income as taxes or pay no income taxes at all, due to special tax treatments or *loopholes* in the income tax laws. Interest income from municipal bonds, for example, is not taxed, in order to allow state and local governments to borrow at lower interest rates. The major beneficiaries (in addition to the municipalities) are the very wealthy who have large sums of money to put into the bonds and are in the highest marginal tax rate brackets. Persons with modest incomes don't realize great tax savings from municipal bonds because they don't make large bond purchases, and because their marginal tax rates are lower. In the 20 percent marginal tax rate bracket, a 5 percent municipal bond pays the equivalent of a 6 percent return per year (interest plus tax saving). In the 50 percent tax bracket, the same 5 percent tax-free bond pays the equivalent of a 7.5 percent rate of return per year.

Not all loopholes benefit only the very rich. For example, federal income tax law allows the deduction of state and local taxes and interest payments from gross income in figuring taxable income. This subsidizes everybody who is paying for a home, because mortgage interest and real estate taxes are deductible. Renters can't make this deduction, even though they pay a share of their landlords' interest and property taxes in their monthly rents. However, even this loophole gives the greatest tax savings to persons in high tax brackets because they generally have more expensive property and the tax savings per dollar of interest and property tax paid are greater because of the higher marginal tax rate.

There is much to be said for reforms that simplify the tax system. On the side of equity, a simpler tax system with fewer (or no) loopholes would result in different families with the same income and dependents paying the same tax. A simpler system would allow lower and more meaningful tax rates. At present the high marginal tax rates on high incomes don't indicate the true tax burden, because they apply to taxable income. There is no question that simplified tax rules would make the existing income tax more progressive.

Promises and proposals for tax reform and closing tax loopholes have become part of the standard American political rhetoric, but really significant simplification of the tax system or large-scale closing of loopholes has yet to materialize. Every special interest tries to protect its own "tax incentives" while calling for elimination of somebody else's "loophole." Also, there are costs involved in elimination of loopholes. Eliminating tax-free interest on state and local bonds, for example, would require states and localities to pay higher interest on their obligations. The final solution of the "tax mess" requires analysis of the costs and benefits of the reforms and intelligent value judgements on equity and fairness of the tax system.

Practical and Political Problems

Fiscal policies aren't decided by economists and models, but by a political process in a very imperfect real world. In addition to all of the analytical and normative questions, there are some significant political and practical considerations.

Political Appeal

To be effective, discretionary fiscal policies have to be flexible. However, the flexibility of fiscal policy is limited by the necessity of coming up with policies that have broad political support. Unfortunately, the political mood and economic expectations of the electorate aren't always in tune with economic reality. Elected officials (like the rest of us) don't wish to be unemployed, so many fiscal policies tend to reflect political realities more than economic realities.

Fiscal policy is like a lever with a ratchet that makes it easy to turn in one direction, but difficult or impossible to reverse. Programs that are initiated or expanded as part of an expansionary fiscal policy develop constituencies that make it difficult to cut them in periods of fiscal restraint. It's easy politically to cut taxes to stimulate demand, but much harder to raise them to fight inflation.

The passage of "Proposition 13" in California in 1978 made fiscal austerity (reduced government spending and reduced taxes) politically popular because many people don't associate severe cuts in government spending with reductions in public services, or at least cuts in the programs that benefit them. Middle and upper income families may support cuts in welfare payments, but not in police and fire protection. Defense contractors may support reduced spending for environmental programs, but not defense. Environmentalists may support cuts in defense, but not in environmental programs. Social Security recipients may support cuts in highways, but not in Social Security benefits.

Time Lags and Information

Time and information are two practical difficulties in using fiscal policy to regulate aggregate demand to minimize unemployment and inflationary pressure. With inadequate information on the effects of changes in fiscal policy, and economic forecasting a highly imperfect art, fiscal policies may do too much or too little to achieve their objectives. Overstimulation of the economy to promote full employment will lead to excessive inflationary pressures; inadequate stimulation won't achieve the objective of full employment. Excessive fiscal restraint to reduce inflationary pressures will probably result in an unacceptably high unemployment rate.

Time lags also limit the success of discretionary fiscal policies. Economic theorists have defined two basic types of lag:

- The **inside lag** is the time that passes before policymakers take action.

- The **outside lag** is the time it takes for a policy to have its effect on the economy.

The inside lag itself has also been divided into three lags:

- The **recognition lag** is the period of time between the actual beginning of a problem and policymakers' recognition that the problem exists. This lag may be lengthened if policymakers for political reasons refuse to admit that there is a problem.

- The **decision lag** includes both the time it takes for policymakers to decide what policy action is needed, and the time needed for legislators to approve that policy.

- The **action lag** is the time it takes for the approved policy action to be put into effect.

Irregular and unpredictable time lags between the enactment of policies and their effects is one dimension of the overall problem of inadequate information which limits the effectiveness of policies and enhances the chance of error. We simply don't have all of the necessary information to predict the exact effects of fiscal policies or the timing of these effects, which would enable policymakers to hit specific targets for unemployment and inflation. By the time the policies actually affect aggregate demand, economic conditions may have changed, and the policies may end up worsening problems of unemployment and inflation.

Applying the Tools

The 1964 Tax Cut

John F. Kennedy's campaign for the presidency in 1960 hit hard on the Republicans' apparent inability to reduce the unemployment rate and "get the economy moving." During his campaign and after he took office, Kennedy's official and unofficial economic advisers included such prominent Keynesian economists as Professor Paul A. Samuelson and Walter Heller. Keynesian economics became the *New Economics* of the 1960s, even though it had been a generation since the publication of the *General Theory*.

For a year after taking office, the President followed a relatively orthodox, non-Keynesian, course in economic policy. The 1960 election was the closest in recent history, and Kennedy was sensitive to criticisms of fiscal irresponsibility. Although his advisers had called for an active expansionary fiscal policy in 1960, the Kennedy administration didn't pursue active expansionary fiscal policies until the summer of 1962. This was due to a combination of political prudence and recognition and decision lags on the part of the administration concerning the proper course for fiscal policy. From January of 1961 until June of 1962, there was mild fiscal expansion as military spending increased without increased taxes.

In the summer of 1962, Kennedy turned to more clearly expansionary fiscal policies that centered on reducing taxes. Investment tax credits and accelerated depreciation encouraged greater levels of investment to stimulate aggregate demand. In January of 1963, the administration pushed for substantial permanent cuts in personal income tax rates to increase disposable income and consumption expenditures.

Congressional reaction to the proposed tax cuts ranged from lukewarm to hostile, and the familiar criticism of fiscal irresponsibility emerged in the debate over the tax cut. The President went beyond Congress to appeal directly to the public for support for the tax cut, but at the time of his death in the fall of 1963, the tax cut still hadn't been enacted. The tax cut finally was enacted with the passage of the Revenue Act of 1964 in February 1964—three years after Kennedy's inauguration and over a year after his first proposal for tax cuts. The *action lag* between proposal and enactment of the tax cut legislation in this case had exceeded one year.

There was still an additional lag—the *outside lag* between enactment of the tax cut legislation and the effects of the tax cuts on aggregate demand and employment. For about three months, the tax cut had no noticeable effect. The short-term effects appeared over a six-month period following their enactment. By the third quarter of 1964, the short-term effect of the tax cut was an increase of GNP of about $1.50 per $1 of tax reduction. By the middle of 1965, this exceeded $2.50 of additional GNP per $1 of tax reduction. The middle of 1965 was a year and a half after the enactment of the legislation and nearly three years after Kennedy had proposed the cuts.[1]

---

1. Facts on the tax cut are from Rudiger Dornbusch and Stanley Fischer, *Macroeconomics*. New York: McGraw-Hill, 1978, Chapter 10.

In the period between Kennedy's inauguration and the full effect of the tax cut, economic conditions had changed. An economic recovery which had been under way in 1960 continued. The escalation of the Vietnam War after 1965 stimulated aggregate demand further as government military spending increased. On top of this, the Johnson administration expanded the number and scope of federal social programs under the banner of the Great Society. The following table summarizes the chronology of the tax cut program and the unemployment rate at each critical point. By the end of 1965, the expansionary effects of the tax cut, the Vietnam War, and the Great Society programs had driven the unemployment rate low enough that there were significant demand-pull inflationary pressures. In other words, by the time the stimulating effects of the tax cut were fully felt, the economy no longer needed stimulation.

	Year/Quarter	Unemployment Rate
Kennedy inaugurated	1961/I	6.8%
Decision to cut taxes	1962/I	5.6%
Tax cut passed	1964/II	5.2%
Tax cut effects	1965/IV	4.1%

Source: Unemployment data from U.S. Department of Commerce.

Summary

1. Fiscal policies are those dealing with government spending and taxes. **Discretionary fiscal policies** are aimed at regulating aggregate demand and GNP to minimize unemployment and inflationary pressures in the economy.
2. Aggregate demand and GNP vary directly with government spending and inversely with taxes. Generally, changes in government spending will affect GNP more than equal changes in taxes.
3. The choice between government spending and taxes depends in part on political ideology. Modern conservatives tend to prefer tax cuts to increased government spending as a means of stimulating aggregate demand, and spending cuts to dampen aggregate demand. Modern political liberals tend to prefer increased spending and expanded programs to stimulate demand and tax increases to dampen it.
4. Stimulating or dampening aggregate demand may require deficits or surpluses in the government's budget. The **full-employment budget** estimates taxes and spending if the economy were operating at full employment.
5. Deficits and surpluses affect the public debt. An **internally held public debt** which finances capital projects imposes no net burden on the community, but may impose a distributional burden on some members of the community.
6. With a **balanced-budget multiplier effect**, equal changes in government spending and taxes may change equilibrium GNP without creating or changing the national debt.
7. Fiscal policies generally require choices and value judgments that can't be evaluated analytically. Among the more important choices that must be made are the choice of priorities in government spending and the distribution of the tax burden.

8. The effectiveness and flexibility of discretionary fiscal policies are limited by **time lags** in the formulation and impact of fiscal policies, inadequacies in information, and the necessity of formulating policies with broad political appeal.

Questions

1. Explain the meaning of the term *discretionary fiscal policy*. Are all fiscal policies *discretionary*? Explain.
2. What are some of the considerations that would enter into a choice between changes in taxes and changes in government spending as a means of regulating aggregate demand?
3. Many state constitutions require that the state budget be balanced— receipts equal to expenditures. Does this make sense for a state government? Would the merits of requiring balanced state budgets apply to arguments that a constitutional amendment should be ratified which requires an annually balanced federal budget?
4. Emma I. Rich has willed her entire estate to the federal government to be applied to the federal debt to lighten the burden of the debt on the citizens instead of leaving her fortune to her spendthrift heirs. Evaluate the wisdom of this act.
5. In the 1976 presidential campaign, candidate Jimmy Carter promised to try to fight unemployment, fight inflation, and balance the federal budget by 1981. In his January, 1979, Budget Message, President Carter stated that the budget for the 1980 fiscal year ". . . meets my commitment to a deficit of $30 billion or less."

   Is the targeted deficit in the budget for fiscal year 1980 inconsistent with his promise to balance the budget? What are some of the implications of drawing up a budget around a long-term commitment to a balanced budget and an immediate commitment to keeping the deficit below some targeted maximum?
6. Some economists use the enormous federal debt incurred during World War II as an example of a public debt that imposes a net burden on future generations. Evaluate the validity of this argument.
7. Explain how each of the following would affect the progressivity of federal taxes.
   a. the imposition of a value added tax, or a national sales tax;
   b. imposing a value added tax in order to reduce income tax rates;
   c. elimination of the tax-exempt status of municipal bonds;
   d. elimination of all itemized income tax deductions, and substituting a standard deduction of 20 percent of all income;
   e. allowing tuition tax credits for college, secondary, and elementary school tuition.

1. The following data represent aggregate expenditure flows for the economy of Farcelonia (all figures are billions of Farcical dollars).

Consumption: $C = 100 + 0.8\ (Y\text{-}T)$
Intended Investment: $I = 50$
Government Purchases: $G = 50$
Taxes: $T = 40$

a. The best estimate of the Farcical Council of Economic Advisors is that full employment would be reached at a GNP of $1000 billion. Should the government pursue an expansionary fiscal course to stimulate aggregate demand or a restrictive course to dampen inflationary pressure? Explain.

b. What change in government spending would be necessary to move equilibrium GNP to the full-employment level?

c. What change in taxes would move equilibrium GNP to the full employment level? How do you explain the difference between this answer and the answer to part b?

d. Could the government achieve full employment by equal changes in government spending and taxes? If so, what change in government spending and taxes would be required?

2. The relationship between taxes and GNP in Utopia is $T = 20 + 0.2Y$. Government spending is $\underline{G} = 100$.

a. If equilibrium GNP is $\overline{Y} = 300$, will the actual budget be balanced, show a deficit, or show a surplus?

b. At what level of GNP will the actual budget be balanced?

c. If full employment is reached at $Y^* = 500$, does the full-employment Utopian budget show a full-employment deficit or surplus? What does this mean?

3. In problems 1 and 2 at the end of the previous chapter, calculate the size of the inflationary or deflationary gaps.

PART FOUR

Aggregate Demand: The Money Market

The chapters in this section bring money into our analysis of aggregate demand. Money is important to us as individuals, of course, but its importance to the economy as a whole is much greater. Without money, economic specialization and indeed modern civilization itself would be impossible. Further, money plays a critical role in determining the level of aggregate demand and is thus the basis of an important set of demand-management tools—**monetary policy**.

Like the product markets described in Chapter 3, the money market is one in which demand and supply interact to achieve an equilibrium. In the first chapter of this section, we'll examine the demand side of the money market by asking why people want to hold money (as opposed to, say, real estate or gold) and how much money they want to hold. The answers to those questions will allow us to construct a **demand curve for money** and to show how equilibrium in the money market affects aggregate demand in the goods market. In the next chapter, we'll look at how the banking system determines the **supply of money** in the economy, and how the money supply influences aggregate output and prices. Finally, we'll examine a variety of issues surrounding the government's use of its power over the money supply as a policy tool for "managing" aggregate demand.

10

Money: What It Is and What It Does

Preview: Money is only one of a variety of possible forms in which people can hold their wealth. In this chapter, we'll explore why people want to hold money. We'll begin by looking briefly at the history of money to see how its role in most modern economies has evolved over time. We'll then focus on the **demand for money** and examine how the interaction between the demand and supply of money in the money market affects aggregate demand and output in the goods market.

Few people need formal training in economics to recognize that money is important. An individual's economic welfare depends largely on his or her purchasing power, which in turn depends on his or her money and real income. The importance of money to individuals is so obvious that it tends to obscure the role of money and monetary policies in the determination of aggregate demand, aggregate output, and the seriousness of the problems of unemployment and inflation. Money and monetary issues have attracted the attention of the greatest economists, as well as the attention of an unusually large number of quacks.

A Brief History of Money	The origins of the use of money go back to the beginnings of economic specialization, exchange, and organized markets. In many primitive and feudal societies, households or small communities were self-sufficient, and the exchange that did take place was *barter exchange*.

- In **barter exchanges**, goods and services exchange directly for other goods and services.

As market economies developed, competition and exchange led to greater economic specialization, and greater specialization required the use of some form of money. By facilitating exchange, the use of money widened producers' markets, and encouraged greater specialization and efficiency than would be possible in a barter system.

If people specialize in producing the things they produce best, this increases the efficiency in the use of the economy's resources. However, the degree of specialization is severely limited in barter economies because of the difficulties of making exchanges. Suppose, for example, that you are a very good pig farmer. In a barter economy, if you needed cloth, you would have to find another person who had cloth to offer in exchange *and* would be willing to accept pigs in exchange. To guard against the possibility of not finding such a person, you'd have to provide your minimal needs of cloth by producing it yourself—i.e., divert some of your time and resources from raising pigs (which you do well) to producing cloth (which you might not do so well).

In a money economy, however, to exchange your pigs for cloth and other goods you need, all you have to do is find somebody who will exchange money for your pigs (whether or not he or she has cloth to offer in exchange). The money from the sale of the pigs could then be used to purchase the cloth and other goods you need from persons who may or may not want to buy pigs. This reduces the possibility that you would be deprived of some of the things you need if you specialized in pig production, and you would be more likely to specialize. If everybody specialized in producing the things he or she produced best and exchanged for other goods, this would make more efficient use of the economy's resources.

Commodity Money

The earliest money was **commodity money**—physical goods with the basic characteristics of money. The most common money commodities were precious metals, particularly gold and silver. These metals have been widely acceptable in exchange since ancient times. They are relatively durable, easily divisible into small units, and (despite the efforts of alchemists and mad scientists) impossible to reproduce.

With commodity money, the *value of money* is determined by the supply of and demand for the money commodity, just like the value of any other scarce commodity. The money prices of other goods and services reflect the relative prices of the goods and the money commodity. The *money price* of a pound of meat, for example, is the amount of money that has to be given up to get it. Changes in the scarcity of the money commodity relative to other goods and services appear as changes in the money prices of the other goods and services.

Close-up

The Price Revolution in Europe

After a long period of economic stability in the late medieval period, there was a rapid inflow of gold into Europe at the end of the fifteenth century as a result of Spanish discoveries in the New World. Some of the gold was brought by the Spanish, and some was brought by pirates who stole it from the Spanish.

Gold was commodity money in Europe, and the rapid influx of gold drove the price of gold downward relative to the prices of other goods. Since gold was less scarce relative to other goods, more gold had to be offered in exchange for goods, and the gold (money) prices of goods rose dramatically.

In a commodity money system, gold or silver currency or coin simply specified and guaranteed the quantity and quality of the gold or silver contained in the coin. In fact, in the British system, the denominations *pound* and *shilling* were originally measures of weight. Exchanging coins was more convenient than assaying and weighing gold and silver each time a purchase was made, but some problems emerged. Devious and enterprising persons would "clip" or shave the edges of coins and sell the gold or silver shavings. Most people can't tell the exact weight of a coin by feel, so the clipped coins could be exchanged at their full face value. Finely serrated edges on coins made it easier to tell whether or not a coin had been clipped. On a larger scale, governments often *debased* or adulterated their currency by reducing the weight of the gold in the coins or mixing other metals (such as lead) with the gold in the coins.

The practices of clipping coins, counterfeiting, and debasement encouraged people to hoard their gold coins (*good* money) or to use it for international purchases, and to use only the debased or adulterated coins (*bad* money) domestically. Several hundred years after this had become a familiar phenomenon, it was given a name—*Gresham's Law*.

- **Gresham's Law** states that *bad* money drives out *good*.

The Gold Standard

Initially, paper currency was fully backed by the money commodity (gold or silver). A piece of **fully backed currency** was a coupon which entitled the holder to a specified quantity of gold or silver. Before 1933, for example, U.S. Gold Certificates would be exchanged by the government for gold coin. Until the late 1960s, Silver Certificates were convertible to silver dollars or metallic silver by the government.

Paper money that was fully backed by gold or silver was, in fact, commodity money. This arrangement is commonly called the *gold standard*—or more generally the *commodity standard*.

- With a **gold standard**, the quantity of currency in circulation is tied to the quantity of gold held by the government.

Paper money is more convenient than gold coins, and the use of paper money kept much of the gold coin out of circulation. This reduced the loss of gold through wear and abrasion of coins in circulation.

Not all backed currency was fully backed by gold or another money commodity. The quantity of **partially backed currency** is limited to a multiple of the value of the gold held by the government. Until the late 1960s, for example, the maximum amount of U.S. currency that could be issued was limited to a rather large multiple of the value of U.S. government gold reserves. This wasn't a true commodity money system, since the currency wasn't converted by the government to gold, but it was designed to limit the discretionary power of the government over the quantity of currency issued.

By the late 1960s, however, the U.S. gold reserve had become so small that it threatened to constrain the money supply, so the last tie between the gold reserves and the quantity of currency issued was severed. Today, U.S. currency isn't backed by any commodity.

Fiat Money

U.S. currency is *fiat money*.

- **Fiat money** is money simply because the law (fiat) says it's money.

Just about every dollar bill in circulation today is a Federal Reserve Note. The government will not redeem a dollar bill for anything except other denominations of currency.

The value of fiat money, like the value of commodity money, is determined by its purchasing power over goods and services. The value of a dollar is the quantity of goods and services that can be purchased with a dollar. However, unlike commodity money, the value of fiat money doesn't depend on the value of any commodity.

Some people attribute every historical catastrophe since the fall of Rome to the abandonment of commodity money or the gold standard. Others are upset because a fiat money system removes a restraint on the power of the government to issue currency. Those who distrust the competence or intentions of government monetary authorities tend to be the most leary of fiat money.

Generally, however, people aren't terribly concerned about fiat money as long as their money is acceptable in exchange for goods and services or there isn't a complete economic and social collapse. If any readers of this book feel that their fiat money is worthless because it isn't backed by gold or silver, the author would be happy to take it off their hands.

The Basic Functions of Money

Money has two basic economic functions. It serves as a *unit of account and exchange*, and as a *store of value*. In fact, money can be defined in terms of these basic functions.

- **Money** is anything that serves as a **unit of account and exchange** and as a **store of value.**

Unit of Account and Exchange

As a *unit of account* or unit of value, money makes it possible to quantify costs, revenue, profits, and national income. Monetary values are common denominators that allow the addition of different goods, services, and resources. Oranges, apples, bobby pins, locomotives, hours of labor, etc., can't be added together without first expressing them as monetary values.

To perform its accounting and exchange function, money must have several basic characteristics. It must be *generally acceptable in exchange*, and it must be *divisible into small units*. If few people accepted money, it couldn't serve its exchange function. If it weren't divisible into small units, it couldn't be an accurate measure of value, nor could it ensure exchange of equal values.

In addition, money must be *scarce* and *difficult or impossible to reproduce*. If money weren't scarce or could be produced easily by individuals, it would not be a meaningful unit of value in exchange.

Store of Value

Generally, one's needs for goods and services don't coincide with the receipt of his or her money income. Money allows households and firms to "store" the values of the goods, services, and productive resources they sell. Obviously, to serve as a *store of value*, money must be relatively durable.

Storing the value of one's goods and services is cumbersome or impossible without money. It's much easier to store the value of a wheat crop by holding the money received from its sale than to store the wheat. The values of highly perishable goods can't be stored for more than a few days without money. The value of services (haircuts, for example) can't be stored at all without the use of money.

Defining Money Aggregates

Money, we have seen, can be just about anything that performs the basic functions of money. When examining the role of money in the aggregate economy, however, it is necessary to use somewhat narrower definitions of *money*.

- **Money aggregates** are formal definitions of money used for studying the influence of money in the economy.

Money aggregates are used in particular when studying the *supply of money* or the *demand for money* in an economy.

Most of us identify money as *currency*, and an increase in the supply of money is seen in our minds' eye as a change in the amount of currency in circulation—an image that is reinforced by the common phrase *printing money* to refer to an increase in the money supply. All money aggregates include currency in their definitions of money, but other things are also included. The dividing line between things that are considered money and those that aren't is drawn on the basis of the ability to be substituted for each other as money.

The Strict Definition

Demand deposits, or checking accounts, are nearly perfect substitutes for currency as money. Checks are generally acceptable in exchange, and can be written for just about any amount. Because demand deposits and currency are close substitutes as money, they are included in even the narrowest definition of money.

- The **strict definition of money** is currency plus demand deposits.

For years, monetary authorities and most economists adopted the strict definition as the relevant definition of the money supply. This definition excludes **time deposits**, or savings accounts, from the definition of money. The basic argument for excluding time deposits has been that time deposits aren't very close substitutes for currency and demand deposits as money. Until recently, persons couldn't write checks authorizing someone else to withdraw funds from a savings account. Some time deposits reserve the bank's right to require advance notice for withdrawals, and some time deposits require that funds remain on deposit for a minimum period of time from 90 days to several years. In short, time deposits generally are less *liquid* than currency or demand deposits—which is one of the reasons that they earn interest.

Recent dramatic changes in banking regulations and practices have caused monetary authorities to reexamine the traditional exclusion of time deposits from the definition of money. New types of savings accounts—Negotiated Order of Withdrawal (or *NOW*) accounts and Automatic Funds Transfer (AFT) accounts—transfer funds automatically from savings to checking accounts. Many banks will transfer funds from savings to checking accounts via depositors' telephone orders. Some savings and loan associations even have checkable savings accounts.

Broader Definitions of Money

The strict definition is, in fact, only one of five official definitions of the money supply. We need to concern ourselves with only three of these definitions.

M_1 (the strict definition) = currency plus demand deposits

$M_2 = M_1$ plus savings and time deposits in commercial banks

$M_3 = M_2$ plus savings and time deposits in nonbank thrift institutions

Because of the changes in banking practices and regulations that make some time deposits close substitutes for currency and demand deposits as money, the definition of M_1 is being altered, and the Federal Reserve has started publishing yet another money aggregate, M_1+

$M_1+ = M_1$ plus savings deposits at commercial banks and checkable deposits at nonbank thrift institutions.

Although all of the money aggregates show a similar pattern of growth over time in Figure 1, the strict supply of money has grown more slowly than the money supply more broadly defined.

Monetary authorities still generally consider M_1 (or M_1+) as the relevant definition of the money supply, but for some monetary policy questions, M_2 or M_3 may be the relevant definition. For example, the funds available for residential mortgages depend heavily on time deposits in commercial banks and savings and loan associations.

The specific monetary aggregate that we define as money isn't crucial for a basic understanding of the relationships between money and the price level and between money and real GNP. To keep the analysis simple, the term *money* in the following chapters will refer to M_1 unless noted otherwise.

Near Monies

Near monies are things with stable monetary values that are easily convertible into money at their full value. Government securities are an example of a near money. There is little risk of loss in holding government securities, and they can be sold for cash easily. Some government securities are *negotiable* and can be assigned from one person to another. However, government securities aren't close enough as substitutes or demand deposits to include them in the definition of money.

Economic uncertainty and inflation in the middle and late 1970s caused many people to turn their attention to gold as a store of value and a hedge against inflation. "Good as gold" is a common phrase, but one never describes something as "good as a Federal Reserve Note" or "good as a personal check." Yet, gold isn't included in any official definition of money. Gold is simply a commodity. In periods of inflation and uncertainty, its value tends to rise as people seek to hold gold rather than money or financial securities. Despite the gold mystique, most heavily promoted by sellers of gold, the value of gold has fluctuated significantly since 1974.

Figure 1   Changes in the Money Supply

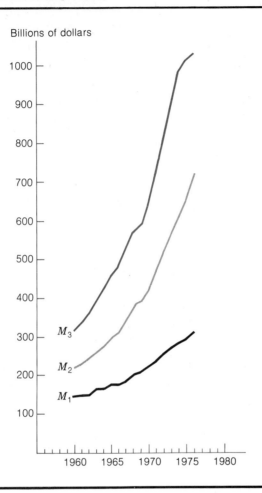

Billions of dollars

Close-up

Are Credit Cards Money?

The credit card has become a familiar fixture in household finances. The use of credit cards has grown dramatically in the past twenty years, and some people even refer to them as "plastic money." One of the large bank credit card companies even tells its card holders to treat the card "like money."

However, credit cards are not money. When a person makes a purchase with a credit card, he or she simply agrees to pay for the purchase in the future, and to pay a substantial rate of interest (typically 18% per year). Like other forms of credit, credit card purchases are a loan to the consumer, and these loans are paid for with money (currency or check).

Credit and credit cards are substitutes for money, rather than a component of the money supply.

Basic Motives for Holding Money

The amount of money demanded for the economy as a whole is the sum of the quantities demanded by individual households, firms, and financial institutions. Households, firms, and financial institutions demand money for three basic reasons—to make transactions, to prepare for unexpected contingencies, and to protect against losses.

Households and firms have to hold some money to make transactions that require money payments—either in currency or by check. The amount of money that must be held for these transactions represents the **transactions demand** for money. The transactions demand for money is determined largely by institutional features of the economy—means of making payments, the availability of credit, etc.

The **precautionary demand for money** stems from uncertainty about the future. Except for a few self-styled clairvoyants, nobody knows when future needs for money will arise. Households and firms hold some money to take care of the unforeseen contingencies that may arise in the future. During periods of economic uncertainty and pessimism, the precautionary demand for money tends to increase.

The **speculative demand for money** also stems from economic uncertainty: the probability of incurring an economic loss by holding money compared with the probability of loss by holding stocks, bonds, and other assets. In periods when the risk of incurring such losses is high, the speculative demand for money tends to be high.

Although we are examining the demand for money, it should be clear that holders of money are interested in their *real balances*—the amount of transactions, precautionary, and speculative benefits that can be purchased with the money. The ability of money balances to purchase these benefits depends, in turn, on the level of prices.

- **Real balances** are money balances divided by the price index.

For example, $1000 in cash and demand deposits would represent a real balance of $1000 if the price index is 1.0.

$$\text{Real balance} = \frac{\text{Money balance}}{\text{Price index}} = \frac{M}{P} \qquad (1)$$
$$= \frac{\$1000}{1.0} = \$1000.$$

If the price index rose to 1.25, the same $1000 represents a real balance of

$$\frac{M}{P} = \frac{\$1000}{1.25} = \$800.$$

For now, we'll assume that the price level doesn't change, so that changes in money balances represent equal changes in real balances.

Money thus offers households, firms, and financial institutions important benefits—the ability to make transactions, to meet future needs, and to minimize economic losses. Why, then, don't individuals simply hold their entire wealth as money? Why not simply fill the mattress with cash and enjoy the benefits? To understand the demand for money, particularly the precautionary and speculative demands, we have to take a closer look at money as an asset and the factors that contribute to choices to hold money and other assets.

Choice of Assets and the Demand for Money

Households, firms, and financial institutions hold their wealth in the form of assets. Money is one of these assets, but not the only one. Individual owners of wealth may decide to hold their wealth in real estate, in corporate bonds, in government securities, in savings accounts, in common stocks, and in many other types of assets in addition to money. Owners of wealth will try to hold the assortment of assets, or **portfolio of assets**, that strikes the best balance among liquidity, rate of return, and risk. Differences in individual circumstances among owners of assets—age, income, willingness to take risks, size of family, etc.—affect individual decisions on the best portfolio of assets. The demand for money depends heavily on the choices of individuals concerning the amount of money to hold in their portfolios.

Liquidity, Risk, and Rate of Return

Liquid assets are assets that can be converted easily into other assets. Money and negotiable securities are very liquid assets that can be converted easily into other assets at virtually no cost. Most owners of wealth will try to achieve some level of **liquidity**, or flexibility, in their asset portfolios. If a household held all of its wealth in real estate (the least liquid of assets), for example, it would be difficult to adjust to changing economic conditions by converting the real estate into other assets—i.e., selling the real estate and using the proceeds to purchase other assets.

Assets that involve a loss of liquidity, other things equal, aren't as desirable as more liquid assets. For example, few people would purchase a one-year certificate of deposit if the interest rate were the same as on passbook savings that can be withdrawn at any time without any interest penalty. To induce people to give up liquidity, then, banks have to pay a higher rate of return on funds that reduce the depositors' liquidity, and this rate of return is higher the longer the term that the money must remain on deposit.

- Other things equal, there is an inverse relationship between the liquidity of assets and the rate of return. The less liquid the asset, the higher the rate of return necessary to induce people to hold it.

Many assets also involve some risk of losing the value of the asset. Common stocks, for example, may depreciate in value after they are purchased, in which case the stockholder suffers a loss of the money value of his or her stock. Few people would accept the same rate of return for owning an asset that involved a low level of risk and another that involved a high risk of loss. Anybody who has gambled knows that high odds are necessary to induce people to bet long shots. Those who bet long shots and win do very well—for example, those who bet on Mohammed Ali (then Cassius Clay) in his first fight against Sonny Liston or who bet on Leon Spinks in his first fight against Ali. However, few successful gamblers bet only long shots because the risk of losing is so great.

- Other things equal, the rate of return on assets varies directly with the risk of loss from holding the asset.

There is a way to avoid risk—simply hold nothing but safe assets with a very small risk of loss. The catch is that these assets offer low rates of return. In inflationary periods, the rate of return on very safe assets may not even keep pace with prices.

Very few owners of assets hold portfolios that achieve the highest possible safety and liquidity, but earn the lowest possible rate of return. Similarly, very few maximize the rate of return on their assets by holding only assets that involve the maximum degree of risk and the minimum liquidity.

- Generally, owners of assets will choose portfolios of assets to achieve some combination of liquidity, safety, and rate of return.

Money as an Asset

Money would be a part of just about any portfolio of assets. The only exceptions would be for asset owners for whom liquidity and safety are unimportant. Money is the most liquid of assets. It can be converted into other assets instantly and at no cost. Holding money offers asset owners liquidity or flexibility to adjust to future needs and to future changes in economic conditions.

Money is also a safe asset, in the sense that the risk of losing the face value of money is nonexistent. Holding $1000 in currency and demand deposits involves no risk that this would be worth less money in the future. The same can't be said for a $1000 corporate bond or $1000 worth of common stock. With these assets, there is a risk of losing the face value of the assets. The corporation could go bankrupt, in which case it would pay off only a percentage of its bonds and other debts, and the stock of a bankrupt corporation is virtually worthless. The price of the bond or the common stock could fall in financial markets, in which case the assets couldn't be redeemed for their full face value.

Since money is the most liquid asset, and the asset with the minimum risk of loss of its face value, holding money involves no loss of liquidity and no risk of loss. Therefore, no return is required to induce people and institutions to hold money (currency and demand deposits). As a reasonable approximation of reality, then, money can be treated as an asset that is completely liquid, completely safe, and earns no interest. Remember that we're still looking at a world in which the price level is constant—rising prices would cause a loss of *real balances* from holding money.

With stable prices, the way to maximize liquidity and safety would be to hold all assets as money. However, money earns no interest. The benefits of liquidity and safety from holding money have a cost—namely, the interest that could be earned in alternative uses that involve no risk. At low interest rates, the opportunity cost of holding money is low, and households and businesses tend to hold relatively large amounts of money in their portfolios. For example, holding $10,000 as money for one year costs $500 if the interest rate is 5%. If the individual decides that it is worth $500 to hold $10,000 for one year, he will do so. However, if the interest rate increases to 8%, the cost of holding $10,000 for one year increases to $800, and the individual will reduce his holdings of money due to the higher cost, as shown in Figure 2a.

- The quantity of money demanded varies inversely with changes in the interest rate, other things constant.

Figure 2 The Demand Curve for Money

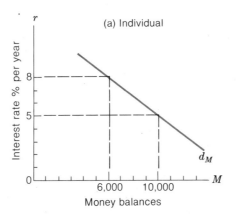
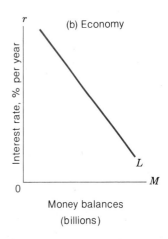

For the economy, the quantity of money demanded at a given interest rate, other things equal, is the economy's **liquidity preference**, or **demand for money**. In Figure 2b, the inverse relationship between the interest rate and the quantity of money demanded is shown by the negatively sloped **liquidity preference function** (L), which is the economy's **demand curve for money**.

Among the variables assumed constant for a given demand curve for money are the price level, aggregate output (or real GNP), nominal GNP (or money GNP), and expectations. Changes in any of these exogenous variables will cause the demand for money to change at any interest rate, and will shift the demand curve for money.

Changes in the Demand for Money

The demand for money will change, and the demand curve for money will shift, if *nominal GNP* changes. Nominal GNP (Y_n) is simply aggregate output (Y) evaluated in current prices (P), or

$$Y_n = P\ Y. \tag{2}$$

At any level of nominal GNP, firms and households will demand sufficient money to make transactions. The money demanded at any given level of nominal GNP will be a fraction or proportion (m) of the nominal GNP. The demand for money won't equal nominal GNP because money is spent more than once. Algebraically, the demand for money at any level of nominal GNP is

$$L = mPY. \tag{3}$$

From this equation, the demand for money at any interest rate would vary directly with the price level (P), the aggregate output (Y), and nominal GNP (PY). For example, if $m = 0.5$ and nominal GNP = \$2 trillion, the demand for money would be

$$L = mPY = 0.5 \times \$2 \text{ trillion} = \$1 \text{ trillion}.$$

If the price level doubled to $P' = 2P$, the demand for money with the same aggregate output (Y) would be

$$\begin{aligned} L' &= mP'Y = 0.5 \times 2P \times Y = 0.5 \times \$4 \text{ trillion} \\ &= \$2 \text{ trillion}. \end{aligned}$$

Similarly, if aggregate output doubled to $Y' = 2Y$ at a constant price level (P), the demand for money would be

$$\begin{aligned} L' &= mPY' = 0.5 \times 2 \times \$2 \text{ trillion} = 0.5 \times \$4 \text{ trillion} \\ &= \$2 \text{ trillion}. \end{aligned}$$

The effect of an increase in nominal GNP (through changes in the price level and in aggregate output) is shown graphically in Figure 3 by a shift of the demand curve for money to the right from L to L'. It should be obvious that declines in nominal GNP would cause the

Figure 3 Change in the Demand for Money

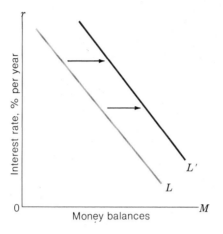

demand for money at any interest rate to fall and the demand curve for money to shift to the left.

Changes in the value of m can change the demand for money at any interest rate. The value of m, in turn, reflects a number of variables.

First of all, the institutional features of the economy that determine the efficiency of money in exchange affect the value of m. For example, if the established practice was for people to be paid their yearly salary once each year (on January 1), people would have to hold large average balances of money (probably in checking accounts) to make transactions over the course of the year. When people are paid monthly, the average amount of money they have to hold to make transactions over the course of the year is much less.

The efficiency of money and the value of m are affected by the ways that payment is made for purchases. In a cash-only society, in which all purchases had to be paid for in cash or check, everybody would have to hold relatively large amounts of currency and maintain large checking account balances to make their purchases. However, the availability of credit for making purchases reduces the amount of money that persons have to hold in order to make their purchases.

The value of m and the demand for money are also affected by economic expectations. If there is widespread economic uncertainty and pessimism, households and institutions may want to hold greater precautionary and speculative balances to provide for future contingencies and to reduce the risk of loss by holding more money. In periods of optimism when the risk from holding assets other than money is low, the owners of wealth will shift some of their assets out of money into other assets, and the demand for money will drop.

The institutional variables that affect the demand for money—such as the frequency of wage and salary payments and the system of making purchases and payments—are relatively stable, and change rather gradually over time. However, unstable expectations can create instability in the demand for money that has serious implications for the stability of aggregate output and employment in the goods sector of the economy and for the success of attempts to regulate aggregate demand through the monetary sector.

Equilibrium in the Money Market

Equilibrium in money markets has important implications for equilibrium aggregate output and employment in the goods sector. In fact, all of the analysis of equilibrium output and employment in the previous section of the text assumed equilibrium in the monetary sector. If money markets aren't in equilibrium, the goods sector won't be in equilibrium either, and disturbances in the monetary sector will affect the equilibrium in the goods sector.

Equilibrium in the money market is determined by the interaction of the demand for money and the supply of money. The basic mechanics are similar to the determination of equilibrium price in any market, except that the price in the money market is the interest rate.

The Supply of Money

We've had a good look at the demand side in the money market, but what about the supply of money? For simplicity, we'll assume that the supply of money (M) is a *policy variable*. This simply means that the supply of money is determined by government policy and not by the interest rate. This assumption is not quite accurate as a picture of the determinants of the money supply in the real world, but monetary policy by the government is the most important determinant of the money supply, and the assumption makes our analysis much simpler than a more comprehensive list of the determinants of the money supply.

If the money supply (M) is determined by government policy, and not by the interest rate, the supply of money doesn't vary with the interest rate. With no changes in monetary policy to alter the supply of money, then, the supply of money can be represented by the vertical supply function, M, in Figure 4.

The Equilibrium Interest Rate

Given the demand for money (L) and the supply of money (M) in Figure 4, the interest will tend to move toward equilibrium at $\bar{r}$ where the quantity of money demanded along L equals the supply of money. If the interest rate were r_1, which is below the equlibrium rate, there would be excess demand for money balances, and this excess demand would drive the interest rate upward. If the interest rate were above equilibrium, say at r_2, excess supply of money would drive the interest rate downward.

The link between the demand for and supply of money and the interest rate is crucial, because the interest rate affects investment expenditures and some types of consumption expenditures. This gives us an important link between the money market and aggregate demand in the goods sector.

Money, Interest, Investment, and GNP: The "Keynesian Connection"

It was shown that the level of investment will increase or decrease until the marginal efficiency of investment (MEI)—the annual rate of return on the last investment made—equals the interest rate. The link between the money markets and aggregate demand is easy to establish. All we have to do is combine the demand curve for money, the marginal efficiency of investment, and the simple Keynesian model.

The demand curve for money (L) and the supply of money (M) determine the equilibrium interest rate ($\bar{r}$) in Figure 5a. In Figure 5b, the equilibrium interest rate ($\bar{r}$) and the marginal efficiency of investment (MEI) determine the equilibrium level of investment at $\bar{I}$, where $\bar{r} = MEI$. Combining the equilibrium level of investment with other expenditure flows gives us the aggregate demand function, $AD = C + \bar{I} + G$ in Figure 5c. Equlibrium GNP ($\bar{Y}$) is reached in Figure 5c where $AD = \bar{Y}$.

If the money market isn't in equilibrium, the interest rate won't be stable, but will be moving toward equilibrium. Without a stable interest rate, we can't have equilibrium in the goods market because the changing interest rate would lead to changes in the level of invest-

Figure 4 Money Market Equilibrium

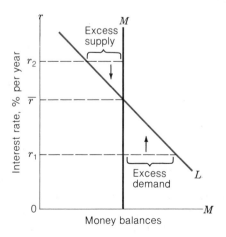

Figure 5 Money Market Equilibrium and the Level of GNP

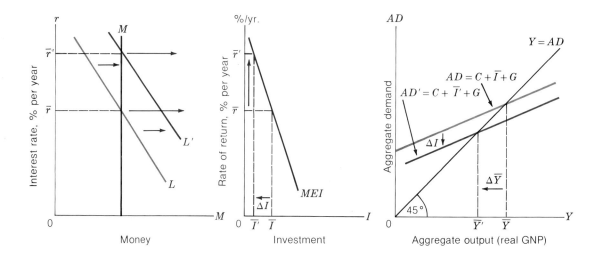

ment, aggregate demand, aggregate output, and employment in the goods sector until the interest rate stabilized at equilibrium and investment stabilized where $\bar{r} = MEI$.

Now, the importance of the stability and predictability of the demand for money should be clear. Suppose that we have equilibrium in the money market at $\bar{r}$ and in the goods market at $\overline{Y}$ in Figure 5. Shifts in the demand for money—due to a change in expectations, for example—will disturb the equilibrium in the money market and this will disturb the equilibrium in the goods market. An increase in the demand for money to L' will drive the interest rate to $\bar{r}'$, which will cause investment to fall to $\overline{I}'$ where $MEI = \bar{r}'$, and this will cause aggregate output to fall to $\overline{Y}' = C + \overline{I}' + G$. Instability in the demand for money over time will be translated into unstable aggregate demand, aggregate output, and employment in the goods sector.

Understanding equilibrium in the money market and the link between equilibrium in the money and goods markets sets the stage for analyzing the effects of changes in the money supply on aggregate demand, aggregate output, and the price level. This is important because government monetary policies seek to regulate or *manage* aggregate demand to minimize instability, unemployment, and inflationary pressure. The link between changes in the money supply and changes in output and prices is taken up in the next chapter.

Summary

1. The origins of money go back to the beginnings of economic specialization and exchange, and the development of the market economy. Money encourages greater specialization by facilitating exchange.

2. The earliest forms of money were **commodity money**—a commodity which possessed the basic characteristics of money. The value or purchasing power of commodity money is determined by the relative scarcity and relative price of the money commodity.

3. **Fiat money** is money because laws define it as money. It isn't backed by any money commodity. The value of fiat money is its purchasing power, but this purchasing power doesn't depend on the value of a money commodity.

4. As a **unit of exchange**, or **unit of account**, money makes it possible to quantify costs, profits, and aggregate output. To serve as a unit of account and exchange, money must be generally acceptable in exchange, divisible into small units, and scarce and difficult to reproduce.

5. As a **store of value**, money allows households to store the values of the goods and resources they sell.

6. The strict definition of the money supply includes currency and demand deposits. Broader definitions include some types of savings and time deposits.

7. **Near monies** have stable money values, and are easily converted to money at their full value. They aren't included in the definition of the money supply.

8. Money or **real balances** is only one of the assets individuals will hold in their portfolios of assets. Individuals hold money for transactions, precautionary, and speculative reasons. The quantity of money demanded tends to vary inversely with the interest rate, which is the opportunity cost of holding money balances.

9. Money affects aggregate demand and real GNP through its effect on interest rates and the level of investment. Changes in the demand for money cause changes in interest rates and thus result in changes in the levels of investment and equilibrium GNP.

Concepts for Review

barter exchange	money aggregate	speculative demand for money
commodity money	demand deposit	
Gresham's Law	time deposit	real balance
gold standard	near monies	liquidity
fiat money	transactions demand for money	portfolio of assets
unit of account		liquidity preference
unit of exchange	precautionary demand for money	demand curve for money
store of value		

Questions

1. Of all the villains in Ian Fleming's "007" novels, none was nastier or more cunning than the infamous Goldfinger, who attempted to make the U.S. gold stock radioactive and useless by detonating a nuclear device in the vault at Fort Knox. (Fortunately, he was foiled at the last moment by "007!")

   a. If a modern Goldfinger were to destroy the U.S. gold stock in Fort Knox today, how would this affect our money supply?

   b. Would the same heinous deed have had the same effect on the money supply if it had been pulled off 100 years ago?

2. Some people are upset because our money isn't backed by any *real* money (such as gold or silver). Is there any historical cause for this concern? Do you think that the fact that our fiat money isn't backed by gold or silver is a serious economic problem today?

3. The line between things that should be included in the definition of money and those that shouldn't is drawn on the basis of their substitutability as money.
   a. What functions does money perform, and what characteristics does money have to have to perform these functions?
   b. Which of the following would you include in the definition of money, and why?

currency	government securities
demand deposits	checkable savings accounts
savings accounts	gold
time deposits	credit cards

4. Deposits in insured passbook savings accounts earn an annual rate of 5¼ percent. Longer term certificates of deposit earn 6 percent if the funds are left on deposit for one year. High-grade, long-term corporate bonds earn about 10 percent per year. Bonds issued by the Last Gasp Uranium Mining Co. pay an annual interest rate of 20 percent.
   a. How do you explain the different annual rates of return for holding these assets?
   b. Which of the interest rates above are reasonable approximations of the opportunity cost of holding money as an asset?
   c. Suppose that the interest rate on insured passbook savings deposits increases to 6 percent. How would this affect individual portfolios of assets? What would you expect to happen to the interest rates on the other assets? How would this change affect the demand for money as an asset?

5. It is possible to have equilibrium aggregate output of goods and services if the money market isn't in equilibrium? How do disturbances of equilibrium in money markets affect equilibrium output of goods and services?

6. "Other things being the same, it is highly plausible that the fraction of assets individuals and business enterprises wish to hold in the form of money, and also in the form of close substitutes for money, will be smaller when they look forward to a period of stable economic conditions than when they anticipate disturbed and uncertain conditions." [Milton Friedman, A *Monetary History of the United States*. New York: National Bureau of Economic Research, 1963 (Published by Princeton University Press), p. 673.]
   a. Explain carefully how the stability of economic expectations affects the demand for money as an asset. How does this affect the stability of aggregate demand and aggregate output in the goods sector?
   b. Based on your knowledge of facts and monetary economics, how would economic expectations have affected the demand for money as an asset during the "new era" prosperity of the mid 1920s, the Great Depression of the 1930s, the World War II and early postwar period (1940–45 and 1945–48)? You can check your answer by consulting the relevant section of the *Monetary History*.

Problems

1. The relationships between the interest rate (r), the level of intended investment (I), and the demand for money balances (L) for the small country of Mammonland are as follows:

Interest Rate (r) (% per year)	Intended Investment (I) (billions $ per year)	Demand for Money (L) ($ billions per year)
20	0	0
18	10	5
16	20	10
14	30	15
12	40	20
10	50	25
8	60	30
6	70	35
4	80	40
2	90	45

a. Write an equation that expresses the relationship between the interest rate and the demand for money. The equation will be of the general form $r = a + bL$. Explain the relationship between the interest rate and the demand for money.

b. Write an equation that expresses the relationship between the interest rate and the level of intended investment. The equation will be of the general form $r = a + bI$. Explain this relationship.

c. If the supply of money is M = $20 billion, find the equilibrium interest rate ($\bar{r}$). What will be the level of investment at this interest rate?

d. The consumption function in Mammonland is C = 50 + 0.8 Y. Government spending is autonomous at G_a = $30 billion. Intended investment is determined by the interest rate and the *MEI*. Write the economy's aggregate demand function as an equation. What is equilibrium aggregate output?

e. Worsening economic expectations double the amount of money that households and firms wish to hold at every interest rate. How does this affect the equilibrium in the money market and the level of GNP that you found in part (c)?

f. Show the effect of the increased demand for money as an asset in part (d) on the aggregate demand function and on equilibrium aggregate output.

11

The Supply of Money

Preview: The relationship between the money supply and the levels of aggregate output and prices is a controversial subject that has fascinated economists for centuries. In this chapter, we'll analyze that relationship as it is explained by the quantity theory of money. We'll also look closely at exactly how the supply of money is determined by the commercial banking system and the Federal Reserve.

The Supply of Money and Aggregate Output

The previous chapter established a link between equilibrium in the money market and equilibrium aggregate output in the goods market. The link is the interest rate. The demand for money and the supply of money determine the equilibrium interest rate, which determines the level of investment demand (and also affects some types of consumption spending). The level of investment, as a component of aggregate demand, is a determinant of equilibrium real GNP or aggregate output. Changes in the demand for money will upset the monetary equilibrium, upsetting equilibrium in the goods sector as well.

What about the supply side of the money market? How do changes in the supply of money affect equilibrium in the money market, aggregate demand, and equilibrium aggregate output in the goods sector? How do changes in the money supply affect the price level? The relationship between changes in the money supply and changes in output and prices has interested economists for centuries, and it continues to be a central issue that divides economists.

Recall from the previous chapter that the demand for money (L) and the supply of money (M) define the equilibrium interest rate ($\bar{r}$) in Figure 1a. At the equilibrium interest rate, investment will increase until the rate of return on the last investment made (MEI) equals the

Figure 1   Changes in the Money Supply and Changes in GNP

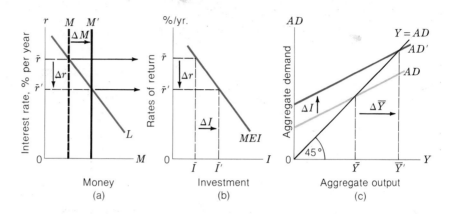

Money
(a)

Investment
(b)

Aggregate output
(c)

interest rate—$\bar{I}$ in Figure 1b. In Figure 1c, the equilibrium level of investment, along with the other intended expenditure flows, determines the level of aggregate demand (AD) and equilibrium aggregate output or real GNP (Y).

Now suppose that the money supply increases from M to M' in Figure 1a. The equilibrium interest rate falls to r'. As a result of the lower interest rate, investment increases to I' where $r' = MEI$. The increase in investment to $\bar{I}'$ causes the aggregate demand function in Figure 1c to rise to AD', and aggregate output to increase to $\bar{Y}' = AD'$. Verify for yourself that reducing the money supply from M' to M would cause aggregate demand and equilibrium real GNP to fall. We have thus identified an important link between changes in the supply of money and changes in aggregate output.

- At a constant price level, aggregate output will vary directly with changes in the money supply.

This relationship is obvious in Figure 2, which compares yearly changes in the money supply (M_1 and M_2) and changes in real GNP (Y) between 1929 and 1978.

The relationship between changes in the money supply and changes in aggregate output, with a constant price level, is easily verified by looking back at the demand for money and equilibrium in the money market. In the last chapter, we saw that the *demand for money at any level of nominal GNP* ($Y_n = PY$), other things constant, is a fraction (m) of nominal GNP, or

$$L = mY_n = mPY. \tag{1}$$

If the money market is in equilibrium, the supply of money equals the demand, or

$$M = mPY. \tag{2}$$

With given values of m and P, aggregate output will vary directly with changes in the money supply.

There is a qualification that has to be made concerning the effects of changes in the money supply on real GNP. If changes in the money supply cause the interest rate to change:

1. The interest rate will vary inversely with the money supply.
2. Investment will vary inversely with the interest rate, and directly with the money supply.
3. Equilibrium GNP will vary directly with investment, and directly with the money supply.

Money Supply, Output, and Prices: The Quantity Theory of Money

Most of us have an intuitive notion that the amount of money in circulation affects prices of goods and services. If the supply of money in circulation increased while the output of goods and services remained constant, or if the money supply increased more rapidly than the output of goods and services, goods and services would be more scarce relative to money. This means that goods and services will command more money in exchange, or more simply that the money prices of goods and services will rise.

If the quantity of money fell while real output remained constant or increased—or if it fell more rapidly than the output of goods and

Figure 2 Changes in the Money Supply and Changes in Real GNP, 1929–1978

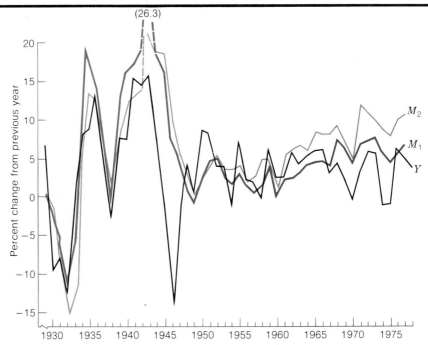

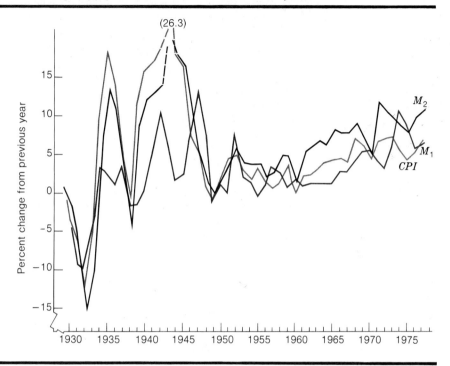

services—money would become more scarce relative to goods and services. In this case, goods and services would command less money in exchange, or the money prices of goods and services would fall.

In the eighteenth century, the British philosopher and essayist David Hume wrote a fable in which everybody's money doubled overnight. As the people rushed out to spend their new wealth, however, the increased demand for goods and services doubled the prices of goods and services. *Hume's Fable* states the "crude" quantity theory of money.

- The *crude* **quantity theory of money** predicts that prices will change in the same direction and by the same proportion as changes in the money supply.

Modern monetary theory also predicts a direct relationship between changes in the money supply and changes in prices, but a less rigid relationship than the one stated in the crude quantity theory.

- The *modern* **quantity theory of money** predicts a direct, but not necessarily proportional, relationship between changes in the money supply and changes in prices.

If the money supply doubled overnight, the modern quantity theory would predict that prices would rise, but not necessarily double.

Figure 3 shows year-to-year changes in the money supply (M_1 and M_2) and the Consumer Price Index (CPI) for the period 1929–1977. Generally, but not always, prices tend to rise most rapidly during periods of rapid increase in the money supply, and tend to rise more slowly or fall in periods in which the money supply is increasing slowly or falling. This generally confirms the predictions that follow from the quantity theory, but it also indicates that the money supply isn't the only variable that affects prices.

The Velocity of Money

The quantity of money in circulation doesn't have to be as large as nominal GNP because money is spent more than once.

- The **velocity of money** is the rate at which money changes hands, or "turns over" in the economy.

If the velocity of money were 2, for example, this means that the supply of money would, on the average, change hands twice during the year. It would also mean that nominal GNP is twice as great as the money supply.

We can measure the velocity of money by dividing the nominal (or "money") GNP in current prices by the supply of money—i.e.,

$$V = \frac{\text{Nominal GNP}}{\text{Money Supply}}. \tag{3}$$

Nominal GNP is real GNP (Y), or aggregate output, multiplied by the current price level (P)—algebraically, *nominal GNP = PY*. Now, the expression for velocity becomes

$$V = \frac{PY}{M}. \tag{4}$$

As noted in the last chapter, there is some disagreement over the best measure of the supply of money—M_1 or M_2. We'll skirt the issue by examining two measures of velocity, V_1 and V_2, where

$$V_1 = \frac{PY}{M_1} \quad \text{and} \quad V_2 = \frac{PY}{M_2}.$$

For example, in 1977,

$$V_1 = \frac{\$1890.4 \text{ billion}}{\$324.5 \text{ billion}} = 5.83$$

$$V_2 = \frac{\$1890.4 \text{ billion}}{777.6 \text{ billion}} = 2.43.$$

Most early monetary theorists paid relatively little attention to velocity. They either ignored it or assumed that it was an institutionally determined constant. However, velocity may change for a number of reasons—institutional changes (such as new arrangements for making payments), changing economic conditions, changing expectations, and changes in households' and firms' preference for holding money over other assets. Figure 4 shows the behavior of V_1 and V_2 between 1929 and 1977.

The rise in V_1 in Figure 4, for example, reflects in part the growing use of checkable savings accounts (such as the NOW accounts). By making it easier to make payments out of savings accounts, the checkable savings account tend to reduce the households' and firms' need to hold currency and demand deposit balances. In other words, M_1 falls relative to nominal GNP, and $V_1 = PY/M_1$ rises.

Although V_2 has been considerably more stable over time than V_1, it hasn't been constant. Dramatic changes in economic conditions tend to increase households' and firms' demand for money balances, and this causes velocity to fall—as it did through much of the Great Depression, during and immediately following World War II, and less dramatically in several recessions since World War II (note 1974 in particular).

The stability and predictability of velocity is important economically. If velocity is unstable or unpredictable, it will be difficult to predict the effect of changes in the money supply on prices.

The Equation of Exchange

One way of expressing the quantity theory of money is with the *equation of exchange*.

- The **equation of exchange** states the relationship among the money supply, velocity, the price level, and real GNP.

Derivation of the equation of exchange is easy, and follows from

Figure 4 Velocity of Money, 1929–1977

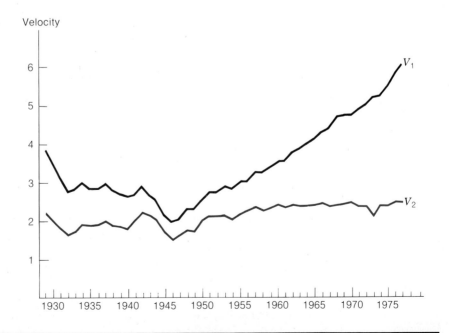

the definitions of nominal GNP (PY) and velocity ($V = PY/M$). Multiplying the money supply (M) by velocity (V),

$$MV = M\left(\frac{PY}{M}\right) = PY.$$

The equation of exchange, then, is

$$MV = PY. \tag{5}$$

Historically, the concern has been the effect of changes in the money supply on the price level, so we can write the equation of exchange as

$$PY = MV.$$

Dividing both sides by Y,

$$P = \frac{MV}{Y}. \tag{6}$$

The general predictions from the equation of exchange are obvious.

1. Prices tend to vary directly with changes in the money supply.
2. Prices tend to vary directly with changes in the velocity of money.
3. Prices tend to vary inversely with changes in real GNP.

The crude quantity theory predicted proportional changes in the money supply and prices by assuming implicitly that output and velocity remain constant while the supply of money changed.

To illustrate the effect of changes in velocity, suppose that the initial supply of money is 200, velocity is 4, real GNP is 800, and the price level is 1—i.e.,

$$P = \frac{MV}{Y} = \frac{200 \times 4}{800} = \frac{800}{800} = 1.$$

Now, suppose that the money supply increases to 400 and that the velocity of money increases to 5. If Y remains at 800, the new price level will be

$$P = \frac{400 \times 5}{800} = \frac{2,000}{800} = 2.5.$$

Because of the change in V, doubling the money supply leads to a 2.5-fold increase in prices.

The equation of exchange predicts that the price level will vary inversely with changes in real GNP. For example, suppose that the money supply and velocity remain at their initial values, while real GNP increases from 800 to 1200. The new price level will be

$$P = \frac{MV}{Y} = \frac{200 \times 4}{1200} = \frac{800}{1200} = 0.75.$$

In reality, of course, these variables don't change one at a time as they did in the examples. If M, V, and Y are changing at the same time, the effect on prices depends on which variables are changing the fastest.

- If MV rises (falls) more rapidly than Y, prices will rise (fall). If Y rises (falls) more rapidly than MV, prices will fall (rise).

Close-up

The Free Silver Movement

Following the Civil War, the U.S. experienced rapid growth of real GNP. However, the supply of gold was fairly stable. Since the U.S. was on a "gold standard," the money supply increased more slowly than real output. In the context of the quantity theory and the equation of exchange, MV was increasing more slowly than Y, and the price level fell.

Inflation has been such a serious matter of concern in the 1970s that the problems of *falling* prices might not be obvious. As prices fall, the dollars that repay loans have greater purchasing power than the dollars originally borrowed. This increases the *real* burden of debts, and debtors (persons who owe debts) are worse off economically when prices are falling. Creditors (persons to whom debts are owed) benefit during periods of falling prices because they receive money in repayment of loans that has greater purchasing power than the money lent.

The *Free Silver* Movement in the U.S. was composed of advocates of greater coinage of silver. More silver money would increase the money supply, and this would stem the deflation. In the 1896 presidential election, the movement gained an eloquent spokesman in the person of William Jennings Bryan (the "silver-tongued orator of the Platte"), who ran on the Democratic ticket. Bryan declared that the gold standard was crucifying mankind on a "cross of gold."

Business and financial interests rallied around the Republicans' promise to preserve the gold standard and "sound money." Creditors who had benefitted from the deflation didn't want to end it by increasing the supply of silver money.

The Democrats' strongest support for "free silver" came from debtor classes —particularly farmers in the South and the West. They lost the election. However, by the end of the century, the deflation was stemmed—not by the free coinage of silver, but by increased production of gold.

The Equation of Exchange and Equilibrium in the Money Market

You may have noticed some similarities between the equation of exchange and the money market equilibrium discussed earlier. This isn't surprising since they are alternative ways of saying about the same thing concerning the effects of changes in the money supply. In fact, the equation of exchange can be derived easily from the equilibrium in the money market.

The money market reaches equilibrium when $M = L$, or

$$M = mPY. \tag{7}$$

The value of m is determined by the same variables that define velocity of money (V), except that the circumstances which define a low value for m define a high value for V. Specifically, m is the *reciprocal* of V. From the previous equation, m is found by dividing both sides of the equation by PY, or

$$m = \frac{M}{PY}. \tag{8}$$

From the equation of exchange, we established that velocity is

$$V = \frac{PY}{M}.$$

Therefore

$$m = \frac{1}{V}. \tag{9}$$

For example, if the velocity of money were $V = 2$, this is simply a way of saying that money changes hands twice during the year, or that the required supply of money would be ½ of nominal GNP, or $m = \frac{1}{2}$.

The two expressions of the modern quantity theory are simply alternative ways of expressing essentially the same thing. If we start with the equation

$$M = mPY,$$

and substitute $(1/V)$ for m, we have

$$M = \frac{1}{V}PY.$$

Multiplying both sides of this equation by V,

$$MV = V\frac{1}{V}PY,$$

or

$$MV = PY.$$

Obviously, the importance of the stability and predictability of velocity applies with equal force to the stability and predictability of m. To the extent that m is unstable or unpredictable, it will be difficult to predict accurately the effects of changes in the money supply on the price level.

Having established the relationship between changes in the money supply and changes in aggregate output, we have to examine the way that the money supply is altered. The most important economic institutions, as far as the supply of money is concerned, are commercial banks and the Federal Reserve (the authority over monetary policy in the United States).

Commercial Banks and the Money Supply

The banking system plays a critical role in determining the supply of money. **Commercial banks** are particularly important. In addition to providing the familiar services of holding demand and time deposits and providing credit to households and businesses, commercial banks *create* money. To see how commercial banks can do this without printing currency and without any legal authority over the money supply, we have to examine the nature and functions of banks more closely.

Goldsmiths and the Origins of Commercial Banking

In addition to making and selling gold objects, goldsmiths were the first commercial bankers. They held gold for their customers for safekeeping against bandits, thieves, and tax collectors, and charged fees for this service similar to the fees charged by modern banks for safe-deposit boxes. The goldsmiths kept accounts showing each customer's deposits, withdrawals, and the balance of each customer's account.

The ancestors of modern checking accounts emerged as depositors wrote *drafts* authorizing third parties to make withdrawals from their accounts. Eventually, drafts played an important role as money. Buyers used them to authorize payments to sellers. Sellers deposited the drafts into their accounts, and the goldsmith simply deducted the amount of the draft from the buyer's account and added it to the seller's account. Very often, no gold physically changed hands. This had a very important result.

Goldsmiths soon discovered that they didn't have to hold all of the gold that had been deposited with them, but only enough to meet the normal demands of customers for withdrawals. As long as the goldsmiths could honor requests for withdrawals of gold, they could loan out the gold they didn't need and earn interest on the loans (in addition to the fees charged to depositors). This type of banking is called *fractional reserve banking*.

- **Fractional reserve banking** is a system in which banks hold only a fraction of their deposits as reserves.

By loaning out part of their reserves, the goldsmiths could *create* money. Say a goldsmith holds $100,000 worth of gold deposits for his customers. But suppose, the goldsmith decides that only 20 percent of this amount needs to be held as **required reserves** to cover normal demands for withdrawals of gold. This means that the goldsmith has $80,000 (80 percent of $100,000) in **excess reserves**— i.e., reserves in excess of those needed to meet customers' withdrawal requests.

Enterprising goldsmiths loaned out their excess reserves, and earned interest on the loans. This put more money into circulation, in addition to the original deposits. If our goldsmith-banker loaned out the $80,000 in excess reserves, the amount of money in circulation (the gold demand deposits, plus the money loaned out) would be

Initial Gold Demand Deposits	$100,000
Gold Loaned Out	80,000
Money in Circulation	$180,000

In other words, the goldsmith *created* an additional $80,000 in money by making loans from his deposits.

The Commercial Bank's Balance Sheet

Like the goldsmith bankers, modern commercial banks hold fractional reserves. Although commercial banks in the U.S. don't issue currency, fractional reserves allow the banks to alter the money supply by increasing or decreasing the quantity of demand-deposit money.

To see how banks can *create* money, we have to take a look at a highly simplified **balance sheet** for a hypothetical commercial bank. A balance sheet is simply an accounting statement that summarizes a firm's **assets**, **liabilities**, and **net worth** (or **equity**). One of the basic axioms of accounting is that *assets must equal liabilities plus owners' equity*. Every change in an asset is accompanied by an equal change in liabilities or equity or offsetting changes in other assets. For example, if you borrow $5000 to buy a new car, you'll acquire a $5000 asset (the car) and a $5000 liability (the loan). If you paid for the car out of your accumulated savings, you'd acquire a $5000 asset (the car), but you'd reduce another asset (savings) by $5000.

The simplified balance sheet for our hypothetical commercial bank —call it Bank A—is shown in Table 1. The bank's *reserves* are money held as vault cash and as a demand deposit with a central reserve bank. Suppose that Bank A must hold 20 percent of its demand deposits as *required reserves* to meet depositors' requests for withdrawals. This bank is *loaned up*—i.e., it holds no *excess reserves* above its required reserves.

Table 1 Simplified Balance Sheet for Bank A

ASSETS		LIABILITIES	
Reserves		Demand Deposits	$20 million
Required	$ 4 million	Time Deposits	5 million
Excess	0	Other Liabilities	5 million
Loans	16 million		
Government Securities	8 million	OWNERS' EQUITY	5 million
Other Securities	7 million		
	$35 million		$35 million

The bank's other assets include loans, government securities, and other securities. These represent obligations of others to make repayments to the bank. On the liabilities side of the sheet, demand deposits and time deposits are liabilities for the bank. They represent the bank's obligations to honor requests for withdrawals from these accounts. All other liabilities are lumped together in a catch-all category, *other liabilities*. The bank's *owners' equity* or *net worth* is the difference between assets and its liabilities, and represents the value of the owners' claims against the bank.

Initially, Bank A is loaned up and holds no excess reserves. This bank couldn't create any additional money unless something happened to increase its reserves.

Creation of Money by the Banks

Suppose that Bank A receives an additional $2 million in new reserves. This could happen if the bank acquired new demand deposits from new depositors or additional demand deposits from old depositors. This increases Bank A's reserves (an asset) by $2 million, and its demand deposits (a liability) by $2 million. If the bank holds 20 percent of its demand deposits as **required reserves**, the additional $2 million in demand deposits will increase required reserves by $0.4 million (20 percent of $2 million).

Additional reserves above required reserves are additional **excess reserves**. So the additional $2 million in demand deposits increase excess reserves by $1.6 million (80 percent of $2 million).

		Bank A	
ASSETS		**LIABILITIES**	
Reserves		Demand Deposits	+ $2 million
Required	+ $0.4 million		
Excess	+ $1.6 million		

The new excess reserves held by the bank can be loaned out to earn interest. Assume that the bank loans out the entire $1.6 million —after all, the excess reserves earn no income as reserves. After loaning out the new excess reserves, the bank is loaned up again. The bank has converted one asset (excess reserves) into another asset (loans).

	Bank A	
ASSETS		**LIABILITIES**
Excess Reserves	− $1.6 million	No Change
Loans	+ $1.6 million	

Firms and households generally take out loans to make purchases. It doesn't make a great deal of sense for a borrower to hold borrowed funds (on which interest must be paid) as currency (which earns nothing) or to deposit them in a savings account at a lower rate of interest than must be paid on the loan.

Whether borrowers deposit borrowed funds in their own accounts or make purchases with the borrowed funds and the sellers deposit them in their demand deposit accounts, the loaned funds eventually find their way back into the banking system as additional demand deposits.

Suppose that the entire $1.6 million in additional excess reserves in Bank A is loaned out, and that the funds are redeposited in Bank B as demand deposits. This increases Bank B's demand deposits and its *reserves* by $1.6 million. Bank B also holds 20 percent of its new demand deposits as required reserves, and the remaining 80 percent represents new excess reserves in Bank B.

	Bank B	
ASSETS	LIABILITIES	
Reserves	Demand Deposits	+ $1.6 million
Required + $0.32 million		
Excess + $1.28 million		

Like Bank A, Bank B loans out its new excess reserves, converting excess reserves into loans.

	Bank B	
ASSETS		LIABILITIES
Excess Reserves	− $1.28 million	No Change
Loans	+ $1.28 million	

If the $1.28 million loaned out by Bank B is deposited in another bank—Bank C—the process is repeated. Bank C's demand deposits and reserves increase by $1.28 million.

The additional reserves are broken down into $0.26 million in required reserves (20 percent of $1.28 million) and $1.02 million in new excess reserves (80 percent of $1.28 million).

	Bank C	
ASSETS	LIABILITIES	
Reserves	Demand Deposits	+ $1.28 million
Required + $0.26 million		
Excess + $1.02 million		

If Bank C loans out the entire $1.02 million in excess reserves, and these funds are deposited in yet another bank—Bank D—demand deposits and bank reserves will continue to increase. To verify your understanding of all of this, construct balance sheets to show the effect of Bank C's new loans on its assets and liabilities, and the effect of the additional demand deposits in Bank D.

In these examples, no bank loaned out more funds than it held as reserves—in fact each bank held some of its additional reserves as required reserves. However, *together* the banks created additional money as bank reserves and demand deposits increased. The total increase in reserves and demand deposit money from the initial increase of $2 million in Bank A's reserves is shown below.

New Reserves in Bank A	$2.0 million
New Reserves in Bank B	1.6 million
New Reserves in Bank C	1.28 million
TOTAL NEW RESERVES	$4.88 million

The banking *system* in this example has *created* nearly $3 million in additional demand deposit money over and above the original increase in bank reserves.

The Banking System Multiplier

How much money will eventually be generated by the initial increase in Bank A's reserves? This is determined by something called the *banking system multiplier*.

- The **banking system multiplier** determines the maximum supply of demand deposit money that can be generated from any level of bank reserves, and the maximum change in the supply of demand deposit money as a result of changes in bank reserves.

The size of the banking system multiplier effect depends on the *reserve ratio* (rr).

- The **reserve ratio** is the proportion of demand deposits (DD) that banks must hold as required reserves (R).

The maximum supply of demand deposit money (DD_{max}) from any given level of bank reserves is

$$DD_{max} = \frac{1}{rr} R. \qquad (10)$$

If bank reserves change by some ΔR, the maximum change in the supply of demand deposit money (ΔDD_{max}) is

$$\Delta DD_{max} = \frac{1}{rr} \Delta R. \qquad (11)$$

The ratio $(1/rr)$ is the banking system multiplier.[1]

---

1. The proportion of an initial change in bank reserves, ΔR, that can be loaned out is $(1 - rr)$. This represents additional reserves for the "second generation bank," and the second generation bank can loan out $(1 - rr)$ of these additional reserves, or $(1 - rr)(1 - rr)\Delta R = (1 - rr)^2 \Delta R$. This amount, in turn represents new reserves for the third generation bank, and the third generation bank can loan out $(1 - rr)(1 - rr)^2 \Delta R = (1 - rr)^3 \Delta R$. If no funds ever leak out of the demand-deposit credit flow, the maximum change in demand deposit money will be

$$\Delta DD_{max} = \Delta R + (1 - rr)\Delta R + (1 - rr)^2 \Delta R + (1 - rr)^3 \Delta R + \cdots$$
$$= \Delta R[1 + (1 - rr) + (1 - rr)^2 + (1 - rr)^3 + \cdots]$$

As the number of rounds increases, the amount of new reserves entering the banking system gets

Bank reserves can fall as well as rise, of course, and the banking system multiplier works in both directions. If bank reserves declined, banks may have to reduce their loans to maintain their required reserves, and this would cause demand deposits in the banking system (and the level of total bank reserves in the system) to fall further.

If banks were required to hold *all* of their demand deposits as required reserves, we wouldn't have fractional reserve banking, but *100% banking*. With 100% banking, there would be no banking system multiplier effect, because the reserve ratio is $rr = 1$, and the banking system multiplier would be $1/rr = 1/1 = 1$.

The Banking System Multiplier: Some Qualifications

The banking system multiplier defines the maximum level of demand deposit money that can be generated by the banking system from a given level of bank reserves, or the maximum change in demand deposit money as a result of a given change in bank reserves, with a given reserve ratio. However, it's highly unlikely that this maximum would ever be reached in practice.

In the examples, no funds leaked out of the demand-deposit credit flow of the banking system. In fact, there are a number of possible leaks out of this flow which reduce the size of the banking multiplier. Leaks into currency are an important leak. To the extent that funds are held as currency instead of being redeposited as demand deposits in the banking system, this reduces the expansion of bank reserves and the banking system's ability to generate demand-deposit money.

In addition, the banks in the examples stayed loaned up, and never held excess reserves. This infers that banks are mechanical and passive in the creation or contraction of the money supply. In fact, banks aren't passive or mechanical in their decisions. Like households and firms, banks may desire to hold some excess reserves for precautionary or speculative reasons. If Bank A in the previous examples had diverted more than 20 percent of its additional demand deposits to reserves, less money would have been loaned out and redeposited in Bank B as demand deposits, and the expansion of demand deposits in Bank B and all subsequent banks would have been smaller.

These qualifications are significant, because the exact size of the banking system multiplier is not easy to predict precisely. The fol-

---

smaller and smaller. The expression in the brackets becomes an *infinite series*, which can be written

$$\frac{1}{1 - (1 - rr)} = \frac{1}{rr}.$$

The maximum change in demand deposits from an initial change in reserves is

$$\Delta DD_{max} = \frac{1}{rr} \Delta R.$$

lowing is a more realistic, but less precise statement of the banking system multiplier.

- With fractional reserve banking, banks can generate demand deposit money from their excess reserves, and changes in bank reserves will produce greater changes in demand deposit money.

But Is It Really Money?

The creation of money through a series of accounting operations looks like a sleight-of-hand trick that violates our common sense. Do the commercial banks really create money?

Demand deposits, as many people point out, are only "money on paper," but they *are* money. Demand deposits are very good substitutes for currency as a means of exchange and a store of value, and are widely acceptable in exchange. Except with *commodity money* (such as gold or fully backed gold certificates), all money is "money on paper." The folding money in your pocket is also "money on paper." In short, when banks alter the supply of demand-deposit money, they *do* alter the supply of money.

The Federal Reserve and the Money Supply

Unlike the hypothetical banks in the previous section of this chapter, commercial banks in the real world aren't completely free to set their own minimum required reserves or to determine the supply of money independently of any central control. In all industrialized countries, the actions of individual banks are restricted by the rules, regulations, and policies of a **central bank**. A central bank is the keystone of the commercial banking system. Central banks play three critically important roles—as the *government's bank*, as the *banks' bank*, and as the *authority over monetary policies*.

The United States hasn't had a true central bank since the demise of the Bank of the United States in 1836. Control over monetary policy and the actions of individual banks were decentralized in the United States through most of the nineteenth century. The United States was on a gold standard in this period, and this stabilized the money supply somewhat, but serious economic panics occurred in 1873, 1884, 1890, 1893, and 1907.

After the Panic of 1907, Congress appointed the National Monetary Commission to study the problem of monetary policy. Unlike most commissions, the National Monetary Commission had some impact. Largely as a result of the research and recommendations of the National Monetary Commission, the Federal Reserve Act was passed and enacted in 1913. This act established the **Federal Reserve System** to perform most of the functions of a central bank in the United States. The formal organization of the Federal Reserve System (the *Fed*) is about the same today as it was in 1913.

The Structure of the Federal Reserve

The country is divided into twelve Federal Reserve Districts, as shown in the map in Figure 5. Each district has a Federal Reserve Bank that serves as a central bank for the member commercial banks in the district. The Federal Reserve Banks hold demand deposits for the commercial banks, make short-term loans, and perform other banking services for member commercial banks.

Federal Reserve Banks act as clearinghouses for commercial banks. Suppose that Emma Turkey buys a new car from Saintly Sam and pays for it with a check drawn on her account at the Ebeneezer Bank & Trust Co. The dealer deposits the check in his account with the Legree Bank, which adds the amount of the check to the dealer's account. The Legree Bank then deposits the check in its reserve account with the Federal Reserve Bank in his district.

The Federal Reserve Bank *clears* the check by adding the amount of the check to the Legree Bank's reserve account and deducting it from Ebeneezer Bank & Trust Co.'s account. The check then proceeds to the Ebeneezer Bank & Trust Co., which deducts the amount of the check from Ms. Turkey's account and returns the paid (or cancelled) check as a receipt. The journey of the check is shown in Figure 6.

Figure 5   The Federal Reserve System

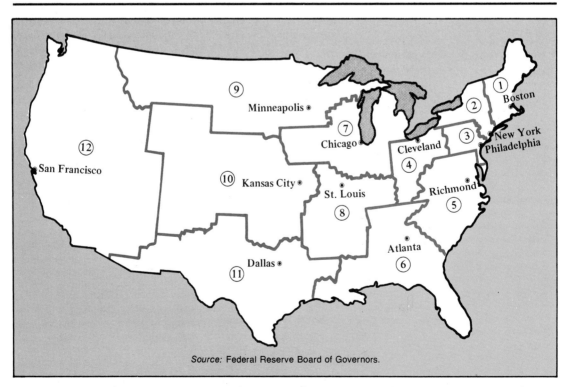

Source: Federal Reserve Board of Governors.

Alaska and Hawaii are in District 12, served by the Federal Reserve Bank of San Francisco.

Clearing operations are important economically. They make transactions by check much easier than they would be if each bank had to send all checks to other banks for payment. By facilitating exchanges by check, clearing operations enhance the monetary function of demand deposits.

Federal Reserve Banks are "owned" by the member commercial banks in their districts. The commercial banks are the "stockholders" in their Federal Reserve Banks, but they don't have all of the rights and powers of stockholders in private corporations. The commercial banks can't, for example, decide on the dividend that will be paid on their stock in the Federal Reserve Bank—this is limited by law to a 6 percent annual rate of return. Unlike private stockholders, commercial banks don't choose all of the directors of a Federal Reserve Bank. Each Federal Reserve Bank has a nine-member board of directors, three of whom are appointed by the Board of Governors of the Federal Reserve System.

Individual Federal Reserve Banks don't determine monetary policies for their districts independently. National monetary policy is determined by the Board of Governors and several committees.

The Board of Governors. The Federal Reserve System is directed by a seven-member Board of Governors, or the Federal Reserve Board. Members of the Board are appointed by the President, with confirmation by the Senate. The President appoints the Chairman of the Board when the post becomes vacant.

Figure 6 Movement of a Check Through the Banking System

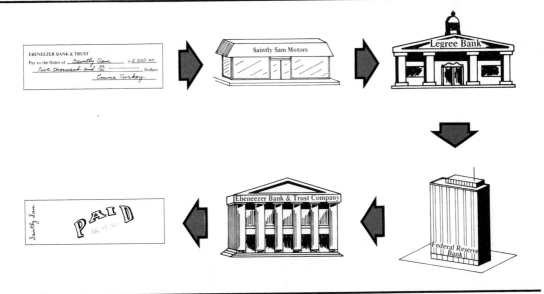

Members of the Federal Reserve Board of Governors are appointed for 14-year terms. The terms of the Governors are staggered, with a vacancy on the Board in every even-numbered year. This seemingly trivial institutional detail is very significant. A President can't fire or demand the resignation of a member of the Board of Governors whose term has not expired, and a President's appointees to the Board of Governors will affect monetary policy after the President is out of office. Also, because the Board will be made up of appointees of at least two different Presidents, this makes monetary policy relatively independent of changing political moods that are reflected in changes in the occupants of 1600 Pennsylvania Avenue.

The Federal Open Market Committee (FOMC).   The Federal Open Market Committee (FOMC) is a potent force in monetary policy. The majority of the twelve-member FOMC are the seven members of the Board of Governors. The other five members are the presidents of five of the twelve Federal Reserve Banks. This committee directs the Fed's purchases and sales of government securities in the open securities market. This is a very important monetary policy tool.

Centralization of Power in the Fed.   On paper, the Fed looks relatively decentralized. However, the centralization of power and influence in monetary policy is considerably greater than the formal organization of the Fed suggests.

The chairman of the Board of Governors is more than the presiding member of the Board. Generally, chairmen dominate the Board, and strong Federal Reserve chairmen have been recognized as the most important spokesmen on monetary policy by the President, the Congress, the media, and the public.

Secondly, to borrow a phrase from George Orwell's *Animal Farm*, some of the Federal Reserve Banks are "more equal" than others in their ability to influence monetary policy. The Federal Reserve Bank of New York is the most influential of the 12 Federal Reserve Banks because New York is the financial capital of the country. The president of the Federal Reserve Bank of New York, is the only Federal Reserve Bank president that holds a voting seat on the FOMC every year.

How Does the Fed Control the Money Supply?   Article I of the U.S. Constitution gives Congress the power to "coin money and regulate the value thereof," but the authority to regulate the supply of money has been delegated by the Congress to the Federal Reserve. Changing the supply of money, however, involves more than coining or printing currency. The Fed has a number of tools that it can use to regulate the supply of money, but the tools aren't equally useful or effective.

The Quantity of Currency in Circulation. Common references in the media and political debates to "printing money" when the Fed expands the money supply are very misleading because they infer that the way the money supply is increased is simply by printing more currency. The Fed *can* order the Treasury and the Bureau of Printing and Engraving to print more currency, but the quantity of *currency* in circulation isn't very significant as a monetary policy tool.

The critical variable is the quantity of *money* in circulation, and currency isn't the largest component of the money supply. In December 1978, for example, currency was only about 27 percent of the narrowly defined money supply (M_1 = currency + demand deposits). Using the broader definition of money, M_2, currency accounted for only about 11 percent of the money supply in December 1978.

Furthermore, the mix of currency and demand deposits depends largely on the public's need or preference for currency and demand deposits. If the Fed tried to put more currency in circulation than firms, households, and financial institutions wanted to hold as money, the excess currency would end up in banks as demand deposits, and eventually back at the Fed.

The Required Reserve Ratio. Commercial banks that belong to the Federal Reserve System can't set their own *reserve ratios*—the proportion of demand deposits held as required reserves. The minimum reserve ratio for commercial banks in the United States is set by the Federal Reserve. Changing the reserve ratio is a powerful monetary tool which can have dramatic effects on the money supply.

The *banking system multiplier* is the ratio $1/rr$, where *rr* is the reserve ratio, and it defines the maximum amount of demand deposit money that banks can generate from a given level of bank reserves. Changing the reserve ratio changes the maximum amount of demand deposit money that can be generated from bank reserves.

The effect of a change in the reserve ratio on the banks' ability to generate money is shown below. At an initial reserve ratio of 10 percent of demand deposits, the bank below holds $2 million in excess reserves.

ASSETS		LIABILITIES
Reserves		Demand Deposits $20 million
Required	$ 2 million	
Excess	2 million	
Loans	$16 million	

If these reserves were loaned out and redeposited as demand deposits in the banking system, this would increase the supply of demand deposit money.

If the Fed raised the reserve ratio from 10 percent to 20 percent (this is an *enormous* change and is only illustrative), the bank's balance sheet would look like this:

ASSETS		LIABILITIES
Reserves		Demand Deposits $20 million
Required	$ 4 million	
Excess	0	
Loans	$16 million	

What happened to the excess reserves? They're gone, because the bank now has to hold the entire $4 million as required reserves (20 percent of $20 million). At the higher reserve ratio, the bank is loaned up, there are no excess reserves to loan out, and this bank can't contribute to an increase in the quantity of demand deposit money.

What if the bank had been loaned up at the lower reserve ratio?

ASSETS		LIABILITIES
Reserves		Demand Deposits $20 million
Required	$ 2 million	
Excess	0	
Loans	$18 million	

The bank holds no excess reserves, and if the reserve ratio rose to 20 percent it would have to increase its reserves to $4 million. The bank may have to take out a short-term loan from the Fed to meet its immediate need for reserves, but eventually it will have to convert some of its other assets (primarily loans) to reserves, and this takes money out of the demand-deposit credit flow.

With a reserve ratio of 20 percent of demand deposits, the bank is loaned up and can't create any demand-deposit money by extending loans from excess reserves. If the reserve ratio were lowered to 10 percent of demand deposits, however, the bank would have excess reserves. With the lower reserve ratio and reduced required reserves, the bank could create demand deposit money by loaning out its excess reserves.

All of this leads to two obvious conclusions.

- *Raising the reserve ratio* reduces the maximum amount of money that can be generated from bank reserves.

- *Lowering the reserve ratio* increases the maximum amount of money that can be generated from bank reserves.

The reserve ratio is a powerful tool with only limited usefulness as a monetary policy tool. Seemingly small changes in the reserve ratio can have dramatic, but not always accurately predictable, effects on the money supply. If banks desire to hold excess reserves or the public desires to hold some of the additional money as currency, the exact effect of changing the reserve ratio on the money supply is hard to predict.

The Fed is limited by law to reserve ratios between 7 percent and 22 percent of demand deposits, and the reserve ratio has been fairly stable around 15 percent in recent years, although the Fed can and does change it by a point or less from time to time. The reserve ratio is most useful for large changes in the money supply, and usually changes in the reserve ratio are accompanied by other monetary policies to soften its short-run impact.

Open Market Operations. The Fed is a large buyer and seller of government securities in the open market.

- **Open market operations** are the purchases and sales of government securities by the Federal Reserve.

The Fed differs from most private buyers and sellers of securities in two important respects. First, the Fed's purchases and sales are large enough to affect the market prices of securities. Secondly, unlike private traders, the Fed's main objective in open market operations isn't to earn the highest possible return on a portfolio of financial securities, but to change the money supply and the interest rate. Open market operations are the most important and widely used monetary policy tools.

- The Fed *buys securities* in the open market to *increase the money supply* and *lower interest rates*.

The sale of the securities to the Fed increases member banks' reserves, and reduces their holdings of government securities.

Member Banks		
ASSETS		LIABILITIES
Government Securities	−$100 million	No Change
Reserves	+$100 million	

The purchase of government securities increases the Fed's holdings of government securities and increases member bank deposits.

Federal Reserve		
ASSETS		LIABILITIES
Government Securities	+$100 million	Member Bank Deposits	+$100 million

If the securities had been sold by households and firms, an extra step is involved. The Fed acquires $100 million in government securities, and pays the sellers by check. As the households and firms deposit their proceeds in commercial banks, bank reserves increase. If the households and firms purchase goods and services with the proceeds from the government securities and the sellers of these goods and services deposit the funds in their demand deposits, this also increases the banks' demand deposits and reserves.

- The Fed *sells securities* in the open market to *reduce the money supply* and *raise interest rates.*

When the Fed sells government securities, its holdings of government securities decline, and member bank deposits (bank reserves) decline as the banks purchase the securities. A sale of $100 million in government securities by the Fed to commercial banks increases the banks' holdings of government securities by $100 million, and reduces bank reserves (which are used to pay for the securities) by $100 million.

Member Banks

ASSETS		LIABILITIES
Government Securities	+$100 million	No Change
Reserves	−$100 million	

The sale of the securities reduces the Fed's holdings of government securities and member bank deposits (reserves) by $100 million.

Federal Reserve

ASSETS		LIABILITIES	
Government Securities	−$100 million	Member Bank Deposits	−$100 million

Again, the effect is similar if the government securities are purchased by households and firms. If the households and firms write checks to pay for the securities, demand deposits in commercial banks and the level of bank reserves fall.

Open Market Operations and Securities Prices.   In addition to their effects on interest rates through changing the supply of money, the Fed's open-market operations affect interest rates and aggregate demand through their effects on the prices of securities.

The size of the Fed's open-market purchases and sales is great enough to affect the prices of securities, and the effective interest rate on a security is determined by its price. For example, a government bond that sells for $20,000 and pays $2000 per year in interest has an effective interest rate or yield of 10 percent per year ($2000 per year/$20,000). If the price of the bond fell to $16,000, the effective interest rate or yield would increase to 12.5 percent per year ($2000 per year/$16,000). If the price of the bond rose from $20,000 to $25,000, the effective interest rate would fall from 10 percent per year to 8 percent per year ($2000 per year/$25,000). Such changes may stimulate aggregate demand in two ways. First, higher securities prices mean lower interest rates, and lower interest rates stimulate investment spending and some forms of consumer spending. Also, the higher securities prices increase the wealth of the holders of the securities. Some of the additional wealth of securities owners may lead to increased spending, and this also stimu-

Figure 7 Effects of the Fed's Open Market Operations

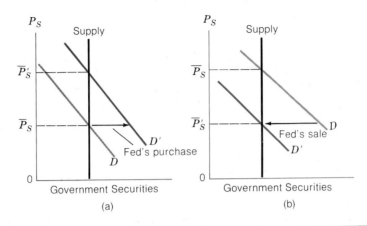

(a)   (b)

lates aggregate demand. The effects of Fed purchases of government securities are illustrated in Figure 7a.

When the Fed sells government securities on the open market, this tends to dampen aggregate demand. In Figure 7b, the sale of government securities by the Fed lowers the price of securities from $\overline{P}_S$ to $\overline{P}_S'$. Lower securities prices dampen aggregate demand and economic activity by raising effective interest rates (which discourages investment and some consumer spending), and by reducing the wealth of securities owners.

The Discount Rate. Federal Reserve Banks extend loans to member commercial banks to meet short-term needs for funds, and charges interest on these loans. The **discount rate** is the interest rate which the Fed charges on loans to commercial banks.

Commercial banks are profit-seeking institutions. If they have to pay more for the short-term funds they borrow from the Fed, they will pass on this higher cost to their customers as higher interest rates on the loans they extend. Also, higher discount rates discourage the commercial banks from borrowing short-term funds from the Fed to cover reserves, and this reduces the availability of credit in the economy. In short, raising the discount rate tends to dampen aggregate demand and economic activity.

Reducing the discount rate tends to stimulate aggregate demand and economic activity. Lower discount rates may encourage commercial banks to lower interest rates on loans extended to their customers. Also, commercial banks may be encouraged to extend more loans and cover short-term reserve requirements with funds borrowed by the Fed if the discount rate and therefore the cost of short-term funds from the Fed is low. These effects of a lower discount rate tend to stimulate aggregate demand.

Direct Controls.   The Fed sets maximum interest rates that commercial banks can pay on savings and time deposits—"the highest interest rates allowed by law." Interest rates on time deposits affect households' allocation of income between consumption and saving and firms' investment decisions. High interest rates on time deposits tend to encourage saving and discourage consumption and investment.

During World War II, the Fed had extensive direct controls over consumer credit, most of which were removed after the War. The Fed retained one important direct control over credit—*margin requirements* on purchases of stocks and other securities. The *margin requirement* is the percentage of a securities purchases that must be paid in cash to the broker. For example, a margin requirement of 50 percent means that a buyer of common stock would have to pay at least half of the amount of the purchase in cash at the time of the purchase.

Low margin requirements and large stock purchases on credit were among the causes of the financial panic and collapse of the stock market in 1929. Many people bought common stocks on very low margins, expecting the stocks to appreciate and to make large returns on their margins. When stock prices fell, the margins disappeared. Brokers sold stocks as losses wiped out the margins, and this drove stock prices even lower. To avoid a repeat performance of October 1929, the Fed has established fairly high margin requirements on most securities purchases.

The Fed's goal in manipulating the money supply is to regulate interest rates and aggregate demand to maintain low levels of unemployment, stabilize aggregate output, and dampen inflationary pressures. Whether or not monetary policies can accomplish these objectives is a central issue among economists, and this issue is examined in some detail in the next chapter.

Summary

1. If changes in the money supply cause changes in the interest rate, then they will also cause changes in the levels of investment and aggregate output.
2. The **quantity theory of money** states the relationships among the money supply, the velocity of money, the price level, and real GNP.
3. The **velocity of money** is the rate at which money "turns over" or changes hands during the year. It is determined by institutional arrangements, economic conditions, expectations, and the preference for money over other assets. Changes in velocity affect the relationship between changes in the money supply and changes in prices.
4. **Commercial banks** can create demand-deposit money because they operate with **fractional reserves,** holding only a fraction of their demand deposits as **required reserves.** The proportion of demand deposits that must be held as required reserves is the **reserve ratio.**
5. The banking system can *create* money as banks extend loans from their excess reserves and these loaned funds are redeposited as demand deposits in the system.

6. The **banking multiplier** is the maximum amount of demand-deposit money that can be generated from each dollar of bank reserves, or the maximum change in demand deposit money from each dollar's change in bank reserves. The banking multiplier varies inversely with the reserve ratio.

7. The exact size of the banking multiplier is hard to predict accurately because of numerous "leaks" out of the demand-deposit credit flow that creates money.

8. **Central banks** or their equivalent serve as the government's bank, the banks' bank, and as the monetary authority. The United States hasn't had a true central bank since 1836. The functions of a central bank are performed by the **Federal Reserve System,** which was established in 1913.

9. The Fed could alter the supply of money by changing the banks' reserve ratio, but this is a powerful and unpredictable tool. The Fed's most important means of regulating the money supply and interest rates is through **open-market operations.** The Fed also regulates interest rates by setting the discount rate on its short-term loans to member banks and to a lesser extent through its authority to set maximum interest rates on savings and time deposits.

Concepts for Review			
crude quantity theory	required reserve	central bank
modern quantity theory	excess reserve	Federal Reserve System
Hume's Fable	asset	Board of Governors
velocity of money	liability	Federal Open Market
equation of exchange	net worth	Committee
commercial bank	banking multiplier	open market operations
fractional reserve banking	reserve ratio	discount rate

Questions

1. What is the essential difference between the crude and modern versions of the quantity theory of money? Explain, and show that the crude quantity theory is a special case of the modern quantity theory.

2. What is the velocity of money? What determines velocity, and why is it important economically?

3. Following the November Revolution in 1917, the Soviet Union experienced serious economic problems. World War I had been an economic disaster, absenteeism among factory workers was very high, many people left the cities because of social and economic chaos, and productivity fell dramatically. In 1918, the government enacted legislation that authorized the printing of as many paper rubles as necessary. The currency in circulation increased from about 22 billion rubles in 1917 to about 61 billion by the end of 1918.
   Using the quantity theory of money and the equation of exchange, what would you predict as the most likely effect of this increase in the money supply?

4. The "classical" economists' concern with the supply of money was almost exclusively a concern with the relationship between the money

supply and the price level. In fact, they generally argued that in the long run, changes in the money supply would affect only prices, and not real output.

How does classical macroeconomics, presented in earlier chapters, lead to this conclusion? Use the quantity theory and the equation of exchange in explaining your answer.

5. If you wrote a check for the full amount of your checking account balance, could your bank cash the check for you immediately? If all checking-account depositors wrote checks for the full amount of their checking account balances, could the banking system cash their checks for them immediately? Explain your answers.

6. When Franklin D. Roosevelt assumed the office of President in 1933, one of his first acts was to declare a "bank holiday" and close the banks.

Based on your understanding of banking and your knowledge of economic conditions in 1933, explain the circumstances that made the holiday necessary.

7. Explain the basic functions of central banks. Why are central banks important economically?

8. When the Federal Reserve increases the money supply, does it simply order the Treasury to print more currency? Explain how the Fed can alter the money supply, and the effectiveness of its basic monetary tools.

9. What could you envision as possible economic consequences of dismantling the Federal Reserve System and decentralizing control over the money supply?

10. Suppose that the Federal Reserve sells $500 million worth of government securities on the open market.
    a. What would be the Fed's objective in making the sale?
    b. Explain how the sale would achieve the Fed's objective.
    c. Could the Fed achieve the same objective by any other means?

Problems

1. Suppose that an additional $10 million is deposited by millionaire-philanthropist Bruce Wayne in his checking account with the Gotham City Bank & Trust Co.
    a. Show and explain the effect on the bank's assets and its liabilities.
    b. The Gotham City Bank & Trust Co. is a member of a system of commercial banks, each of which holds 25 percent of its reserves as required reserves. What is the maximum change in demand deposit money that the banking system could generate from the additional $10 million deposited in the Gotham City Bank & Trust? Show the effect through 3 "generations" of banks in the system.
    c. What conditions are necessary for the change in demand deposit money to reach the maximum you identified in part b? Is it likely that the maximum would be reached? Explain carefully.

12

Monetary Policy: Mechanics, Problems, and Issues

Preview: Discretionary monetary policies are changes in the money supply and interest rates aimed at minimizing unemployment and inflation. Like fiscal policies, monetary policies are a form of **demand management**, whose usefulness as a tool in controlling the economy has been a subject of considerable controversy in recent years. In this chapter, we'll explore the basic mechanics of monetary policy and the controversies surrounding its use as a tool for controlling the economy.

For many years, a battle raged over the question of the effectiveness of discretionary monetary policies in achieving the objectives of full employment, stable prices, and stability. *Keynesians*, who emphasized the importance of fiscal policies, were portrayed as arguing that "money doesn't matter" (or "doesn't matter much"). *Monetarists*, who emphasized the importance of monetary policy, found themselves associated with arguments ranging from "money matters" to "money is all that matters."

Today, fortunately, there is little disagreement that money matters. However, the issue of the effectiveness and necessity of *discretionary* monetary and fiscal policies remains unsettled.

- **Discretionary monetary policies** alter the supply of money and the interest rate with the goal of altering aggregate demand, real GNP, employment, and inflation.

Discretionary Monetary Policy: The Mechanics

As you will recall from the last chapter, changes in the money supply affect aggregate demand, real GNP, and the strength of inflationary pressure primarily via their effects on interest rates.

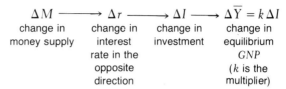

$$\Delta M \longrightarrow \Delta r \longrightarrow \Delta I \longrightarrow \Delta \overline{Y} = k\,\Delta I$$

| change in money supply | change in interest rate in the opposite direction | change in investment | change in equilibrium GNP (k is the multiplier) |

The object of discretionary monetary policies is to change the money supply in a way that brings equilibrium real GNP to its full employment level (i.e., to achieve $\overline{Y} = Y^*$).

Unemployment and Expansionary Monetary Policy

If the economy experiences unemployment as a result of inadequate aggregate demand, monetary policies will seek to stimulate aggregate demand, and monetary authorities will pursue *expansionary monetary policies*.

- **Expansionary monetary policies** are deliberate increases in the money supply aimed at stimulating aggregate demand and relieving unemployment.

Increasing the money supply from M to M' in Figure 1a lowers the interest rate from $\bar{r}$ to $\bar{r}'$. In Figure 1b, the lower interest rate causes investment to increase to $\overline{I}'$, where the marginal efficiency of invest-

Figure 1 Effects of Expansionary Monetary Policy

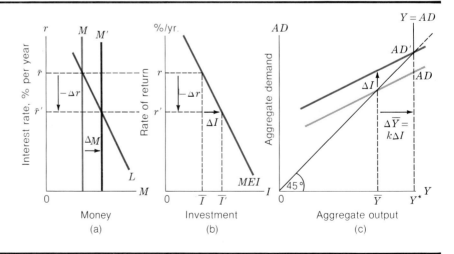

ment (MEI) equals the lower interest rate. The increased investment, of course, raises aggregate demand (AD) in Figure 1c, narrowing or closing the *deflationary gap* and bringing GNP closer to the full-employment GNP.

$$+ \Delta M \longrightarrow - \Delta r \;-\!- \; + \Delta I \longrightarrow + \Delta \overline{Y} = k\,\Delta I$$

Inflation and Restrictive Monetary Policy

If the problem facing the monetary authorities is inflationary pressure as a result of excess aggregate demand, *restrictive monetary policies* may dampen aggregate demand and the inflationary pressure.

- **Restrictive monetary policies** are deliberate decreases in the money supply aimed at lowering aggregate demand and relieving inflationary pressures.

Reducing the money supply from M to M' in Figure 2a raises the interest rate from $\bar{r}$ to $\bar{r}'$. In Figure 2b, the higher interest rate reduces investment from $\bar{I}$ to $\bar{I}'$, where $MEI = \bar{r}'$. Finally, in Figure 2c, the lower level of investment lowers aggregate demand to AD', reducing equilibrium GNP and closing the *inflationary gap*.

$$- \Delta M \longrightarrow + \Delta r \longrightarrow - \Delta I \longrightarrow - \Delta \overline{Y} = k\,\Delta I$$

Of course, if the real world operated as neatly as the models, there wouldn't be any dispute over the effectiveness and necessity of discretionary monetary policies. Unfortunately, the real world is considerably "messier."

Figure 2 Effects of Restrictive Monetary Policy

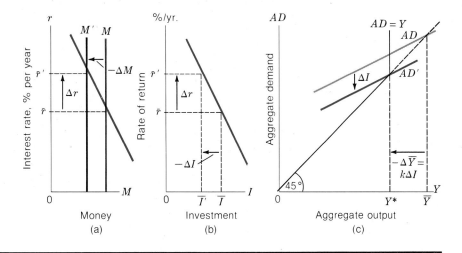

Close-up

Political Business Cycles?

Economic conditions play an important part in the political fortunes of incumbent presidents seeking re-election. Professor Ray Fair of Yale University has found that incumbents have traditionally had a much greater chance of re-election if aggregate output and employment are rising during the election year.[1] If this is in fact the case, an incumbent president seeking re-election would do well to pursue monetary and fiscal policies that would ensure the maximum rate of expansion during the election year. One way to do this would be to apply monetary and fiscal restraint to put the economy into a contraction in the year before the election year, and then pursue expansionary monetary and fiscal policies during the election year. This would generate what some observers have called *political business cycles*—fluctuations in economic activity that can be explained by the domination of political concerns of incumbents over other goals of discretionary monetary and fiscal policy (such as price stability).

There are a number of cases consistent with the political-business-cycle scenario. In 1972, for example, the money supply grew at a rapid rate—over 8 percent. In 1972, of course, Richard Nixon was also seeking re-election. The Chairman of the Board of Governors of the Federal Reserve, and the dominant voice in monetary policy at the time, was Arthur Burns. Burns and Nixon were very close ideologically and members of the same party. This combination of events, of course, doesn't necessarily mean that Burns' motives in monetary policy were to aid the re-election efforts of Nixon, but policy certainly was consistent with this aim.[2]

It is probably a bit of an exaggeration to predict that incumbents will invariably follow expansionary monetary and fiscal policies in election years, even at the expense of excessive inflation, or that such policies would be the most important factor affecting the outcome of the election. President Ford opposed many expansionary policies in 1975 and 1976, and the economic expansion in 1976 didn't result in his election. Many factors besides economic growth affect the outcomes of elections—ideology, candidates' personalities, foreign policy issues, and other political issues (such as President Ford's pardon of Richard Nixon). Also, after several inflationary expansions to gain voter support, excessive inflation may well become the dominant issue for voters—this clearly was the case by mid-1979 as the Carter administration geared up for the 1980 election.

---

1. Ray C. Fair, "Growth Rates Predict November Winners," *New York Times*, January 25, 1976.
2. On the 1972 election, see Carol J. Loomis, "The New Questions About the U.S. Economy," *Fortune*, Vol. 89, No. 1 (January 1974), pp. 69–73ff.

Choice of Objectives

The ultimate objective of discretionary monetary policy is to minimize unemployment and inflationary pressure. In pursuit of this goal, the

Federal Reserve has to shoot at two "targets" in its policy decisions—a **money supply growth target** and an **interest rate target**. Once it has determined the proper direction for monetary policy, the Fed establishes a targeted range for changes in the money supply and for the interest rate.

In some cases, the monetary and interest rate targets are competing goals. The Fed may have to sacrifice its targeted growth of the money supply to keep the interest rate in the desired range, or it may have to sacrifice its interest rate objective to keep changes in the money supply within the targeted range. When push comes to shove, the Fed appears more willing to sacrifice the money supply objective than the interest rate objective, and this willingness can have some serious consequences.

The basic economic logic behind reducing instability of interest rates is sound and easy to follow. Unstable interest rates lead to unstable investment, aggregate demand, and GNP, which in turn lead to unstable expectations and further instability of aggregate demand. However, if economic conditions dictate a change in the interest rate, trying to keep it from changing by adjusting the money supply can create problems. Suppose that the economy is experiencing rising aggregate demand and is approaching full employment. Since income is increasing, money demand will also be increasing, and interest rates will tend to rise (perhaps rather sharply). The Federal Reserve, concerned about the rising interest rates, may increase the money supply, thus intensifying inflationary pressures. If the interest rate had been allowed to rise, the increase in aggregate demand would have been dampened as the economy moved toward full employment.

Consider the opposite case. A sharp economic downturn reduces the level of investment and the demand for money. The decline in the demand for money reduces interest rates. If the Fed tries to stabilize interest rates, it will have to reduce the money supply. However, reducing the money supply in a recession will tend to amplify the deflationary forces—probably lengthening and deepening the recession. The proper course of action would be to let interest rates fall, which would dampen the decline in aggregate demand.

Close-up

The "Credit Crunch" of 1966

The period between 1960 and 1965 was one of steady and strong economic recovery and expansion. In 1964, demand was stimulated further by the enactment of a major cut in federal income taxes, and in mid-1965 the escalation of the Vietnam War caused still greater increases in aggregate demand. The economic expansion increased the public and private demand for funds in credit markets, and interest rates began to rise.

The Federal Reserve, concerned about the prospects of high interest rates, moved in mid-1965 to increase the money supply more rapidly to accommodate the increased demand for funds. Since the increase in the money supply added to the inflationary pressures building in the economy, the Fed moved in 1966 to reduce inflationary pressures by reversing their expansionary monetary policies. Between the second and third quarters of 1966, M_1 fell at an annual rate of 0.7 percent after four consecutive quarters in which M_1 had increased at annual rates in excess of 4.5 percent.

The sharp reversal of monetary policy created severe shortages of loanable funds in money markets—or, as it was called at the time, a severe **credit crunch**. The crunch undoubtedly would have been less severe had the Fed simply allowed interest rates to rise and restrained the growth of the money supply more gradually in 1965.

The Effectiveness of Monetary Policy

The effectiveness of monetary policy is a two-part question. First, there is the question of the strength of the effects of monetary policies on aggregate demand, output, employment, and prices. The second question is the practical usefulness of monetary policy as a means of regulating demand. Obviously, monetary policy wouldn't be very effective if it had very weak effects on aggregate demand. Nor would it be very useful if its effects on aggregate demand were erratic and unpredictable.

Money and Depression: The Liquidity Trap

In the depths of an economic disaster of the magnitude of the Great Depression of the 1930s, monetary policies alone may not be very effective in stimulating aggregate demand. In an extreme situation, called a *liquidity trap*, changing the money supply won't stimulate aggregate demand at all.

- A **liquidity trap** is a situation in which increasing the money supply *only* increases the amount of money held by households and firms and does not cause the interest rate to fall.

Bleak and uncertain economic expectations encourage firms, households, and financial institutions to be as liquid as possible—i.e., to hold money for precautionary and speculative reasons. In Figure 3, the money supply is increased from M to M' in an attempt to stimulate demand and output. However, worsening expectations increase the precautionary and speculative demands for money, shifting the money demand curve from L to L' in Figure 3. Instead of spending the money supplied, individuals simply hold the additional money as precautionary and speculative balances to provide for needs in a grim economic future and to minimize the risk of loss. As a result, the

Figure 3 Liquidity Trap

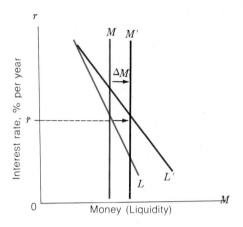

interest rate doesn't change and the increase in the money supply cannot stimulate aggregate demand via higher levels of investment.

The liquidity trap has been presented as a key concept in Keynesian economics and in the Keynesian explanation of the Great Depression. In fact, Keynes himself recognized only the theoretical possibility of liquidity traps and argued that liquidity traps probably never had been observed. The Great Depression is the only economic catastrophe in this century in which a liquidity trap might have been observed, but the money supply in fact *fell* during the worst years of the Depression.

Economists in the classical and monetarist tradition deny even the theoretical possibility of liquidity traps—except at interest rates approaching zero. The classical argument goes all the way back to Adam Smith's assertion that "A man must be perfectly crazy who, where there is tolerable security, does not employ all the stock which he commands."[1] This implies that people would put their money into interest-bearing assets as long as these assets earn any interest at all.

Weak Effects of Monetary Policy

Short of severe depressions and the highly unlikely liquidity trap situations, there are conditions in which monetary policy alone would have relatively weak effects on aggregate demand, real GNP, and employment. This situation is likely to occur when aggregate demand is low and GNP is considerably below the full employment level—as in Figure 4.

In Figure 4a, the low level of GNP generates a low transactions demand for money, and the interest rate ($\bar{r}$) is relatively low. Increasing

1. Adam Smith, *An Inquiry into the Nature and Causes of the Wealth of Nations*, Book II, Chapter 1.

Figure 4 Weak Effects of Monetary Policy

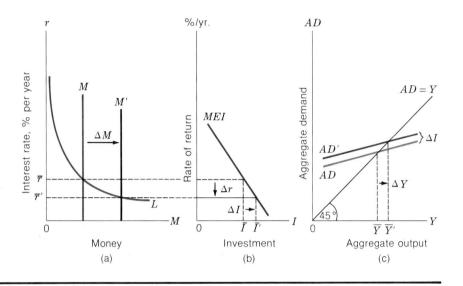

the money supply to M' lowers the interest rate to $\bar{r}'$, a small reduction from a substantial increase in the money supply. The small drop in the interest rate, coupled with the low response of investment to changes in the interest rate in Figure 4b, results in a small increase in investment from $\bar{I}$ to $\bar{I}'$. Thus, in Figure 4c, the large initial increase in the money supply has yielded a relatively small increase in equilibrium GNP from $\bar{Y}$ to $\bar{Y}'$.

In periods of low output and high unemployment, as portrayed in Figure 4, the Fed's other monetary policy tools may not be very effective either. The discount rate on loans from the Fed to commercial banks could be lowered, but the Fed can't force the banks to extend more loans at lower interest rates. In a severe recession, there may not be many opportunities to make loans at the banks' minimum acceptable interest rate, and banks won't lower the interest rate if the lower rates don't compensate them for the loss of liquidity.

The effectiveness of monetary policy in stimulating recovery from a recession has thus been described as trying to "push a string." Though the phrase is fairly descriptive of the problem, it shouldn't be interpreted as meaning that "money doesn't matter," but rather that monetary policy *alone* may not be very effective in these circumstances.

Strong Effects of Monetary Policy Not surprisingly, the conditions in which monetary policies are likely to have strong effects on aggregate demand are basically the opposite of the conditions in which the effects are weak. High aggregate output, high transactions demand for money, a steep demand curve for money, a relatively flat *MEI* curve, and a strong expenditure multiplier will contribute to strong effects of monetary policy on aggregate demand.

In Figure 5a, the transactions demand for money is high relative to the supply of money, resulting in a high initial interest rate $(\bar{r})$ in the portion of the money demand curve (L) where the interest rate is most sensitive to changes in the money supply. A relatively small increase in the money supply from M to M' causes a substantial decline in the interest rate in Figure 5a, leading to a large increase in investment in Figure 5b. The increase in investment causes a large increase in equilibrium GNP from $\bar{Y}$ to $\bar{Y}'$ in Figure 5c as a result of the initial small increase in the money supply in Figure 5a.

Thus, the impact of monetary policies on aggregate demand, GNP, employment, and inflationary pressures varies with economic conditions. As a general rule, monetary policies have the weakest effects in periods in which aggregate demand, GNP, and initial interest rates are low; and the strongest effects when aggregate demand, GNP, and initial interest rates are high.

Another lesson is that discretionary monetary policies are more useful for some problems than others. Pushing the string to stimulate recovery from a deep recession by monetary expansion alone will be difficult. However, pulling on a string is more effective, and monetary restraint is a strong tool for dampening inflationary pressures caused by excess demand.

Figure 5 Strong Effects of Monetary Policy

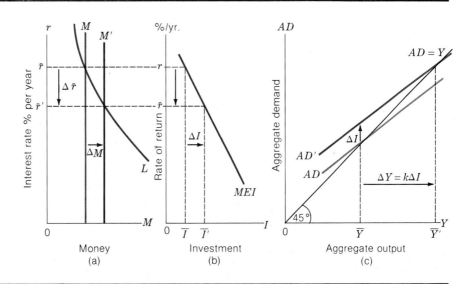

Information Problems

"The best laid schemes o' mice and men," wrote the Scottish poet Robert Burns, "gang aft agley" ("often go awry"). The same thing could be said of many of the best laid schemes of the Federal Reserve. One reason that many well-designed monetary policies "gang aft agley" is the inadequacy of information.

What pieces of information would be required to achieve minimum unemployment and inflationary pressures via monetary policies? First, a reasonably good estimate of the demand curve for money is needed to predict the effects of changes in the money supply on the interest rate. Policies should be based on the best empirical estimates possible, but even the best estimates may not be accurate.

In Figure 6a, suppose that the estimated money demand curve is L_e, but that actual money demand is represented by the darker curve L_a. The interest rate will be more sensitive to changes in the money supply than the estimate would predict. If the Fed increased the money supply from M to M' to stimulate aggregate demand, it would expect the interest rate to fall from $\bar{r}$ to $\bar{r}'$ in Figure 6a. However, such an increase in the money supply would actually cause the interest rate to fall from $\bar{r}$ to $\bar{r}''$, stimulating investment and aggregate demand more than the Fed's estimate. This overstimulus could lead to inflationary pressure, even if all of the other information required is 100% accurate (which it isn't).

What if the Fed tries to dampen aggregate demand and *underestimates* the sensitivity of the interest rate to changes in the money supply? In Figure 6b, the estimated money demand curve is L_e and actual

Figure 6   Information Problems: Estimating Money Demand

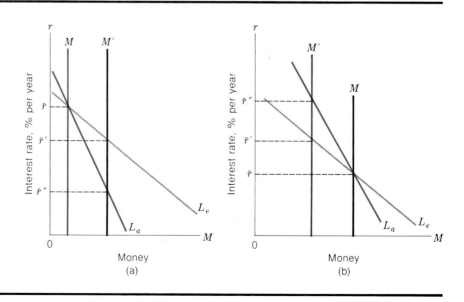

Money
(a)

Money
(b)

money demand is represented by L_a. If the Fed cuts the money supply from M to M', expecting the interest rate to rise from $\bar{r}$ to $\bar{r}'$, the interest rate would actually increase to $\bar{r}''$. In this case, the error in estimated money demand would depress investment and aggregate demand more than predicted, resulting in greater unemployment than expected.

Money demand is only one piece of the puzzle that monetary authorities must solve. The Fed also needs a good estimate of the responsiveness of investment changes in the interest rate, or the marginal efficiency of investment (MEI). In Figure 7, the estimated marginal efficiency of investment function is MEI_e, and the actual marginal efficiency of investment function is MEI_a. In this case the level of investment is more responsive to changes in the interest rate than the estimate suggests. If the Fed's actions lower the interest rate from $\bar{r}$ to $\bar{r}'$, in Figure 7, the expected increase in investment would be from $\bar{I}$ to $\bar{I}'$. However, because of the error in the estimated MEI curve, the level of investment actually increases to $\bar{I}''$—more than predicted and possibly enough more to create unacceptable inflationary pressure. Similarly, if the Fed tries to dampen inflationary pressure by increasing interest rates, the decline in investment would be greater than predicted, possibly resulting in an unacceptable rise in unemployment.

Even if the Fed knew the money demand and marginal efficiency of investment functions fairly accurately, there could be problems. To estimate the increase in aggregate demand that would yield an ac-

Figure 7 Information Problems: Estimating the Responsiveness of Investment

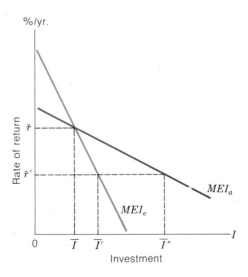

ceptably low unemployment without excessive inflationary pressure or dampen inflationary pressure without creating an unacceptable unemployment rate, the Fed must have a good estimate of the multiplier effect of a change in investment on equilibrium GNP.

Expectations

To make matters worse, the money demand and *MEI* curves have a nasty habit of shifting in response to changes in expectations, making even the best estimates from previous data inaccurate. Suppose that the estimated money demand curve (*L*) in Figure 8 is an accurate estimate based on data from past years. The Fed increases the money supply from *M* to *M'*, expecting to lower the interest rate from $\bar{r}$ to $\bar{r}'$ and stimulate investment and aggregate demand. But if economic expectations have worsened, demand for precautionary and speculative balances will have increased, shifting the money demand curve to *L'*. Increasing the money supply to *M'* thus causes a smaller reduction of the interest rate (to $\bar{r}''$) than expected.

Expectations also affect the expected rate of return on investments and therefore the *MEI* curve. Suppose that monetary authorities increase the money supply and lower the interest rate from $\bar{r}$ to $\bar{r}'$, expecting that investment will rise to $\bar{I}'$ in Figure 9. If worsening expectations have shifted *MEI* leftward to *MEI'*, the increase in investment will be much smaller than expected.

Changes in expectations are hard to predict, and because they affect the responsiveness of interest rates and investment to changes in the

Figure 8 Effects of Expectations on Money Demand

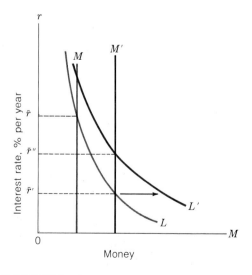

Figure 9 Effects of Expectations on Investment Decisions

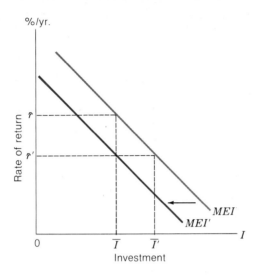

supply of money, unstable expectations increase the chance that monetary authorities will make mistakes. Frequent mistakes in monetary policy, in turn, make expectations still less stable.

Leads and Lags   Imagine that you own an extremely powerful car that can reach speeds of over 200 miles per hour. The car has a strange quirk, however: when you step on the accelerator, the car will speed up, but you can't be sure when or how much. If you let up on the accelerator and apply the brake, the car will slow down, but you can't be sure when. Furthermore, the time lags between your actions and the car's reactions aren't always the same. How should you drive such a machine? If you drove it at all, you should do so *very* cautiously. In fact, many would urge you not to drive it at all.

What does all of this have to do with monetary policy? Like the car, money and monetary policy are powerful machines. Also like the car, there is generally some lag between a change in monetary policy and the full effect of this change. Finally, the lags between the policy and its full effect aren't always the same, and the same acceleration or braking of monetary policy won't always have the same ultimate effect. Monetary policy is thus a machine to be operated with some caution. Frequent rapid acceleration, deceleration, and braking can lead to serious accidents.

When aggregate demand and economic activity change, monetary authorities don't know about it immediately. The information doesn't reach the authorities until the relevant data has been compiled and published. This **data lag** is usually about two months—inflationary pressures that develop in January become apparent when January data becomes available in late February or early March.

Authorities generally don't act on the basis of a one-month change in economic conditions, but wait to see if there is a trend. If the data show very slow growth or a decline in aggregate output for January, for example, policymakers will probably wait for February and maybe March data to see if the economy is truly in a recession. In short, there is a **recognition lag** between the publication of data and the recognition of a need for discretionary policies. This lag may be on the order of two to three months.

For fiscal policies, there are significant **decision lags** and **action lags** because it takes time for Congress and the President to decide upon, enact, and implement legislation and appropriate spending and tax policies. With monetary policies, these particular elements of the **inside lag** are virtually nonexistent. The Open Market Committee and the Board of Governors can make policy decisions much more quickly than the Congress and the President. Once the Fed decides on a change in monetary policy, it can act almost immediately.

The inside lag thus tends to be much shorter for monetary policy than it was for fiscal policy. Unfortunately, the same cannot be said for the **outside** or **effectiveness lag**. The impact of fiscal policy on aggregate output is quite direct: an increase in government spending represents (in theory) a direct increase in aggregate demand which will lead directly to an increase in output. The effects of monetary policy, on the other hand, are indirect: a change in the money supply changes the interest rate, which changes the level of investment, which changes aggregate demand, which changes output. The outside lag between the implementation of a change in monetary policy and its full economic impact may be as long as six to ten months.

If all of these lags were regular, predictable, and short, they wouldn't pose a serious problem for discretionary monetary policy. However, if they are long, variable in length, and unpredictable, the problems of effective discretionary policy are much more serious. Adding the lags together, there may be a lag of a year or more between the time that economic conditions change and the full effects of corrective policies are felt. Many other changes can occur in the course of a year, and by the time that the full effects of a change in policy are felt, they may worsen a new problem that has arisen in the meantime.

Relationship Between Monetary and Fiscal Policies

Monetary and fiscal policies are under the jurisdiction of separate authorities—monetary policy under the Federal Reserve and fiscal policy under the President and Congress. However, the two are not independent economically. The economic effects of discretionary fiscal policies depend heavily—some argue exclusively—on supportive monetary policies. How are monetary and fiscal policy related? Can one work without the other?

Unsupported
Fiscal Expansion

Suppose that the President and Congress embark on a course of expansionary fiscal policy—increasing government spending or cutting taxes—but the Fed doesn't go along. To stimulate aggregate demand, the government runs or increases a deficit in the Federal budget, and has to increase borrowing to finance the deficit.

To see how deficits and government borrowing affect interest rates and aggregate demand, we have to take a look at the market for **loanable funds**. Loanable funds are funds available for loans to borrowers. The price of loanable funds is the interest rate that has to be paid for the use of the funds.

As the interest rate rises, households and businesses reduce their holdings of money balances and convert more of their money balances into assets that earn interest. Thus, more loanable funds become available as the interest rate rises, so there is a direct relationship between the interest rate and the quantity of loanable funds supplied along S_{LF} in Figure 10a. But a rise in the interest rate also represents an increase in the price of loanable funds, so the quantity of loanable funds demanded will fall along D_{LF}. The loanable funds market is in equilibrium when the quantity of loanable funds demanded equals the quantity supplied—i.e., at the equilibrium interest rate ($\bar{r}$) in Figure 10a.

Figure 10 Unsupported Fiscal Expansion

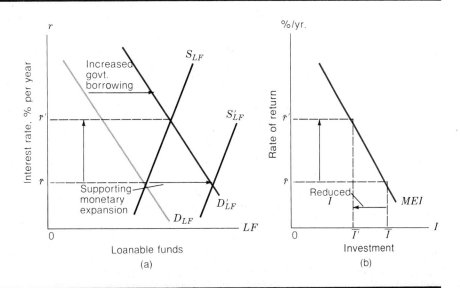

If the government increases its borrowing to finance a larger deficit due to expansionary fiscal policies, the demand for loanable funds increases to D_{LF}' in Figure 10a and driving the interest rate upward to $\bar{r}'$. The rising interest rate chokes off investment, as shown in Figure 10b. As the interest rate rises to $\bar{r}'$, investment falls to $\bar{I}'$, dampening aggregate demand and working against the goal of expansionary fiscal policy. In other words, some private spending is *crowded out* by the higher interest rates that followed the fiscal expansion.

- **Crowding out** is the tendency of expansionary fiscal policies to reduce private investment demand by raising interest rates.

Expansionary monetary policies would increase the supply of loanable funds, shown in Figure 10b by the shift from S_{LF} to S_{LF}'. This would support the expansionary fiscal policy by reducing or offsetting the effect of government borrowing on the interest rate. By keeping the interest rate from rising, the supporting monetary policy reduces or eliminates the crowding out of private investment.

Unsupported Fiscal Restraint

Suppose that the President and Congress try to restrain inflationary pressure by reducing government spending or raising taxes. This would reduce the government deficit and government borrowing. Less government borrowing reduces the demand for loanable funds from D_{LF} to D_{LF}' in Figure 11a, causing the interest rate to fall to $\bar{r}'$. The lower interest rate encourages more investment in Figure 11b, and this at least partially offsets the dampening effect of fiscal restraint on aggregate demand.

Figure 11 Unsupported Fiscal Restraint

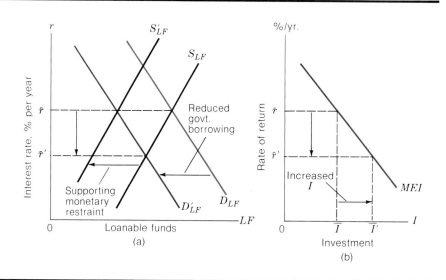

(a)

(b)

The Fed could support fiscal restraint by restrictive monetary policies. Restrictive monetary policies reduce the supply of money and the supply of loanable funds from S_{LF} to S_{LF}' in Figure 11a. By keeping the interest rate from falling, or at least reducing the decline in the interest rate, supporting monetary restriction reinforces the effect of the restrictive fiscal measures.

There is a fairly broad consensus that fiscal policy and monetary policy will be more effective if they aren't pulling in opposite directions. However, the question of the proper degree of coordination and consolidation of monetary and fiscal policy is not easy to answer.

Consolidation of Monetary and Fiscal Policy: Pro

Conflicting monetary and fiscal policies make both less effective. If the Fed were required to support fiscal policies with appropriate monetary policies, there would be no conflict between them and fiscal policy would be more effective. This would eliminate conflicts among the Fed, the Congress, and the President such as those in the 1930's, the mid-1960's, and the mid-1970's in which the Congress and the President followed expansionary fiscal policies to stimulate demand and reduce unemployment, while the Fed pursued anti-inflationary monetary policies.

Greater formal coordination of monetary and fiscal policy would make monetary policy more responsive to the electorate. The President and the Congress have the responsibility for fiscal policy and must run for re-election periodically. Therefore, fiscal policy is likely to follow as closely as possible the needs and wishes of a majority of voters. Monetary policy, on the other hand, is in control of the Board of Governors of the Fed, who are appointed (not elected) for long terms. This makes it much easier to pursue monetary policies that run counter to the views of the popular majority. If monetary policy were tied formally to fiscal policy, monetary policy would be more "democratic" in the sense of conforming more closely to majority sentiment.

Consolidation of Monetary and Fiscal Policy: Con

Consolidation of monetary and fiscal policy would indeed make fiscal policy more potent, but the negative side of this is that mistakes in monetary or fiscal policy would be magnified if the two were coordinated. If the President and Congress follow the wrong fiscal policies, the Fed would have to magnify the error by following a supportive monetary policy.

Making monetary policy more responsive to the popular will is consistent with the tradition of majority rule, but may not be a good thing economically. The long and staggered terms of the members of the Board of Governors of the Fed and the independence of the Fed give the Fed greater freedom to pursue monetary policies which may be necessary but unpopular. The long terms of members also contribute to greater consistency of monetary policy over time.

Political considerations make it difficult for Congress and the President to pursue necessary fiscal policies which may be unpopular—especially anti-inflationary policies which reduce government spending or raise taxes. To limit the flexibility of the Fed with similar political considerations would put similar pressures on monetary policy.

If frequent changes in the political climate led to frequent changes in monetary policy, monetary policy would be less consistent over time, thus contributing to instability and uncertainty. Uncertainty, especially if accompanied by pessimistic expectations, is not a favorable economic environment.

Formal consolidation of monetary and fiscal policy could have some disastrous economic effects. The President and the Congress could take a relatively casual view toward the enactment of new programs if they could be sure that the programs could be financed by expansionary monetary policy without following the politically dangerous course of raising taxes.

The question of the proper degree of consolidation of monetary and fiscal policy will not be settled overnight. The final solution ultimately depends on the strength of the positive and negative aspects of more or less coordination. If there is too little coordination and too much conflict between monetary and fiscal policy, both may be relatively ineffective. If there is too much coordination, mistakes in monetary or fiscal policy will be magnified.

Close-up

Carter and the Chairmen

Every President inherits Federal Reserve Board members who were appointed during previous administrations. When President Carter assumed office, he inherited not only Federal Reserve Board members who had been appointed by President Nixon, but one of the strongest willed Chairmen of the Federal Reserve Board, Arthur F. Burns. The politically and economically conservative Burns is a widely respected monetary economist, and a former director of the National Bureau of Economic Research. While the President followed an expansionary fiscal course in 1977 to stimulate aggregate demand and reduce unemployment, Burns not only didn't go along with supporting monetary policies, but followed his own independent course of monetary restraint to reduce inflationary pressure. When Burns' term as Chairman expired in 1978, President Carter's decision not to reappoint him surprised nobody (least of all Burns).

When President Carter appointed G. William Miller as Chairman, most observers saw this as a move that would reduce the Fed's independence from the Executive and Legislative branches of the government. Miller's scholarly credentials as a student of monetary theory and policy didn't approach those of Burns, and he was not a well-known public figure. However, Federal Reserve Board appointees have a way of surprising the President who appoints them.

Chairman Miller followed a monetary course which he described as "steady as you go," i.e., avoiding dramatic changes in the money supply. After having trouble getting Chairman Burns to go along with expansionary policies, the President had some trouble getting Chairman Miller to support fiscal restraint with discretionary restrictive monetary policies. The friction between the two was not enough, however, to prevent Miller's joining the Carter cabinet as Secretary of the Treasury in July, 1979.

The Monetarist Prescription

With a firm grounding in the economics of monetary and fiscal policy, we can take a closer look at **monetarism**, which was introduced briefly in an earlier chapter. Monetarism is a school of economic thought that emphasizes private market forces and changes in the money supply as the critical determinants of aggregate demand, output, employment, and prices. Monetarist economic arguments are based on several basic propositions.

1. In the long run, freely operating market forces will yield equilibrium real GNP at full employment.
2. In the short run, changes in the money supply can affect real GNP. The effects of fiscal policy on real GNP are weak and short-lived unless supported by monetary policy.
3. In the long run, real GNP is determined by the economy's capacity to produce, and changes in the money supply affect only prices and nominal GNP. Fiscal policy only determines the division of income and output between the public and private sectors.
4. Incomplete information and irregular lags between changes in monetary policy and the full effect of these changes make it hard to predict the size and timing of the effects of monetary policies.

These basic propositions have led the monetarists to a policy strategy that is dramatically different from the strategy followed by monetary authorities. This strategy is most fully and clearly developed and expressed in the works of the monetarists' most famous and eloquent spokesman, Milton Friedman.

No Discretionary Monetary Policy

One fundamental goal of the monetarist strategy is to strip the Fed of its discretionary power over the money supply. Friedman and many other monetarists would replace the discretionary power of the Fed with a legislative rule requiring a constant annual rate of growth of the money supply. The constant rate would be tied to the long-term trends in growth of real GNP and velocity of money.

If the money supply grew at a rate that just offset the effects of economic growth and changing velocity, it would have no long-range effect on prices. Temporary shifts of aggregate demand could cause short-term variation of prices, but inflationary or deflationary pressures wouldn't be worsened by monetary policy. Friedman has estimated that an annual rate of growth of three to five percent would accomplish this objective.

It might seem odd that Friedman and the other monetarists attach such great importance to changes in the money supply but advocate the elimination of discretionary monetary policy. Friedman's basic argument is that the history of discretionary monetary policy is one of mistakes by monetary policy authorities—"Too late and too much has been the general practice."[2]

Monetarists attribute the destabilizing effects of monetary policy to a number of causes—incompetence of monetary authorities, inadequate information, irregular and unpredictable lags between changes in policy and the effects of these changes, political pressure on monetary authorities, or some combination of these. In short, in the monetarist framework, the Fed is almost certain to make mistakes in monetary policy and the effects of these mistakes are destabilizing. Thus, the proposal to eliminate discretionary monetary policy isn't inconsistent with the view that money is the most potent economic variable.

Fiscal Policy

Most monetarists reject discretionary fiscal policies as a means of reducing unemployment and inflationary pressures. In the short run, fiscal policy has very little effect on aggregate demand, GNP, employment, or inflationary pressure unless it is supported by accommodating monetary policies—i.e., *crowding out* is virtually complete. In the long run, fiscal policy doesn't affect equilibrium real GNP because in the monetarist view of the world, real GNP tends toward the full employment level in the long run. Thus, the only effect of fiscal policy is to determine the division of aggregate output and income between the private and public sectors of the economy.

Monetarists generally advocate a minimal role for the government in the economy, so it isn't surprising that they would reject discretionary monetary and fiscal policies as a means of promoting full employment and stable prices. Friedman would limit fiscal policy to government spending projects that are determined by the community's need for them, and argues that all government spending should be financed by taxes—i.e., that the budget should be balanced. In fact, Friedman has advocated a form of "balanced-budget amendment" to the Constitution.

Employment

How would problems of unemployment be handled without discretionary monetary and fiscal policies to regulate the level of aggregate

2. Milton Friedman, "The Role of Monetary Policy," *American Economic Review*, vol. 58, no. 1 (March 1968), p. 16.

demand? Monetarists tend to accept the classical view that the economy will tend toward equilibrium at full employment in the long run if the government doesn't interfere in the free working of market forces. If the long-run level of employment is full employment without discretionary policies, the discretionary policies are unnecessary.

Of course, monetarists—like their classical predecessors—recognize the possibility of unemployment in the short run. However, if government tries to cure unemployment through discretionary fiscal and monetary policies, the long-run effect would be inflationary. Expansionary fiscal policies to reduce unemployment have to be supported by expansionary monetary policies to be effective, and expansionary monetary policies will contribute to inflation as the economy moves toward its long-run equilibrium at full employment.

Critique of the Monetarist Program

Monetarists constitute a minority of contemporary economists—an important minority, but still a minority. Most economists would accept some of the monetarists' arguments about the importance of money, but not their attachment to laissez faire and their desire to disarm monetary and fiscal policy authorities.

The monetarist program described briefly above rests on an implicit assumption that the private sector of the economy is inherently stable and that it would deal with unemployment and inflationary pressures on its own. However, as we have seen, some components of aggregate private spending—specifically, investment and consumer durables— tend to be unstable. To the extent that there is an *accelerator effect*, investment will tend to be less stable than GNP over time.

The monetarist-classical argument that the natural long-run equilibrium of the economy is only at full employment requires that prices of goods and resources be flexible—downward as well as upward. In a period of slack demand, for example, prices must move downward to clear goods markets of unsold goods and labor markets of unemployed workers. There are a number of forces in the economy, however, that contribute to price rigidity, or at least sluggish adjustments of prices, especially downward adjustments. In most basic industries, for example, there are only a few large firms, and these firms tend to avoid *price wars*. The aversion to vigorous price competition in these industries contributes to downward rigidity of prices.

Labor unions try to use their market power to get their members the maximum economic benefits possible in periods of brisk demand, and to guard against reductions in these benefits in periods of slack demand. This means that wages in organized industries where unions have bargaining power are likewise extremely slow to adjust downward.

Friedman argues that wages and prices can remain rigid downward only if they are supported by monetary policy. If wages are too high to clear the labor market, for example, monetary authorities are under pressure to pursue expansionary monetary policy to reduce full employment, thus supporting the high wages.

The monetarist view of the world is a long-run view. In the long run, market forces will deal effectively with unemployment and inflation without discretionary monetary and fiscal policies. However, as Keynes once observed, "In the long run, we all are dead." The monetarist program would eliminate some important policy tools to deal with short-run problems of unemployment and inflation.

The Monetarist Controversy: Who's Right?

The running debate between the monetarist minority and the nonmonetarist majority isn't between an entrenched intellectual establishment and a vocal but insignificant minority. The Presidency of the American Economic Association is perhaps the clearest evidence of esteem from the economics establishment. The following are excerpts from the 1968 Presidential Address of Professor Friedman and the 1976 Presidential Address of Professor Franco Modigliani of M.I.T.

> My own prescription is still that the monetary authority go all the way in avoiding swings in monetary policy by adopting publicly the policy of achieving a steady rate of growth in a specified monetary total. . . . It would be better to have a fixed rate that would on the average produce moderate inflation or moderate deflation, provided that it was steady, than to suffer the wide and erratic perturbations we have experienced.[3]

> All I am arguing is that (i) there is no basis for the monetarists' suggestion that our postwar instability can be traced to monetary instability—our most unstable periods have coincided with periods of relative monetary stability; and (ii) stability of the money supply is not enough to give us a stable economy, precisely because there are exogenous disturbances.[4]

In the currently unsettled state of the debate, is there any reason to accept the basic monetarist or basic nonmonetarist arguments? One possible reason to choose one over the other is a basic confidence that the private sector is inherently stable (which would lean one toward monetarism) or that the private sector is inherently unstable (which would lean one toward nonmonetarist activism in monetary and fiscal policy). Similarly, the choice between the monetarists' laissez-faire prescription and discretionary monetary and fiscal policies depends on one's confidence in the ability of monetary and fiscal authorities to gather and evaluate all of the necessary information and take the appropriate actions to deal effectively with unemployment and inflation.

A second basis for choosing monetarism or nonmonetarist activism is more political, ideological, and normative than analytical. If one feels that there are unmet social needs that can be dealt with effec-

---

3. Milton Friedman, "The Role of Monetary Policy," *American Economic Review*: vol. 48, no. 1 (March 1968), p. 16.
4. Franco Modigliani, "The Monetarist Controversy or, Should We Forsake Stabilization Policies?" *American Economic Review*: vol. 67, no. 2 (March 1977), p. 12.

tively only through the public sector—national health insurance, improved mass transit, etc.—this suggests an active role for fiscal policy in meeting social needs as well as promoting full employment. If, on the other hand, one feels that individuals should be free to spend their incomes as they see fit, and that the ultimate test of goods and services society should have is the market test, he or she will tend more toward the monetarist view of the world. These, obviously, are very important considerations. Unfortunately, there is no positive, analytical resolution of these types of issues.

Summary

1. **Discretionary monetary policies** try to regulate aggregate demand by changing the money supply and the interest rate.
2. Monetary policy affects aggregate demand, output, employment, and the price level through its effects on interest rates and investment expenditures.
3. The Federal Reserve gears its monetary policies to two targets—a targeted rate of growth of the money supply and an interest rate target.
4. A **liquidity trap** is a situation in which changes in the money supply have no effect on the interest rate, and therefore no effect on aggregate demand, output, or employment.
5. The effectiveness of monetary policy in regulating aggregate demand and achieving unemployment and inflation goals is limited by information problems and lags between changes in monetary policy and the economic effects of these changes in policy.
6. Without supporting monetary policies, fiscal policies may be relatively ineffective in regulating aggregate demand. Unsupported fiscal policies to stimulate aggregate demand tend to raise interest rates and crowd out some private spending. Unsupported fiscal restraint will cause interest rates to fall, at least partially offsetting the effects on aggregate demand.
7. Modern monetarism emphasizes the importance of private markets and changes in the money supply as the critical determinants of aggregate output, employment, and prices. Monetarists argue for a minimal role of government demand-management policies and a constant rate of growth of the money supply as an alternative to discretionary monetary policy.

Concepts for Review

discretionary monetary policy	restrictive monetary policy	credit crunch liquidity trap
expansionary monetary policy	money supply growth target interest rate target	crowding out loanable funds monetarist program

Questions

1. Suppose that the Federal Reserve sticks closely to a strategy of keeping interest rates stable by changing the money supply.
   a. In a period of rising aggregate demand and aggregate output, what should the Fed do to keep the interest rate stable? Explain how these policies would stabilize interest rates. Would the policies have any

effects beyond stabilizing the interest rate?

   b. Answer the questions in part (a) for a period of falling aggregate demand and aggregate output.

2. Stimulating recovery from severe recessions has been characterized as "pushing on a string," or, as Keynes advised President Roosevelt in 1936, "trying to get fat by buying a bigger belt."

   a. Explain why the effects of expansionary monetary policy tend to be weak in severe recessions. Under what circumstances might expansionary monetary policies alone be completely ineffective in stimulating aggregate demand and output?

   b. Do the weak effects of monetary policy alone in recessions apply to the effects of monetary policy in periods of high output and inflationary pressure?

3. Supporters of discretionary monetary policy have argued that monetary policy stabilizes aggregate demand and output by "leaning against the wind." Friedman and other monetarist critics of discretionary monetary policy have replied that monetary policy authorities have to decide now on policies to lean against whatever wind is blowing in the future.

   a. Explain the meaning of the term "leaning against the wind." How could monetary policy do this?

   b. Explain the basis of the monetarists' counterargument. What are the merits and weak points of the argument? What are the implications of the monetarist critique for discretionary monetary policy?

4. What is meant by the term *crowding out*? What does it imply about the effectiveness of unsupported fiscal policies in stimulating aggregate demand and output? What (if anything) could monetary policy do to reduce crowding out? Explain carefully.

5. "Restricted growth in Federal spending, combined with the revenues yielded by a moderately growing economy, will reduce the budget deficit to $29 billion in 1980, less than half its size in the year before I took office . . . These measures of fiscal policy are being complemented by firm and careful monetary restraint on the part of the Federal Reserve Board . . . ." (President Carter, January 1979).

   a. What kinds of monetary policy would support the efforts of restrictive fiscal policies in dampening aggregate demand?

   b. What would be the probable effects of the Fed's refusing to complement fiscal restraint?

6. If Friedman and the monetarists argue that the money supply and changes in the money supply are such potent economic variables, why do they advocate a constant rate of growth of the money supply to replace discretionary monetary policies?

7. Consider the following proposals:

   a. Make the Federal Reserve completely independent of the executive and legislative branches of the government—i.e., make it an institution similar to the Supreme Court.

   b. Make the terms of members of the Federal Reserve Board of Governors identical to the presidential term of office.

   c. Select members of the Federal Reserve Board of Governors by popular vote.

What would you predict as the effects of these proposals on the nature and effectiveness of monetary policy? Explain.

APPENDIX

Money, Interest, and GNP: The *IS-LM* Approach

Equilibrium aggregate output of goods and services is reached when the aggregate demand for goods and services—or intended spending—is just equal to aggregate output or real GNP. Equilibrium also requires that the expenditure outflows (or leaks) from the spending stream equal the expenditure inflows into the spending stream. However, equilibrium in the goods sector and equilibrium aggregate output requires equilibrium in money markets as well. If money markets aren't in equilibrium, the interest rate will move toward its equilibrium, and this will affect investment, some consumption expenditures, and aggregate demand. In 1939, Sir John Hicks derived a model to show how equilibrium real GNP and equilibrium in money markets are interrelated, and to show how changes in one sector affect equilibrium in the other.

The Goods Sector and Real GNP

Recall that equilibrium GNP is reached in a closed private economy where *intended investment* (I) equals *intended saving* (S). Intended investment depends on the interest rate (r). Given an interest rate of 7% in Figure A–1a, intended investment comes to rest at $\overline{I} = 250$, where the interest rate (r) equals the *MEI*.

Equilibrium GNP ($\overline{Y}$) is reached when $I = S$. The saving function (S) in Figure A–1b shows the relationship between GNP (Y) and intended saving (S). Equilibrium GNP is reached at $\overline{Y} = 500$ in Figure A–1b where $\overline{I} = S = 250$. In other words, the interest rate, the *MEI* function, and the saving function have determined an equilibrium GNP that is consistent with an interest rate of 7%. In Figure A–1c, then, if the interest rate is $r = 7\%$, $I = S$ at $\overline{Y} = 500$.

If the interest rate fell to $r' = 6\%$ in Figure A–1a, intended investment would rise to $I' = 500$. Equilibrium GNP with $I = S$ would be reached at $\overline{Y} = 1000$ in Figure A–1b. In Figure A–1c, an interest of 6% is consistent with an equilibrium real GNP ($\overline{Y}$) of 1000. We now have two points on the *IS* curve in Figure A–1c.

- At all points on the ***IS* curve**, the goods sector is in equilibrium with $I = S$.

The Monetary Sector

Equilibrium in money markets is reached when the quantity of money (or liquidity) demanded equals the supply of money in circulation.

For a given level of GNP, the quantity of money demanded will vary inversely with the interest rate (r) along the demand curve for money (L) in Figure A–2a. At a higher level of GNP, the demand for money will be greater at every interest rate. Suppose that the supply of money is $M = 400$ in Figure A–2a. At a GNP of 1000, the money market would reach equilibrium where

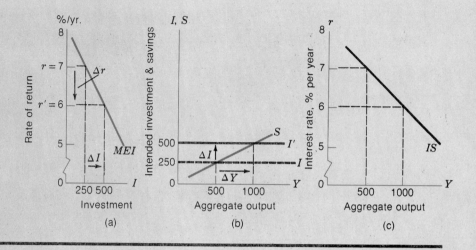

L = M at an interest rate of 5%. In Figure A–2b, then, we have a monetary
equilibrium (L = M) at an interest rate of 5% and a GNP of 1000.

If GNP increased to 1500, the demand for money would shift from L to L' in
Figure A–2a. With the same supply of money (M = 400), the money market
would now reach equilibrium (L' = M) at an interest rate of 7%.

Combinations of GNP (Y) and interest rates (r) that generate equilibrium
in money markets (L = M) with the given supply of money (M = 400) will
define points on the LM *curve* in Figure A–2b.

Figure A–2 Deriving the LM Curve

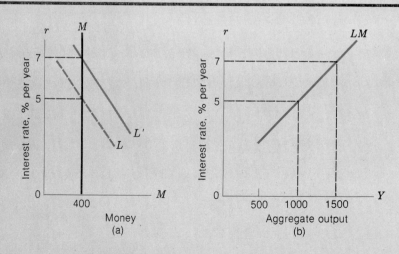

- At all points on the **LM curve** the demand for money equals the supply of money ($L = M$), and the money market is in equilibrium.

A word of caution concerning the interpretation of *IS* and *LM* curves: they resemble supply and demand curves, but in fact they are entirely different. The *IS* curve represents combinations of GNP and interest rates that generate equilibrium in the goods market ($I = S$). Similarly, the *LM* curve shows combinations of GNP and interest rates that generate equilibrium in money markets ($L = M$).

Equilibrium in Goods and Money Markets

To have a macroeconomic equilibrium, we must have equilibrium in both the goods sector and the monetary sector. Equilibrium is reached at the interest rate ($\bar{r}$) and real GNP ($\bar{Y}$) where the *IS* and *LM* curves intersect in Figure A–3— i.e., at $\bar{Y} = 1000$ and $\bar{r} = 5\%$. Any other combination of interest rate and GNP will be unstable because of disequilibrium in goods or money markets.

For example, consider $Y = 500$ and $r = 7\%$ in Figure A–3. We have equilibrium in goods markets ($I = S$), but money markets aren't in equilibrium. Monetary equilibrium with a GNP of $Y = 500$ would be reached with an interest rate of only 3%. An interest rate of 7% at a GNP of 500 is above the interest rate that would clear money markets of excess demand or excess supply of money. In this case, with the interest rate above equilibrium, there will be an excess supply of money in money markets, and this excess supply will cause the interest rate to fall. As the interest rate falls, this tends to stimulate investment and aggregate demand, causing GNP to increase along *IS*.

If the initial interest rate were 7% and GNP were $Y = 1500$, we have equilibrium in money markets ($L = M$ on *LM*), but not in goods markets. At this GNP, goods market equilibrium would be reached at an interest rate of $r = 3\%$. In this case, at $Y = 1500$ and $r = 7\%$, the interest rate is too high to achieve equilibrium in the goods market at a GNP of 1500. Since the interest rate is above the interest rate necessary to get $I = S$ at $Y = 1500$, this means that the level of investment at an interest rate of 7% must be less than intended saving, and

Figure A–3 The IS-LM Model

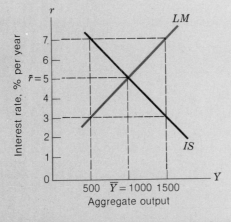

unintended investment will cause GNP to fall. As GNP falls, the interest rate to maintain goods market equilibrium rises along IS, and the interest rate to maintain monetary equilibrium falls along LM.

All of this leads to an obvious condition for equilibrium in goods and money markets.

- Equilibrium in goods and money markets is reached at the interest rate and GNP where $I = S$ and $L = M$, or where $IS = LM$.

Effects of Fiscal and Monetary Policies

Adding the public sector to the income determination model, you will recall, adds expenditure flows for government spending (G) and net taxes (T) and changes the equilibrium conditions for real GNP from

$$I = S$$

to

$$I + G = S + T,$$

where I is intended investment, S is intended saving, G is government spending, and T is net taxes. The public sector is incorporated in the IS–LM model in Figure A–4.

In Figure A–4a, autonomous spending includes I, which varies with the interest rate (r), and government spending which is independent of the interest rate. At a given interest rate, $r = 6\%$, autonomous spending is the sum of equilibrium investment ($\bar{I} = 200$) plus government spending ($G = 100$), or $\bar{I} + G = 300$.

Equilibrium GNP ($\bar{Y}$) is reached in Figure A–4b where $\bar{I} + G = S + T = 300$

Figure A–4 Fiscal Policy and the IS Curve

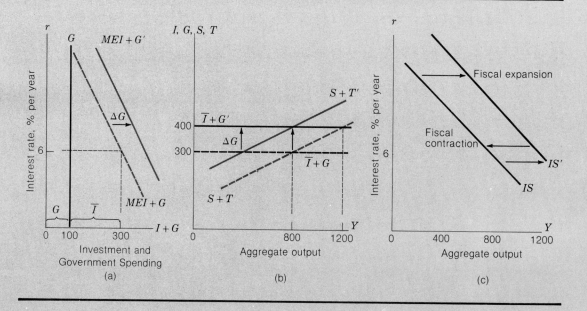

at $\overline{Y} = 800$. Finally, in Figure A–4c, we have a point on the *IS* curve where GNP = 800 and $r = 6\%$.

Changes in Government Spending

Now, suppose that government spending increases from 100 to 200—i.e., $\Delta G = 100$ per year. This shifts the autonomous expenditure curve from *MEI* + G to *MEI* + G' in Figure A–4a, increasing autonomous spending to $\overline{I} + G' = 400$ in Figures A–4a and A–4b. In Figure A–4b, the new equilibrium GNP is at 1200 where $I + G' = 400 = S + T$. In Figure A–4c, equilibrium in the goods sector is now reached with an interest rate of $r = 6\%$ and an equilibrium GNP of 1200, so the *IS* curve has shifted to the right to *IS'*.

- Increases in government spending will shift the *IS* curve to the right. Reductions in government spending will shift the *IS* curve to the left.

You should be able to verify in Figure A–4 that reducing government spending from G' to G would bring *IS'* back to *IS*.

Changes in Taxes

Changes in taxes also affect the *IS* curve. Suppose that equilibrium is reached in Figure A–4b with $S + T = I + G'$ at 1200. Now suppose that taxes are increased, shifting $S + T$ upward to $S + T'$. Equilibrium GNP falls to 800. In other words, the tax increase reduces the equilibrium GNP to 800 at the interest rate $r = 6\%$, shifting the *IS* curve to the *left* from *IS'* to *IS*.

- Tax increases shift the *IS* curve to the left. Tax reductions shift the *IS* curve to the right.

You should be able to verify in Figure A–4 that cutting taxes sufficiently to bring $S + T'$ back to $S + T$ would shift the *IS* curve from *IS* to *IS'*.

The effects of shifts of the *IS* curve on equilibrium GNP and equilibrium interest rates are shown in Figure A–5.

Figure A–5 Shifts in the IS Curve

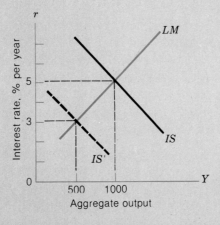

- If the *IS* curve shifts to the right, equilibrium GNP and the equilibrium interest rate will tend to rise.
- If the *IS* curve shifts to the left, equilibrium GNP and the equilibrium interest rate will tend to fall.

Changes in the Money Supply

At all points on the *LM* curve in Figure A–6, the monetary sector is in equilibrium. Changes in the money supply will disturb equilibrium in money markets and cause the *LM* curve to shift. Suppose that the supply of money is increased from *M* to *M'* in Figure A–6a. This causes the interest rate to fall to 5%, which is consistent with a GNP of 1500. In Figure A–6b, then, the effect of the greater money supply is a shift of *LM* to the right.

- The *LM* curve shifts in the same direction as changes in the money supply.

The effect of shifts of the *LM* curve on equilibrium GNP and the interest rate is shown clearly in Figure A–7.

- If the *LM* curve shifts to the right, equilibrium GNP tends to increase and the equilibrium interest rate tends to fall.
- If the *LM* curve shifts to the left, equilibrium GNP tends to fall, and the equilibrium interest rate tends to rise.

Unsupported Fiscal Policy

For GNP to be at its equilibrium level, both the goods sector and the monetary sector must be in equilibrium. Changes in fiscal policy will disturb equilibrium in the goods sector and cause shifts of the *IS* curve. However, shifts of the *IS* curve will cause disequilibrium in the monetary sector as well. The

Figure A–6   Monetary Policy and the LM Curve

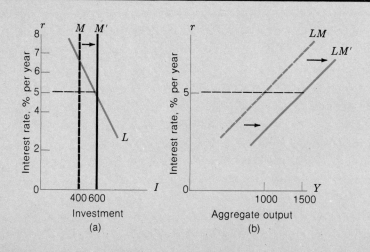

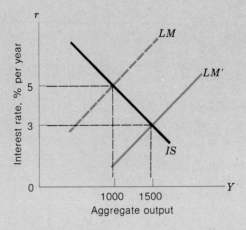

effectiveness of unsupported fiscal policies in altering equilibrium GNP and dealing with unemployment or inflation depends on the shape of the *LM* curve.

Unsupported Fiscal Expansion and "Crowding Out"

In Figure A–8, an expansionary fiscal policy (increased government spending or tax cuts) shift the *IS* curve to the right to *IS'*. However, the Fed decides not to change the money supply, so *LM* doesn't change.

If the interest rate remained at $r = 6\%$, the fiscal expansion would cause equilibrium GNP to increase to 1200. However at a GNP of 1200, an interest

Figure A–8   Unsupported Fiscal Policy

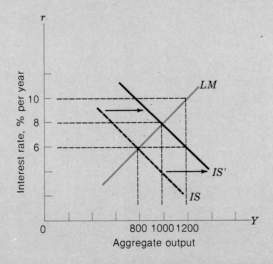

rate of 10% would be required for equilibrium in the monetary sector—i.e., there would be excess demand in money markets which would pull the interest rate upward toward 10% at a GNP of 1200. As the interest rate rises, the economy moves along IS' until equilibrium is reached at an interest rate of 8% and an equilibrium GNP of 1000. The rising interest rate has crowded out private spending of 200 (1200 − 200) as a result of the fiscal expansion.

The strength of the crowding-out effect and the effectiveness of expansionary fiscal policy in raising equilibrium GNP depends on the slope of the LM curve, and this slope isn't the same at all levels of real GNP and employment of capacity. In Figure A–9, the LM curve is relatively flat at low levels of output and employment. If there is a liquidity trap, it will be horizontal at the minimum interest rate. As real GNP and the employment of capacity increase, the LM curve generally gets steeper because it gets increasingly difficult to increase real output. At full employment, the LM curve becomes vertical because real GNP can't be increased at all.

In Figure A–9, if the initial position of the economy is with $IS_1 = LM$ at $Y = 400$, fiscal policy that shifts the IS curve from IS_1 to IS_2 will increase real GNP from 400 to 750, while increasing the interest rate from 4% to 5%. If the interest rate hadn't risen, the new equilibrium GNP on IS_2 would have been 800, so rising interest rates crowded out private spending of only 50.

However, if the initial position had been at $Y = 1600$ and $r = 12\%$ —where $IS_3 = LM$—the same fiscal expansion would have a much smaller effect on real GNP and a much larger effect on the interest rate. Fiscal expansion that shifts IS from IS_3 to IS_4 (the same shift as from IS_1 to IS_2) causes the interest rate to rise to 18.5% while real GNP increases only from 1600 to 1700. If the

Figure A–9 The Strength of the *Crowding Out* Effect

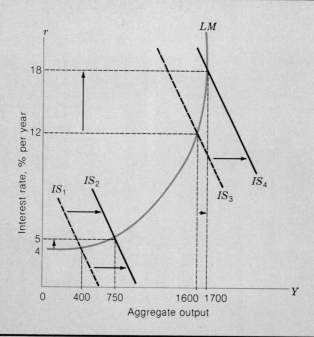

interest rate hadn't risen, this fiscal expansion would have led to a real GNP of 2000, so rising interest rates due to the fiscal expansion crowded out private spending of 300.

- Unsupported fiscal policies have a smaller effect on real GNP, and crowding out is greater, the higher the level of real GNP and employment.

The strongest monetarist arguments that unsupported fiscal expansion can't affect real GNP at all implies that the economy will be operating in the vertical region of the *LM* curve. If unsupported expansionary fiscal policies shift the *IS* curve beyond IS_4 in Figure A–9, the only effect will be rising interest rates and crowding out will completely offset the expansionary effect of the fiscal policies. Of course, by crowding out private spending, the expansionary fiscal policy means that a larger share of aggregate output and income will be accounted for by public spending.

**Unsupported
Fiscal Restraint**

The effectiveness of unsupported fiscal restraint in dampening demand-related inflationary pressure also depends on the responsiveness of GNP and interest rates to shifts of the *IS* curve. Since demand-related inflation occurs at high levels of output and employment, where the *LM* curve is steep, unsupported fiscal restraint is likely to have greater effects on interest rates than on reduced real GNP.

Suppose, for example, that the economy depicted in Figure A–9 is operating at $Y = 1700$ where $IS_4 = LM$, and that demand-related inflationary pressures are unacceptably great. Fiscal authorities estimate that these inflationary pressures would be minimized at a real GNP of 1200, and raise taxes and reduce government spending to shift *IS* from IS_4 to IS_3. However, shifting the *IS* curve to the left lowers interest rates from 18.5% to 12%, and GNP falls only from 1700 to 1600. Unless this fiscal restraint were supported by restrictive monetary policies, it would require a much larger shift of *IS* to get GNP to 1200—verify this in Figure A–9.

Even relatively mild fiscal restraint—cutting government spending or raising taxes—has serious political implications. The strong fiscal restraint necessary to curb demand-related inflationary pressures at high levels of output and employment may be politically impossible to achieve unless milder fiscal restraint is accompanied by supporting monetary restraint.

**Supported
Fiscal Policy**

Expansionary or restrictive fiscal policies will have a larger impact on aggregate demand and real GNP if they are supported by monetary policies. In fact, monetarists argue that fiscal policy alone will be ineffective unless supported by monetary policy.

In Figure A–10, expansionary fiscal policy shifts *IS* to the right to *IS'*. To avoid rising interest rates and crowding out, the expansionary fiscal measures are supported by expansionary monetary policies that shift *LM* to the right to *LM'*. As a result of the fiscal expansion and supporting monetary expansion, GNP increases to 1200, while the interest rate remains at 8%. Because of the expansionary monetary policy, there has been no crowding out. If the monetary authorities hadn't gone along with the expansion, the interest rate

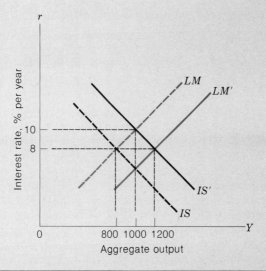

would have risen to 10%, and crowding out would have resulted in a smaller increase in real GNP (to 1000 instead of 1200).

The same argument works in reverse. If fiscal restraint shifted *IS* to the left from *IS'* to *IS*, and the monetary authorities didn't cooperate, interest rates would fall to 6% and GNP would fall to 1000. However, with a restrictive monetary policy supporting fiscal restraint, *LM* also shifts to the left (from *LM'* to *LM*), and the fiscal restraint has a stronger effect on GNP.

The potential and the dangers of supporting monetary policy should be fairly obvious. Coordinating monetary policy with fiscal policy makes discretionary policies more potent. However, coordination will also amplify the effects of mistakes in policy. If there is a political bias toward the expansion of public programs and against increasing taxes, the ability to "finance" fiscal expansion with monetary expansion and inflation may be very tempting politically.

PART FIVE

Inflation and Unemployment

The overriding economic theme of the 1970s was the problem of unacceptably high rates of inflation and unemployment occurring at the same time. The issue came to a head in the period 1974–75, when unemployment reached its highest level since the Depression, while the Consumer Price Index rose at its fastest annual rate since the lifting of price controls after World War II. The persistence of the problem raised serious doubts about the validity of a significant portion of traditional macroeconomic theory, and even led some critics to point to the 1970s as proof of the "death" of macroeconomics.

This view, like Mark Twain's premature obituary, appears to be somewhat exaggerated. Macroeconomics *is* in a state of flux, however, and many of the traditional analytical tools have had to be abandoned in favor of newer ones that more accurately describe the world as it really is. In this section, we'll explore the dual problem of inflation and unemployment, using the **aggregate demand–aggregate supply model** introduced earlier. We will examine the sources of the problem, some possible solutions to it, and the important question of whether policymakers can "trade off" higher rates of inflation for lower unemployment rates (and vice versa).

Several words of caution and encouragement are in order before you tackle this section. Some of the analysis approaches the frontiers of current economic thinking and can thus be quite tricky at times. Many of the waters are uncharted, and controversy in this area is the rule rather than the exception. However, your efforts in these chapters will reap substantial rewards in terms of understanding the contemporary problem of inflation and unemployment.

13

Inflation and Unemployment: Defining the Problem

Preview: The notion that inflation and unemployment *are* in fact problems is one that most people accept without very much question. But why exactly are they problems? Does an unemployment rate of five percent *really* mean that five million Americans can't find jobs? Is everybody *really* getting poorer during times of inflation? In order to gain a clearer picture of the costs these problems impose on society as a whole, we have to look at precisely how inflation and unemployment are defined and measured. This, in turn, will allow us to set reasonable policy goals for minimizing those costs.

The Meaning and Significance of Inflation

Inflation, as everybody knows, refers to rising prices. However, a rise in the price of baseball tickets or of any other single product isn't necessarily cause for concern about inflation.

- **Inflation** refers to a sustained rise in the general price level, as measured by some price index.

The two most common summary indicators of the price level are the Consumer Price Index (CPI) and the Implicit Price Deflator for GNP (IPD).

- The **Consumer Price Index** *(CPI)* estimates the cost of a given bundle of goods and services as a percentage of the cost of the same bundle in a base year.

- The **Implicit Price Deflator** *(IPD)* estimates the average change in prices of all final goods and services between a base year and a given year.

These price indexes were explained in some detail in a previous chapter. Since the CPI is used to estimate the change in the cost of living for a typical household, it is the most commonly cited price index.

In Figure 1, the black line shows the year-to-year percentage changes in the CPI. Obviously, *stable prices* (no change in the CPI from one year to the next) have been rare—1950 and 1955 are the only years in the past half-century in which prices remained virtually unchanged from the previous year. Most of us have lived our entire lifetimes in a period of rising prices. Figure 1 also explains our increasing concern with the problem of inflation over the past twenty years: since the mid-1950s, the trend in price changes has clearly been upward.

Inflation: Winners and Losers

In his 1979 *Economic Report*, President Carter suggested that "inflation injures every person in our country." This sort of statement makes good press when inflation is the most important problem of the day and solutions are likely to be unpopular, but it isn't accurate.

Figure 1 Unemployment and Inflation, 1930–1980

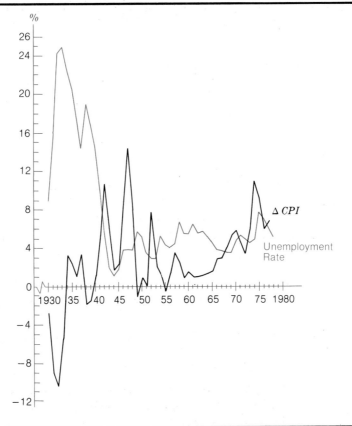

- Nobody whose money income at least keeps up with increases in prices is worse off economically during periods of inflation.

First of all, many persons are protected against inflation by *escalator clauses* that adjust their money incomes to changes in the CPI. Social security recipients, military and civilian federal pensioners, retired state government employees, and workers whose contracts contain cost-of-living-adjustment (COLA) clauses are not injured by inflation.

Furthermore, in some industries, the power of firms in the product market and of unions in the labor market can produce wage increases that exceed the rate of price increase; workers in these industries will be better off economically because their *real wages* are increasing. Such firms may also be able to protect the incomes of stockholders and suppliers of nonlabor resources by raising the prices of their products. The ability of firms and unions to push wages and prices upward depends heavily on outside support—from regulations that limit competition and allow firms to pass on higher costs as higher prices, or from government monetary and fiscal policies that accommodate their higher wages and prices.

Inflation also redistributes real income among various groups in the economy. Borrowers who owe long-term debts typically gain as a result of inflation because the dollars that they use to repay the loans have lower purchasing power (or are *cheaper*) than the dollars they borrowed. The borrowers' gains, of course, are the lenders' losses. The lender receives *"cheaper"* dollars in repayment of loans than were lent out.

Any person or institution whose money income rises *less* rapidly than prices does suffer a loss of real income as a result of inflation. Workers in weak bargaining positions, many welfare recipients and private pensioners, and probably the person teaching this course all lose real income during inflationary periods. Likewise, many banks and bond-holders who earn interest income from bonds suffer real losses from inflation. Persons on fixed money incomes are hurt worst of all, since their money incomes don't increase to offset even partially the corrosive effects of inflation.

If inflation actually did injure "every person in our country," no value judgment would be needed to conclude that inflation is unambiguously bad for the country and that reducing it would be unambiguously good for the country. Since inflation *doesn't* injure all of us economically, however, such sweeping statements about inflation require at least implicit value judgments concerning the importance of those who lose as a result of inflation vs. those who don't.

Furthermore, some policies that reduce inflation will impose significant costs on some groups in the population—for example, those who become unemployed if the government decides to fight inflation through monetary and fiscal contraction. Thus, those who lose as a result of inflation may sometimes lose even *more* as a result of efforts to fight inflation.

Inflation and Savings

Inflation alters *real interest rates* and *real interest income*. It also erodes the purchasing power of savings and principal on loans. For example, suppose that a family of modest means has managed to accumulate savings of $10,000 which it has deposited in a savings account that pays an interest rate of 6% per year. At the end of a year, the money value or *nominal* value of the principal and interest is $10,000 × 1.06 = $10,600. This increase in the nominal value of principal and interest is an illusion, however, unless prices are stable. If prices rose by ten percent over the year, the purchasing power of $10,600 would be about $9600—$400 less than the purchasing power of $10,000 a year earlier. In other words, the saver has earned *real interest* of −$400, or a *real interest rate* of −4% per year. The effect would be the same on a lender who lent out $10,000 at 6% interest under the same conditions.

Obviously, the prospects of very low or negative real interest rates are a deterrent to saving and lending. Under the circumstances above, the household would have an incentive to consume its $10,000 rather than save it at a negative real interest rate. Inflationary expectations lead lenders to charge an *inflation premium* as part of the nominal interest rate on loans to protect against a loss of purchasing power. Even this premium, however, is no guarantee against loss if the rate of inflation turns out to be higher than anticipated by lenders.

Inflation and Taxation

Inflation imposes a tax on our incomes in two ways. In the first place, it reduces the purchasing power of the dollars we receive as money income. For example, if the price level rises by 10%, the purchasing power of a $300 per week wage is the same as the purchasing power of a $273 per week wage at the old price level.

But inflation imposes taxes in another, more subtle way. The Federal Income Tax is a *progressive tax*—i.e., high incomes are taxed at higher *rates* than low incomes. Income taxes are calculated on our money incomes, not our real incomes. The family of four in the table below, for example, has an income of $20,000 in year 1 and pays a federal tax of $2536, or about 12.7 percent of income. Suppose that in year 2 the household's money income rises 10 percent to $22,000, but that prices also rise 10 percent. The household's *real* income has remained constant, but the federal tax on $22,000 is $3036, or 13.8 percent. As a result, despite the apparent $2000 increase in the family's income, its *real* after-tax income has actually fallen $224, from $17,464 to $17,240.

	Money Income	Real Income	Tax Rate	Money Taxes Paid	Real Taxes Paid	After-Tax Money Income	After-Tax Real Income
Year 1	$20,000	20,000	12.7%	2536	2536	17,464	17,464
Year 2	$22,000	20,000	13.8%	3036	2760	18,964	17,240

Taxes that depend on money incomes create a windfall gain of tax revenue for the government during inflationary periods—a gain that requires no politically risky legislation. If and when public pressure to reduce the tax burden becomes irresistible, the government can enact popular "tax cuts" that don't cut taxes at all. If in the previous example the government cut taxes in year 2 by 5 percent, it would still receive about $2884, a *real* gain of $86 over the previous year's revenue.

Applying the Tools

The Granddaddy of Inflations

Hyperinflation, as its name implies, is extreme or super inflation. It is the bogey man of all persons who fear inflation. There isn't a clear-cut line to divide serious inflation from hyperinflation, although Professor Philip Cagan has drawn the line at annual price increases of 50 percent or more. However serious a 50 percent annual inflation might seem, though, some actual hyperinflationary episodes make Cagan's standard look modest. One of the most severe hyperinflations in history occurred in Germany between 1921 and 1923, in which prices rose by a factor of one trillion—or an average rate of 102 percent per *day*!

What Caused the Inflation?
Wars are generally inflationary, particularly for countries in which the war is fought. During World War I (1914-18), the Germans financed their wartime expenditures by government deficits and borrowing. Following the war, the German government continued to run budget deficits and to finance them by printing money.

The Germans ran balance of payments deficits in foreign exchange markets because the war had destroyed most international commercial relations and much of the ability to produce for export. In addition, the Germans had to make postwar reparations payments in *gold marks*—i.e., in currency that could be converted for gold in international markets. Since the Germans couldn't finance these payments by trade surpluses (excess of exports over imports), they sold paper marks (currency not backed up by gold) in international markets. This caused the value of the mark to fall in international markets, and this tends to be inflationary. After the mark had depreciated initially, foreign currency speculators bought the marks, expecting the value of the mark to rise (they were wrong). German currency speculators sold marks, betting that the value of the mark would continue to fall (they were correct). Eventually, all currency speculators dumped their paper marks in international markets, and the value of the mark fell to virtually nothing.

At home, the German government followed expansionary monetary and fiscal policies. The government budget continued to run deficits, the availability of credit to businesses was expanded dramatically, interest rates were too low to restrain aggregate demand, and printing money (literally running the printing presses to print paper marks) went on 24 hours a day. New currency, unbacked paper marks, removed all constraints on the government's ability to increase the money supply. All of this, you should keep in mind, was taking place in an economy whose productive capacity had *shrunk* as a result of the war effort.

Speculative business activity ran rampant in Germany. The availability of business credit, negative real interest rates on loans, and the government's seemingly unbounded commitment to increasing the money supply encouraged firms to finance speculative ventures on borrowed funds, since the marks they would use to repay the loans would have a tiny fraction of the purchasing power of the marks they had borrowed.

The rapid acceleration of the rate of inflation encouraged people to spend their marks as quickly as possible. Holding marks for a day or two would reduce their purchasing power by 50 to 75 percent. Workers were paid twice a day so that they could spend their morning's wages before their purchasing power evaporated. The velocity of money was basically the speed at which people could run to spend their marks. This, of course, added to the inflationary pressures.

Effects of the Hyperinflation

Surprisingly, not all of the effects of the inflation were bad—at least, not bad for everybody. During the 1920–1922 postwar depression in Europe, for example, employment and output rose in Germany in spite of the inflation. Businesses who read the signals correctly made enormous gains during the inflation through speculative ventures and acquisition of other firms. Landholdings that were financed by mortgages were paid for in worthless marks, and many landowners made out handsomely. Anybody who could earn foreign currency (for example, exporters) was in good shape, since small amounts of foreign currency could finance large purchases of property and assets in Germany.

Output wasn't growing fast enough to allow the great economic gains to some Germans without imposing losses on others. Persons whose incomes couldn't keep up with the rate of inflation suffered losses of real income, and persons who were on pensions or fixed salaries were quickly reduced to desperation. Most wage and salary workers and much of the German middle class suffered losses during the hyperinflation because their incomes couldn't keep up with prices, and they had to sell property and assets at a fraction of their value to survive. The group that suffered under the inflation was a large part of the German population, and this provided a political base for Hitler's National Socialists (Nazis).

Albert Speer, who later became Hitler's chief architect and city planner during the Third Reich, was a student during the inflation in 1923:

> I had to draw my allowance weekly; by the end of the week the fabulous sum had melted away to nothing. . . . shortly before the end of the inflation, a restaurant dinner cost ten to twenty billion marks, and even in the student dining hall over a billion. I had to pay between three and four hundred million marks for a theater ticket.[1]

The End of the Inflation

By the end of 1923, the German monetary system had simply collapsed. Money had become worthless, and many exchanges were barter exchanges. There was no

---

1. Albert Speer, *Inside the Third Reich*. New York: Macmillan, 1970, pp. 9–10.

way that monetary and fiscal policies could restore order to the economy with the worthless paper currency. In 1924 the German government issued new currency that could be converted for the old marks at a rate of 1 trillion old marks = 1 new mark. The new *reichsmark* was convertible to gold or dollars, and one *reichsmark* (which was equivalent to 1 trillion paper marks) could be converted for $0.24!

Most of the facts in this discussion are from Dudley Dillard, *Economic Development of the North Atlantic Community*. Englewood Cliffs, N.J.: Prentice-Hall, 1967, pp. 512–20.

The Meaning and Significance of Unemployment

Our concern with high unemployment rates goes back to the Great Depression of the 1930s when the unemployment rate reached astronomical levels (the highest was 25.2 percent of the labor force, in 1933). For many, unemployment meant real and severe economic hardships. Breadlines, displaced families, and economic desperation are indelible images of that era in the public mind.

Fortunately, the unemployment rate hasn't reached depression levels since the 1930s, although it did exceed 9 percent briefly in 1975. Does unemployment carry the same connotations of hardship in the 1980s that it did in the Depression?

How Unemployment Is Measured

Government labor force data are based on statistical estimates made by the Bureau of Labor Statistics. Each month, the BLS surveys a sample of households which reflects the characteristics of the total population. The sample is rotated so that any given household is in the sample for a few months.

Interviewers ask the sample households a series of questions, and the responses determine the labor force status of members of the households. The sample results are then "blown up" to estimate the size of the labor force, total employment, total unemployment, and the unemployment rate.

- Persons who were employed for pay are defined as **employed.**

- Persons who weren't employed for pay, but were able to work and actively seeking work or awaiting recall from layoffs are defined as **unemployed.**

- Persons who weren't employed for pay because of inability to work or weren't actively seeking work are defined as **not in the labor force.**

The **labor force** is the sum of total employment and total unemployment, and the unemployment rate is the percentage of the labor force that is unemployed. Persons who are disabled, have full-time home responsibilities, or are not able to work or seek work for any number of other reasons are not in the labor force, and therefore don't enter into the calculation of the unemployment rate.

Many people misinterpret unemployment data and the meaning of the unemployment rate—in particular, politicians and others who talk about achieving *zero* unemployment or equate all unemployment with suffering and misery. The fact that an average of six million persons was unemployed in 1978 doesn't mean that six million persons stood in breadlines or lived off their savings for the entire year. The overall unemployment rate hides two very important dimensions of the unemployment problem—the duration of unemployment and the reasons that persons were unemployed.

The Duration of Unemployment

If the unemployment rate is stable at, say, 6 percent of the labor force for a number of years, this does *not* mean that the same 6 percent of the labor force remains unemployed for the entire period. In 1978, the annual average number of unemployed workers was slightly more than six million persons (5.2 percent of the labor force), but the average duration of unemployment in 1978 was only 11.9 weeks. In other words, the same six million workers weren't unemployed for the entire year. In fact, 2.8 million persons (2.4 percent of the labor force) were unemployed for fewer than five weeks in 1978.

Over time, persons move among labor force categories, as summarized in Figure 2. There is a steady flow of *new entrants* into the civilian labor force—i.e., persons going to work for the first time. In addition, there

Figure 2 Changes in the Labor Force

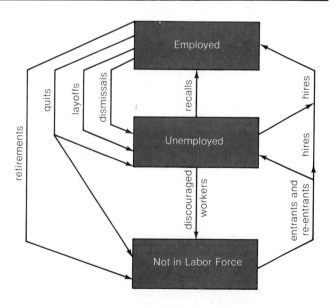

are *re-entrants*—persons who had been in the labor force but had dropped out temporarily. Some entrants and re-entrants will be hired immediately and others will be unemployed while they seek work.

If unemployed workers, new labor force entrants, or re-entrants are hired, the level of employment rises.

There are also flows of workers out of the labor force. Some persons quit their jobs to leave the labor force temporarily—for example, women who leave work during the periods of their lives when family demands are heaviest. Retirees represent another flow out of the labor force. Finally, discouraged workers who give up the search for employment represent a flow out of the labor force.

Quits, layoffs, and dismissals represent flows out of employment. Some of the persons who quit or are dismissed from employment leave the labor force completely, but most become unemployed as they seek other employment. Employment increases if laid-off workers are recalled by their employers.

The point here is that even in periods when the unemployment rate is stable, there are continual movements of persons among labor force categories. Seeking a goal of keeping the unemployment rate at 5 percent doesn't condemn a stable group of persons to perpetual unemployment. Also, because of the continual movements among labor force categories, the measured unemployment rate *cannot* be reduced to zero.

Kinds of Unemployment

Average unemployment figures can be misleading in another way. Although the same six million persons weren't unemployed for all of 1978, due to the relatively short duration of unemployment, more than six million persons experienced periods of unemployment during the year. If all of this unemployment could be explained by insufficient aggregate demand, it would be bad news, but at least such unemployment would respond to monetary and fiscal measures. However, several types of unemployment are not caused by low aggregate demand.

Frictional Unemployment. Some persons are unemployed because they are "between jobs," or temporarily unemployed. Workers on temporary layoff from their regular jobs are unemployed until they are recalled. Others who are dissatisfied with their jobs quit to seek other employment, and these workers are unemployed until they are employed on new jobs. These are examples of *frictional unemployment*.

- **Frictional unemployment** can be explained by imperfections, or "friction," in the labor market.

Specific causes of frictional unemployment include geographic or occupational immobility of labor, the time necessary to find new employment, the time required to acquire new skills, and inadequate market information. Because of these frictions, people don't move instantly from one job to another, and during the time between jobs they are frictionally unemployed.

Job Search Unemployment. Just because workers are unemployed doesn't mean they will necessarily take the first job they find. Most workers have a *reservation wage*, or a minimum acceptable wage. Jobs that offer wages below a worker's reservation wage will be rejected, and the worker will search for work until finding a job that offers a wage equal to or greater than the reservation wage. As long as the job search continues, a worker is considered unemployed.

- **Job search unemployment** is due to unemployed workers' choosing to continue their job searches until their reservation wage is met.

As long as the worker expects a wage offer equal to or greater than the reservation wage to turn up through continued searching, he or she will choose to continue to search rather than accept a wage offer below the reservation wage. However, as the number of weeks of unemployment and job search increases, the worker tends to lower the reservation wage.

The inverse relationship between the weeks of unemployment and the worker's reservation wage is shown graphically in Figure 3. At the end of week 1, the worker's reservation wage is $5 per hour. This is the wage that would be necessary to get the worker to cease searching

Figure 3 Time and the Reservation Wage

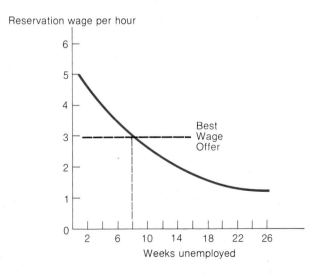

and accept employment. If a week of searching turns up a best wage offer of $3, the worker won't accept it because he or she expects to find a better wage offer by further searching. However, as further searching fails to turn up a $5 wage offer, the worker lowers his or her reservation wage. If after eight weeks of unemployment and searching, the best wage offer is still $3 per hour, the worker will accept the offer because the reservation wage has fallen to $3.

Structural Unemployment. Some unemployed workers don't have the skills and training necessary to fill the jobs that are in demand. For example, unemployed teenagers and persons with less than high-school educations won't be hired to fill vacancies for computer technicians, tool and die makers, accountants, or other jobs that require substantial education and training. Others with highly specialized skills are unemployed because technological change or shifting demand has eliminated the need for these skills. Revolutionary changes in typesetting and printing, for example, eliminated or sharply reduced the demand for many skilled printing crafts. These are examples of *structural unemployment*.

- **Structural unemployment** is the result of basic differences between the characteristics of unemployed workers and the characteristics of the jobs in demand.

The magnitude and significance of structural unemployment is a long-standing controversy among economists. In long periods of relatively high unemployment rates, the structural element tends to look quite large because of the large number of workers unemployed for long periods of time. In periods when the demand for labor is high, however, some of what appeared to be structural unemployment usually disappears. To the extent that structural unemployment does exist, stimulating aggregate demand will be ineffective in reducing unemployment because structural unemployment would exist regardless of the level of aggregate demand.

The key point of this discussion is that unemployment is due to a number of causes. The disturbing corollary of this is that no single approach will be effective against all types of unemployment. Stimulating aggregate demand will be effective against demand-deficiency unemployment, but not against structural unemployment. Retraining the structurally unemployed without adequate attention to aggregate demand won't do much to alleviate demand-deficiency unemployment. Too much attention to the overall unemployment rate probably won't do much to reduce the tragically high unemployment rates among specific groups in the labor force. In short, complex problems require complex solutions.

**What the
Unemployment
Rate Hides**

We have seen that, in one sense, the overall unemployment rate over-states the seriousness of unemployment because some unemployment is voluntary (for example, choosing to continue job search rather than accept employment at the best current wage offer), and because most persons are unemployed for short rather than long periods of time. However, the unemployment rate also *understates* some other serious dimensions of the problem of unemployment.

Minority and Female Unemployment. The unemployment rate for the total labor force is a convenient summary indicator of macroeconomic performance, but it doesn't tell us much about the employment status or the severity of unemployment for specific subgroups in the labor force. In 1978, for example, the unemployment rate for the total labor force was 6 percent. However, unemployment rates for individual subgroups in 1978 ranged from 3.7 percent for white males ages 20 and older to 38.4 percent for non-white females ages 16-19. For married men, the unemployment rate in 1978 was only 2.8 percent.

Unemployment rates have been consistently higher for blacks than for whites—a long-standing source of social tension. For many years, blacks were discriminated against in hiring and retention. Where workers were protected by seniority rules, blacks tend to be at the bottom of the seniority ladder and hence the first workers laid off in periods of slack demand. For young blacks, the unemployment rates in the 1970s were higher than the overall unemployment rates in the depths of the Great Depression.

Discouraged Workers. In some cases, when unemployment rates have remained unusually high for long periods of time, many unemployed workers become discouraged and stop looking for employment. These *discouraged workers* are officially defined as not in the labor force, even though they would be able to work and would be likely to seek employment if they were more optimistic about their prospects. The **discouraged worker effect** tends to understate the seriousness of unemployment in economically depressed geographic areas, during severe recessions and depressions when unemployment rates remain high for long periods, and among demographic groups where unemployment rates are chronically high.

Underemployment. Persons who are employed for pay are counted as employed whether or not they are fully employed. There are two basic types of **underemployment** of labor.

Some workers are underemployed because they are unable to find employment that utilizes their training, skills, and talents fully. Many Ph.D.s have been unable to find suitable academic or research employment because of the shrinking demand for college teachers and the overexpansion of graduate education in the 1950s and 1960s. A Ph.D.

in history who has to settle for a full-time job pumping gas or in routine clerical work is employed, but underemployed.

Part-time employment is another form of underemployment. Persons who are unable to find full-time employment may have to settle for part-time or casual employment. Since the BLS data don't measure underemployment—in fact, it may be difficult or impossible to measure accurately—the data don't reflect the loss of production of goods and services due to underemployment of labor.

The Costs of Unemployment

Unemployment imposes severe costs on the community. Some of the costs are borne by those who are unemployed. Persons who are unemployed as a result of layoffs, dismissals, and quits and are unable to find other employment suffer losses of income. Entrants and reentrants into the labor force who are unable to find employment are unable to earn income. Recent studies in other disciplines—sociology, psychology, and even medicine—have identified some other costs borne by the unemployed. Groups that suffer chronically high unemployment show higher incidences of mental disorders and physical illnesses than the general population. The suicide rate, for example, is considerably greater among the unemployed than it is for the general population. Social instability and tensions are common in urban ghettoes where high unemployment rates are the norm.

The community as a whole also loses economically when workers are unemployed—even when that unemployment doesn't mean economic desperation for the unemployed workers themselves. For example, relatively affluent housewives and teenagers who seek supplementary income probably won't be in a desperate situation if they don't find employment. However, their unemployment does impose a cost on the community. An unemployed worker, regardless of economic need, represents an unemployed resource, and the community loses the benefits of the goods and services he or she could have produced if employed.

The way the government estimates the value of these lost benefits to the community requires a bit of explanation. The President's Council of Economic Advisers (CEA) bases many of its predictions and policy recommendations on estimated *potential GNP.*

- **Potential GNP** is the estimated real GNP (in constant dollars) that would be produced with low unemployment rates and high rates of utilization of capacity.

The first step in defining potential GNP is to establish the measured unemployment rate that in fact constitutes full employment, or a **benchmark unemployment rate.** Since 1975, the benchmark unemployment rate for calculating potential GNP has been 5.1 percent.

Potential GNP isn't stable over time, but grows as a result of several economic forces. As population and the labor force grow, the capacity to produce expands due to the additional labor resources. Potential GNP also grows as a result of innovations, technological change, and other forces that increase the productivity of labor and other resources. The broken line in Figure 4 is the estimated trend of potential GNP between 1968 and 1978.

The solid line in Figure 4 is the path of actual real GNP (in 1972 prices) between 1968 and 1978. For brief periods, actual GNP exceeded potential GNP, which simply means that unemployment fell below the benchmark rate. For most of the period, however, actual GNP fell below potential GNP, creating a *GNP gap*.

- The **GNP gap** is the difference between potential GNP and actual GNP.

In 1978, for example, the GNP gap (in billions of 1972 dollars) was

$$\text{Potential GNP} - \text{Actual GNP} = \$1,422.9 \text{ billion} - \$1,385.1 \text{ billion}$$
$$= \$37.8 \text{ billion.}$$

The GNP gap shows one of the costs of unemployment to the community—the loss of goods and services that would have been produced if the economy were at full employment. In other words, unemployment in 1978 cost the U.S. $37.8 billion (1972 dollars). The loss of goods and services due to excessive unemployment for the decade 1968–1978 is represented in Figure 4 by the shaded area *below* the broken line.

Figure 4 Actual and Potential GNP, 1968–1978

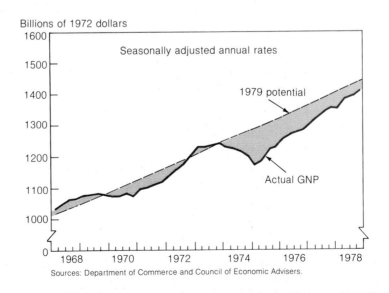

Sources: Department of Commerce and Council of Economic Advisers.

Setting an Employment Goal

Because unemployment is such a complex problem, setting a goal for policies to deal with the problem is no easy matter. Full employment is a desirable goal, but the definition and meaning of full employment isn't clear-cut. The only non-arbitrary definition is a measured unemployment rate of zero, but this is impossible to reach. The lowest measured unemployment rate recorded in the United States was 1.2 percent of the labor force in 1944, a year of peak wartime demand, a civilian labor force depleted by military manpower needs, complete mobilization, and extensive economic controls. Nobody reasonably expects to lower measured unemployment to the 1944 level, and we should be thankful that we don't face the situation that drove the unemployment rate so low.

Since a zero measured unemployment rate can't be reached, full employment has to be defined in terms of a measured unemployment rate that in fact constitutes full employment. This can be tricky. Depending on one's optimism and the weight one attaches to inflation as a problem, full employment may be defined very optimistically as a measured unemployment rate of 3 or 4 percent of the labor force, or less optimistically as 5, 6, or even 7 percent. Obviously, the measured unemployment rate that we accept as full employment isn't a precise standard.

One consideration in defining the measured unemployment rate that constitutes full employment is the rate of inflation we're willing to accept. Look back at Figure 1. Except in periods of stringent price controls during World War II, sudden drops in the unemployment rate generally have been accompanied by more rapid rates of price increase. In the late 1950s and 1960s, there was a clear pattern of falling unemployment rates and rising rates of increase in the Consumer Price Index.

- Most economists define **full employment** as the lowest measured unemployment rate that can be sustained without excessive inflation.

However, there is no unambiguous standard that defines the rate of inflation that is *excessive*. The historical record summarized in Figure 1 and common sense suggest that complete price stability is an unreasonable goal for an economy that is continually changing and buffeted by economic shocks. On the other hand, few would accept a sustained period of double-digit rates of price increase as a reasonable goal for price stability. Within this very broad range, what is an excessive rate of inflation—2, 4, 5, 8 percent per year? There is no absolute analytical standard.

A more fundamental question is whether there is, in fact, any long-run tradeoff between inflation and unemployment. That's a question we'll explore in some depth in the next chapter.

Summary

1. **Inflation** refers to sustained increases in the price level as measured by a price index.

2. Inflation imposes losses of income on those whose money incomes don't keep up with price increases. Those whose money incomes increase more rapidly than prices gain real income during inflationary periods. Inflation generally redistributes real income from those who lose real income to those who gain.

3. Since many taxes are tied to money income or the value of real estate, inflation generally increases government tax revenue without any alternation of tax rates. With progressive taxes, the effective tax rate on incomes rises with inflation.

4. **Unemployment** data are estimated from sample surveys of households which define persons into one of three categories—*employed*, *unemployed*, and *not in the labor force*. The overall unemployment rate doesn't show the seriousness of the unemployment problem for specific labor force groups, nor does it tell us much about the duration or type of unemployment.

5. Unemployment is caused by a combination of deficiency of aggregate demand, friction and immobility in labor markets, and structural mismatch between the characteristics of the unemployed and the jobs available.

6. Employment at jobs that don't utilize workers' skills or abilities fully and part-time employment are forms of underemployment. Unemployment data don't include the loss of employment or production from underemployment.

7. Unemployment imposes economic costs on those who are unemployed and on society in the form of lost production of goods and services that could have been produced by the unemployed workers. The loss of production due to unemployment is estimated as the difference between the estimated potential GNP and actual GNP.

8. As a practical goal, full employment with stable prices is unrealistic. Employment goals tend to be defined in terms of measured unemployment rates that we accept as full employment. There is no single, unambiguous analytical standard for defining a single rate of unemployment as "the" full-employment standard.

Concepts for Review

inflation	frictional unemployment	underemployment
real interest	job search unemployment	potential GNP
hyperinflation	structural unemployment	GNP gap
labor force	discouraged worker effect	full employment

Questions

1. Evaluate the following statement:
"We know a lot about unemployment and how to deal with it, but we don't know much about inflation. Therefore, we should follow

a course of trying to achieve full employment and let the inflation take care of itself."

a. What kinds of policies would follow from this way of looking at unemployment and inflation? What would be the effects of such policies?

b. Are there any normative arguments implicit in the statement? Explain.

2. Job vacancy data estimate the number of unfilled jobs available. What would be the merits of defining full employment as a situation in which the number of unemployed equals the number of job vacancies?

3. What is *job search unemployment*? In what respect is it voluntary unemployment? How would each of the following affect the level and average duration of job search unemployment?

a. Improved transmission of labor market information.

b. Increased economic optimism concerning economic conditions in the near future.

c. Increased economic pessimism concerning economic conditions in the near future.

d. Higher unemployment compensation benefits and extended coverage under unemployment insurance.

4. Some critics of official unemployment data argue that the data overstate the seriousness of unemployment by including as unemployed many who don't suffer any financial hardship as a result of unemployment— teenagers living at home, middle-class housewives entering the labor force for the first time, etc.

a. What would happen to the measured unemployment rate if definitions included financial need in the definition of unemployed— i.e., those not working who don't need the income would be classified not in the labor force?

b. In terms of the economic welfare of society, and the costs of unemployment to society, is economic need a relevant criterion for defining unemployment?

5. The Council of Economic Advisers uses a *benchmark unemployment rate* of 5.1 percent in estimating potential GNP. Some critics argue that this benchmark is too high and others argue that it is too low.

a. Why should any measured unemployment rate be accepted as *full employment*?

b. What factors would affect the choice of a measured unemployment rate to serve as full employment?

c. What are the implications of accepting a 7 percent unemployment rate as full employment? How about 4 percent as the full employment standard?

6. Although income tax rates were cut in 1979, many people found that they were paying more income tax in 1979 than they did in 1978, and that their after-tax incomes bought less in 1979 than in 1978. How could you explain this?

Problems

1. Suppose that prices rise by 8 percent this year. What effect will this have on each of the following people?
   a. A farmer who borrowed $10,000 at 10 percent interest for the year, and the banker who made the loan.
   b. A person with $10,000 deposited in a savings account that pays 6 percent annual interest.
   c. A person who pays an interest rate of 7 percent per year on the unpaid balance of a home mortgage.
   d. A person who received a raise from $20,000 annual salary last year to $21,000 this year.
   e. A pensioner who receives a fixed pension of $1,000 per month.
   f. Persons covered by escalator clauses that adjust their money incomes for changes in the price level.

2. The duchy of Idlehandia uses the same labor force definitions as the United States, since its earliest settlers were people who had retired from the U.S. Bureau of Labor Statistics. At the end of the year 1979, the labor force was 100,000 persons, of whom 95,000 were employed. During 1980, the following events occurred:
   i. 11,000 persons entered the labor force for the first time. Of these, 6,000 found employment immediately—although 1,000 of these were persons with Ph.D.s who took unskilled jobs. The remaining entrants continued to search for employment for the rest of the year.
   ii. A survey of households showed that 8,000 persons were willing to work, able to work, and desired to work, but didn't look for work because they were too pessimistic about their employment prospects.
   iii. Layoffs and dismissals totaled 5,000. Of these 3,000 found other work or were recalled during the year, 1,000 continued to search for employment for the rest of the year, and 1,000 gave up searching for employment.
   a. How many were unemployed and what was the unemployment rate at the end of 1979?
   b. Find employment, unemployment, labor force, and the unemployment rate at the end of 1980.

14

Aggregate Demand and Aggregate Supply

Preview: The Keynesian income determination model presented in earlier chapters showed how aggregate demand would determine equilibrium GNP or aggregate output at a *given* price level. But what if the price level isn't fixed? In this chapter, we'll "rebuild" the **aggregate demand–aggregate supply model** introduced earlier and show how and why aggregate output demanded and aggregate output supplied will vary with the price level, how the interaction of the two will determine equilibrium levels of GNP and prices, and how disturbances from either side of the economy will affect employment, output, and prices.

The great contribution of Keynesian economics was its explanation of aggregate demand and of the importance of aggregate demand as a determinant of aggregate output and employment. However, the basic Keynesian income determination model, with its assumption that the price level remains stable until full employment is reached, seriously understates the difficulty of our contemporary problems of unemployment and inflation. To understand the existence of unemployment and inflation *at the same time*, we have to drop the assumption of price stability and take a close look at the aggregate supply side of the economy, which is largely overlooked in the simple Keynesian model. This will allow us to see how aggregate demand and aggregate supply interact to determine the price level and the rate of inflation, as well as the level of aggregate output.

The first step is to restate aggregate demand and aggregate supply in terms of real GNP and the price level. The basic model was introduced briefly in Chapter 4, but without much explanation. This chapter takes a much closer look at aggregate demand and aggregate supply. Some of the analysis is difficult, but the rewards—in terms

Figure 1 Aggregate Output and the Price Level

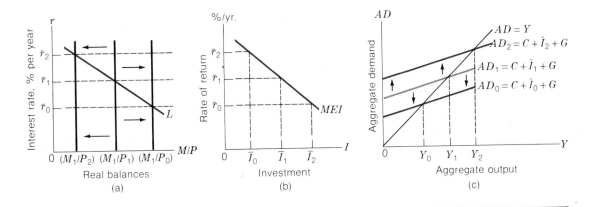

of understanding contemporary problems of unemployment and inflation and evaluating policies to deal with them—are very great.

Another View of Aggregate Demand

In the analysis of aggregate demand up to this point, we have defined
aggregate demand as the level of intended spending by households,
firms, and the government at various levels of real GNP with a fixed
price level. Equilibrium GNP was reached when intended spending
equaled real GNP in the goods sector and when money demanded
equaled money supplied in the money sector. A change in the price
level disturbs this equilibrium and generally causes a change in the
level of aggregate demand.

The initial money supply (M_1) and the price level (P_1) define the
supply of real balances, M_1/P_1, in Figure 1a. Real balances, you will
recall, represent the purchasing power of the money in circulation.
Given GNP, the demand for real balances at any interest rate is shown
by the demand curve for money (L). Equilibrium is reached in money
markets when the quantity of real balances demanded equals the
supply—at $\bar{r}_1$ in Figure 1a.

The interest rate, you will recall, is a major determinant of the level
of investment. Investment will increase or decrease until the rate of
return from the last investment (MEI) equals the interest rate—i.e.,
until investment reaches $\bar{I}_1$ in Figure 1b. Investment is a component
of aggregate demand, along with consumption and government spending. In Figure 1c, consumption (C), investment (I_1), and government
spending (G) define the aggregate demand function (AD_1) and determine aggregate output demanded[1] where $Y = AD$ at Y_1.

---

1. With a fixed price level, we could say that aggregate demand alone determined **equilibrium
aggregate output**. If we allow the price level to change, then aggregate demand *alone* will
only determine **aggregate output demanded**.

Aggregate Demand and the Price Level

Now, suppose that the price level falls from P_1 to P_0. The supply of real balances in Figure 1a will increase from M_1/P_1 to M_1/P_0—the purchasing power of the money in circulation is greater due to the drop in the price level. This increase in the supply of real balances causes the equilibrium interest rate to fall to $\bar{r}_0$, increasing the level of investment to $\bar{I}_2$ in Figure 1b. The higher level of investment in turn increases aggregate output demanded to Y_2 in Figure 1c.

If the price level rose from P_1 to P_2, the effects would be just the opposite. Real balances would fall to M_1/P_2, raising the interest rate to $\bar{r}_2$. The higher interest rate in turn would cause investment to fall, and aggregate output demanded would drop to Y_0.

In short, a decline in the price level increases the aggregate output demanded from Y_1 to Y_2, while an increase in the price level lowers aggregate output demanded from Y_1 to Y_0. This inverse relationship between the price level and aggregate output demanded defines the *aggregate demand curve* in Figure 2.

- The **aggregate demand curve** shows the level of aggregate output demanded at any price level.

To make it clear when *aggregate demand* refers to the relationship between aggregate output demanded and the price level, we will again label this curve YD instead of AD.

The aggregate demand curve in Figure 2 resembles the demand curve for a commodity, but there is an important difference. Points on YD represent equilibrium in the money market ($L = M/P$) and in the goods sector ($Y = AD$) at each price level. Thus, the points on YD and the shape of YD are determined for a given consumption function (C), a given aggregate demand function (AD), a given MEI function, and a given demand curve for money.

Figure 2   The Aggregate Demand (YD) Curve

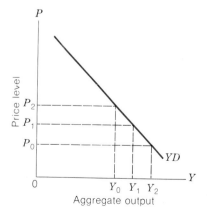

The Slope of the Aggregate Demand Curve

The slope of the YD curve reveals the responsiveness of aggregate output demanded to changes in the price level. Along a steep aggregate demand curve like YD in Figure 3, large changes in the price level result in relatively small changes in the aggregate output demanded. On the other hand, if the aggregate demand curve is relatively flat like YD', much smaller changes in the price level will result in relatively large changes in aggregate output demanded. What determines the responsiveness of aggregate output demanded to changes in the price level?

The demand curve for money. If the demand for real balances is highly responsive to changes in the interest rate—i.e., the demand curve for money is relatively flat—large changes in the price level and the supply of real balances with a given money supply will cause small changes in the interest rate. If the interest rate is highly responsive to changes in real balances—i.e., the demand curve for money is steep—small changes in the price level and real balances will cause relatively large changes in the interest rate. The size of the change in investment, aggregate demand, and equilibrium GNP as a result of a given change in the price level depends on the change in interest rates, so

• Aggregate output demanded is more responsive to changes in the price level the more responsive the interest rate is to changes in real balances.

The *MEI* curve. If the *MEI* curve is relatively flat, intended investment is more responsive to a given change in the interest rate than it is along a relatively steep *MEI* curve. The magnitude of the change in aggregate demand depends on the magnitude of the change in investment.

Figure 3 The Slope of the *YD* Curve

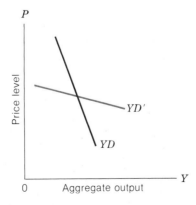

- Aggregate output demanded is more responsive to changes in the price level the more responsive investment is to changes in the interest rate.

The multiplier effect. If the multiplier effect is weak, aggregate output demanded is less responsive to a given change in investment than it is with a strong multiplier effect.

- Aggregate output demanded is more responsive to changes in the price level the greater is the multiplier effect of changes in investment.

Shifts of the Aggregate Demand Curve

Any exogenous change that affects aggregate demand will cause the aggregate demand curve to shift. Any number of exogenous changes can cause these shifts—shifts of the consumption function, altered expectations, different preferences for current consumption vs. future income, to name just a few. There is a simple, general rule for the effect of *any* exogenous change on the aggregate demand curve.

- Any exogenous change that increases aggregate demand shifts YD to the right, and any exogenous change that reduces aggregate demand shifts YD to the left.

From the policymaker's point of view, the most important changes are those in government monetary and fiscal policies. A close look at the mechanism by which such changes shift the aggregate demand curve will illustrate the effects of all exogenous changes. In Figure 4a, increasing government spending by ΔG raises AD to AD′ and increases aggregate output demanded in Figure 4a to Y′. Thus, in Figure

Figure 4 Fiscal Policy and the YD Curve

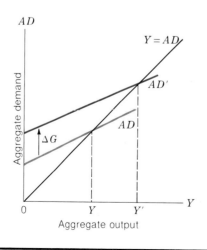 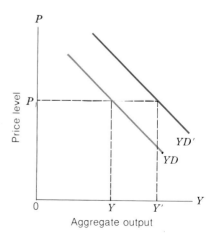

4b, the increased government spending increases aggregate output demanded to Y' at price level P_1, shifting YD to the right to YD'.

- Expansionary fiscal policies—increasing government spending or cutting taxes—shift the aggregate demand curve (YD) to the right.

Restrictive fiscal policies—cutting government spending or raising taxes—will have just the opposite effect. You should verify and explain for yourself how a reduction of government spending of ΔG in Figure 4 causes the aggregate demand curve to shift from YD' to YD.

- Restrictive fiscal policies—cutting government spending or raising taxes—shift the aggregate demand curve (YD) to the left.

Changes in the money supply also cause the aggregate demand curve to shift. In Figure 5a, expansionary monetary policies increase the money supply from M to M' and the supply of real balances from (M/P_1) to (M'/P_1) at the given price level P_1. Increasing the supply of real balances lowers the equilibrium interest rate to $\bar{r}'$. The lower interest rate causes investment to increase to $\bar{I}'$, where $MEI = \bar{r}'$ in

Figure 5 Monetary Policy and the *YD* Curve

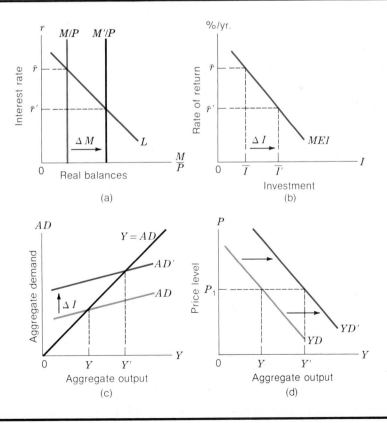

(a)

(b)

(c)

(d)

Figure 5b. The increased level of investment, in turn, causes aggregate output demanded to increase to Y' in Figure 5c. Thus, in Figure 5d, the aggregate demand curve shifts from YD to YD' as a result of the expansionary monetary policy.

- Expansionary monetary policies—increasing the money supply in order to reduce the interest rate—shift the aggregate demand curve (YD) to the right.

Again, you should verify and explain for yourself how reducing the money supply from M' to M would shift the aggregate demand curve in Figure 5d from YD' to YD.

- Restrictive monetary policies—reducing the money supply in order to raise the interest rate—shift the aggregate demand curve (YD) to the left.

Aggregate Supply: Output and the Price Level

With the wide acceptance of Keynesian economics in the 1940s, 1950s, and most of the 1960s, macroeconomics became preoccupied with aggregate demand. The high unemployment rates of the 1930s, wartime and post war inflationary pressures between 1940 and 1947, and the periodic episodes of recession and inflation in the 1950s and 1960s could be explained reasonably well in terms of aggregate demand. Furthermore, discretionary monetary and fiscal policies—**demand management policies**—did a fairly good job of regulating aggregate demand and keeping unemployment and inflation rates low.

In the past decade, however, aggregate demand has proved insufficient by itself as a means of explaining unemployment and inflation or of charting appropriate policies to deal with these problems. While changes in aggregate demand could explain rising prices with rising employment or falling employment with falling prices, they could not adequately account for falling employment with rising prices, a persistant problem in recent years. As a result, the *macroeconomics* of the 1970s has paid increasing attention to the *microeconomics* of aggregate supply in the search for an explanation of the problems of unemployment and inflation.

Employment and Output: The Aggregate Production Function

The first step in understanding aggregate supply is to understand the relationship between the employment of labor and the level of output. We can start with a simple example. Suppose a farmer uses labor (ℓ) and a fixed amount of capital (k^*) to produce wheat. The output of wheat (q) varies with the input of labor, and we can express this relationship with the function

$$q = f(\ell, k^*). \tag{1}$$

This is the wheat farm's **production function**.

Adding labor to a fixed input of capital won't yield equal increases in output for every additional unit of labor—if it did, an infinite amount of wheat could be produced by adding labor to a backyard garden. Eventually, the farm will produce under conditions of **diminishing returns**, with successive additional units of labor adding less and less output, as in Figure 6a. The **principle of diminishing returns,** one of the most universally valid propositions in economics, holds that eventually all goods must be produced under conditions of diminishing returns.

The relationship between the aggregate employment of labor (N) and the level of aggregate output (Y) is defined by the economy's *aggregate production function*.

- The **aggregate production function** shows the relationship between the level of employment and the level of aggregate output.

Since all goods must be produced under diminishing returns, it follows that the aggregate output of goods and services will show diminishing returns as employment increases with a given capital stock and a given state of technology, as in Figure 6b.

The aggregate production function defines a level of aggregate output (Y) for each level of employment (N), and conversely, a level of employment consistent with each level of aggregate output. In Figure 6b, for example, an aggregate output of Y_1 requires employment of N_1. At the level of employment that we accept as full employment (N*), we have the full-employment real GNP (Y*).

Figure 6 Aggregate Production Function

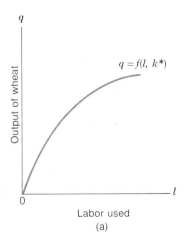

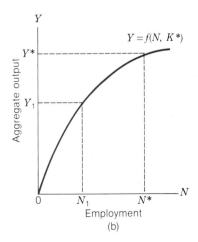

Labor used
(a)

Employment
(b)

Equilibrium in the Labor Market

In competitive labor markets, the supply of labor by households and the demand for labor by firms determine the equilibrium level of employment and the equilibrium wage. Profit-maximizing firms will increase or reduce the number of workers they employ until the last worker employed adds the same amount to the firm's revenue that he or she adds to the firm's cost. If adding a worker would increase the firm's revenue by $100 per day, and the firm would have to pay the worker a wage of $75 per day, hiring the worker would cause the firm's revenue to rise more than its costs, so profit would rise. Thus the firm should hire more labor until the last worker's addition to the firm's revenue is equal to the additional cost of hiring the additional worker.

The additional revenue from an additional unit of labor, or the revenue added by the last worker employed, is called the **marginal revenue product of labor** (MRP_N), and is $100 in the case above. The MRP of additional labor employed depends on the additional output produced by the additional labor, or the **marginal physical product** (MP_N), and the price at which that additional output is sold. For the economy as a whole, MP_N is the additional aggregate output produced by the additional labor employed. The value of this additional output is defined by the price level (P), so that

$$MRP_N \equiv MP_N \times P. \qquad (2)$$

With diminishing returns and a given price level, MP_N and MRP_N will both fall as employment increases, since each additional worker hired produces less additional output.

At any **money wage** (W), firms will maximize profit by hiring labor until

$$W = MRP_N. \qquad (3)$$

In other words, firms will hire workers until the value of the output the last worker produces is equal to the cost of hiring that worker. At any **real wage** (money wage divided by price level, or W/P), labor will be hired until[1],

$$\frac{W}{P} = MP_N. \qquad (4)$$

At a real wage of $(W/P)_1$ in Figure 7a, firms will want to employ N_1 units of labor, where the MP_N equals the real wage. If the real wage fell to $(W/P)_0$, firms would want to increase their employment to N_2. The falling MP_N curve thus represents the **demand curve for labor** (D_N).

---

1. These two conditions are really the same. Firms hire until $W = MRP_N = MP_N \times P$. Dividing both sides of the equation by P, we get

$$\frac{W}{P} = \frac{MRP_N}{P} = \frac{MP_N \times P}{P} = MP_N.$$

The decisions of households in allocating their time between leisure and working for pay determines the **supply of labor**. Workers try to allocate their time between work and leisure to achieve the combination of leisure and income that maximizes their utility. If the real wage rises, an hour's work for pay will buy more goods and services, and an hour's leisure will require a larger sacrifice of goods and services. The higher real wage will therefore encourage workers to consume less leisure and to work more.

At a real wage of $(W/P)_1$ in Figure 7b, workers will be willing to supply N_1 of labor. At a higher real wage of $(W/P)_2$, workers are willing to supply more labor, N_2 in Figure 7b. This direct relationship between the real wage and the aggregate quantity of labor supplied defines the **supply curve of labor** (S_N) in Figure 7b. It is important to note, though, that in the real world workers generally make labor-supply decisions on the basis of the money wage and an *expected* price level—i.e., on the basis of an **expected real wage**.

Figure 7c combines Figures 7a and 7b to show how demand and supply determine the equilibrium wage $(\overline{W/P})$ and the equilibrium level of employment $(\overline{N})$. At a higher real wage, such as $(W/P)_2$, workers are willing to supply more labor than firms want to hire. At a lower real wage, such as $(W/P)_0$, firms want to hire more labor than workers are willing to supply.

Prices, Employment, and Output

The key to aggregate supply is the relationship between the aggregate output supplied by all firms in the economy and the price level. This relationship is determined largely by the aggregate production function and the labor market equilibrium we've just looked at.

Figure 7 Labor Market Equilibrium

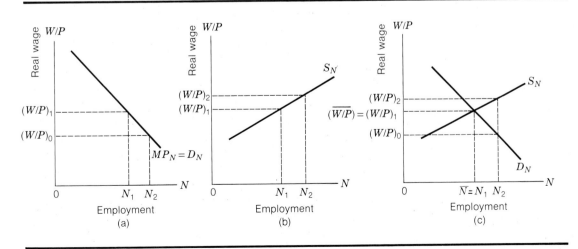

Given the price level P_1 in Figure 8a, labor market equilibrium will be reached at an equilibrium level of employment of $\overline{N}_1$ and an equilibrium real wage of $(\overline{W/P})_1$. Note, however, that this equilibrium real wage is in fact defined by an equilibrium money wage $(\overline{W})$ and the given price level (P_1). Thus,

$$(\overline{W/P})_1 = \overline{W}/P_1. \tag{5}$$

In Figure 8b, employment of N_1 generates an aggregate output of Y_1 on the aggregate production function. Thus, the combination of aggregate output supplied (Y_1) and price level (P_1) define point A in Figure 8c.

Now suppose that the price level rises to P_2 and that workers' price level expectations do not adjust immediately. At the original equilibrium money wage $(\overline{W})$ and employment level $(\overline{N}_1)$, the real wage falls to $= \overline{W}/P_2$. This change is represented graphically in Figure 8a as a downward shift in the labor supply curve to $S_N{}'$. In other words, workers are now supplying any quantity of labor at a lower real wage than before. Because of the lower real wage, firms will want to increase employment, but to do so they must raise the money wage, leading some workers to think they are getting a higher real wage and thus to supply more labor. A new equilibrium will be reached at employment level $\overline{N}_2$ and real wage $(\overline{W/P})_2 = \overline{W}'/P_2$ in Figure 8a. Notice that while the new equilibrium money wage is higher than it was before the increase in the price level (i.e. $\overline{W}' > \overline{W}$), the new real wage is lower than the original real wage (i.e., $(\overline{W/P})_2 < (\overline{W/P})_1$).

At the new higher level of employment $(\overline{N}_2)$, firms will a higher level of aggregate output (Y_2) in Figure 8b. Thus, this second combination of price level (P_2) and aggregate output supplied (Y_2) defines point B in Figure 8c.

Figure 8 Deriving the Aggregate Supply (YS) Curve

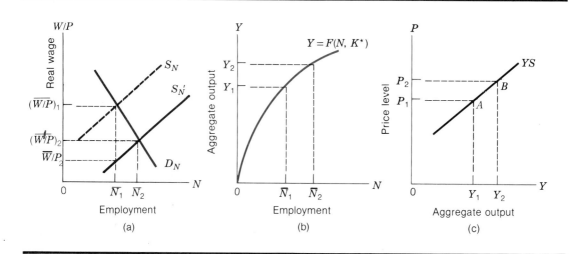

Any change in the price level should cause this same chain of events as long as workers' price level expectations do not adjust.

$$+ \Delta P \longrightarrow - \Delta(W/P) \longrightarrow + \Delta N \longrightarrow + \Delta Y$$

| Increase in Price Level | Decrease in Real Wage | Increase in Employment | Increase in Aggregate Output Supplied |

Graphically, this chain of events defines the upward-sloping *aggregate supply curve* (YS) in Figure 8c.

- The **aggregate supply curve** (YS) shows the relationship between the price level and the aggregate output supplied, other things constant.

The aggregate supply curve in Figure 8c depicts a *short-run* relationship between the price level and aggregate output supplied. Initially, many workers may not recognize that rising prices have lowered the real wage. Unemployed workers holding out for a higher reservation wage, for example, generally respond to a higher money wage even if the real wage has fallen. For many employed workers, there may be a lag between a rise in the price level and a full recognition of the effect of higher prices on their real wage. Because of multi-year contracts, there may also be a lag between the workers' recognition of the drop in the real wage and their ability to demand a compensating change in the money wage. Once workers do catch on, however, raising their expected price level and demanding a higher money wage at every level of employment, the labor supply curve will shift upward from S_N'.

To keep our analysis simple, however, we'll assume for now that workers aren't aware of the effect of higher prices on the real wage, so that the labor supply curve remains at S_N' in Figure 8c. This assumption will be relaxed in the next chapter, which extends the analysis of prices, employment, and output to the long run.

The Shape of the Aggregate Supply Curve

There is little disagreement over the existence of an aggregate supply curve, but little agreement on its shape. The shape of the aggregate supply curve is not a trivial question, however. If the aggregate supply curve is vertical—as YS_1 in Figure 9—equilibrium aggregate output and employment will be the same regardless of the level of aggregate demand, and changes in aggregate demand will affect only the price level. At the other extreme, if the aggregate supply curve is horizontal—as YS_2 in Figure 9—changes in aggregate demand would cause aggregate output and employment to change without changing the price level. A relatively steep aggregate supply curve (YS_3) translates changes in aggregate demand into small changes in output and employment and large changes in the price level. A relatively flat aggregate supply curve (YS_4) would translate changes in aggregate demand into

Figure 9 The Shape of the *YS* Curve

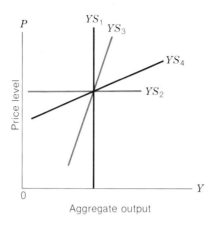

large changes in output and small changes in the price level.

Controversies among economists notwithstanding, empirical evidence strongly suggests (in the short run, at least) a direct relationship between the price level and the level of aggregate output. For this reason, we will make the not unreasonable assumption that the aggregate supply curve is upward-sloping, like YS_3 and YS_4 in Figure 9.

Shifts of the Aggregate Supply Curve

The relationship between aggregate output and the price level may change as a result of a number of exogenous changes. Higher input prices (for example, higher oil prices), changes in weather (such as prolonged drought), and changes in international relations that affect the supply of inputs are examples of **supply shocks** that would cause the aggregate supply curve to shift.

The dramatic rise in energy costs in the 1970s is one of the clearest examples of a supply shock. Just about every form of energy—oil, coal, gas, and nuclear—has become more expensive to produce in recent years. This has raised the price of energy and increased the cost of producing everything that requires energy in production—i.e., everything we produce. These higher costs of production are passed on to consumers as higher prices, so the price level rises at every level of aggregate output, shifting YS upward or to the left to YS' in Figure 10.

Changes in the labor market may also shift the aggregate supply curve. In Figure 11a, the labor supply curve shifts upward from S_N to S_N'. This shift could be due to any number of exogenous changes—stronger preference for leisure over income and other goods, greater optimism on the chance of finding higher wages through job searches, higher unemployment benefits, etc. To maintain employment at N_1

Figure 10 Shifts in the YS Curve

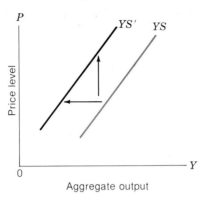

and real GNP at Y_1, the wage would have to rise from $(W/P)_1$ to $(W/P)_2$ on the new supply of labor S_N'. This would cause higher costs and higher prices at every level of aggregate output, shifting the aggregate supply curve to YS' in Figure 11b.

Technological change can also shift the aggregate supply curve. Suppose that a technological breakthrough results in a practical and inexpensive means of using solar energy to meet most of our energy needs for production and consumption. This would lower energy costs and thus the costs of producing goods and services, causing the price level to fall at every level of aggregate output. As a result, the aggregate supply curve would shift downward.

Figure 11 Labor Market Changes and the Aggregate Supply Curve

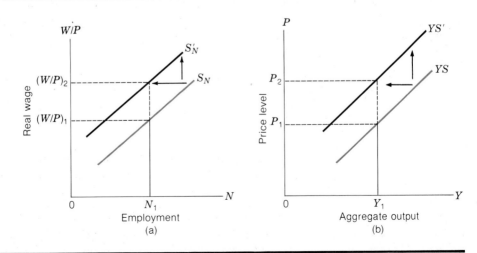

Summing all of this up,

- Exogenous changes that increase the cost of producing goods and services will shift the aggregate supply curve upward.

- Exogenous changes that lower the cost of producing goods and services will shift the aggregate supply curve downward.

Equilibrium Employment, Output, and Price Level

We now have all of the pieces of the puzzle. All that remains is to put them together to see how aggregate demand and aggregate supply interact to determine not only equilibrium aggregate output and employment, but also the equilibrium price level.

In Figure 12, the aggregate demand (YD) and aggregate supply (YS) curves determine equilibrium aggregate output at $\overline{Y}_1$ and an equilibrium price level at $\overline{P}_1$. If the price level were above or below $\overline{P}_1$, with the given YD and YS curves, the price level and aggregate output would not be in equilibrium. At P_2, for example, output supplied along YS exceeds output demanded along YD, and inventories of goods will increase. Firms will reduce their inventories by lowering prices to sell more and by reducing current output and employment. As prices fall real balances rise and more output will be demanded along YD.

At P_0 in Figure 12, current output falls short of aggregate demand, and inventories will fall. To maintain inventories and meet the demand for products, firms will increase current output and employment, causing wages and costs to rise with employment and raising the price level as output increases along YS. As the price level rises, real balances fall and the aggregate output demanded falls along YD.

Figure 12 The *YD-YS* Model

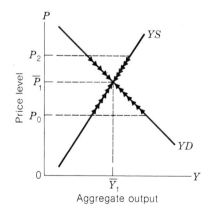

Aggregate output

With flexible wages and prices, output will move toward $\overline{Y}_1$ and the price level toward $\overline{P}_1$. Once attained, there will be no tendency for output or the price level to change unless there is a shift in the aggregate demand or aggregate supply curves.

Demand Shifts

Suppose that an exogenous change—for example, expansionary monetary and fiscal policies—shifts aggregate demand from YD to YD' in Figure 13a. As a result of the increased demand for output, the economy faces demand-pull pressures on the level of output and on the price level. With YD' and YS, there is excess aggregate demand at Y_1 and P_1. As the producers increase employment and output and buyers compete for goods and services, the price level will rise until a new equilibrium is reached at $\overline{Y}_2$ and $\overline{P}_2$.

- Exogenous increases in aggregate demand generally cause aggregate output, employment, and the price level to rise.

If an exogenous change had caused aggregate demand to fall from YD' to YD in Figure 13a, the result would be just the opposite. Inventories would increase at Y_2 and P_2, the price level would fall and output would contract until equilibrium were restored at $\overline{Y}_1$ and $\overline{P}_1$.

- Exogenous decreases in aggregate demand generally cause aggregate output, employment, and the price level to fall.

Supply Shifts

In Figure 13b, an exogenous change causes the aggregate supply curve to shift upward from YS to YS'. Whatever the cause of this shift— more aggressive wage demands by workers, natural disasters that af-

Figure 13 Changes in Equilibrium Output and Price Level

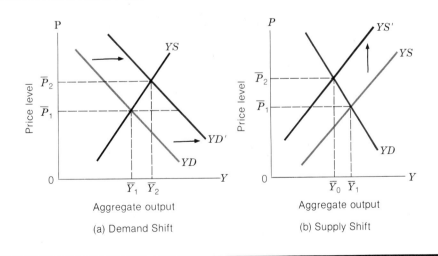

(a) Demand Shift

(b) Supply Shift

fect production of critical goods, political and economic decisions by OPEC, etc.—the upward shift of YS means that every given level of aggregate output will be supplied only at a higher price level than before. At Y_1 and P_1, excess demand results from the shift of YS, causing the price level to rise until a new equilibrium is reached at a higher price level ($\overline{P}_2$) and a smaller aggregate output ($\overline{Y}_0$).

- Upward shifts of the aggregate supply curve, or reductions in aggregate supply, cause the aggregate price level to rise and the level of output and employment to fall.

If aggregate supply increases, or the aggregate supply curve shifts downward, the results would be just the opposite. If aggregate supply shifted from YS' to YS in Figure 13b, there would be excess aggregate supply and rising inventories at Y_0 and P_2. As the price level falls, aggregate output demanded will increase along YD until equilibrium is restored at $\overline{Y}_1$ and $\overline{P}_1$.

- Downward shifts in the aggregate supply curve, or increases in aggregate supply, cause the price level to fall and aggregate output and employment to increase.

We have come a long way on a rough road, but we now have a framework within which we can analyze the effects of aggregate demand and aggregate supply on output, employment, and the price level. We are no longer in the rarified world in which prices remain constant until full employment is reached. We can attack the real world problem of excessive unemployment and excessive rates of inflation.

One lesson is clear, and will preview the discussion in the next chapter. Since unemployment and inflation are determined by aggregate demand and aggregate supply forces, traditional demand-management policies—primarily discretionary monetary and fiscal policies—won't be adequate by themselves in attacking unemployment and inflation at the same time.

In the next chapter, we'll examine the relationship between the rate of inflation and the unemployment rate. For many years economists have argued that there is a trade-off between unemployment and inflation—i.e., to reduce unemployment we have to accept a greater rate of inflation, and vice versa. The next chapter tackles the nature of the unemployment-inflation trade-off and the question of whether such a trade-off exists at all.

Summary

1. The Keynesian income determination model and the analysis of equilibrium in money markets show how aggregate demand affects aggregate output or real GNP, assuming a fixed price level.

2. To understand contemporary unemployment and inflation, the first step is to drop the assumption of stable prices, and to examine the relationships between the price level and the aggregate demand for goods and services and between the level of output and the price level.

3. Other things equal, aggregate output demanded varies inversely with the price level. As the price level falls, money markets adjust to a new equilibrium interest rate, and investment, aggregate demand, and aggregate output demanded increase, defining an **aggregate demand curve**.

4. Exogenous changes that increase aggregate demand cause the aggregate demand curve to shift to the right. Exogenous changes that reduce aggregate demand shift the aggregate demand curve to the left.

5. Aggregate output supplied varies in the short run directly with the price level, defining an **aggregate supply curve**. When the price level rises, the **real wage** falls and firms will hire more labor to increase output and profit.

6. Exogenous changes that increase costs at any level of output or that reduce the output that will be produced at a given price level shift the aggregate supply curve upward or to the left. Exogenous changes that lower costs or increase the output that can be produced at a given level of prices shift the aggregate supply curve downward or to the right.

7. Aggregate output and the price level reach equilibrium when the aggregate output produced (aggregate supply) equals the aggregate output demanded.

8. Exogenous changes that shift aggregate demand or aggregate supply curves will disturb equilibrium aggregate output and the price level.

Concepts for Review	aggregate demand curve
	aggregate supply curve
	production function
	diminishing returns
		aggregate production
		  function
		marginal revenue
		  product of labor
			supply of labor
			demand for labor
			real wage
			supply shock

Questions

1. Explain the relationship between the aggregate demand curve as it was presented in the discussion of income determination and as it is presented in this chapter.

2. How would each of the following affect the aggregate demand for goods and services? In each case, explain whether the changes are along the aggregate demand curve or are shifts of the aggregate demand curve.

   a. The Federal Reserve reduces the supply of money.

   b. Households increase consumption expenditures at every level of income.

   c. The Consumer Price Index rises from 200 (1967 = 100) to 210.

   d. Investors become more pessimistic about future economic conditions.

   e. The federal government increases its purchases of goods and services from the private sector.

3. Describe the conditions that would make aggregate demand highly responsive to changes in the price level, and the conditions that would make aggregate demand relatively unresponsive to changes in the price level. Why is the responsiveness of aggregate demand to changes in the price level significant?
4. What determines the economy's aggregate production function? What does it show? What are diminishing returns? How do diminishing returns affect the production function, and what do they imply about the relationship between aggregate output and the price level?
5. How would each of the following affect aggregate supply? Explain whether each would cause a change along an aggregate supply curve or would cause the aggregate supply curve to shift.
   a. OPEC raises the price of oil in world markets from $23.50 to $30.
   b. Output per worker and money wages both rise by 10 percent.
   c. Output per worker rises by 5 percent, and money wages by 10 percent.
   d. A technological breakthrough makes it possible to generate massive amount of electric power with solar powered generators at one-half the cost per kwh with existing methods.
6. If aggregate output is greater or less than its equilibrium level, explain how aggregate demand and aggregate supply will bring it to its equilibrium level. What is the significance of assuming that prices are flexible in this analysis?
7. What are the implications of each of the following for aggregate output and employment, the price level, and the ability of aggregate demand and aggregate supply to produce equilibrium aggregate output and prices?
   a. Firms in basic industries (steel, oil, aluminum, etc.) agree not to precipitate price wars and uncertainty by cutting prices.
   b. A comprehensive minimum wage law prohibits any employer from hiring any worker at less than $4 an hour.
   c. To avoid excessive inflation the government freezes all wages and prices at their current level.
   d. Maximum interest rates are imposed on time deposits and on business and commercial loans.

Problems

1. Econometricians in the small country of Aggregatania have found the following empirical relationships. The data are very accurate and the econometricians are very smart, so we can accept these as accurate relationships.
   Demand for money (real balances) (L): $r = 20 - 0.8\ (M/P)$
   Investment demand (MEI): $MEI = 20 - 0.5\ I$
   Government purchases: $G = 27$
   Consumption: $C = 50 + 0.8\ (Y - T)$
   Taxes: $T = 20$
   Pricé level: $P = 1.00$
   Money supply: $M = 20$.
   a. Find the equilibrium interest rate (r) and the level of investment (I) from the above information. This can be done algebraically or graphically by drawing an accurate demand curve for real balances (L) and an accurate MEI curve.

b. From the answer to part (a) and the other information given, find equilibrium aggregate output or real GNP ($\bar{Y}$). This can be done algebraically or graphically. What does this tell you about the aggregate output demanded at $P = 1.00$ with the other information given? Show *this* graphically.

c. Now, suppose that the price level rises to $P' = 2.00$, and that nothing else changes. Repeat parts (a) and (b) with the new price level.

d. Draw the aggregate demand (YD) curve, showing the relationship between aggregate output demanded and the price level over this range of price levels. How is this aggregate demand curve different from the demand curve for a single commodity that shows the quantity demanded at various prices?

e. The government increases the money supply to $M' = 30$. Repeat (a) and (b) with the new money supply and the price level $P' = 2.00$. What has happened to the aggregate demand curve you found in part (d)?

f. The government increases its spending to $G' = 40$. How does this affect the results you got from parts (a) and (b)? How has the change affected the aggregate demand curve? How would the existence of crowding out affect this result?

2. Given the following labor supply information for the economy of Ewessay.

Money wage per worker per year	Employment (N) (millions of workers)	Real output produced (millions)
$ 7,000	15	$200,000
8,000	20	300,000
9,000	25	390,000
10,000	30	470,000
11,000	35	540,000
12,000	40	600,000
13,000	45	650,000
14,000	50	690,000
15,000	55	720,000

a. Assuming that the economy's price level is equal to one, find the marginal product of labor (MP_N) at each level of employment. What is the demand for labor?

b. Find the equilibrium wage and level of employment in the economy. What level of aggregate output will be produced at this level of employment?

c. Suppose now that the price level doubles overnight, and that workers remain unaware of the change. At what real wage will the former equilibrium employment level be reached? How will firms react to this change? What will be the new equilibrium wage and employment level in the economy? How long would you expect this equilibrium to continue?

3. In the small country of Fernland, an aggregate output (or real GNP) of $600 billion (1972 dollars) is consistent with a price level of 2.80 on the YS function. However, the aggregate output demanded at this price level is $500 billion on the YD function. Every change in the price level by 0.2 points causes the aggregate output supplied to change in the same direction by $10 billion and the aggregate output demanded to change in the opposite direction by $10 billion.

a. Draw the economy's aggregate demand (YD) and aggregate supply (YS) curves for the range of aggregate output between $500 billion and $600 billion.

b. Is $600 billion the equilibrium aggregate output? Is $500 billion the equilibrium aggregate output? How do you know? What adjustments (if any) would bring aggregate output and the price level to equilibrium?

c. Find the equilibrium aggregate output and price level (if you haven't already).

d. An increase in energy prices adds 0.8 points to the price level at each level of aggregate output produced. What effect will this have on aggregate output and the price level? Find the new equilibrium aggregate output and price level.

e. Every increase or decrease of aggregate output by $1 billion causes employment to increase or decrease by 10,000 workers per year. What effect will the higher energy prices in part (d) have on employment in Fernland? If the government undertakes monetary and fiscal policies to bring employment back to the original level, what will happen to the price level? Why?

15

Inflation and Unemployment: Is There a Trade-off?

Preview: This chapter examines the relationship between the unemployment rate and the rate of inflation. The aggregate demand and aggregate supply model from the previous chapter is modified to show how aggregate demand and aggregate supply determine the level of aggregate output, employment, the unemployment rate, and the rate of inflation. The chapter also discusses the difference between the short-run and long-run relationships between unemployment and inflation.

Aggregate Demand, Aggregate Supply, Inflation, and Unemployment

The 1960s was a decade of steadily declining unemployment rates and increasing rates of inflation. In 1960, the unemployment rate was 5.5 percent, and the Consumer Price Index (CPI) was about 1.5 percent above it's level in 1959. In 1969, the unemployment rate had fallen to 3.5 percent, and the CPI had risen about 5.4 percent between 1968 and 1969.

The experience of the United States with unemployment and inflation in the 1960s—coupled with the pioneering studies in the 1950s by the late British economist, A. W. Phillips, of unemployment rates, wages, and prices in England—led many economists and others to see an inverse relationship or *trade-off* between the apparently conflicting goals of full employment and stable prices. The emphasis in economic policy discussions turned to finding the best, or most acceptable, compromise between low unemployment rates and low rates of inflation. Since the costs of unemployment and inflation aren't borne equally by all groups within society, finding the best trade-off between unemployment and inflation involves value judgments.

In the 1970s, the debate over the relationship between unemployment and inflation took a new twist. The data showed a very loose and unstable relationship between the unemployment rate and the rate of inflation, so that even identifying the trade-off is a sticky problem. Furthermore, new theoretical and empirical work in the 1970s suggests that there is no trade-off between unemployment and inflation in the long run—only the choice between higher and lower rates of inflation—and that the apparent trade-off in the 1960s had been a short-run phenomenon.

Obviously, the relationship (if any) between the unemployment rate and the rate of inflation is central to our ability to achieve an acceptably low rate of inflation and an acceptably low unemployment rate through discretionary policies. To understand how unemployment and inflation are affected by aggregate demand and aggregate supply, we have to restate aggregate supply and aggregate demand to show how aggregate output supplied (*YS*) and aggregate output demanded (*YD*) are related to the **rate of inflation**. These aren't different from the aggregate demand and aggregate supply relationships presented in the previous chapter, but merely a slightly different way of looking at them.

Aggregate Supply and the Inflation Rate

In the last chapter, we saw that when the price level rises and the real wage falls, firms will want to hire more labor and increase output, and by offering higher money wages, they will be able to do so until workers' expectations adjust to the higher price level. As the economy approaches full capacity, however, equal increases in the price level result in smaller and smaller increases in output. Conversely, equal increases in output require successively larger increases in the price level. In short, there is an apparent relationship between the level of aggregate output supplied and the percentage change in the price level, or the **inflation rate**.

This result occurs mainly for two reasons. In Figure 1a, the aggregate production function shows the relationship between employment

Figure 1 Aggregate Production Funciton and Employment Per Dollar of Real GNP

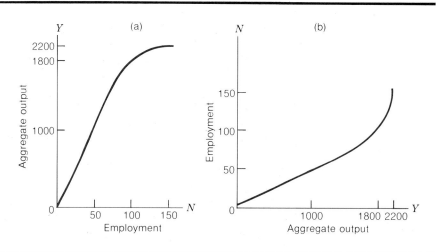

(N) and aggregate output or real GNP (Y). Because of diminishing returns, Y increases at a diminishing rate as N increases. Figure 1b is simply Figure 1a turned on its side. It shows that the number of workers required to produce an additional dollar of real GNP rises at an increasing rate as output increases. Such successively larger increases in employment can come about only through successively larger declines in the real wage. These, in turn, can result only from larger and larger increases in the price level.

The behavior of the money wage augments this effect. Figure 2 shows the quantity of labor supplied as a function of the money wage, with given price level expectations. To call out additional labor, firms must increase the money wage, partially offsetting the decline in the real wage. At low levels of output, with many unemployed workers holding out for reservation wages and employed workers anxious for overtime, relatively small increases in the money wage will be required to produce a given increase in employment. As the economy approaches full capacity, however, fewer workers remain unemployed and employed workers are less and less willing to sacrifice additional leisure time for additional income. As a result, equal increases in employment require successively larger increases in the money wage. Thus, the increase in the price level required to bring about a given decline in the real wage and corresponding rise in employment will be greater the closer the economy is to full capacity.

In short, with a large gap between actual output (Y) and full-capacity output (Y*), aggregate output supplied will be relatively responsive to changes in the price level. As that gap shrinks, however, the combined effect of diminishing returns and rising money wages means that the price level must rise at an increasing rate with respect to aggregate output supplied. Therefore, given any gap between Y and Y*, we can associate a percentage change in the price level, or *infla-*

Figure 2 Supply Curve of Labor

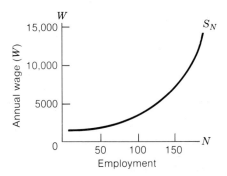

Figure 3 Aggregate Supply, Aggregate Demand, and the Rate of Inflation

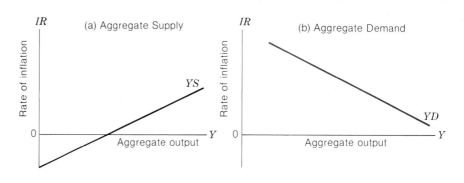

tion rate (IR), with any change in the size of that gap. This, of course, allows us indirectly to relate a rate of inflation to the level of aggregate output supplied, as illustrated in Figure 3a. As aggregate output increases, the gap between actual and full-capacity output gets smaller and the rate of inflation rises.[1]

Aggregate Demand and the Inflation Rate

You will recall from the last chapter that aggregate output demanded (YD) varies inversely with the price level, other things constant. Suppose that the money supply this year is the same as it was last year, but that the price level has increased by 10 percent. This will produce the following familiar sequence of events:

1. A 10 percent increase in the price level with a constant money supply cause real balances (M/P) to fall by about 10 percent.
2. The 10 percent drop in real balances causes the interest rate to rise.
3. Higher interest rates reduce investment and aggregate spending and cause the aggregate demand for goods and services to fall.

Now, suppose that the price level had risen by 5 percent instead of 10 percent since last year, with a constant money supply. Compared with the effects listed above for a 10 percent increase in the price level,

1. There will be a smaller reduction in real balances—about 5 percent instead of 10 percent.
2. There will be a smaller rise in the interest rate.
3. There will be smaller reductions in investment, aggregate spending, and the aggregate demand for goods and services.

---

1. This relationship is meant only to simplify our analysis of unemployment and inflation, and should *not* be misinterpreted. The YS curve in Figure 3a shows the relationship between output and the inflation for *given values of Y and Y** and *given price level expectations.* Since Y, Y*, and price expectations are constantly changing, we can't interpret Figure 3a as saying that a particular level of aggregate output supplied (say, $2 trillion) will *always* be associated with a particular rate of inflation (say, 12 percent).

4. Aggregate output demanded this year will be greater than it would be with a 10 percent rate of inflation.

In short, given an initial level of aggregate output, we can define an inverse relationship between the rate of inflation (IR) and the level of aggregate output demanded.[2] This relationship is shown graphically by the negatively-sloped YD curve in Figure 3b.

Aggregate Output and the Inflation Rate

We now have the pieces to assemble part of the unemployment-inflation picture. Combining Figures 3a and 3b, aggregate demand (YD) and aggregate supply (YS) determine a level of aggregate output ($\overline{Y}_1$) and a rate of inflation ($\overline{IR}_1$) in Figure 4.

If aggregate output were greater than $\overline{Y}_1$—for example, Y_2 in Figure 4—the rate of inflation as a result of producing this level of output (IR_2 along YS) would be greater than the rate of inflation that would clear the market of this aggregate output. Looked at another way, the aggregate output demanded at a rate of inflation of IR_2 is less than Y_2—i.e., aggregate demand is insufficient to clear the market of the aggregate output produced. Unintended increases in inventories would cause the rate of inflation to fall as firms either lowered prices or reduced price increases to sell their unsold goods.

At an aggregate output below $\overline{Y}_1$ in Figure 4—for example, Y_0—the rate of inflation is IR_0 (from YS). At this rate of inflation, the aggregate output demanded (from YD) is greater than the output of goods and services, and the economy will experience excess aggregate demand. Producers will respond to unfilled orders and declining inventories by increasing output, causing the aggregate output to increase from Y_0 and the rate of inflation to rise above IR_0.

Figure 4 The *YD-YS* Model and the Rate of Inflation

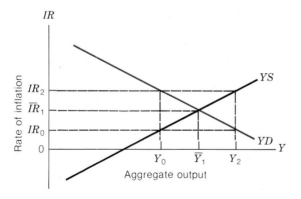

2. In other words, aggregate output demanded *this year* depends on aggregate output *last year* and the rate of change in the price level *since last year*.

Figure 5 Unemployment and the Rate of Inflation

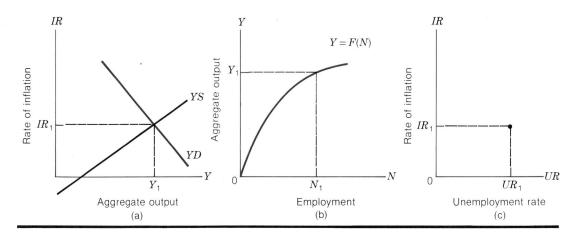

Inflation, Output, and Unemployment

The final piece that has to be put in place is the relationship between the rate of inflation and the unemployment rate. Actually, that is relatively simple. In Figure 5a, YS and YD determine the level of aggregate output (Y_1) and the rate of inflation (IR_1). The aggregate production function in Figure 5b shows the level of employment (N_1) consistent with an aggregate output of Y_1. We now know that a rate of inflation of IR_1 is consistent with aggregate employment of N_1.

What about inflation and *un*employment? If we let N^* be full employment, then unemployment at N_1 is

$$U_1 = N^* - N_1. \tag{1}$$

The **unemployment rate** is simply unemployment as a percentage of the labor force or full employment, so the unemployment rate at N_1 is

$$UR_1 = \frac{N^* - N_1}{N^*}. \tag{2}$$

Our basic model is now complete. Aggregate demand and aggregate supply determine aggregate output and the rate of inflation in Figure 5a and the level of employment in Figure 5b. The level of employment defines the level of unemployment and the unemployment rate in Figure 5c. Putting it all together, we have aggregate demand and aggregate supply determining the unemployment rate (UR_1) and the rate of inflation (IR_1) in Figure 5c. Now we are ready to turn to the trade-off between the unemployment rate and the rate of inflation.

The Phillips Curve

The **Phillips curve** shows the relationship between the unemployment rate (UR) and the rate of inflation (IR). The term recognizes the con-

tributions made by a British economist—the late A. W. Phillips—
in the 1950s in his studies of the relationship between unemployment rates, wage increases, and inflation in Britain.

The Phillips curve can be derived directly from the aggregate demand–aggregate supply model. Aggregate demand (YD) and aggre-
gate supply (YS) in Figure 6a determine a level of output $\overline{Y}_1$ (with an
unemployment rate of 6 percent) and an annual rate of inflation of 5
percent. Now, suppose the government undertakes expansionary monetary and fiscal policies to lower the unemployment rate. Such policies shift the aggregate demand curve to YD' in Figure 6a, raising
aggregate output to $\overline{Y}_2$ (with an unemployment rate of 5 percent) and
the rate of inflation to 8 percent. These two combinations of inflation
rate and unemployment rate (shown as points A and B) lie on the
negatively-sloped Phillips curve PC in Figure 6b.

Figure 6 The _YD-YS_ Model and the Phillips Curve

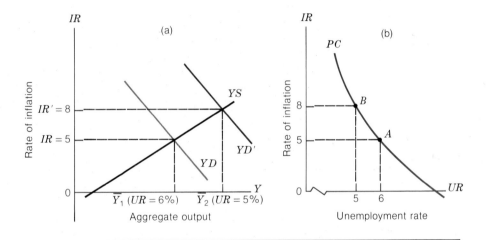

**Unemployment
and Inflation in
the 1960s**

The Phillips curve can be estimated empirically by constructing a
scatter diagram with each point in the scatter representing the unemployment rate and the rate of inflation in a given year.[3] Figure 7
is a scatter diagram showing unemployment rates and the rate of inflation (percentage changes in the Consumer Price Index) for the United
States in the years 1960–1969.

It's easy to see in Figure 7 why the notion of a trade-off between
the unemployment rate was so prevalent in the 1960s. Simply connecting the points year-to-year traces out a Phillips curve for the
1960s, and shows a stable and predictable relationship between the
unemployment rate and the rate of inflation.

---

3. For more detail on statistical estimation, see the appendix to Chapter 1.

The Breakdown of the Trade-off in the 1970s

The stable relationship between the unemployment rate and the rate of inflation that seemed so clear in the 1960s came apart in the 1970s. Figure 8 adds the unemployment rates and rates of inflation for the years 1970–1977 to the scatter diagram for the 1960s. It should come as no surprise after looking at Figure 8 that the notion of a stable and predictable trade-off between the unemployment rate and the rate of inflation lost ground rapidly in the 1970s. No single Phillips curve of the general shape of the Phillips curves in Figures 6 and 7 fits all of the points in Figure 8 very well—indicating a very loose relationship or an unstable trade-off.

If we continue the year-to-year path of unemployment and inflation from the 1960s to the 1970s, we get a very different picture for the 1970s than we saw for the 1960s. Between 1969 and 1970, the unemployment rate and the rate of inflation both increased. There was an apparent trade-off between 1970 and 1971, but both rates fell between 1971 and 1972. After an increase in the rate of inflation between 1972 and 1973, the pattern repeats in the period 1974–1978. If we put the 1960s and 1970s together, the path of unemployment and inflation traces out a *spiral*.

Amid all of the gnashing of teeth and breast-beating over how little we know about unemployment and inflation in the 1970s, several important points went largely unnoticed outside the ranks of professional economists. First, a stable and predictable Phillips-curve relationship between unemployment rates and the rate of inflation depends on a stable aggregate supply curve. In the 1970s, there were a number of supply shocks that made the relationship between aggre-

Figure 7 Phillips Curve, 1960–1969

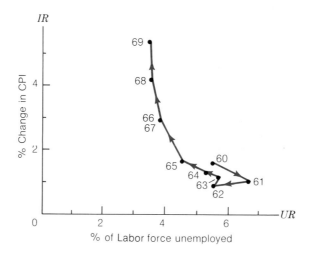

gate output supplied and the price level unstable—for example, the imposition and removal of a price freeze in 1971–1972 and the dramatic increase in the prices of oil imports. Secondly, the inverse relationship between unemployment rates and the rate of inflation in the 1960s apparently was a short-run relationship. The long-run relationship between the unemployment rate and the rate of inflation is quite different from the short-run trade-off we saw in the 1960s—in fact, there may be no trade-off in the long run.

Figure 8 Phillips Curve, 1960–1977

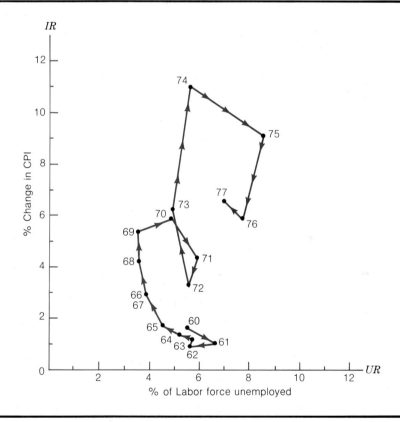

Is There a Long-Run Trade-off?

Why would the relationship between unemployment and inflation be different in the long run than in the short run? What factors contribute to this difference? Is there a trade-off between unemployment and inflation in the long run? These questions are central to the success (or lack of success) of policies to combat unemployment and inflation.

Expectations, Aggregate Supply, and the Natural Unemployment Rate

What firms and households expect to happen in the economy has an impact on what actually does happen in the economy. For example, if firms expect a rapid increase in prices in the future, they may withhold products from market now in order to receive higher prices later. The resulting reduction in supply contributes to rising prices. Likewise, if unions expect rapid inflation, they will bargain for large money wage increases to offset the expected inflation. These reactions of firms and households to expected inflation will contribute to actual inflation.

Expecting something to happen, of course, doesn't mean that it will happen, and economic expectations may turn out to be wrong. People and businesses aren't dumb, and there is no reason to believe that they will cling indefinitely to unfulfilled expectations. Rather, individuals and firms will adapt their economic expectations to actual economic conditions. For example, if the expected rate of inflation is 5 percent per year, and the price level actually rises by 10 percent per year, businesses and households will adjust their inflationary expectations upward. These changes in expectations show up in our aggregate demand–aggregate supply model as shifts in the aggregate supply curve.

- Changes in the expected rate of inflation will shift the labor supply curve and the aggregate supply curve.

The labor supply and aggregate supply curves will stabilize only when the actual rate of inflation (IR_a) equals the expected rate of inflation (IR_e)—that is, when there are no unexpected changes in the price level. Suppose, for example, that the expected rate of inflation is $IR_e = 0$. In other words, households and firms expect stable prices.

Figure 9   The Natural Rate Hypothesis

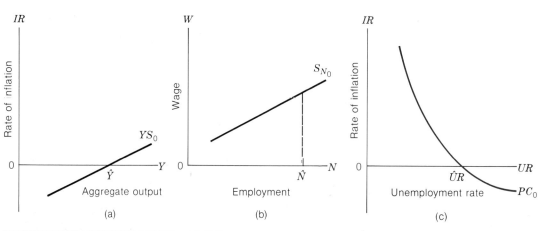

With $IR_e = 0$, the aggregate supply curve (YS_0) in Figure 9a shows the relationship between aggregate output (Y) and the actual rate of inflation (IR_a). At output $\hat{Y}$, the actual rate of inflation equals the expected rate ($IR_a = IR_e = 0$). $\hat{Y}$ is referred to as the *natural level of aggregate output*.

- When the actual rate of inflation equals the expected rate of inflation, the economy is producing its **natural level of aggregate output**.

The labor supply curve S_{N_0}, in Figure 9b shows the relationship between the level of employment and the wage level if workers expect stable prices ($IR_e = 0$). $\hat{N}$ in Figure 9b is the level of employment consistent with the natural aggregate output, or the level of employment at which the actual and expected rates of inflation are equal. $\hat{N}$ is referred to as the **natural level of employment**.

If the actual and expected rates of inflation are equal, the economy is producing the natural level of aggregate output, $\hat{Y}$ in Figure 9a, at the natural level of employment, $\hat{N}$ in Figure 9b. This means that the unemployment rate will also be at its natural rate in Figure 9c.

- The **natural unemployment rate** is the unemployment rate at which the actual rate of inflation equals the expected rate of inflation.

In Figure 9c, the natural unemployment rate is $\hat{UR}$, where $IR_e = IR_a = 0$. As long as the expected rate of inflation stays at $IR_e = 0$, there will be a trade-off between unemployment and inflation represented by the curve PC_0 in Figure 9c. Note that the rate of inflation equals the expected rate on PC_0 at the natural unemployment rate, $\hat{UR}$.

Before moving on, several points have to be cleared up concerning the natural unemployment rate. First of all, contrary to its name, it is not determined by natural forces. The natural unemployment rate is affected by such things as unemployment compensation laws, immobility and friction in labor markets, and institutional relationships in the economy. Secondly, the natural unemployment rate is not permanently fixed, but can be changed through changes in economic institutions, legislation, and improvements in the working of labor markets. Finally, the natural unemployment rate will never be zero, and may even exceed the unemployment rate that is politically acceptable as full employment.

In what sense are natural employment, output, and unemployment rate *natural*? These are simply the rates toward which the economy will *naturally* move as economic expectations adjust the expected rate of inflation to the actual rate. In Figure 10a, YD and YS_0 determine equilibrium aggregate output at $\overline{Y}$ which is greater than natural aggregate output ($\hat{Y}$). This means that the unemployment rate ($\overline{UR}$) is less than the natural rate ($\hat{UR}$) in Figure 10b, and that the actual rate of inflation ($IR_a = 3\%$) exceeds the expected rate ($IR_e = 0$). As workers find that prices are rising more rapidly than they expected, the money wage will rise at every level of employment, increasing costs and raising the aggregate supply curve in Figure 10a.

The aggregate supply curve will continue to shift upward until the actual and expected rates of inflation are equal—i.e., until aggregate output reaches its natural level. In Figure 10a, natural output is reached again when $IR_e' = IR_a = 6$ percent. In Figure 10b, the increase in the expected rate of inflation and the shift of the aggregate supply curve to YS_6 shifts the Phillips curve upward in Figure 10b until the actual and expected rates of inflation are equal, or until unemployment reaches the natural rate $(\hat{UR})$ with a $IR_e' = IR_a = 6$ percent.

Figure 10   Adjustment to the Natural Rate

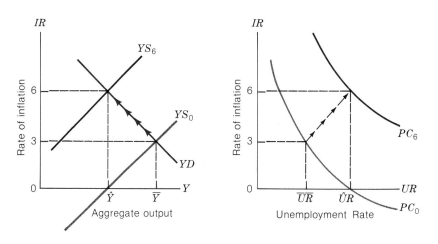

If aggregate demand and aggregate supply determine a level of aggregate output below the natural level, prices will rise more slowly than the expected rate of inflation, and the unemployment rate will exceed the natural rate. In Figure 11a, for example, the equilibrium aggregate output determined by YD and YS_6 ($IR_e = 6$ percent) is below the natural rate, and prices are rising at 4.5 percent rather than at the expected rate of inflation of 6 percent. In Figure 11b, the unemployment rate exceeds the natural rate with prices rising at 4.5 percent. As the expected rate of inflation adapts to the actual rate, the aggregate supply curve falls until the actual rate of inflation equals the expected rate at $IR_e' = IR_a = 3$ percent. The shift of the aggregate supply curve due to weaker inflationary expectations shifts the Phillips curve from PC_6 to PC_3. Again, it's important to note that $IR_e' = IR_a = 3$ percent on PC_3 at the natural unemployment rate $\hat{UR}$.

Long-Run Aggregate Supply and the Long-Run Phillips Curve

In the long run, allowing enough time for expectations to adapt to actual rates of inflation, aggregate output will always readjust to its natural level. This suggests that the *long-run aggregate supply curve* (LYS) will be vertical at the natural level of aggregate output, as in Figure 11a. This implies that in the long run, aggregate output will be at $\hat{Y}$, regardless of the level of aggregate demand. The only thing that aggregate demand determines in the long run is the rate of inflation.

The long-run aggregate supply curve in Figure 11a also suggests a vertical *long-run Phillips Curve* (LPC) at the natural rate of unemployment, as in Figure 11b. The short-run Phillips curves, such as PC_4 and PC_3 in Figure 11b, indicate the inverse relationship between the unemployment rate and the rate of inflation that occurred in the United States in the 1960s. However, if expectations adjust fully to changing economic conditions, the vertical Phillips curve at the natural unemployment rate indicates that there is no long-run trade-off between the unemployment rate and the rate of inflation—only a choice between higher and lower rates of inflation at the natural unemployment rate.

The notion of a natural unemployment rate is a source of controversy among economists, and the lines in the controversy are fairly sharply drawn. The strongest supporters of the **natural rate hypothesis** are monetarists and others who are skeptical of the ability of discretionary monetary and fiscal policies to achieve full employment and price stability. Monetary and fiscal activists who assign a large role to discretionary monetary and fiscal policy are the most critical of the natural rate hypothesis.

The notion that the unemployment rate will move toward its natural rate in the long run has serious implications for the long-run effects

Figure 11 Long-Run Aggregate Supply and the Long-Run Phillips Curve

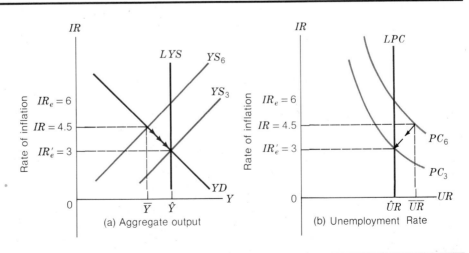

(a) Aggregate output

(b) Unemployment Rate

Figure 12 Inflation, Unemployment, and Government Policy

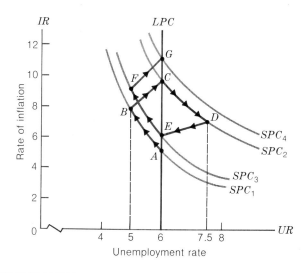

of discretionary monetary and fiscal policies—particularly if these policies are aimed at a target unemployment rate below the natural rate. Suppose that the desired rate of employment ("full employment") is defined as 5 percent, and that the government is committed to a goal of full employment. Initially, suppose that the unemployment rate is at the natural rate of 6 percent with prices increasing at 5 percent per year, as shown by point A in Figure 12.

To get the unemployment rate down to 5 percent, which it has defined as full employment, the government undertakes expansionary monetary and fiscal policies to stimulate aggregate demand. The short-term effect of the expansionary policies is to reduce the unemployment rate to 5 percent and to raise the rate of inflation to 8 percent along SPC_1. The acceleration of the rate of inflation, however, will soon lead consumers, producers, and workers to adjust their expectations. As the expected rate of inflation increases, the short-run Phillips curve shifts upward to SPC_2. If no further monetary or fiscal actions were taken, and if the expected rate of inflation didn't change, the unemployment rate would return to the natural rate of 6 percent, with a rate of inflation of 9.5 percent.

If the government were committed to an unemployment rate below the natural rate at any cost, the net result of discretionary monetary and fiscal policies to achieve this objective would be hyperinflation. However, hyperinflation is a highly unlikely result because society and the government are concerned about the rate of inflation as well as the unemployment rate. Suppose that the 9.5 percent annual rate of price increase at C in Figure 12 is considered excessive. The government's economic policy turns to monetary and fiscal restraint to dampen inflation. The short-run effect is to move from C to D on SPC_2. The rate of price increase falls to 7 percent per year and the unemployment rate increases 7.5 percent. But now the actual rate of inflation is *below* the expected rate, so firms and households will adjust their expectations downward, shifting the short-run Phillips curve to SPC_3. If no further actions are taken, the unemployment rate falls back to the natural rate at E with prices increasing at 6 percent per year.

Having succeeded in lowering the rate of inflation, the government now turns its attention to unemployment, since the unemployment rate has stopped falling before reaching the desired "full employment" rate of 5 percent. If expansionary monetary and fiscal policies are undertaken to push the unemployment rate down to 5 percent from point E, the process starts over, and a second "loop" begins. As the government deals alternately with unemployment and inflation, and expectations constantly adjust to changes, unemployment and inflation rates trace a series of clockwise loops, or a **price spiral** around the natural unemployment rate.

This analysis enables us to make some sense out of the behavior of unemployment and inflation in the 1960s and 1970s. The path $ABCDEFG$ in Figure 12 bears a striking resemblance to the spiral traced out by unemployment rates and rates of inflation for the United States in the 1960s and 1970s in Figure 8. Figure 8 suggests a spiral around an unemployment rate in the neighborhood of 5.5 percent, which is consistent with most estimates of the natural unemployment rate for the United States.

What does all of this suggest for policies to deal with unemployment and inflation? One possible conclusion is that no discretionary monetary and fiscal policies will be successful in keeping unemployment rates below the natural rate without excessive rates of inflation because the policies themselves will alter expectations in a way that offsets the effects of the policies. Another, not much more reassuring, implication is that monetary and fiscal policies will work only as long as people are fooled—i.e., until their expectations adjust to what's actually happening. Yet another implication is that traditional monetary and fiscal policies that are directed at the demand side of the problem of unemployment and inflation must *at the very least* be accompanied by other policies that affect unemployment and inflation from the aggregate supply side and by policies that reduce the natural unemployment rate. The problem, then, is not that economists don't know anything about the problem of unemployment and inflation or how to deal with it, but that what we do know isn't very pleasant or appealing. Some policy strategies to deal with unemployment and inflation are discussed in the next chapter.

Applying the Tools

Rational Expectations

Abraham Lincoln once asserted that "You can fool all of the people some of the time, and some of the people all of the time, but you can't fool all of the people all of the time." In the 1970s, a major innovation in macroeconomics by Professors Robert E. Lucas, Thomas J. Sargent, and Neil Wallace carries Lincoln's argument one step further by arguing in effect that "You can't fool anybody anytime"—at least as far as monetary and fiscal policies are concerned.

The **theory of rational expectations** derived by Lucas, Sargent, and Wallace argues that individuals and firms know what to expect from monetary and fiscal policies and adjust their expectations to announced or predicted changes in monetary and fiscal policies before the changes actually take place. For example, if workers and employers know that the government always increases the money supply and enacts expansionary fiscal measures if the unemployment exceeds 5.5 percent, they will expect these measures whenever the unemployment rate exceeds 5.5 percent, and will alter their economic expectations to take into account the forthcoming changes in monetary and fiscal policy. When the expected monetary and fiscal measures actually occur, according to this line of argument, they will have no effect because expectations have already anticipated them!

Figure A is a simplified sketch of the way that rational expectations offset the effect of discretionary monetary and fiscal policies on aggregate demand, output, and the unemployment rate. Initially, suppose that aggregate output is at $\hat{Y}$ and that the unemployment rate is at $\hat{UR}$. The government feels that the unemployment rate is too high, and announces that it will act to reduce the unemployment rate to UR^*. From previous experience, firms and households know that this means expansionary monetary and fiscal policies are on the way, and they expect a higher rate of inflation as a result. When the government expresses its concern with the unemployment rate and its commitment to reduce it, then, the expected rate of inflation increases from IR_e to IR_e', shifting the aggregate supply curve upward to YS' and the Phillips curve to PC'.

When the expansionary monetary and fiscal policies actually take place, aggregate demand increases to YD'. However, because the aggregate supply curve has already shifted to YS', the expansionary policies and the increase in aggregate demand have *no effect* on the aggregate output or the unemployment rate. They simply increase the rate of inflation at the same level of aggregate output and at the same unemployment rate. Since expectations had taken account of the effects of the policies, they don't even have any short-run effect on aggregate output or the unemployment rate.

The implications of the rational expectations hypothesis for discretionary monetary and fiscal policies are even stronger than the implications of the natural rate hypothesis. According to the natural rate hypothesis, discretionary monetary and fiscal policies have no effect on output or employment in the long run because they will move to their natural levels as expectations adapt to economic conditions. The implication of the rational expectations hypothesis is that, unless they come as a total surprise to the public, discretionary monetary and fiscal policies will have no effect *at all* on aggregate output or the employment rate.

Figure A

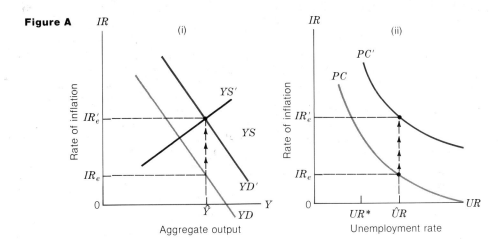

What types of monetary and fiscal policies are consistent with the rational expectations hypothesis? Since discretionary policies are defeated by changing expectations, monetary and fiscal policies should not attempt to regulate aggregate demand or alter output and unemployment. A constant rate of growth of the money supply should replace discretionary monetary policies. Fiscal policy should provide necessary services through the public sector, and pay for them with tax revenue—i.e., balanced government budgets should replace discretionary fiscal policy.

The rational expectations hypothesis is a highly controversial proposition. It is anathema to those who see an active role for discretionary monetary and fiscal policy in achieving acceptable unemployment rates and rates of inflation. Even monetarists, who tend to be highly critical of discretionary monetary and fiscal policies, have serious reservations about carrying the argument as far as the rational expectations hypothesis does.

Summary

1. Aggregate demand and aggregate supply will determine an equilibrium aggregate output and an equilibrium rate of inflation. Since aggregate output determines the level of employment and the unemployment rate, aggregate demand and aggregate supply will also determine the **unemployment rate**.

2. **Phillips curves** show the relationship between the unemployment rate and the rate of inflation. Through the 1960s, the most commonly held view of the Phillips curve was an inverse relationship, or trade-off, between unemployment and inflation.

3. In the long run, expectations define a **natural unemployment rate** where the actual and expected rates of inflation are equal. If the actual rate of inflation deviates from the expected rate, expectations will adjust to move the unemployment to the natural rate.

4. According to the **natural rate hypothesis,** the long-run supply curve is vertical at the natural level of aggregate output and the **long-run Phillips curve** is vertical at the natural unemployment rate.

5. If economic policy is committed to an unemployment goal below the natural rate of unemployment and to minimizing the rate of inflation, discretionary monetary and fiscal policies will alternate between stimulating aggregate demand to lower the unemployment rate and reducing aggregate demand to lower the rate of inflation, leading to a **price spiral** around the natural rate of unemployment.

Concepts for Review

rate of inflation	natural level of	long-run aggregate
aggregate output	aggregate output	supply curve
per worker	natural level of	long-run Phillips
productivity of labor	employment	curve
unemployment rate	natural rate of	price spiral
Phillips curve	unemployment	theory of rational
	natural rate hypothesis	expectations

Questions

1. Explain how increases and decreases in aggregate output would affect each of the following. Where possible, explain the long-run effects as well as the short-run effects.
   a. Aggregate employment.
   b. Output per worker.
   c. Demand for labor.
   d. Wage per worker.
   e. Costs incurred by producers.
   f. The rate of inflation.

2. Would you expect the aggregate output demanded this year to be greater if the price level had risen 10 percent since last year or if the price level had risen 20 percent since last year? Why?

3. How does the level of aggregate output affect the rate of inflation? What relationship do you expect between the level of aggregate output and the rate of inflation?

4. What is a Phillips curve? How is the Phillips curve related to aggregate demand and aggregate supply? How well does the Phillips curve explain the relationship between the unemployment rate and the rate of inflation in the United States in the 1960s? How well does it do for the relationship between unemployment and inflation in the 1970s? How can you explain the difference?

5. "The notion of a trade-off between unemployment and inflation is pure bunk, promoted by reactionary economists. During the past year, the unemployment rate fell and the rate of inflation slowed. Therefore, the way to deal with unemployment and inflation is to do whatever is

necessary to lower the unemployment rate, and the rate of inflation will fall along with it" (Senator A. Gass Bagg).

Analyze and evaluate the above statement on unemployment and inflation. If you think the senator is incorrect, how do you explain the fact that unemployment and inflation both fell? What would be the most likely consequences of following the senator's proposed policies to deal with unemployment and inflation?

6. Most estimates of the natural unemployment rate for the United States place it in the neighborhood of 5.5 to 6.0 percent.

   a. What would happen if society and the government were committed to a single goal of achieving and maintaining an unemployment rate of 5.0 percent through traditional discretionary monetary and fiscal measures?

   b. How would your answer to part (a) be different if society and the government set their goals for monetary and fiscal policy as maintaining an unemployment rate of 5.0 percent without excessive inflationary pressure?

   c. What would be some of the effects of accepting the natural rate of unemployment as the unemployment goal? How would monetary and fiscal policies be affected? What would be the implications for policy if we accepted the natural unemployment rate as our unemployment goal and we also accepted the rational expectations hypothesis?

   d. Would accepting a current natural unemployment rate of 5.5 percent necessarily mean that we could never achieve and maintain an unemployment rate of 5.0 percent without accelerating rates of inflation? Explain.

16

Inflation and Unemployment: Attacking the Problem

Preview: We have seen that unemployment and inflation may result from disturbances on either the demand side or the supply side of the economy. Not surprisingly, policies to deal with these problems may also be directed toward either demand or supply. Traditional Keynesian macroeconomics has tended to focus on aggregate demand management through discretionary fiscal and monetary policies as the key to the problems. In earlier chapters, we've looked closely at such policies to deal with inflation and unemployment through the manipulation of taxes, government spending, and the money supply. In this chapter, we turn our attention to a number of alternative strategies.

Monetarism and the Market Solution

The proper role of markets and government in the economy is one of the longest-running controversies in economics. Adam Smith's *Wealth of Nations*, the work that marks the birth of modern economics, was in large part a laissez-faire attack on 18th-century economic orthodoxy that stressed the importance of policy (economic "statesmanship") and economic controls. Contemporary laissez-faire critics of government policy argue that reducing the microeconomic and macroeconomic role of government to a minimum would contribute to lower unemployment rates and greater price stability.

The basic argument is that because of the absence of incentives to reduce costs or improve productivity in providing public services, the government is an inefficiently large and complex bureaucracy. Expanding the role of government shifts more of society's resources from the efficient private sector to the inefficient public sector, creating both unemployment and inflationary pressure. By reducing the scope of government in the economy, the proponents of laissez-faire assert, we'll make more efficient use of our resources, market forces will operate freely, and unemployment and inflation will diminish.

Further, according to advocates of laissez-faire and monetarism, government policies seldom achieve their objectives and tend to be destabilizing. If fiscal policies were limited to providing and financing only the services that the public needs, and not aimed at managing aggregate demand, the destabilizing effects of fiscal policy would be eliminated or at least minimized. Likewise, tying the change in the money supply to a *constant-growth-rate rule* would stabilize monetary policy and expectations.

On the microeconomic side, *laissez-faire* critics advocate the removal or drastic reduction of government regulations that reduce wage and price flexibility and competition. The specific targets are government regulation of particular industries or occupations, regulated prices, minimum wage laws that keep wages from adjusting to levels that would clear the market, and unemployment compensation laws that encourage workers to remain unemployed or keep searching for employment rather than accept their best wage offer. The underlying assertions in this strategy are that public regulations are the cause of unemployment and inflation, and that removing the regulations would allow competitive market forces and prices to clear markets of unsold goods and unemployed workers.

In the long run, real GNP and the unemployment rate would move to their natural levels, and prices would change at a constant rate. Disturbances due to exogenous shocks could cause the unemployment rate to fall below the natural level, accelerating the rise in prices, or to exceed the natural unemployment rate in which case inflation would slow down. However, the free operation of market forces and flexible wages and prices would restore the natural unemployment rate and a constant rate of price change more quickly and smoothly than would discretionary monetary and fiscal policies.

Is the laissez-faire prescription correct? Frankly, at the present state of our knowledge, there isn't a clear-cut answer to this question. The monetarists' predictions depend heavily on the assumption of flexible wages and prices, and such flexibility, particularly in a downward direction, is limited by a number of economic and institutional variables in the real world.

Modern corporations, like government agencies, are managed by large and complex bureaucracies, and contain some of the same sources of bureaucratic inefficiency that the proponents of laissez-faire attribute to the public sector. Most key industries in our economy are controlled by small numbers of large firms who share a common interest in avoiding vigorous price competition (or *price wars*), which contributes to downward inflexibility of prices in these industries. Most trade unions try to keep their members' wages from falling in periods of slack demand, and this contributes to downward rigidity of wages in organized industries.

If wages and prices were completely rigid downward, the classical adjustment mechanism to maintain full employment wouldn't work. If wages and prices are flexible but *sticky*, market adjustments will tend to be slow—perhaps too slow to be very appealing as a solution to the problems of unemployment and inflation. Even if wages and prices were totally flexible, the natural rate of unemployment and a constant rate of price change are *long-run* results. Short-run disequilibria and movements toward the long-run equilibrium may involve fairly long periods of calendar time with unacceptable levels of unemployment, inflation, and instability.

Proponents of laissez-faire, monetarists in particular, argue that eliminating the errors inherent in discretionary monetary and fiscal policy is desirable because monetary and fiscal policies won't amplify the effects of exogenous shocks. However, the activist reply to this argument is that discretionary monetary and fiscal policies are necessary for the simple reason that exogenous shocks *do* exist and discretionary policies can soften their impact on real GNP, unemployment, and inflation.

Managing Aggregate Demand: Fine Tuning

In periods of unacceptably high unemployment, the traditional activist prescription has been to stimulate aggregate demand through expansionary monetary and fiscal policies. In periods of high inflation, activists urge tight monetary and fiscal policies to dampen aggregate demand and inflationary pressures. Such discretionary stabilization policies have seemed quite successful in dealing with massive disturbances of aggregate demand—the Great Depression or World War II, for example.

The past two decades have witnessed dramatic developments in quantitative economics, or *econometrics*, and in the technology of gathering, synthesizing, and processing economic data. Sophisticated *econometric models* of the economy express economic relationships as statistically estimated equations. By feeding actual or projected data into the model, econometric models yield predictions of GNP, employment, interest rates, prices, and other key economic variables.

The development of such sophisticated econometric modeling techniques and the apparent success of demand management policies in dealing with major disturbances in aggregate demand led a substantial number of economists during the 1960s to argue that the impact of much less dramatic fluctuations could be smoothed out by relatively small changes in spending and the money supply—i.e., that the economy could be *fine tuned*.

- **Fine tuning** refers to discretionary monetary and fiscal policies to reduce the impact of relatively minor fluctuations in aggregate demand, employment, and prices.

The success of fine tuning, or the lack of it, depends on the ability of forecasting models to make accurate and specific economic predictions. The models must be sensitive enough to identify the kind and magnitude of fine tuning needed to achieve acceptable unemployment and inflation rates. Not surprisingly, fine tuning was most widely accepted in the 1960s, when the track record of economic forecasters was good, discretionary monetary and fiscal policies apparently were successful in achieving their objectives, and unemployment rates and rates of inflation were relatively modest. Unfortunately, the success of fine tuning didn't carry over into the 1970s. The relationship between unemployment rates and the rate of increase of the price level was less stable and predictable in the 1970s, and the track record of the economic forecasters wasn't nearly as strong.

Why were the forecasting models that were successful in the 1960s less so in the 1970s? One reason is that econometrics and econometric models can't foresee exogenous economic shocks. Econometric models are based on data from the recent past and work best when economic conditions and relationships aren't dramatically different from those of the recent past. The models tend to do worse when conditions and relationships are different from those in the recent past, and ironically this is when economic forecasts and policy prescriptions are most important.

No econometric model, for example, could estimate and predict the political tensions in the Middle East that produced the export embargo on oil shipments by the Arab members of the Organization of Petroleum Exporting Countries (OPEC) in 1973–1974. Furthermore, instead of a one-shot price hike on oil exports, OPEC raised prices on exported oil continually through the 1970s, generating and intensifying cost-push inflationary pressures—another variable even the best model couldn't foresee.

Second, economic policies are shaped ultimately by political forces as well as economic forces, and it is difficult if not impossible to incorporate political variables in empirical models. The Vietnam War was escalated and then ended in 1973, direct controls were instituted then removed during Nixon's New Economic Plan, and numerous shifts occurred in monetary and fiscal policies.

In addition to these problems with the forecasts on which the fine tuners relied, fine tuning in the 1970s suffered from many of the same problems as other demand management policies—lags in implementation and effect, uncertainty about timing and results, and expectations. Also, fine tuning may require more flexibility in monetary and fiscal policies than political institutions permit. There is no guarantee that better models would have resulted in better economic policies during the 1970s; politicians are often unwilling or politically unable to undertake the policies prescribed by the forecasters and fine tuners.

If econometric models, forecasts, and fine tuning took too much credit for the economic successes of the 1960s, they also took too much of the blame for the serious problems of unemployment and inflation of the middle and late 1970s. Few economists seriously argue that econometric models should be ignored or that econometrics should be relegated to the status of a black art. The only alternative to systematic quantitative forecasting is playing hunches, based on individuals' subjective feel for economic conditions. Improving quantitative methods and forecasting tools should remain a high priority item in the fight against unemployment and inflation.

Managing Aggregate Supply: Incomes Policies

The mixed record of traditional stabilization policies in maintaining acceptable levels of unemployment and inflation has led some economists and policymakers to take a closer look at *incomes policies*.

- **Incomes policies** aim to reduce inflation by restraining the ability of wages and prices to rise.

Incomes policies attack cost-push inflation by regulating aggregate supply. To the extent that they keep wages and prices from rising, they hold the aggregate supply curve down. Since they attack the supply side of the unemployment-inflation problem, incomes policies are *supply management* policies. Incomes policies range from persuasion and voluntary guidelines to mandatory controls of wages, prices, rents, profits, and interest income.

Voluntary Guideposts and Guidelines

In 1962, President John Kennedy's Council of Economic Advisers proposed the use of voluntary wage and price guideposts as a means of controlling inflation. The guideposts tried to eliminate cost-push inflation by tying the average rate of increase in compensation per worker-hour to the average rate of increase of output per worker hour. This would stabilize the *average unit labor cost* (*ULC*) of goods and services produced. Unit labor cost is

$$ULC = \frac{WR}{(Q/H)}, \qquad (1)$$

where WR is the wage rate per worker hour and (Q/H) is output per worker hour. If the wage rate rose at the same rate over time as output per worker, ULC would remain constant, and one of the cost-push pressures would be eliminated.

Voluntary wage-price standards rely heavily on persuasion, moral suasion, and the force of public opinion for compliance. When firms and unions deliberately ignore or violate guidelines, government officials (typically the President) use the force of their offices to turn public pressure against the violators. The haggling and persuasive effort by the President to promote compliance with voluntary standards is called **jawboning**—presumably referring to the dialogue between the President, unions, and firms, although critics have been quick to point to the Old Testament account of Samson's slaying of a thousand Philistines with ". . . a fresh jawbone of an ass."

Bringing the weight and influence of the Presidency against wage and price actions of unions and firms can be a potent force. Perhaps the most dramatic example of that force was John Kennedy's famous 1962 showdown with the steel industry in which the companies finally backed off and rescinded their price increases. It seems naive, however, to expect moral suasion and voluntary compliance alone to keep powerful unions and firms from exercising their market power, especially in periods where there are strong demand-pull forces. By and large, Presidents haven't been as effective in jawboning unions and corporations as Samson apparently was in jawboning the Philistines.

Close-up

The Carter Wage-Price Guidelines

The voluntary guidelines–jawboning strategy emerged again in 1978, as the Carter administration turned its attention from unemployment to inflation. The 1978–1979 guidelines simply stated targets for wage and price increases.

> The voluntary wage and price standards call for an average rate of pay increase of 7 percent or less (in 1979). I also have asked businesses to hold their average rate of price increase to at least one-half percentage point below the average rate of increase in 1976–77. Where such price deceleration is not possible, the standards provide for limitations on profit margins.[1]

President Carter appointed a special chief inflation fighter, Alfred E. Kahn (who had been a Professor of Economics at Cornell, head of the New York State Public Utilities Commission, and Chairman of the Civil Aeronautics Board). In his public acceptance of his position, Kahn asserted that the only alternative to voluntary compliance with the wage and price standards was a massive recession, or a "deep, deep depression." When the White House expressed concern that Kahn's strong language would be alarmist, he agreed to substitute the word "banana" for recession and depression.

Some firms and unions agreed to comply with the standards, but the rate of inflation continued to accelerate in the first quarter of 1979. The du Pont Co., which had agreed to comply with the price guideline, announced in April 1979 that it might not be able to comply if inflation continued to accelerate.

The reaction of organized labor to the standards ranged from cool to frigid. George Meany and other key leaders in the AFL-CIO rejected the guidelines as unfair to labor, and large increases in corporate profits in early 1979 didn't make the AFL-CIO any more receptive to the guidelines. A Teamsters' strike in April of 1979 produced tragicomic episodes of Teamsters officials rejecting the guidelines and government officials attempting to show that the Teamsters' wage demands really were consistent with the guidelines. The Rubber Workers' Union opened its contract negotiations in the spring of 1979 with a demand for a 40 percent wage increase over the three-year term of the new contract, and the massive United Auto Workers Union also announced its intention to bargain very hard on wages.

By the spring of 1979, there was growing public admission that the most likely means of restraining inflation would be monetary and fiscal restraint which would produce a recession (or "banana"). Although the guideline program had had

---

1. *Economic Report of the President* (Washington: Government Printing Office, 1979), p. 9.

some success (most notably when Sears was convinced to cancel a scheduled price increase), and although the Supreme Court in June of 1979 had upheld the President's right to enforce his program by denying government contracts to violators, inflation continued at a rate well above ten percent.

Mandatory Wage and Price Controls

Some critics of guidelines and voluntary compliance advocate tougher measures to restrain wage and price increases and mandatory compliance with standards. Usually, these proposals for mandatory controls extend them to cover increases in all types of income—profits, interest, and rents as well as wages.

It isn't reasonable to expect unions to keep wage demands within wage guidelines if they can't be confident that price increases also will stay within price guidelines. Similarly, firms won't be likely to keep price increases within guidelines if workers demand excessive wage increases. The advocates of wage and price controls argue that making noncompliance with standards more difficult would lower the inflationary expectations and uncertainty of workers and employers and would thus weaken inflationary pressures without excessive unemployment.

Unless something is done that gets at the causes of inflationary pressure, however, wage and price controls may end up merely suppressing inflation. Wages and prices would remain stable or increase slowly, while inflationary pressure took such forms as empty shelves, waiting lists, and non-price rationing (formal or informal).

Mandatory wage and price standards have to be enforced to be effective, and enforcement isn't free. Manpower and other resources have to be allocated to enforce the controls, and these resources have alternative uses. Even during World War II, when the country faced very real external threats and there was almost unprecedented unity of purpose, enforcing of the price controls set by the Office of Price Administration (OPA) required a massive bureaucracy, plus thousands of volunteers who worked in the enforcement effort without pay. Enforcement of stringent controls certainly wouldn't be any easier in the political and economic climate of the 1980s.

Very stringent controls on wages and prices—such as a wage-price "freeze"—is like pinching a hose with the water turned on. Price increases slow down during the freeze, but inflationary pressures continue to build. When the freeze is lifted, the general pattern is for prices to take a sudden jump and then follow a more moderate rate of increase. There is very little evidence that temporary price and wage freezes have any long-term effect on inflation, so the only reasonable result to expect is a temporary slowing of price increases, followed by a short burst of rapid inflation and a return to the long-term price trend.

**Can Incomes
Policies Work?**
To be effective, an incomes policy would have to reduce inflationary expectations. Households, workers, firms, and financial institutions have to be convinced that the policies will reduce the expected rate of inflation. If this happens, then the natural rate could be maintained with a lower rate of inflation. In Figure 1, for example, if the actual rate of inflation equals the expected rate of 10 percent per year at the natural unemployment rate of 6 percent, lowering the expected rate to 5 percent will result eventually in the natural rate of unemployment being maintained with a constant 5 percent per year rise in the price level.

Of course, if attempts at limiting inflation through incomes policies have a poor success record, a new incomes policy may not generate very widespread confidence, in which case it would have little if any effect on expectations. It's even possible that very stringent controls could raise inflationary expectations if people and institutions expect the typical pattern of rapid price increases after the controls are relaxed.

The final consideration in assessing the probable effectiveness of incomes policies is more political than economic. Well-heeled special interests will lobby hard for exceptions to the standards, and the interest groups and industries with the most economic and political clout will be the most successful in getting exceptions. This means that the standards will be enforced unevenly, with enforcement being the most stringent in the industries with the least influence.

Figure 1 Lowering the Expected Rate of Inflation

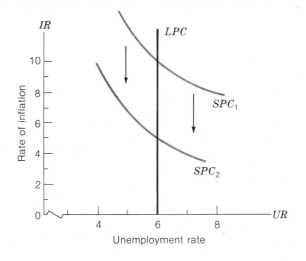

**Managing
Aggregate
Supply:
Indexing**
Inflation erodes the purchasing power of money, and can create unforeseen windfall gains and losses. A worker whose money wage increases by less than the rate of inflation incurs an unexpected loss in real income. Lenders will suffer losses if the real value of the repay-

ments of interest and principal are less than the real value of the original loan. Savers suffer losses of real wealth if the interest on their accounts is below the inflation rate. Since income taxes are based on money wages and money profits, inflation tends to produce unexpected increases in taxes—especially with progressive taxes. Further, efforts by those affected to anticipate future inflation through higher wage demands and interest rates only worsen the problem.

One way to eliminate unforeseen effects of inflation on purchasing power and real income is to tie money payments to the Consumer Price Index or some other measure of changes in the price level.

- **Indexing** of money payments would tie the value of money payments to an index of prices.

Proposals for comprehensive indexing of money payments aren't new. Alfred Marshall proposed indexing in the late 19th century. However, indexing remains a nontraditional approach to inflation. It has been tried in countries suffering chronic inflation (such as Brazil) with some success, but it doesn't have much of a record on which to base its likelihood of success.

Escalator Clauses

One form of indexing is relatively familiar, namely, the *escalator clause*.

- **Escalator clauses** adjust money payments automatically to changes in the price level.

Escalator clauses in collective bargaining agreements provide for adjustments to money wage rates to compensate for changes in the Consumer Price Index. For example, suppose that a contract provides for an initial wage of $10 per hour, and a three percent annual wage increase, with an escalator clause that adjusts money wages for changes in the Consumer Price Index. If there were no change in the Consumer Price Index after the first year of the contract, the wage would be $10.30 per hour in the second year—i.e., ($10 × 1.03 = $10.30). However, if the CPI increased ten percent during the first year of the contract, the money wage for the second year would have to be increased by ten percent as well. Thus the wage escalator would result in a three percent increase in the real wage, but the money wage for the second year would be ($10 × $1.13 = $11.30). Escalator clauses could thus reduce the tendency to push for large increases in money wages by guaranteeing the rate of increase in real wages.

A number of money payments in our economy are tied to the Consumer Price Index by escalator clauses. Social Security payments are adjusted for changes in the Consumer Price Index. Most public pension payments—military and civilian employees' pensions—provide for cost-of-living adjustments that index them to the Consumer Price Index. Many collective bargaining contracts provide for escalation of money wages if prices rise during the term of the contract.

Indexing Taxes

Because of the progressive structure of the Federal Income Tax, the American government is the biggest winner from inflation. Every rise in the price level means a huge increase in tax revenues. Some critics have even charged that the government has a vested interest in maintaining an inflationary economy.

Milton Friedman and other advocates of indexing have argued that indexing taxes would reduce the government's windfall revenues and would eliminate the false tax cuts that reduce tax rates but not total tax payments or revenue. One way to do this would be by indexing dependents' allowances, standard deductions, and tax brackets to compensate for changes in the Consumer Price Index. If prices rose by ten percent, for example, the dependents' allowance would be increased from $800 to $880, the standard deduction for a joint return would be increased from $1500 to $1650, and the $20,000 to $20,050 bracket which specifies a tax of $2536 would become the $22,000 to $22,050 bracket with a tax of $2790 for a family of four.

Indexing Interest Rates

Indexing proposals generally include indexing principal and interest payments to guarantee a real rate of interest. Suppose, for example, that a saver could buy a **purchasing power bond** for $10,000 that paid three percent yearly interest, adjustable to changes in prices. If, at the end of one year, the price level had risen by ten percent, the value of the interest and principal and interest would be $10,000 × 1.03 × 1.10 = $11,330, which is the equivalent of $10,300 at the original prices. In other words, indexing guarantees a *real interest rate of three percent a year*. Obviously, the incentive to save in periods of inflation will be greater if savers can be guaranteed a positive real interest rate.

The real value of interest payments and principal on loans could be guaranteed by issuing **purchasing power loans** indexed to the Consumer Price Index. If a bank loaned $20,000 for a year at four percent interest, and the Consumer Price Index rose by ten percent, the borrower would repay $20,000 × 1.04 × 1.10 = $22,880 after one year. The borrower would pay and the lender would receive a *real interest rate* of four percent a year. If loans were indexed, proponents of indexing argue, there would be no need for lenders to guess at the inflation premium component of nominal interest rates.

Control of Inflation or Surrender to It?

Critics of indexing argue that it would, in effect, strengthen inflationary pressures. Every buyer, seller, worker, employer, saver, borrower, and lender would be compensated for changes in prices. This, it is argued, would reduce the public pressure on government to fight inflationary pressure through monetary and fiscal restraint and other politically unpopular means.

Advocates assert that indexing would reduce cost-push inflationary pressures by stabilizing inflationary expectations. Uncertainty about future real income would be reduced by indexing money payments to changes in the piece level. Indexing would also reduce the unexpected windfall gains and losses, redistribution, and tax increases that accompany inflation.

Close-up

TIPs

One form of indexing that has received considerable attention in recent years is TIPs. *Tax-based incomes policies* (TIPs) attempt to limit the rate of increase of wages and costs through the tax system. There are two basic versions of TIPs —the "carrot" and the "stick."

Arthur Okun, formerly Professor of Economics at Yale and a Chairman of the Council of Economic Advisers under President Johnson, is the best-known proponent of the "carrot" approach. This approach seeks to limit wage increases by providing tax incentives to employees who keep wage increases below a specified rate. Workers who receive wage increases below the target rate would receive tax credits to bring their wage increases up to the target rate. President Carter's ill-fated "wage insurance" program was a variant of this approach. The logic is that workers will accept smaller wage increases as a result of the tax credits, and that this will slow the increases in labor costs and dampen cost-push pressures.

Henry Wallich is a widely respected economist and a Governor of the Federal Reserve. He is a proponent of the "stick" approach to TIPs which would impose tax penalties on corporations that paid wage increases above a targeted rate. The logic of the stick approach is that excessive wage increases and cost-push pressures would be lessened as employers try to avoid tax penalties by keeping wage offers down.

TIPs haven't been implemented on a meaningful scale, so we don't know how effective they would be against cost-push inflation. However, there are some potential problems. Workers who could get wage increases above the target rate would have no incentive to accept wage increases below the target rate and a tax credit that would bring their wage increases up to the target rate. At the same time, those who would receive wage increases below the target rate anyway could gain by receiving tax credits that bring their wage increases up to the targeted rate. The "stick" approach could add to cost-push pressures by levying tax penalties on firms. Tax penalties are added to the cost-push pressures of excessive wage increases, and higher costs have a habit of getting passed on as higher prices.

Won't Anything Work?

Where does our understanding of macroeconomics leave us on the problem of unemployment and inflation? Do we conclude that nothing we try will work? Can the analytical tools tell us anything about the problem and policies to deal with it or does macroeconomics simply lead us astray?

These are fair questions, and competent people have come up with different answers to each of them. However, one thing does seem clear—no simplistic solution will serve as a cure-all for the problem of unemployment and inflation. Also, the course of action we choose to attack the problem will not be without cost, and many measures that could be effective will be unacceptable on political or normative grounds. What follows is a brief sketch of the elements of what seems necessary to deal with unemployment and inflation. An effective policy has to attack the microeconomic and macroeconomic roots of unemployment and inflation, and must convince society that the policies will be effective against unemployment and inflation. This is a tall order, and no single policy will be effective by itself.

Monetary and Fiscal Policy

Discretionary monetary and fiscal policies can be effective shock absorbers to soften the effect of sudden economic changes on output, employment, and prices. However, these policies by themselves won't be effective against unemployment and inflation.

Fiscal policies should provide and finance society's needs that can't be met effectively through the public sector. Expenditures and revenues should aim at maintaining a balanced *full-employment budget*. Time lags, political controversy, and numerous mandated expenditures reduce the effectiveness and flexibility of fiscal policy as a means of fine tuning the economy.

Wide swings in monetary and fiscal policy should be avoided. Monetary policy should follow a stable course over time, although not necessarily a fixed rate of growth of the money supply. Rapid acceleration followed by hard braking in monetary policy has produced inflationary "booms" alternating with high unemployment "busts." This leads to unstable economic expectations which reduce the effectiveness of any monetary and fiscal measures. Also, the costs of wide swings in economic activity and employment usually impose the greatest human costs on the poor and those in chronically high-unemployment groups.

The Unemployment Target

If the unemployment rate is kept below the natural rate, prices will accelerate over time. If this acceleration is slow, we may well decide that the lower unemployment rate is worth the cost of slightly accelerating prices. However, if the rate of inflation continues to accelerate over time it will eventually reach a rate that society finds excessive and will have to be dealt with.

Setting the unemployment rate target at the natural rate of unemployment is one way of stabilizing the rate of inflation, and there may be some movement in this direction. Most estimates of the natural unemployment rate place it in the neighborhood of 5.5 percent. Since 1973, the Council of Economic Advisers has raised its "benchmark" unemployment rate for estimating potential GNP from 4.9 percent to 5.1 percent. Maintaining an unemployment rate of 5.5 percent doesn't relegate the same 5.5 percent of the population to perpetual unemployment, though, since persons move among labor force categories over time.

Reducing the Natural Unemployment Rate

The natural unemployment rate isn't determined by nature or etched in stone. If society decides that the natural rate of 5.5 percent is excessive, it is possible to lower the natural rate. Some means of lowering the natural rate will be popular and have broad appeal, but others will be controversial and unpopular. Also, programs that will be effective in lowering the natural rate are likely to be expensive.

Training and retraining programs can provide unemployed workers with employable skills and enhance their chances of finding employment. Increasing the mobility of labor out of economically depressed areas or encouraging employers to locate in these areas could reduce some chronic unemployment that contributes to the natural unemployment rate. Equal employment opportunity and affirmative action legislation and programs can reduce unemployment related to discrimination. Improved public employment services can improve the flow of labor market information and make job searches shorter and more effective. Some of these measures are controversial (affirmative action in particular) and all are expensive to implement and enforce. Society would have to decide whether the effectiveness of such programs is worth the cost.

The most controversial proposals for lowering the natural unemployment rate are those that would reform minimum wage legislation and unemployment compensation programs. Critics of minimum wages have argued for years that they restrict the employment opportunities of the young, the unskilled, and the untrained, and this argument has some empirical support. The implication is that the natural rate would fall if minimum wage laws were revised to exempt some groups and thus improve their prospects for employment.

Similar criticisms have been directed at unemployment compensation, which provides workers with income during periods of unemployment. Critics argue that the current unemployment compensation programs give the worker a strong incentive to keep searching and keep his or her reservation wage high until the benefits run out. Some have suggested that the natural unemployment rate would fall if unemployment compensation programs were modified in a way that shortened job searches and encouraged workers to accept employment —for example, by shortening the benefit period, lowering benefits, or including the benefits as taxable income.

Modifications of minimum wage legislation and unemployment compensation to reduce the natural unemployment rate carry obvious normative questions. In all but the most conservative constituencies, these measures would be politically treacherous.

Wage and Price Standards

Incomes policies have had a sorry record in controlling inflation, but publication of wage and price standards and of the firms and unions that choose to ignore the standards may have some effect on wages and prices through the force of public opinion. Standby authority to intervene in wage and price decisions may have a moderating effect if the workers and the firms want to avoid government intervention. However, it's not reasonable to expect such measures to have a dramatic effect on inflation.

Reducing Inflationary Expectations

Whatever combination of policies is chosen, its success in reducing unemployment without unacceptable increases in unemployment depends on its effectiveness in reducing inflationary expectations. If the expected rate of price increase falls, the rate of inflation at the natural rate of unemployment should also fall.

A long period of recession and high unemployment might reduce inflationary expectations, but the costs are high. It takes time for expectations to adjust to a declining rate of price increase, and in the meantime high unemployment imposes high costs on the unemployed and on the community in the form of lost output.

Selective indexing could reduce some of the inflationary expectations that contribute to cost-push inflation. Escalator clauses could reduce the incentive to push aggressively for high money wage increases, high nominal interest rates, etc. The escalators would guarantee the purchasing power of future money payments.

The success in reducing inflationary expectations may raise a "Catch 22" situation. To reduce inflation without high unemployment, inflationary expectations must be lowered. However, the most effective means of lowering inflationary expectations is to have a past record of success in reducing inflation without excessively high unemployment.

Summary

1. Monetarists assign a minimal role to discretionary monetary and fiscal policies as a means of achieving and maintaining full employment and stable prices. The monetarist strategy centers on the importance of market forces and flexible prices to achieve the objectives of full employment without unacceptable rates of inflation.
2. The traditional Keynesian approach to macroeconomic policies to achieve and maintain full employment or stabilize prices is *demand management* —i.e., regulating aggregate demand via discretionary monetary and fiscal policies.
3. **Fine tuning** refers to demand management policies that stabilize aggregate demand, output, and inflation through small changes in discretionary monetary and fiscal policies to minimize the instability of the economy over time. The success of fine tuning efforts depends heavily on the quality of information and the accuracy of economic forecasts.
4. **Supply management** policies attack unemployment, inflation, and instability that can be explained by instability of aggregate supply.
5. **Incomes policies** attempt to regulate aggregate supply by restraining increases in wages, prices, and costs. Incomes policies range from volun-

tary guidelines to compulsory controls.
6. **Indexing** would tie all wages, interest, and other payments to the Consumer Price Index. The object is to guarantee purchasing power and to reduce the incentive for workers, banks, and others to push for high nominal incomes to compensate for the effects of inflation. Since it attacks the cost-push forces, it is a supply management policy.
7. Any successful macroeconomic strategy must attack *all* of the forces that contribute to unemployment and inflation.

Concepts for Review

market solution	supply management	indexing
econometrics	tax-based incomes	escalator clauses
fine tuning	policies	purchasing power bond
incomes policies	jawboning	purchasing power loan

Questions

1. Which of the following are demand management policies, and which are supply management policies? Explain how each could affect aggregate demand or aggregate supply.
   a. government subsidies of research and development activities to stimulate technological change;
   b. restrictive monetary and fiscal policies;
   c. compulsory wage and price controls;
   d. tax cuts;
   e. retraining and relocation programs for unemployed workers.
2. According to Professor Friedman and many other monetarists, cost-push inflation from aggressive wage demands of unions is impossible unless the monetary authorities go along.
   a. What implications does this argument have for the probable success of wage and price controls as a means of reducing inflation?
   b. What type of macroeconomic strategy follows from this argument?
3. "Our tools of economic policy are much better tools than existed a generation ago. We are able to proceed with much greater confidence and flexibility in seeking effective answers to the changing problems of our changing economy." (President Lyndon B. Johnson, *Economic Report of the President*, January 28, 1965)
   a. What type of macroeconomic strategy is implied in this quote? Why was this strategy so appealing in 1965?
   b. Would the strategy implied in Johnson's statement be as likely to succeed now as it was in 1965? Why?
4. Suppose that the natural unemployment rate is 5.5 percent, and that the unemployment rate would remain at 5.5 percent with prices rising at a constant rate of 8 percent per year. The government has established goals of lowering the unemployment rate to 5 percent and the annual rate of price increase to 5 percent.
   Is there *any* way that these unemployment and inflation goals could be achieved? Explain, and put together a "package" of policies that would be necessary to achieve the unemployment and inflation goals.

PART SIX

The World Economy

The OPEC oil embargo of 1973 opened many people's eyes to the fact that the economies of the world have in recent years grown increasingly dependent upon one another. Gone are the days when a nation could close its doors to the rest of the world and hope to solve the problem of scarcity on its own. With the opening of relations with China, the decline of Cold War tensions between East and West, and the growth of multinational firms, trade today probably plays a more important role internationally than at any other time in history.

In this section, we'll explore the meaning and significance of **international trade**. The first two chapters lay the theoretical groundwork. We begin by asking the fundamental questions of *why* nations wish to trade with each other. What benefits do they derive from trade? We then move to the question of *how* nations trade, examining the role of national currencies in the international setting.

International trade is strongly influenced by *national* governments, through the **trade policies** they choose to enact. Increasingly in recent years, trade has been used as much more than merely a source of mutual benefit among nations. Import and export policies, for example, have been suggested and used as tools for achieving domestic goals—for controlling inflation and raising employment. Trade has also been employed more and more as a political weapon—a way of rewarding "friends" and punishing "enemies." In the last chapter of the section, we'll explore the effects and implications of various uses and abuses of trade policy.

17

The Gains
from Trade

Preview: We live in an economically interdependent world, and international trade is increasingly important economically. We import nearly half of the oil we consume. Some goods—bananas and coffee, for example—wouldn't be available at all in the absence of international trade. The agricultural sector and some industries (such as machinery, aircraft, and transportation) are large-scale exporters. Foreign trade is a fact of life, but *why* do countries trade with each other?

The roots of international trade are about the same as the roots of trade within a country. Trade exists because it makes the traders better off than they could be without trade. In this chapter, we'll explore the motivation, terms, and impact of international trade in order to get a basic understanding of the gains from trade.

Specialization, Trade, and Efficiency

A few rather simple propositions lie at the heart of international trade theory.

- Specialization leads to greater efficiency in production.

- Specialization requires the ability to trade.

- Trade encourages greater specialization and greater efficiency.

These propositions comprise the *classical* case for free trade, which was stated first by Adam Smith in *The Wealth of Nations* two hundred years ago.

Smith built his free trade case on his famous pin factory example. In the example, initially each worker produced a complete pin—drew the wire, cut it, polished it, sharpened the point, attached the head, and put the pins in a box or on a card. Then production was reorganized so that each worker performed only one operation. With this **specialization**, each worker became better at his particular task, and the pin factory became more efficient. Smith used this example to show that specialization, or *division of labour*, leads to greater efficiency in production.

Specialization makes no sense without trade, and Smith argued that specialization is encouraged by trade, or by "the extent of the market." Since efficiency depends on specialization, and specialization depends on the ability to trade, it follows that expanding the ability to trade encourages greater efficiency.[1]

The classical case for free trade follows from this notion. Removing barriers to international trade will increase the "extent of the market," encourage greater specialization, and lead to greater efficiency.

Comparative Advantage

David Ricardo, and later John Stuart Mill, laid the groundwork for the modern theory of international trade in the nineteenth century with the **principle of comparative advantage.** Suppose that a renowned brain surgeon is a hunt-and-peck typist. Clearly, he should devote his time and energy to brain surgery and hire a secretary to do his typing.

But what if the brain surgeon can type 150 words per minute with no errors? Should he hire a secretary, or should he do his own typing? He still should hire a secretary, because he has a **comparative advantage** in brain surgery. He is a better typist than the typical secretary, but he is a *much* better brain surgeon than the typical secretary. Imagine what would happen if the doctor hired a secretary and they divided all duties equally. The doctor would do a good job on the letters and bills, but imagine the brain surgery performed by the secretary! This illustration of comparative advantage can be applied to the production of goods to show the gains from specialization on the basis of comparative advantage.

Comparative Advantage and Specialization

Oranges can be grown in Maine—with heated greenhouses, artificial fertilizers, and artificial sunlight. Very few oranges are grown in Maine, of course, because it is much cheaper and more efficient to grow them in California and Florida where the climate makes the artificial sunlight and heated greenhouses unnecessary. The crops that can be grown commercially in Maine, potatoes for example, don't require the sunlight and warm weather that oranges do, and Maine is more suited to potato production than orange growing.

Comparative advantage is easy to identify if the cost of producing oranges is lower in Florida and the cost of producing potatoes is lower in Maine. Clearly, Florida has a comparative advantage over Maine in oranges and Maine has a comparative advantage over Florida in potatoes. Florida should specialize in oranges and buy its potatoes from Maine, and Maine should specialize in potatoes and buy its oranges from Florida. Potatoes and oranges will be produced more efficiently

1. See Adam Smith, *An Inquiry into the Nature and Causes of the Wealth of Nations,* Book I, Chapter 3.

with specialization and trade than they would be if both states tried to be self-sufficient.

But what if both goods could be produced more cheaply in Florida than in Maine? In Table 1, oranges and potatoes can be grown at a lower cost per bushel in Florida than in Maine. It appears that there would be no gains from specialization because Florida is a more efficient producer of both goods, but this is not the case.

Assume initially that some oranges and some potatoes are grown in both states. Now suppose that orange production is reduced by one bushel in Maine and increased by one bushel in Florida. The change in combined orange production in the two states is

$$\begin{array}{r} 1 \text{ bushel increase in Florida} \\ - \quad 1 \text{ bushel decrease in Maine} \\ \hline 0 \text{ change in combined orange production.} \end{array}$$

Reducing orange production by one bushel in Maine frees $100 that could be used for potato production. The cost of producing a bushel of potatoes in Maine is $4, so Maine could increase its potato production by $100/$4 per bu. = 25 bushels by reducing its orange production by one bushel.

In Florida, producing an additional bushel of oranges requires that $2 be diverted from potato production. The cost of producing a bushel of potatoes in Florida is $2, so increasing orange production by one bushel would cause potato production to fall by $2/$2 per bu. = 1 bushel.

The change in combined potato production in Maine and Florida is the difference between the increase in Maine and the reduction in Florida, or

$$\begin{array}{r} 25 \text{ bushel increase in Maine} \\ - \quad 1 \text{ bushel decrease in Florida} \\ \hline 24 \text{ bushel change in combined potato production.} \end{array}$$

In other words, with the same resources, combined potato production increased by 24 bushels with *no* reduction in combined orange production.

Clearly, Maine should specialize in potatoes and Florida should specialize in oranges. Maine has a *comparative advantage* over Florida in

Table 1   Comparative Advantage

	Cost per bushel	
	Maine	Florida
Oranges	$100	$2
Potatoes	$ 4	$2

potatoes, and Florida has a *comparative advantage* over Maine in oranges. Florida is a better potato producer than Maine, but a *much* better orange producer than Maine.

Comparative Advantage and International Trade

Comparative advantage in international trade is the same as it is in the simple examples above. There will be gains in efficiency if countries specialize on the basis of comparative advantage and trade with each other, compared to efficiency in a world of economically self-sufficient countries.

To illustrate the effects of comparative advantage in international trade, consider two countries—call them America (A) and Japan (J). Assume that they produce and trade two goods—our old friends food (F) and clothing (C). Table 2 shows the cost per unit of food and clothing in the two countries. Could America and/or Japan benefit from specialization and trade? The first reaction might be that American producers couldn't compete with the Japanese in either good because the cost per unit is lower for both goods in Japan than in America, but a closer look will show potential gains from specialization and trade.

Comparative advantage depends on the *relative* costs in the two countries, or the ratio of the costs per unit. According to the table above, the cost per unit of clothing in the United States is 10 times as great as the cost per unit of food. This means that the **internal marginal rate of transformation** (MRT) in America is

$$MRT_A = -\frac{10\,F}{1\,C} \quad \text{switch}$$

By reallocating its own resources without trade, America could get 10 units of food for every 1 unit reduction in clothing, or 1/10 unit of clothing for every 1 unit reduction in food.

In Japan, the cost of producing a unit of clothing is three times as great as the cost per unit of food. The Japanese without trade, would have to give up 3 units of food for every additional unit of clothing, and 1/3 unit of clothing for every additional unit of food produced. The Japanese marginal rate of transformation without trade (MRT_J), then, is

$$MRT_J = -\frac{3\,F}{1\,C}.$$

Table 2 Comparative Advantage and International Trade

	Cost per unit		Opportunity cost per unit	
	America	Japan	America	Japan
Clothing	$50	$12	10 F	3 F*
Food	$ 5	$ 4	1/10 C*	1/3 C

*Comparative advantage

Relative costs and *MRT* define the **opportunity cost** of increasing production of one good in terms of the amount of the other good that has to be given up in a fully employed economy.

In America, the opportunity cost of an additional unit of clothing is the 10 units of food that have to be given up, and the opportunity cost of an additional unit of food is the 1/10 unit of clothing that has to be given up. In Japan, the opportunity cost of an additional unit of clothing is 3 units of food and the opportunity cost of an additional unit of food is 1/3 unit of clothing. The *opportunity costs* of producing the two goods in the absence of trade are also shown in Table 2.

In Table 2, the opportunity cost of a unit of clothing is less than the opportunity cost of a unit of clothing in America, but the opportunity cost of a unit of food is less in America than in Japan. In other words, *America has a comparative advantage over Japan in food*, and *Japan has a comparative advantage over America in clothing*. This means that there are potential gains in efficiency and economic welfare in both countries from specialization and trade. America should specialize in food, and Japan should specialize in clothing. America should export food and import clothing, and Japan should export clothing and import food.

Terms of Trade

Comparative advantage shows *potential* gains from trade between two countries. However, the actual gains from trade, the distribution of the gains from trade between the two countries, and whether the countries would trade with each other at all depend on the *terms of trade*.

- The **terms of trade** define the rate at which goods will exchange for each other in international trade.

In the above examples, the terms of trade would be the rate at which food and clothing exchange for each other in international trade.

Terms of Trade and Gains from Trade

For trade between America and Japan, or between any two countries, to take place, the terms of trade have to lie between the countries' internal *MRT*s. In Table 2, for trade to take place between America and Japan, the international terms of trade would have to lie between $3F:1C$ (MRT_J) and $10F:1C$ (MRT_A).

The terms of international trade are determined by world prices of goods. America and Japan aren't the only trading countries in the world, and world prices are determined by the demand for goods by all buyers and the supply of goods by all sellers in world markets. Suppose that the world price of clothing (P_C) is \$30 and the world price of food (P_F) is \$5. Since the price of clothing is six times as great as the price of food, it takes 6 units of food to buy 1 unit of clothing in international trade, or the terms of trade are $6F:1C$.

Table 3 Comparative Advantage and the Terms of Trade

| | Opportunity cost with (without) trade | | | |
| | 6F : 1C | | 2F : 1C | |
	America	Japan	America	Japan
Clothing	6F (10F)*	6F (3F)	2F (10F)**	2F (3F)**
Food	1/6C(1/10C)	1/6C(1/3C)*	1/2C(1/10C)	1/2C(1/3C)

*Commodity country should import
**Commodity country should export

The terms of trade are determined by the ratio of prices. In the example, the terms of trade for food and clothing are

$$\text{Terms of Trade} = \frac{\Delta C}{\Delta F} = \frac{P_F}{P_C}.$$

The terms of trade define the opportunity cost of each good in international trade in terms of the amount of the other good that must be given up. With the given prices of food and clothing, the opportunity cost of an additional unit of clothing with trade is $6F$, and the opportunity cost of an additional unit of food with trade is $1/6C$. Table 3 shows the opportunity costs of food and clothing in America and Japan with trade at the given prices and without trade.

In the situation shown in Table 3, America should export food and import clothing because the opportunity cost per unit of clothing is lower with trade than the opportunity cost of producing it at home. Likewise, Japan should export clothing and import food because the opportunity cost of a unit of food with trade is less than the opportunity cost of producing it at home. In this situation, trade between America and Japan would be mutually beneficial.

Terms of Trade and Trade Between Countries

The terms of trade determine countries' gains from trade and whether or not any pair of countries will trade with each other at all.

• A country will not gain from trade if the international terms of trade are equal to the internal MRT without trade.

Suppose that the American MRT is $10F{:}1C$ and the Japanese MRT is $3F{:}1C$, as in Table 2, and that the world prices are $P_F = \$6$ and $P_C = \$60$. The international terms of trade are $P_F/P_C = 1C/10F$—the same as the American MRT without trade. In this case America would not gain from trading at all.

Japan's gains from trade with the international terms of trade $= 10F{:}1C$ would be greater than they were with the international terms of trade = $6F:1C$. At the new prices, Japan would have to give up $1/10$ F per unit of C by trading—clearly more advantageous than $1/3F$ per unit of C without trade or $1/6F$ per unit of C at the old terms of trade.

If the international terms of trade were equal to Japan's internal MRT, this would eliminate Japan's gains from trade. The American gains from trade, on the other hand, would be greater if the international terms of trade were $3F:1C$ than with the international terms of trade = $6F:1C$.

These examples illustrate a very important point concerning the gains from trade.

- A country's gains from trade will be greater the greater the difference between the international terms of trade and the country's internal MRT.

If the international terms of trade lie outside the range between the American and Japanese internal MRTs, the Americans and Japanese would not trade with each other because they would gain by exporting or importing the same goods, as in the second part of Table 3 which shows the opportunity costs with and without trade with the international terms of trade = $2F:1C$. At these terms of international trade, both countries will gain by specializing in and exporting food and importing clothing. Obviously, America and Japan wouldn't trade with each other at these international terms of trade.

Trade and Welfare

Gains from trade make it possible for countries to reach higher levels of economic welfare with trade than they can reach without trade. Trade does not expand the country's *production possibilities*, but it expands the number of goods that a country can *consume*.

Production Possibilities in a Closed Economy

As you may recall from Chapter 2, the production possibilities curve (*PPC*) defines feasible combinations of goods than can be produced in a closed economy (no international trade) with given resources and technology. The *PPC* in Figure 1 defines feasible combinations of wheat (*W*) and steel (*S*) in a hypothetical closed economy. The slope of the *PPC*, $\Delta S/\Delta W$, is the economy's internal *MRT*, which shows the rate at which output of one good must be reduced to increase output of the other by reallocating the economy's resources internally.

Suppose that the best combination of wheat and steel for the country is combination A on the *PPC*, with 5 million tons of steel and 17 million bushels of wheat. The means by which the community decides that this is "best" is not important at this point. The main point is that combination A is the best the economy can do without trade. The slope of the line tangent to the *PPC* at A is the economy's internal *MRT* at A.

The Impact of Trade

If the country could trade at given world prices, how would this affect the community economic welfare, compared to the situation without trade? Without making value judgments, it is possible to say that the economy is doing "better" if it can increase its production of one good without reducing the output of other goods, or increase its output of both goods.

Suppose that the world wheat price is $P_W = \$5$ per bushel, and that the world price of steel is $P_S = \$10$ per ton. These aren't accurate approximations of actual world prices, but are only illustrative. The value of combination A at these prices is

$$V_1 = P_W W + P_S S$$
$$= \$5 \times 17 \text{ million} + \$10 \times 5 \text{ million} = \$135 \text{ million}.$$

Other combinations of wheat and steel that have the same value as combination A lie on the negatively sloped line, $V_1 = \$135$ million through A. The slope of V_1 is the ratio $-(P_W/P_S)$.

Combinations of wheat and steel outside the V_1 line have a value greater than $135 million at prevailing world prices, and will lie on other value lines that are parallel to V_1.

- The greatest value of wheat and steel the economy can produce with trade is the combination for which the internal *MRT* equals the international price ratio.

In Figure 1, the combination on the *PPC* with the greatest value at prevailing prices is combination B with 9 million tons of wheat and 13 million tons of steel. Combination B lies on the line $V_2 = \$175$ million which is tangent to the *PPC* at point B.

Figure 1 Trade and Economic Welfare

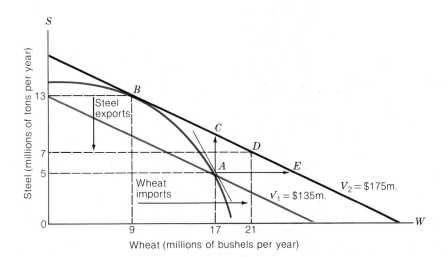

We cannot say that combination B on the PPC is better economically than combination A without making some kind of value judgment. However, with trade, the country can trade and consume any combination of goods on the line V_2. This line lies outside the PPC at all points except point B.

From point B, the country could export steel and use the revenue from the exports to import wheat. Any combination between C and E on V_2 is better than A economically because all combinations in this range have more of one good and no less of the other than combination A. If the community found that combination D were the best combination on V_2 with trade, it would be better off than at A (the best combination without trade) because it would have more wheat and more steel. To reach D, the country would export 6 million tons of steel and import 12 million bushels of wheat.

Figure 1 shows a theoretical result that has very important implications. First of all, the results show the gains from trade, the relationship between the international terms of trade and the gains from trade, and the degree to which the country will specialize in the good in which it has a comparative advantage at prevailing terms of trade. The results are more realistic because they portray one of many countries in world trade, while the earlier examples dealt primarily with bilateral trade between a pair of countries.

Applying the Tools

"The Importance of Being Unimportant"

The eighteenth and nineteenth centuries were a period in which the strong industrialized countries colonized and exploited the economies of the pre-industrial world. This development is described by the summary term *imperialism*. The imperialist epoch led many to the logical conclusion that the big gainers from international trade would be large, powerful economies with extensive resources, and that these gains would come at the expense of the smaller, weaker economies. This conclusion confuses the gains from trade with the political and military domination of small countries by large countries. In fact, the big gainers from trade are small countries without extensive and diverse resources.

To illustrate, classify goods as *farm products* (F) and *manufactures* (M). Figure A(i) shows the PPC for a large agricultural and manufacturing country, such as the United States or the Soviet Union. Figure A(ii) shows the PPC for a country, such as Japan, that has a substantial manufacturing capacity, but a small agricultural capacity. Combination A in Figure A(i) is the best combination of goods without trade for the large country, and combination A' in Figure A(ii) is the best combination of goods without trade for the smaller country.

Now, suppose that the countries can buy and sell farm products and manufactures at given prices, P_M and P_F. With trade, the large country would maximize the value of the goods it produces at point B on its PPC. From point B it moves to its preferred combination (C) on V_2. There are gains from trade, but they are fairly small compared to the best no-trade position for the large country.

Figure A

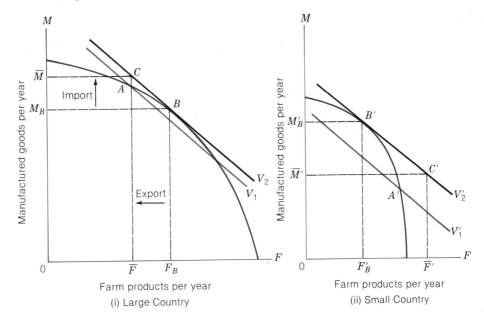

Farm products per year
(i) Large Country

Farm products per year
(ii) Small Country

By trading at given world prices, the small country would produce combination B' in Figure A(ii). By importing farm products and exporting manufactures, the small country moves to its best position (C') on V_2'. The gains from trade are much greater for the small country because the ratio of world prices and the international terms of trade are much different than the internal MRT at the small country's best no-trade position. Another factor contributing to the ability of small countries to realize large gains from trade is their inability to affect world prices. If the large country in Figure A(i) tried to specialize heavily in one good, it would lower the world price of the good, and its gains from trade would fall.

Because the smaller country gains more by trading over the best it could do without trade than the larger country, trade accounts for a larger share of the smaller country's national income than it does in the larger country. There is, of course, another side of the coin. Although small countries without diverse resources can gain the most from trade, fluctuations in international markets and international prices will have the greatest economic impact in these countries. This is especially true for countries that rely heavily on a single export to generate income.

Summary

1. International trade extends a country's markets, encourages international specialization, and raises the efficiency of the use of the world's economic resources.
2. The **principle of comparative advantage** identifies potential gains from specialization and trade, and the possibility of mutually beneficial trade between countries.
3. World prices determine the international **terms of trade,** or the rate at which goods will exchange for each other in international markets.
4. Countries will gain from trade if their **internal *MRT*** is different from the international terms of trade.
5. The potential gains from trade are greatest for relatively small countries without diverse resources, and international economic fluctuations have the greatest impact in these countries.

Concepts for Review

specialization
principle of comparative advantage
comparative advantage

internal marginal rate of transformation
terms of trade

Questions

1. Try to list some of the specific ways that international trade affects your economic welfare. What would be the effects of a complete abolition of the barriers to trade on your welfare? How would a complete cessation of international trade affect your economic welfare? Do you think that either more liberal foreign trade or cessation of trade would have the same impact on the economic welfare of all segments of society?
2. Suppose that Japan could produce all industrial goods at a lower average cost than the United States. Does it follow that the United States should import all industrial goods from Japan? Explain.
3. Some people argue that international trade is a means by which large countries exploit small countries because the small countries always lose in their trade with large countries. Is this notion consistent with the law of comparative advantage? Explain.
4. Countries with very narrow resource bases may have to specialize in the production of a single product for export. These countries stand to realize the greatest gains from trade, but trade also may lead to some serious economic problems in these countries. How could you explain this statement?

Problems

1. Never-Never Land and Almost-Never Land produce Bibles and rum. In Never-Never Land the cost of producing a Bible is $15 and the cost of producing a barrel of rum is $10. In Almost-Never Land, the cost of producing a Bible is $10 and the cost of producing a barrel of rum is $5.

a. In which good (if any) does each country have a comparative advantage over the other? Explain.
b. If the world price of Bibles were $18 and the world price of rum were $10, would it pay these countries to specialize and trade on the basis of comparative advantage?
   If so, in which good should each country specialize? Would they trade with each other?
c. Would your answers to part b be the same if the world price of Bibles were $25 and the world price of rum were $10? Explain.

18

International Exchange

Preview: In international trade as in any other trade, goods go one way and money expenditure goes the other way. If we import goods from abroad, goods flow into our country and money flows out to pay for the goods. If we export goods to another country, the goods flow out of and money flows into our economy. The first requirement for any trade is the ability of traders to make exchanges. But since different countries use different currencies, international trade requires some means to enable buyers and sellers to deal with each other.

Exchange Rates and International Currency

Until 1973, the international monetary system was based on gold. Gold was universally acceptable as money in international trade. **Convertible currencies,** such as the British pound and the American dollar, could be converted to gold by purchasing gold at guaranteed prices. Currencies were convertible for each other because they could be converted to gold at guaranteed prices, and this made it possible for buyers and sellers in different countries to deal with each other. Although the international gold standard no longer exists, the international economy still uses convertible currencies.

To see how convertible currency works, suppose that you buy a British sports car from a British seller. The price of the car will be expressed in pounds (£). Your money, of course, is dollars. To buy the British car, there must be some means for either the buyer or the dealer to convert dollars into pounds. The conversion of one currency for another is accomplished by the sale and purchase of currency in international currency markets.

Purchasing the sports car from Britain will have the following effects:

1. The car will be imported into the United States, and represents a *U.S. commodity import.*

2. The car represents a *British commodity export.*
3. *Pounds must be purchased* in international currency markets to pay for the car.
4. *Dollars must be sold* in international currency markets to buy the pounds to pay for the car.

The number of dollars sold and the number of pounds purchased depend on the *exchange rate* between the pound and the dollar.

- The **exchange rate** between currencies is the rate at which one currency exchanges for another in international markets, or *the price of one currency in terms of another.*

   With an international gold standard, exchange rates were defined by the official prices of gold in various currencies. Governments no longer guarantee the purchase and sale of gold at official prices, and exchange rates are determined by the market forces of supply and demand in international markets. The financial sections of some newspapers and the *Wall Street Journal* publish the exchange rates between the dollar and other currencies, expressed as the prices of other currencies in dollars.

Exchange Rates and the Prices of Exports and Imports

Exchange rates determine the prices that American buyers pay for imports and the prices that foreign buyers have to pay for U.S. exports. If the price of the British sports car in the previous example is £3000, how much will it cost in dollars? If the exchange rate of dollars per pound is $2.00/£, the dollar price of the car is

$$\$2.00/£ \times £3000 = \$6000.$$

If a British firm imported a piece of machinery from the United States, the price of the machinery in pounds would be the exchange rate of pounds per dollar, multiplied by dollar price. If the price of the dollar in pounds is $2.00/£, the price of the pound in dollars is £0.5/$. If the price of the machine is $2000, its price in pounds is

$$£0.5/\$ \times \$2000 = £1000.$$

Currency Appreciation and Depreciation

Changes in exchange rates affect the prices of imported goods to domestic buyers and exported goods to foreign buyers. If the dollar *appreciates* relative to another currency, the price of the dollar in that currency rises.

- **Appreciation** of a country's currency makes imported goods cheaper and exported goods more expensive.

   Suppose that the price of the dollar rose from £0.5/$ to £0.8/$. The price of the pound would fall to $1.25/£ as a result of the appreciation of the dollar. The dollar price of the £3000 British car would be

$$\$1.25/£ \times £3000 = \$3750.$$

The price of the exported U.S. machine in pounds would rise to

$$£0.8/\$ \times \$2000 = £1600.$$

Depreciation of a currency refers to a fall in the price of the currency in international markets.

- **Depreciation** of a country's currency makes its imports more expensive and its exports cheaper.

Suppose that the price of the dollar in pounds falls from £0.5/\$ to £0.25/\$, and therefore that the price of the dollar in pounds rises from \$2.00/£ to \$4.00/£. As a result of the depreciation, the price of the British sports car in dollars rises to

$$\$4.00/£ \times £3000 = \$12,000.$$

The price of the exported American machinery in pounds falls to

$$£0.25/\$ \times \$2000 = £500.$$

How Exchange Rates Are Determined

Exchange rates are currency prices, and like other prices they are determined by supply and demand forces in international currency markets. The supply and demand of currencies, in turn, depends on countries' imports and exports.

Foreign buyers must purchase dollars in international markets to pay for U.S. exports.

- The *demand* for a country's currency in international markets varies directly with its exports.

The demand curve for dollars in Figure 1a ($D_\$$) is negatively sloped, indicating an inverse relationship between the price of the dollar and the quantity of dollars demanded. As the exchange rate rises, U.S. exports become more expensive, and exports tend to fall. As exports fall, so does the quantity of dollars demanded to pay for them. If the price of the dollar falls, exports become cheaper, exports tend to increase, and the quantity of dollars demanded increases.

To pay for imports into the U.S., dollars have to be sold to purchase foreign currencies.

- The *supply* of a country's currency in international markets varies directly with its imports.

The supply curve for dollars in Figure 1b ($S_\$$) is positively sloped, indicating a direct relationship between the exchange rate (£/\$) and the quantity of dollars supplied. As the exchange rate rises, imported goods become cheaper in the United States, and U.S. imports will tend to rise. As more goods are imported, more dollars must be sold to pay for them. If the dollar depreciated relative to the pound, the results would be just the opposite.

Figure 1 Determination of Equilibrium Exchange Rates

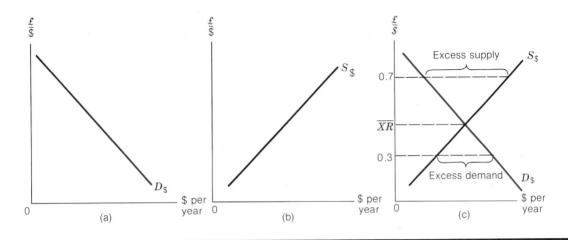

In the absence of restrictions, flexible exchange rates tend toward equilibrium, just as other flexible prices do. The equilibrium exchange rate is reached when the quantity of the currency supplied just equals the quantity demanded in international markets. The equilibrium exchange rate in Figure 1c reflects the U.S. demand for imports (in the $S_\$$ curve) and the foreign demand for U.S. exports (in the $D_\$$ curve).

If the exchange rate were below the equilibrium (for example, at £0.3/$ in Figure 1c) the dollar is **undervalued** relative to the pound, and there is an excess demand of dollars, or a *dollar shortage*. If the exchange rate were above equilibrium (at £0.7/$ in Figure 1c) the dollar is **overvalued,** and there is excess supply of dollars, or a *dollar glut*, in international markets.

The Balance of International Payments

The **balance of payments accounts** summarize the payments a country makes to the rest of the world and payments it receives from the rest of the world. A detailed look at the 1977 U.S. balance of payments accounts will be found in the appendix to this chapter. The following discussion uses a very simplified set of balance of payments accounts, containing only three accounts—a **merchandise** account, a **capital** account, and an **international settlements** account.

The Merchandise Account

The merchandise account shows the exports of goods to other countries and imports of goods from other countries. Exports are a *credit* item in the merchandise account.

- **Credits** are transactions that add to a country's assets or reduce its liabilities.

If the exports are paid for with convertible currencies, the exporting country's holdings of convertible currencies (an asset) increase. If the foreign buyers borrow to purchase exports, this increases the foreign obligations to the exporting country (also an asset).

Merchandise imports are *debits* in the merchandise account.

- **Debits** are transactions that reduce a country's assets or increase its liabilities.

When goods are imported, foreign sellers have to be paid, and paying them reduces the importing country's holdings of convertible currencies (an asset). If the imports are financed by borrowing, this increases the importing country's liabilities to foreign governments.

The **balance on the merchandise account** is the sum of the values of merchandise exports (+) and merchandise imports (−), or

$$\text{Balance on Merchandise Account} = \text{Merchandise Exports} - \text{Merchandise Imports.}$$

This is sometimes called **net exports** (as in the aggregate demand function) or the **balance of trade.**

The Capital Account

The capital account summarizes the capital flows between the United States and the rest of the world. An American firm's investment of capital abroad is a *capital export*. Foreign capital invested in the United States is a *capital import*.

There is a difference between entries in the capital account and the merchandise account.

- *Exports of capital* are debits (−) in the capital account.
- *Imports of capital* are credits (+) in the capital account.

If an American investor invests funds in another country, the funds have to be converted into the other country's currency, so dollars will be sold in international markets as a result of the capital export, and this sale will reduce U.S. holdings of convertible currencies (an asset). When foreign funds are invested in the U.S., the investment would have to be made in dollars, thus requiring purchases of dollars in international markets.

The balance on the capital account is the sum of capital exports and imports—i.e.,

$$\text{Balance on Capital Account} = \text{Capital imports} - \text{Capital exports.}$$

If capital imports exceed capital exports, the capital account will show a positive balance or surplus. If capital exports exceed capital imports, on the other hand, the capital account will show a negative balance or a deficit.

The International Settlements Account

Although the merchandise and capital accounts can show surpluses or deficits, the balance of *all* international payments must equal zero. The corollary of *There ain't no such thing as a free lunch* is *Everything bought or sold must be paid for.* Any difference between credits and debits in the merchandise and capital accounts must be made up for by some form of **international settlement.** With the international gold standard, imports and exports of gold and convertible currencies were important international settlements. Since the U.S. suspended gold payments in 1973, however, changes in the U.S. gold stock have been quite small, and other settlements (changes in reserves of convertible currencies, borrowing, and lending) have become the primary means of making international settlements.

The **settlement account** simply shows the amount that has to be settled with the rest of the world, and how these international settlements are made. Suppose, for example, that the United States exports goods and services worth $300 million, and that we import goods and services worth $250 million. The balance on the merchandise account in this case is

$$\text{Merchandise Exports} - \text{Merchandise Imports} =$$
$$\$300 \text{ million} - \$250 \text{ million} = \$50 \text{ million.}$$

In addition, suppose that capital imports are $100 million, and capital exports are $75 million. The balance on the capital account is

$$\text{Capital Imports} - \text{Capital Exports} = \$100 \text{ million} - \$75 \text{ million} =$$
$$\$25 \text{ million.}$$

The sum of the balances on the merchandise and capital accounts is the balance to be settled with the rest of the world, or the amount of international settlements to be made. In this example, international settlements are

$$\text{Balance on Merchandise Account} + \text{Balance on Capital Account} =$$
$$\$50 \text{ million} + \$25 \text{ million} = \$75 \text{ million.}$$

The surplus of $75 million means that the United States will receive payments or obligations from foreigners to make up for the surplus. To keep things simple, assume that imports and exports of convertible currencies are the only international settlements. The United States would import $75 million in convertible currencies from abroad. Imports of convertible currencies are debits, so the balance of all international payments in this example is $75 million (surplus on merchandise and capital accounts) − $75 million (currency imports) = 0.

It's a fairly common view that deficits in the merchandise and capital accounts are bad economically and surpluses good. In one sense, this is correct. Deficits in the merchandise and capital accounts must be settled by exporting convertible currencies, and convertible currency holdings are a precautionary asset for the country. When there are surpluses on the merchandise and capital account, convertible currency holdings rise, increasing a precautionary asset.

However, the effects of deficits in the merchandise and capital accounts on aggregate demand aren't necessarily bad, and the effects of surpluses aren't necessarily good. During periods of demand-pull inflation, deficits in the merchandise and capital accounts tend to dampen aggregate demand and inflationary pressure. Surpluses may stimulate aggregate demand and amplify inflationary pressures related to demand.

Capital flows create a potential conflict between the balance of payments position and domestic economic problems. Unemployment may suggest increases in the money supply and lower interest rates. However, lower interest rates discourage capital inflows into the country and encourage capital exports to countries where capital earns a higher return. Either of these results would reduce a surplus or increase a deficit in the capital account.

Exchange Rates and the Balance of Payments

Since exchange rates determine the prices of imports and exports, they will affect the country's balance of payments position by affecting merchandise imports and exports. With flexible exchange rates, changes in imports and exports will cause changes in the exchange rate. With fixed, or *pegged* exchange rates, changes in imports and exports will not affect the exchange rate, but will have other effects on the economy.

Pegged Exchange Rates

At a conference at Bretton Woods, New Hampshire, in 1944 the basic shape of the postwar international monetary system was established. One of the features of the Bretton Woods Agreement was fixed or *pegged* international exchange rates. The architects of the agreement, including John Maynard Keynes, saw flexible exchange rates and international currency speculation as one of the causes of the economic disasters of the 1930s, and fixed exchange rates were established to stabilize the international economy.

Exchange rates were pegged by pegging the dollar price of gold at $35 per ounce. The United States guaranteed foreign banks the conversion of dollars for gold at this price. The dollar prices of other currencies were also pegged. In short, exchange rates among currencies were pegged by pegged dollar prices of currencies and the exchange rates between currencies and gold were pegged by the pegged dollar price of gold.

Pegged exchange rates are not free to adjust to changes in currency demand and supply in international markets. Suppose that the price of the dollar is pegged at its equilibrium price $\bar{P}_\$$, in Figure 2a. Now suppose that the demand for U.S. exports increases, increasing the demand for dollars to $D_\$'$. With flexible exchange rates, the dollar would *appreciate*, and the price of the dollar would rise to $\bar{P}_\$'$. However, since the exchange rate is pegged at $P_\$^*$, the dollar is **undervalued** at $P_\$^*$.

Figure 2 Effects of *Pegged* Exchange Rates

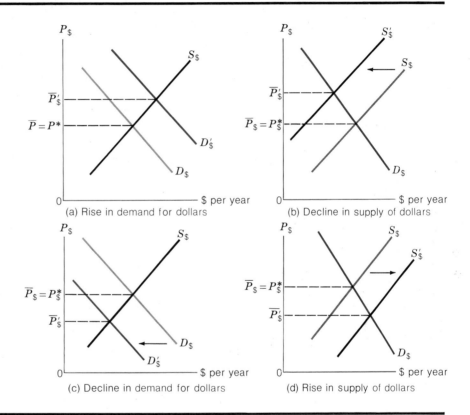

(a) Rise in demand for dollars

(b) Decline in supply of dollars

(c) Decline in demand for dollars

(d) Rise in supply of dollars

The dollar would likewise appreciate as a result of a decline in the U.S. demand for imports. As imports fall, the supply of dollars would shift to the left to $S_\$'$ in Figure 2b. With the smaller supply of dollars and the pegged exchange rate, $P_\$^*$, the dollar would again be undervalued.

Reduced demand for a country's exports or increased demand for imports will cause its currency to depreciate with flexible exchange rates. In Figure 2c, reduced demand for U.S. exports would shift the demand for dollars from $D_\$$ to $D_\$'$ and lower the equilibrium price of the dollar to $\bar{P}_\$'$. At the pegged exchange rate, $P_\$^*$, the fall in U.S.

exports makes the dollar an **overvalued** currency. In Figure 2d, increased demand for imports in the United States increases the supply of dollars in international markets to $S_\$'$, and the equilibrium price of the dollar falls to $\bar{P}_\$'$. Again, with the exchange rate pegged at $P_\$^*$, the dollar is *overvalued*.

How can exchange rates be kept above or below equilibrium? One way is the purchase and sale of currency by the government. If there were excess demand for dollars, for example, the U.S. government could sell dollars in international markets to eliminate the excess demand. With an overvalued currency, the government could sell other currencies to buy up the excess supply of its currency.

What if a country's reserves of convertible currencies aren't sufficient to allow it to maintain a rate that overvalues its currency? It can borrow convertible currencies from other countries or from the International Monetary Fund to enable it to buy enough of its currency to maintain the exchange rate. Every country also has a predetermined quota of **special drawing rights** (SDRs) which serve as reserves to allow it to purchase other currencies to maintain exchange rates.

Overvalued currency in international markets may contribute to domestic unemployment problems. An overvalued currency makes imports a bargain for domestic buyers, and makes exports expensive to foreign buyers in export markets. This will tend to depress the level of domestic employment.

Pegging the exchange rate *below* the equilibrium level, or undervaluing the currency, has the opposite effects. It gives the sellers of underpriced exports an advantage in world markets and makes imports relatively expensive to domestic buyers. In periods of brisk aggregate demand, this may add to inflationary pressures.

In short, something has to give to keep the exchange rate above or below its equilibrium level. If the currency is overvalued, a country's reserves of convertible currencies will be depleted or it will have to incur a foreign debt by borrowing foreign currencies to buy up the excess supply of its own currency. An overvalued currency may be maintained at the expense of domestic employment. Keeping the exchange rate pegged below equilibrium will eventually contribute to inflationary pressure in the economy.

Further, there is no guarantee that even the most heroic efforts to maintain a pegged exchange rate will work. In the mid 1960s, the British government went to great lengths to maintain the value of the pound in international markets. At $2.80/£, the pound was seriously overvalued. The British instituted incomes policies, bought surplus pounds in international markets, and borrowed heavily from the International Monetary Fund and the U.S. to buy pounds. All of these actions were to no avail, however, and eventually the pound was devalued anyway.

Applying the Tools

Pegged Exchanged Rates and the U.S. Balance of Payments, 1946–1972

The period 1946–1972 was one of massive changes in the international economy. Though decimated by World War II, the European and Japanese economies had by the 1960s been through a dramatic reconstruction and become major international economic powers. These changes had dramatic effects on U.S. exports and imports and on the demand for and supply of dollars in international markets, but the exchange rate between the dollar and other currencies was pegged for the entire period.

In 1946, the United States was the only major economy that had come through the war intact. The decimated economies of Europe and Japan were able to produce very little, so U.S. exports and U.S. dollars were in great demand. The supply of dollars in international markets was fairly low because of the low U.S. demand for imports.

With flexible exchange rates in 1946, the dollar would have appreciated dramatically. In Figure A, the demand for dollars (D_{46}) and the supply of dollars (S_{46}) would have determined a high price of the dollar (gold per dollar) at $\overline{P}_{46}$. However, the price of the dollar was pegged at $P^*_\$ = 1/35$ ounce of gold per dollar. This undervalued the dollar, and resulted in a *dollar shortage* in international markets. Foreign buyers settled with the United States by shipping gold and convertible currencies to the United States.

The U.S. gold stock increased during World War II and continued to increase after the war. Between 1946 and 1949, U.S. gold reserves increased from about $21 billion to about $24.5 billion. After 1949, a *gold drain* began. The U.S. gold stock was $17.8 billion in 1960, $13.8 billion in 1965, and $10.5 billion in 1972. Some blamed the gold drain on greedy American workers and unions that were "pricing our goods out of world markets." Others blamed greedy, shortsighted

Figure A

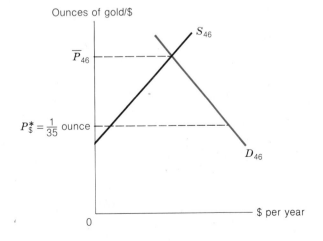

industrialists. Others blamed government deficits that were alleged to raise prices and "price our goods out of international markets." In fact, none of the popular explanations was sufficient to explain the gold drain.

As the European and Japanese economies recovered and grew in strength, their need for U.S. exports fell. By the 1960s competition from Japanese and European exports reduced world demand for U.S. exports, and U.S. producers faced increasing competition in domestic markets from imports.

The effect of the European and Japanese *economic miracle* on the demand for, and supply of, dollars is shown in Figure B. Falling demand for U.S. exports reduced the demand for dollars to D_{72} by 1972. Increased U.S. imports increased the supply of dollars to S_{72}. If the exchange rates had been flexible, the price of the dollar would have fallen to $\overline{P}_{72}$ by 1972.

Figure B

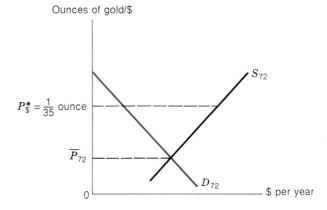

At the pegged exchange rate, however, there was excess supply of dollars or *dollar glut*, because the pegged exchange rate overvalued the dollar relative to other currencies. The United States settled with the rest of the world by exporting gold and convertible currencies. Thus, the gold drain was caused at least in part by the pegged exchange rate that overvalued the dollar. The overvalued dollar may also have contributed to domestic problems of sagging aggregate demand and unemployment in the United States.

Floating Exchange Rates

By the late 1960s, the international monetary system based on gold, the dollar, and pegged exchange rates had come under severe strain. At its pegged exchange rate, the dollar was an overvalued currency (its price in other currencies was too high to clear the market of dollars), and U.S. gold reserves were declining. Capital flows from the United States to Europe and Japan increased the number of dollars held by foreigners, and these foreign dollar holdings represented increased claims against the United States.

The failure of the British to support the overvalued pound through austerity and controls in the domestic economy and intervention in

Figure 3 Results of the 1973 Dollar Float

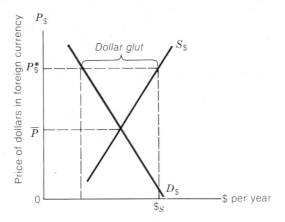

international monetary markets wasn't reassuring to those who supported fixed exchange rates. In January of 1973, the Italians allowed the value of the lira to float in international markets. The float of the lira was followed quickly by the float of the Swiss franc. In March, 1973, the Japanese allowed the value of the yen to float upward. The dollar was depreciated in 1973, and finally allowed to float. The international monetary system that had prevailed since the Bretton Woods Agreement in 1941 had collapsed.

When the dollar was allowed to float in 1973, it actually sank—i.e., its exchange rate fell against most convertible currencies. The reason is easy to understand in terms of simple supply and demand analysis. In Figure 3, the pegged exchange rate (or price of the dollar) is $P_\$^*$, above the equilibrium price P. Fixing a price above equilibrium created an excess supply of dollars, or a dollar glut, and removing the fixed price caused the price of the dollar to drop in international markets.

Although exchange rates aren't officially fixed or pegged, they aren't completely free to fluctuate either. The current exchange rate system is a **dirty float.** Governments and central banks intervene periodically in international currency markets to avoid what they see as excessive fluctuations in exchange rates. For example, when the United States floated the dollar, Germany and Japan bought large quantities of dollars in an attempt to keep the dollar from depreciating too rapidly or too far. In late 1978 and early 1979, the United States took a number of actions to bolster the value of the dollar in world currency markets— most notably raising interest rates and borrowing foreign currencies to buy dollars. The rationale behind the dirty float is that wide fluctuations in exchange rates will be destabilizing in international markets and will disrupt international trade.

A New International Monetary System?

The international monetary arrangements that had been established at Bretton Woods in 1941 were largely demolished by 1973. The current system is a mixture. Exchange rates aren't pegged, but they aren't completely flexible either. A stable monetary system and some form of international currency is essential for trade, but we only have clues concerning the shape of the international monetary system of the future.

Special Drawing Rights (SDRs)

In 1969, the International Monetary Fund (IMF) introduced Special Drawing Rights (SDRs) for making international settlements. Member countries are allocated SDR units on the basis of their share of international trade. The value of an SDR unit is based on the average value of the leading international currencies and therefore doesn't depend on the value of a money commodity (gold) or a single national currency (the dollar). The original purpose of the SDRs was to economize on gold as an international currency and to increase international liquidity. In a world in which the basic reserve currency (the dollar) floats, however, the SDRs have become increasingly important as a form of international currency.

The decline of the value of the dollar since the float in 1973 has caused concern about the stability of an international economy in which the dollar is the basic currency. This concern has been particularly strong among the oil-exporting countries. To understand this concern, suppose that an OPEC country agrees to sell oil to the United States at a specified dollar price—say, $20 a barrel. However, suppose that between the time of the agreement and payment by the U.S. importer the value of the dollar in international markets falls by 10 percent. In real terms, the exporter will receive 10 percent less than the agreed price for the oil. If the exporter and importer had agreed on a price in SDRs, depreciation of the dollar against other currencies wouldn't reduce the purchasing power received by the exporter for a barrel of oil, and this could reduce the incentive of oil exporters to increase the dollar price per barrel of oil to compensate for expected depreciation of the dollar. Of course, SDR prices would make oil more expensive for U.S. buyers because the SDR payments would be worth more dollars as the dollar depreciated.

The European Monetary System

On January 1, 1979, another clue concerning the shape of the future international monetary system appeared with the European Monetary System (EMS) and the European Currency Unit (ECU). The members of the EMS agreed to allow their currencies to float against the dollar, but set narrow limits within which the values of their currencies could fluctuate against each other.

The value of the ECU is a weighted average of the values of the currencies of EMS members, similar to the SDRs. The ECU floats against the dollar, and the range of fluctuations of EMS currencies against each other is defined by their values in ECU. If the exchange rate of, say, the French franc depreciated against the ECU and the German mark appreciated in ECUs so that the exchange rate between marks and francs went beyond the specified limits, the Germans and the French would agree to take appropriate policies to raise or lower the value of their currencies. The goal is to stabilize exchange rates within limits among EMS members.

What Next?

The increasing importance of SDRs in world trade and the introduction of the ECU seem to indicate a trend toward an international currency whose value is a composite of the values of all convertible currencies. This would reduce the importance of the dollar or any other single national currency as an international reserve currency.

Even if there were a new international currency for making international settlements and setting the exchange rates among countries, there is still the question of the degree of flexibility of these exchange rates. Critics of flexible exchange rates argue that some regulation or limits are necessary to prevent the destabilizing effects of fluctuations in exchange rates on international commerce. The proponents of flexible exchange rates argue that they would in fact be stabilizing in the long run, since currencies wouldn't become so overvalued that they encouraged massive speculation on their inevitable depreciation (as was the case with the dollar in the 1960s).

The choice of fixed or flexible exchange rates involves yet another issue—the independence of countries in their own monetary policies. With fixed exchange rates, or with limits on changes in exchange rates, countries with large trade deficits or surpluses would have to alter their domestic monetary policies to support the fixed rate or to keep the rate within prescribed limits. For example, if a large trade deficit put downward pressure on a country's currency, the country would have to follow a restrictive monetary policy to reduce its deficit and support the international value of its currency, and this may well lead to greater domestic unemployment. If trade surpluses caused the currency to appreciate beyond the prescribed limits, expansionary monetary policies (for example, lowering interest rates) would be needed to bring the exchange rate down, and this could lead to domestic inflation.

Summary

1. International trade requires an internationally acceptable currency. Historically, gold has been a basic international currency, but recently convertible currencies have been the basic international currency.
2. The exchange rate between currencies is the price of one currency in terms of the other.
3. Flexible exchange rates will tend toward equilibrium where the quantity of the currency demanded equals the quantity supplied in international

markets. From World War II, the exchange rates between the world's major currencies were not flexible, but fixed by international agreement.

4. The balance of payments accounts summarize payments between a country and the rest of the world. The balance of all of a country's international payments must equal zero.

5. Flexible exchange rates will tend to reduce surpluses and deficits in a country's balance of trade.

Concepts for Review

convertible currency	merchandise account	floating exchange rate
exchange rate	balance of trade	dirty float
appreciation	capital account	European Monetary
depreciation	international settlement	System (EMS)
overvaluation	settlement account	European Currency
undervaluation	pegged exchange rate	Unit (ECU)
currency glut	special drawing right (SDR)	

Questions

1. When the exchange rate between the dollar and other currencies was allowed to float, the price of the dollar fell in international currency markets.
   a. What does this tell you about the previously pegged exchange rate between the dollar and other currencies?
   b. Can you explain why the Japanese bought a large quantity of dollars to keep it from depreciating?
   c. What would you normally expect to happen to the balance of trade as a result of the depreciation of the dollar in international markets?
   d. A harder question: Under what conditions could the actual effect of depreciation of the dollar on the balance of trade be the opposite of the effects one would normally expect?

2. An article in the *Washington Post* in October 1978 contained the following statement: "Bad news for the dollar could not, in fact, be better news for the European market potential of the Detroit automobile industry."
   a. Explain how "bad news for the dollar" could affect the European sales of American cars.
   b. Could this same "bad news" affect the domestic sales of American cars? If so, how?

3. In June of 1979, Mr. Rene Ortiz of Ecuador—the Secretary General of OPEC—said that the OPEC *benchmark price* of crude oil should be raised from $14.55 to at least $20.00 a barrel. He asserted that "we (OPEC) still aren't at all fully compensated for our losses" as a result of the depreciation of the dollar in world markets and U.S. inflation. Explain carefully how U.S. inflation and the depreciation of the dollar would impose "losses" on OPEC.

4. The annual report of the Bank for International Settlements in Switzerland asserted that a U.S. recession would reduce worldwide inflationary pressure, reduce the U.S. trade deficit, and restore stability to international exchange markets. Specifically, the report

called for tighter monetary and fiscal policies and higher interest rates for the United States.

   a. Explain carefully how tight monetary and fiscal policies and a recession in the United States could affect worldwide inflation, the U.S. balance of payments, the strength of the dollar in international markets, and the stability of international exchange markets.

   b. Would monetary and fiscal restraint and a recession in France or Belgium have the same effect on worldwide inflation and the stability of international exchange markets? Why?

   c. Would the measures be necessary if international exchange rates were completely free to float? Why?

5. Although gold no longer serves as an international reserve currency, the price of gold in world markets remains important. When a currency *weakens* against gold, it means that the price of gold in that currency has gone up.

   a. When OPEC announced another price increase in 1979 on its oil exports, the dollar *weakened* against gold. How could higher OPEC oil prices cause the dollar to weaken against gold in international currency markets?

   b. Sometimes the price of gold in all major currencies will rise or fall. How would you interpret and explain a rise in the price of gold in all currencies? How would you interpret and explain a fall in the price of gold in all currencies?

Problems

1. The small country of Sokituya made the following international transactions in 1980. All figures are millions of cronies (the local currency).

Travel by foreigners to Sokituya	200
Private and public purchases of bonds in foreign companies	250
Foreign purchases of Sokituian bonds	100
Sales of military goods abroad	125
Pensions and unilateral transfers to foreigners	50
Purchases of corporate bonds in Sokituya by foreigners	500
Foreign travel by Sokituyans	150
Merchandise imports	750
Misc. services, net	−100
Income from foreign investments	100
Income paid to foreign investors	150

   a. Identify the credits and debits above, and put the appropriate sign (+ or −) before each.

   b. Find the balances for the merchandise, goods and services, current, and capital accounts.

   c. Sokituya makes all international settlements in dollars. Will it import dollars, export dollars, or neither? What value of dollars (if any) will it import or export?

   d. What is the balance of *all* international payments for Sokituya in 1980? Is this unusual?

APPENDIX

U.S. International Transactions, 1977

Most references to the balance of payments in the media and in political debate refer to the balance on the *merchandise account*, the *goods and services account*, or the entire *current account*. These are convenient summary figures, but they represent only a part of our transactions with the rest of the world.

Table A-1 is a summary of U.S. international transactions for 1977.

Table A-1 Summary of U.S. International Transactions, 1977 (millions of $)

Merchandise exports (+) and imports (−), net	−$31,130
Investment income, net	17,507
Net military transactions	1,334
Net travel and transportation	−3,044
Other services	4,749
BALANCE ON GOODS AND SERVICES	−$10,585
Remittances, pensions, and other unilateral transfers	−4,708
BALANCE ON CURRENT ACCOUNT	−$15,292
Change in U.S. assets abroad	−$34,419
Change in foreign assets in the U.S.	50,869
Errors, omissions, discrepancies	−927
BALANCE ON CAPITAL ACCOUNT	$15,523
COMBINED BALANCE, CURRENT AND CAPITAL ACCOUNTS	231
Official Reserve Assets	−231

Source: *Economic Report of the President, 1979.*

The Current Account

The *merchandise account* is fairly straightforward, and needs little explanation—it simply shows the difference between merchandise exports and merchandise imports. The United States showed a deficit in the merchandise account in 1977 of $31,130 million. This means that the value of our merchandise imports from other countries exceeded our merchandise exports to other countries by about $31 billion. The merchandise account showed surpluses (exports greater than imports) in every year between 1946 and 1970, and deficits in five of the years between 1971 and 1977. We don't have to look far for an explanation of this shift. In 1977, we imported nearly $45 billion worth of petroleum and petroleum products—$33 billion from the OPEC countries alone. By comparison, in 1972, our petroleum imports amounted to $4.7 billion, about $3 billion of which came from OPEC. If we excluded petroleum (or even excluded OPEC) imports, the remainder of the merchandise account would show a surplus.

Military transactions include the sales of military goods to other countries and direct military expenditures in other countries. Military sales (for example, international sales of arms and military hardware) are credits in the balance of payments, like any other commodity export. Direct military expenditures, on the other hand, are deficits in the balance of payments accounts. Direct military expenditures include such items as direct military assistance to other countries, maintaining troops abroad, etc. Direct military expenditures, in contrast to sales, involve the sale of dollars in international markets, and are therefore debit items. The military transactions account showed deficits every year from 1946 through 1975, and surpluses in 1976 and 1977.

The *travel and transportation* account is another one that consistently shows deficits—1951 and 1952 were the only postwar years in which this account showed a surplus. When an American travels abroad, he or she must exchange dollars for other currencies, and this increases the supply of dollars in international markets. When a foreign tourist visits the United States, on the other hand, he or she must purchase dollars. In short, Americans' travel expenditures abroad are debits and foreigners' travel expenditures are credits. Places like Athens, Greece, are apparently more attractive to American tourists than are Athens, Georgia, or Athens, Michigan, to foreign tourists.

Remittances, pensions, and other unilateral transfers are, like direct military transactions, unilateral payments abroad. Dollars are sent abroad, sold for other convertible currencies, and no payments flow back to the United States. Nonmilitary foreign economic aid is included in this account. Pension payments to American retirees who live in Ireland or other garden spots abroad also represent unilateral transfers.

Investment income (but not the investments themselves) are included in the current account. Payments of income to foreign investors on their investments in the United States are debits (−) because the dollars paid to foreign investors must be sold for the investors' own currencies. Similarly, income to U.S. investors on their investments abroad is a credit (+), because the foreign currencies must be sold for dollars by U.S. investors.

The sum of the balances on the merchandise, military transactions, investment income, travel, and unilateral transfers accounts is the *balance on the current account.*

The Capital Account

The *capital account* summarizes the international capital flows between the United States and the rest of the world. Actually, since all international payments except international settlements are either current or capital expenditures, the capital account basically includes the items that aren't included in the current account.

Capital flows are summarized as U.S. assets abroad and foreign assets in the United States. Just remember that *capital imports* are credits (+) and *capital exports* are debits (−). If a U.S. company builds a plant in Europe, this is a capital export, and it requires the sale of dollars at some point. On the other hand, if a Japanese company builds a plant in the United States, this is a capital import and it will require a purchase of dollars. The sum of the balances for capital flows and errors and omissions gives us the *balance on the capital account.*

International Settlements

Deficits and surpluses in the current and capital accounts are settled by changes in *official reserves*—government holdings of gold, convertible currencies, special drawing rights, and reserves with the International Monetary Fund. If the combined current and capital account balance shows a deficit (−), this is settled by exporting official reserves. Exports of official reserves are credits (+) and offset the deficit in the current and capital accounts. If the combined current and capital account balance shows a surplus (+), this is settled by importing official reserves (a debit) to make up for the surplus.

In 1977, the combined current and capital account balance showed a surplus ($231 million) due to the large surplus in the capital account. This was settled by importing official reserves from foreign governments (−$231 million). The balance of *all* international transactions and payments in 1977, as in any year, was zero.

19

Trade Policy: Mechanics, Problems, and Issues

Preview: The extent to which our trade with the rest of the world is "free" depends to a large extent on the **trade policies** enacted by the federal government. The government has the power to encourage imports and exports through subsidies, or to discourage them through tariffs and quotas. It may use this power for a variety of reasons: to achieve domestic economic goals, to gain political ends, to maintain national security. In this chapter, we'll examine the most important trade policy tools and assess the arguments for and against various trade policies.

Trade policy problems are nearly as old as international trade itself. International rivalries among emerging nation-states led to a basic economic strategy called **mercantilism** that stressed national economic, political, and military power. In international trade, mercantilist policies emphasized restriction of imports, encouragement of exports, and national economic self-sufficiency. Much of the classical economics of Smith, Ricardo, and Mill was an attack on mercantilist economic policy.

In U.S. history, too, trade policy has been important. The American colonies were restricted to trading almost entirely with England. A British tax on tea shipped to America was one of the catalysts that led to the American Revolution. In the nineteenth century, the United States imposed tariffs to encourage domestic economic development, protect domestic producers, and become as independent as possible economically.

Many of the old trade policy questions are still debated today. Can we reduce unemployment by imposing trade restrictions? Can our workers compete with cheaper foreign labor? Does national security demand economic self-sufficiency? Can we dampen inflationary pressures by restricting exports?

Tariffs and Import Quotas

A country may follow policies that restrict imports for a number of reasons. Some people believe that restricting imports will reduce domestic unemployment. Others advocate import restrictions in the interests of national self-sufficiency and national security. The merits of these and other arguments for restricted imports cannot be evaluated without some understanding of the effects of import restrictions on the economy.

The two basic ways to restrict imports are the imposition of **import quotas** that set maximum quantities of goods that can be imported and the imposition of a *tariff* on imported goods.

- A **tariff** is an excise tax on imported goods. It may be a tax per unit of a good imported or a percentage of the value of a good imported (*ad valorem*).

Tariffs and Efficiency

A British tariff on agricultural imports in the nineteenth century (the Corn Laws) was one of the critical issues that led to the development of classical free-trade arguments. Consider two countries—America (A) and Britain (B). Both countries can produce wheat, but the cost and therefore the supply price of any quantity of wheat produced in America is lower than in Britain because America has superior resources for growing wheat. In Figure 1, the American supply function (S_A) lies below the British supply function (S_B) at every quantity of wheat. Figures 2a and b show the equilibrium prices of wheat in America and Britain without trade. The price is higher in Britain because the inferior land makes wheat scarcer relative to the demand than in America.

Figure 1 Supply Curves for Wheat, Britain and America

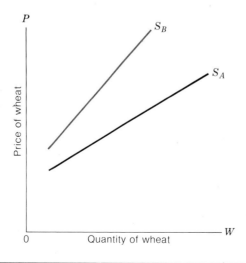

Figure 2 Equilibrium Prices Without Trade

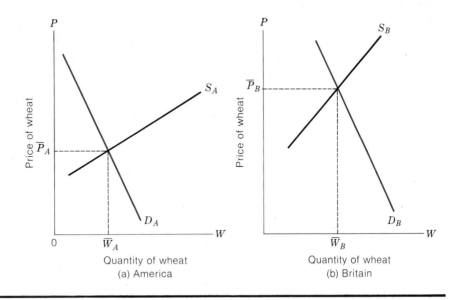

(a) America

(b) Britain

Suppose that American wheat growers are free to deal with British buyers.[1] With trade, there will be a single supply curve for the combined wheat produced in America and Britain—$S_W = S_A + S_B$ in Figure 3. Similarly, with trade, there will be a combined demand curve for America and Britain that shows the combined quantity demanded by American and British buyers at every price—$D_W = D_A + D_B$ in Figure 3. The combined demand and supply curves with trade determine an equilibrium price, $\overline{P}_W$, in Figure 3. This is the price at which British and American growers can sell wheat, and the price for which British and American buyers can buy wheat with trade.

In America, the wheat trade raises the price of wheat from $\overline{P}_A$ (without trade) to $\overline{P}_W$ in Figure 4a. The higher price of wheat reduces the American quantity of wheat demanded and increases American wheat production. The wheat in excess of the domestic quantity demanded is exported to Britain. In Britain, the effects are the opposite of those in America. Trade lowers the British price from $\overline{P}_B$ (without trade) to $\overline{P}_W$ in Figure 4b. At the lower price, British buyers will demand a larger quantity of wheat than at the higher price, but British growers will reduce the quantity of wheat supplied. The excess demand for wheat in Britain at $\overline{P}_W$ is filled by importing American wheat.

The wheat trade between America and Britain thus had the following effects:

1. To keep things simple, ignore the costs of shipping wheat between America and Britain.

Figure 3 Equilibrium Price with Trade

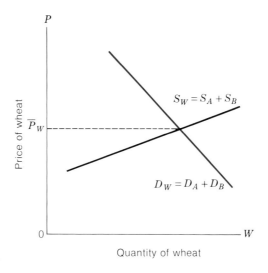

1. Wheat production became more efficient. Trade encouraged higher levels of output from the superior American resources and lower levels of output from the inferior British resources.
2. The price of wheat rose in America as a result of the export demand.
3. The price of wheat fell in Britain as a result of wheat imports from America.

In terms of efficiency of wheat production, the wheat trade was a good thing, but efficiency isn't the only thing involved in assessing the effect of trade on the community's welfare.

The wheat trade benefited American farmers, suppliers of resources needed in American wheat production, and British consumers. American growers received higher prices, produced more wheat, and purchased more resource inputs than without trade. British consumers paid lower prices as a result of the trade.

However, trade didn't make everybody in Britain and America better off. In fact, it made some people in each country *worse* off than they were without trade. American consumers paid higher prices for wheat products. British wheat growers suffered as a result of lower prices, and the suppliers of resource inputs to British wheat production were worse off as production fell.

In short, since trade made some people better off and others worse off in each country, value judgements are required to say that trade is good or bad. The inability to resolve normative questions analytically accounts, in large part, for the durability of controversies concerning trade policy.

Now suppose that the British impose a tariff that protects all of the wheat farmers who were growing wheat prior to trade. This tariff would make imported wheat just as expensive as wheat grown in Britain. The tariff would reduce British wheat imports to zero, increase the quantity of wheat supplied by British farmers, and return Britain to the same position it was in without trade in Figure 2a.

The tariff also returns America to its no-trade position in Figure 2b. With the export demand gone, American producers will face the American demand curve only. The price of wheat in America falls, and the quantity of wheat produced in America declines as a result of the British tariff.

Effective tariffs tend to reduce efficiency. By shutting off the wheat trade, less wheat is produced with the superior American resources, and more wheat is produced with the inferior British resources. However, a value judgement is needed to say that the tariff is a good thing or a bad thing. The British farmers, the suppliers of inputs to British farmers, and American consumers are better off as a result of the tariff. American wheat farmers, the suppliers of inputs to American wheat farmers, and the British consumers of wheat products are worse off as a result of the tariff.

Tariffs and Gains from Trade

Tariffs tend to reduce the volume of a country's trade, the efficiency of production of affected goods, and the country's gains from trade. Without trade, the country in Figure 5a can consume any combination of wheat (W) and steel (S) on or inside its production possibilities curve. Suppose that combination A (11 million tons of wheat and

Figure 4 Effects of Trade

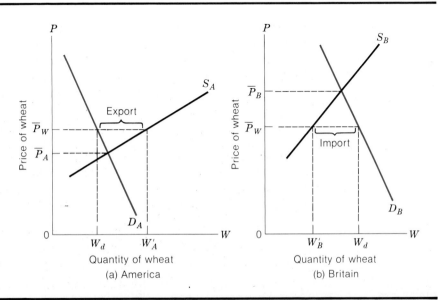

(a) America

(b) Britain

17 million tons of steel) achieves the highest possible level of economic welfare for the country without trade.

Given world prices of wheat (P_w = $40 per ton) and steel ($P_S$ = $20 per ton), the maximum value of wheat and steel the country can produce is combination B (19 million tons of wheat and 12 million tons of steel). The value of combination B is V_1 = $1,000 million. All combinations on the line V_1 also have this value at the given prices, so the country can use trade to move to any position along V_1. We'll assume that the country chooses to move to combination C by exporting 5 million tons of wheat and importing 10 million tons of steel.

Now, suppose that the steel producers' lobby convinces the government to impose a tariff of $20 per ton on imported steel. The tariff raises the price of imported steel to domestic buyers from $20 per ton to $40 per ton ($20 world price + tariff of $20), and makes imported steel more expensive relative to wheat. The terms of trade shift from

$$\frac{\Delta S}{\Delta W} = \frac{P_W}{P_S} = \frac{\$40 \text{ per ton wheat}}{\$20 \text{ per ton steel}} = \frac{2S}{1W}$$

without the tariff to

$$\frac{\Delta S}{\Delta W} = \frac{P_W}{P_S + \text{tariff}} = \frac{\$40 \text{ per ton wheat}}{\$40 \text{ per ton steel}} = \frac{1S}{1W}$$

with the tariff.

With the new terms of trade in Figure 5b, the economy moves from point B on the production possibilities curve to point D as a result of

Figure 5   Tariffs and the Gains from Trade

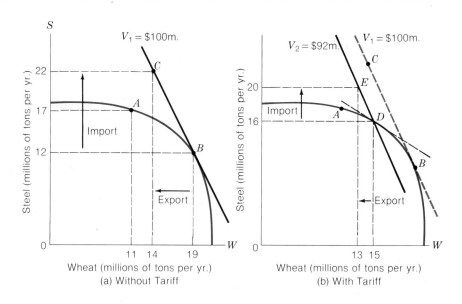

(a) Without Tariff

(b) With Tariff

the tariff. At point D, the domestic marginal rate of transformation (MRT) equals the terms of trade with the tariff (the slope of the line segment tangent to the production possibilities curve is the terms of trade with the tariff. In world prices, the value of combination D (15 million tons of wheat and 16 million tons of steel) is $V_2 = \$92$ million. By exporting wheat and importing steel along V_2 to point E (the best combination for the community on V_2), steel imports fall by 2 million tons (from 22 million to 20 million), and domestic steel production increases from 12 million tons without the tariff to 16 million tons as a result of the tariff. This is a desirable result for the steel industry, but it is not the only effect of the tariff.

The tariff lowers the total value in world prices of wheat and steel produced from \$100 million to \$92 million, reducing the country's gains from trade. If the community chooses combination E on V_2, it will consume less steel and less wheat than with free trade. A reduction in both goods represents a loss of economic welfare to the community.

The tariff thus reduces but does not eliminate trade and the gains from trade. Combination E is better than combination A (the best for the community without trade), but not as desirable as combination C.

Import Quotas

Import quotas reduce imports by setting maximum quantities of goods that may be imported. Obviously, effective import quotas must be set below the level of imports with free trade.

The results of import quotas are the same as those of tariffs. Quotas restrict the supply of imported goods and thus tend to raise the prices of imported goods to domestic consumers. The increase in import prices reduces import competition for domestic producers.

Quotas also reduce the gains from trade. Suppose that, instead of a tariff, the country in Figure 5 limits steel imports to 4 million tons per year by a quota. The quota reduces steel imports by the same amount as the tariff in the previous example. Reducing steel imports raises domestic steel prices, and moves the economy along its production possibilities curve to point D. The terms of trade are altered by the higher prices of steel, just as they were by the tariff. However, at world prices, the value of combination D is only $V_2 = \$92$ million in Figure 5b. The effect of the reduction of imports by 2 million tons with a quota is the same as the effect of the tariff that reduced imports by 2 million tons.

The Case for Import Restriction

Most of the common arguments for policies to restrict imports sound plausible at first, but break down on closer examination. Import restrictions create winners who benefit from them and losers who are worse off, so most arguments for restricting imports involve value judgements at some point. Some arguments for restricting imports are valid in special circumstances but must be examined closely.

Protecting American Workers from Cheap Foreign Labor

Perhaps the most common argument for restricting imports asserts that imports force American labor to compete with foreign workers whose wages and living standards are much lower than those of American workers. The argument asserts that competition with "cheap foreign labor" from Japan, Taiwan, Hong Kong, or Singapore will force American workers out of work. A point usually not stated explicitly is that restricting imports would protect the managers and owners in affected industries as well as the workers.

Although the claim seems plausible, it is one of the weakest arguments for restricting imports. In the first place, one reason wages are comparatively high in the United States is that labor is scarce in the United States relative to other resources. American workers have more land and capital to work with, and thus output per worker-hour of labor will be higher than in the countries where labor is very abundant.

Generally, the workers and industries in the United States that have suffered as imports increased are *labor-intensive*—i.e., production uses large labor inputs relative to other resources. In such industries—for example, cameras, radios, stereo equipment, and textiles—the high wages of U.S. workers make it difficult to compete with imported goods from countries where labor is much cheaper.

On the other hand, the United States has a comparative advantage over countries with abundant labor in the production of goods that require large inputs of land and capital relative to the labor input. For example, the United States can produce most agricultural products more efficiently than Japan because of the abundance of land and capital in the United States. Agriculture and *capital-intensive industries* that use large capital inputs per unit of output would be hurt by import restrictions because their output would decline.

What if most of the goods we consumed could be produced more cheaply abroad and imported than they could be produced at home? Even in this case, the cheap foreign labor argument for import restrictions breaks down on closer examination. First of all, as we saw in the discussion of comparative advantage, it is possible (even likely) that the United States would have a comparative advantage in some products. But what if differences in costs were such that we imported much more from Japan than we exported to Japan? As this continued, the exchange rate between dollars and yen would change—the dollar would depreciate relative to the yen, and the yen would appreciate relative to the dollar. As the yen appreciates relative to the dollar, Japanese goods become more expensive to American buyers. Appreciation of the yen would thus offset the effects of low wages on the cost of imported goods from Japan.

Fair Competition As a variation of the cheap foreign labor argument, some people advocate import restrictions to put domestic producers on equal footing with foreign producers, or to ensure fair competition between domestic products and competing imports. As in the cheap foreign labor argument, one of the most glaring omissions is the effect of cost advantages on exchange rates. If a country had a distinct cost advantage over the United States in the production of goods, and U.S. imports increased, the dollar would depreciate in international markets and make the imports more expensive to U.S. buyers.

If a tariff were enacted to equalize the cost of imports and domestically produced goods—consistent with the notion of fair competition—there would be no gains from trade. With no gains from trade, there would be no trade, and domestic producers would face no import competition.

Tariffs and Full Employment: "Beggar-My-Neighbor" Tariffs are often argued for as possible solutions to sagging aggregate demand and unemployment in the domestic economy. This is an appealing argument intuitively and makes some sense in the context of the basic Keynesian model. Aggregate demand, you will recall, is $AD = C + I + G + X - M$. Aggregate demand varies directly with exports (X) and inversely with imports (M). It appears that reducing imports would raise aggregate demand and equilibrium income and reduce unemployment. What could be wrong with the *beggar-my-neighbor* approach to the unemployment problem?

In the first place, there is the important qualification so frequently left out—*other things must remain unchanged*. For the beggar-my-neighbor policy to work, exports must not fall as a result of the policies that reduce imports. If the United States restricts imports to raise aggregate demand, other countries are likely to respond by restricting their imports from the United States, reducing U.S. exports.

Even in the absence of retaliatory policies abroad, our import restrictions may cause aggregate demand to fall. For foreign countries, U.S. imports are their exports. If U.S. imports fall, exports and aggregate demand will fall in other countries. As aggregate demand falls in other countries, their demand for our exports will fall too. The decline in foreign demand for our exports would at least partially offset the effect of reduced imports on aggregate demand.

The fatal flaw in the beggar-my-neighbor approach is that import restrictions tend to reduce the export flow as well. Also, it is difficult to export unemployment if unemployment is a common problem in other countries—as it was in the 1930s when this argument for import restriction was most popular.

Tariffs as a Source of Tax Revenue Tariffs are excise taxes on imports. Why not use tariffs to raise government revenue, and get foreign producers to help us pay our taxes? First, tariffs are excise taxes, and at least part of an excise tax is passed on to buyers as a higher price. So domestic consumers end up paying at least a share of the tax. Also, there is an obvious conflict between the effectiveness of a tariff as a means of protecting domestic producers and as a source of tax revenue. If the tariff effectively excluded imports, tax revenue from the tariff would be zero.

Infant Industries

A country may have the resources to develop an industry that could compete against import competition and compete successfully in world export markets, but the industry is so poorly developed that it may not even be able to compete against imports at home. If such an *infant industry* were protected by a tariff, it could develop and mature. As the infant matures under the protection of the tariff and becomes more efficient, the tariff would become unnecessary because imports would not be any cheaper than domestically produced goods. Also, once it matured, the industry could compete successfully in international markets.

As a temporary measure to stimulate development of an infant industry, import restrictions may be beneficial, especially in underdeveloped countries. There are some potential problems, however. The most obvious is to identify an infant industry that has a chance of maturing successfully with the country's resources. Also, the gains to the community in the future after the industry matures must be weighed against the cost to the community of protecting it temporarily from import competition. Finally, of course, there is the problem of deciding when the infant has grown up enough to be on its own. There is a danger that an overprotected infant industry may not mature at all.

National Security

Import restrictions have been advocated for some industries in the interest of national security. For industries that *are* critical for national security, protecting them to allow us to meet our minimal needs makes some sense, but there is a catch. What industries really *are* critical for national security? No self-respecting lobbyist would miss a chance to argue that his industry is essential to the national security, and that it should be protected from foreign competition.

Further, what are our minimal needs of critical materials and products? Industries seeking protection on the grounds of national security generally seek exclusion of import competition. In fact, it may be possible to provide for national security without import restrictions by stockpiling critical materials and products.

National security arguments for import restrictions have to be analyzed as closely as others. All import restrictions involve losses of both efficiency and gains from trade. Are the gains in national security worth the cost to the community? Is the industry really essential to the national security? Can minimal needs of critical products be met without import restrictions?

Export Policies

Trade policies don't deal exclusively with imports. Governments may enact policies that affect the level of a country's exports, in order to stimulate aggregate demand or dampen inflationary pressures.

Export Subsidies

A subsidy is just the opposite of an excise tax on producers. By paying producers a subsidy per unit of output, firms may be able to sell at a lower price. Figure 6 shows hypothetical demand and supply curves for wheat *exports*. With no subsidy, the equilibrium price of wheat exports is $\overline{P}$, and wheat exports are $\overline{W}$. Subsidizing wheat exports drives the supply curve downward by the amount of the subsidy, and the price falls to $\overline{P}'$, where the subsidized supply curve intersects the demand curve. Wheat exports increase from $\overline{W}$ to $\overline{W}'$ as a result.

The logic behind such subsidies is that lower prices on exports will increase exports and increase aggregate demand. There are, however, a number of questions and potential problems involved in export subsidies. First of all, it is possible that the entire subsidy will not be passed on as lower prices. In Figure 6, for example, the equilibrium price does not fall by the amount of the subsidy. The difference between $(\overline{P}' + s)$ and $\overline{P}$ is retained by sellers as a higher price than they received without the subsidy.

Secondly, lower prices for exports may not increase the country's revenue from exports. If the volume of our exports rises by a smaller percentage than the percentage decline in the price of exports, lower

Figure 6 Effects of Export Subsidy

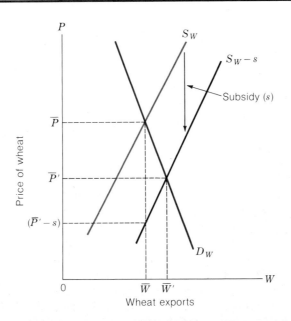

prices will reduce export revenue. Only if a given percentage reduction in export prices leads to a greater percentage increase in exports would lower prices raise export income, other things constant.

A third potential problem is international retaliation in response to our export subsidies. Countries that are affected adversely by a U.S. export subsidy may impose higher tariffs on their imports from the United States or subsidize their exports that compete with U.S. exports in world markets. These reactions would reduce the demand for the subsidized exports and at least partially offset the effect of the subsidy on U.S. exports and export income.

Most arguments for export subsidy overlook the important question of the source of the funds to pay the subsidy. Subsidy payments will increase government spending. If they are covered by additional taxes, the additional taxes tend to offset any effect the export subsidy would have on aggregate demand. If taxes are not increased, the subsidy may have to come at the expense of spending on other public sector projects with a fixed budget. If the additional spending simply increases the deficit in the government budget, it may contribute to inflationary pressures, and domestic inflation may offset the effect of the subsidy on the price of the exports subsidized.

Like tariffs, export subsidies cause the prices and terms of trade to diverge from the world prices and terms of trade. They tend to reduce the value of goods produced by the economy (in world prices), and to reduce the country's gains from trade. Finally, like tariffs, export subsidies benefit those associated with the subsidized industries at the expense of others in the community. This, of course, means that value judgements concerning gains to winners vs. losses to losers are implicit in arguments that export subsidies are good or bad for the community.

Restricting Exports

In recent years, a number of export restrictions have been imposed on certain goods (wheat, logs, and soybeans for example) to dampen inflationary pressures in the domestic economy. The logic behind arguments for export controls is fairly clear. On the macroeconomic side, if demand-pull inflationary pressures can be traced to export demand, reducing exports and export income will dampen aggregate demand and demand-pull inflation. On the microeconomic side, heavy export demand in specific industries may contribute to rising domestic prices in these industries and to cost-push inflation in related industries and an export quota may reduce this pressure. Unfortunately, such results may be a matter of wishful thinking.

Consider, for example, the possible effects of an imposition of export quotas on wheat. Figure 7 shows the demand for U.S. wheat exports, the supply of U.S. wheat exports, the price of wheat exports, and the equilibrium level of wheat exports. Now, suppose that exports are restricted to W* in order to dampen inflationary pressures. The effect of the restriction on aggregate demand and demand-pull

Figure 7 Effects of Export Quota

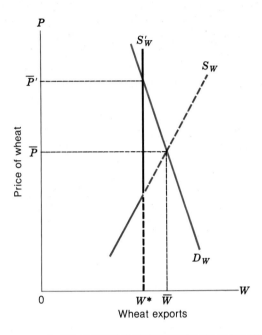

inflationary pressures depends upon its effect on world wheat prices, and upon the responsiveness of world demand for American wheat exports to changes in price. The U.S. is a major wheat exporter, and restricting American wheat exports would tend to raise prices of wheat in world markets. Note in Figure 7 that restricting wheat exports to W^* raises wheat export prices from $\overline{P}$ to $\overline{P}'$. If wheat exports fall by a smaller percentage than price rises, then U.S. income from wheat exports would rise as a result of the export restriction and higher price, increasing inflationary pressures. Also, of course, effective export restrictions reduce the country's gains from trade.

The effectiveness of export controls in reducing cost-push inflationary pressures depends on their effects on domestic production and on international reaction to the export controls. Export controls on wheat, for example, would encourage farmers to divert their land to other crops—or conceivably to nonagricultural uses. These actions would reduce the supply of wheat to domestic consumers and raise wheat prices.

Like import restrictions, export controls may have unfavorable international repercussions. Suppose, for example, that the OPEC countries responded to reductions of United States wheat exports with an embargo on oil exports to the United States. This would drive oil prices and the prices of all oil products upward and generate cost-push inflation in the United States. The same thing would happen if the

OPEC nations raised the price of oil exported to other countries to compensate for the higher prices of wheat in world markets as a result of U.S. export restrictions.

Finally, of course, there are value judgements implicit in arguments for export controls to fight inflation. Export controls shift the burden of fighting inflation to the industries whose exports are restricted and the suppliers of inputs to those industries. This doesn't mean that export controls are bad for the community, but it does require a value judgement concerning the losses in the affected industries vs. gains to the rest of the community.

Trade Policy Problems and Issues of the 1980s

Trends in trade policy in the 1970s were schizophrenic. On the one hand, the trend toward liberalization of trade that had begun in the 1960s continued in the 1970s, culminating in a new multilateral trade agreement in 1979 that lowered tariff and nontariff barriers to trade. On the other hand, slowing economic growth and recessions in the industrialized countries led to growing sentiment for protectionism to deal with domestic unemployment. These conflicting forces of liberalization and protection will continue to shape trade policy in this decade, and perhaps for the remainder of the century. Within this framework, there are a number of key issues and problems facing trade policy.

Dealing with OPEC

When Iran, Iraq, Kuwait, Saudi Arabia, and Venezuela formed the *Organization of Petroleum Exporting Countries* in 1960 to protect the interests of the oil producing countries against those of the multinational corporations who extracted and refined the oil, almost no attention was paid to it. Certainly, there was no alarm that OPEC could affect economic conditions in the United States. In 1970, OPEC (which had grown to 13 countries) agreed on a unified pricing system for oil exports, marking the birth of OPEC as a *cartel*.

- **Cartels** are groups of sellers who agree formally on common prices and terms of sale for their product.

During the 1970s a series of events pushed the OPEC benchmark price from $1.80 per barrel in 1970 to a maximum of $23 a barrel by mid 1979. Although it had been largely unnoticed in the 1960s, OPEC has emerged as the most important force in the international economy, and OPEC decisions are important determinants of prosperity or recession in the industrialized countries that depend on imported oil.

Anger and frustration have led many to propose "trade war" responses to OPEC actions—embargoes on exports to OPEC, boycotting OPEC oil imports, an international cartel of oil importers, etc.—to counter the power of OPEC as a seller of oil. None of these stand much chance of success in breaking the power of OPEC in world markets, and each would impose great costs on the oil importing countries. Countries that have no domestic oil sources can't become self-sufficient, and the costs of self-sufficiency in countries like the United States that can provide a substantial part of their own oil would be very great. Shutting off exports of agricultural and manufactured goods to OPEC countries isn't a realistic alternative because it would depress employment and income in the industrial countries. Cartels are only as strong as their weakest link, and a cartel of oil importers would be only as strong as the willingness of the countries with the greatest need for imported oil to hold out.

What then is the best way of dealing with the high prices of imported oil? It's easy to blame OPEC for our energy problems, but OPEC couldn't command such high prices for their oil if the demand by oil importing countries weren't so great. We have to recognize that the only way to respond effectively to high oil prices is to economize on the use of oil, a solution that is both obvious and unpleasant. At the Tokyo economic summit in 1979, the major industrial importers of oil—the United States, Japan, France, Germany, Britain, and Canada—agreed to put ceilings on future oil imports as a response to the decision of OPEC in June, 1979, to raise the price of oil exports for the second time during that year. What does this imply for the economies of these countries?

It would be nice if the demand for oil could be replaced easily by alternative sources of energy that are safe and clean, but this isn't likely. Alternatives to oil are in an early stage of development and are expensive. Extracting oil from shale, for example, wouldn't be economical unless the price of OPEC oil rose another fifty percent or so. Increased use of coal is an economically feasible solution, if we ignore or undervalue the environmental costs of extracting and burning more coal. The social costs and risks of nuclear power became painfully obvious in the Three-Mile Island "incident" in 1979. Massive use of solar and wind power and the development of clean and safe synthetic fuels has great potential as a source of energy in the twenty-first century, but not now.

For the majority of the population in the industrialized countries, oil conservation will take the forms of slow economic growth, changes in living standards and lifestyles, and more modest economic expectations. Smaller cars, smaller and more energy-efficient houses, less heat in the winter, less air conditioning in the summer, more mass transit, and less recreational automobile travel are some of the less appealing forms that energy conservation will take for most of us.

Dumping

Dumping is a rather uncomplimentary term for exporting goods at "unfair" prices. The criteria for identifying dumping vary somewhat from case to case, but the most typical criteria are charging prices for exports below the cost of production and charging lower prices for exports than the prices of the goods in the exporting country's domestic market. Legislation allows the President and the Congress to take specific actions against the dumping of exports in the United States. If dumping is confirmed, anti-dumping penalties are assessed equal to the difference between the price of the good in the exporters' home market and the price paid by American importers.

Why would exporters dump their goods at a low price? If they face greater competition in export markets than in domestic markets, and if the domestic and export markets can be separated, it may be more profitable to sell at a lower price in the export market than in the domestic market. Producers who overestimate demand for their goods and over produce may temporarily dump the goods by charging a low price to reduce inventories—in the same way that department stores "dump" goods by holding sales to reduce inventories.

Most anti-dumping arguments are standard protectionist fare—specifically, variations of the unfair competition arguments for protection. The standard argument against dumping is that the American economy is injured as a result of losing employment and income to unfairly priced imports. This argument fails to answer two basic questions that are central to its validity. First, what is the line that divides unfair dumping and vigorous price competition in export markets, and who is to decide what's fair? Secondly, what is so harmful to the economy about a form of price discrimination that benefits consumers in the United States?

There is one reasonable case that can be made for anti-dumping actions. Even though foreign firms may dump goods with no other purpose than reducing inventories by lowering price, this can create temporary disruptions for American producers who compete with the imports for sales. Anti-dumping penalties reduce the ability of the foreign seller to do this and reduce the disruptions of employment in import-competing industries in the United States. There is a cost, of course. American consumers won't be able to take advantage of temporary bargains offered by importers.

Routine anti-dumping complaints by import-competing industries, however, stem from basically protectionist motives. If the anti-dumping actions are successful, exporters will be hesitant to offer lower prices for the goods they ship to the United States. Even if anti-dumping suits aren't successful, however, they can create a negative public image of the imported goods as harmful of American economic welfare and can be relatively effective means of harassing foreign exporters and domestic importers from cutting prices on imports.

Trade Policy and International Politics

International trade, trade policy, and international politics have been intertwined for centuries. In some cases, trade policies are enacted to bring pressure and hardship on politically hostile regimes, such as the United States embargo on trade with Cuba since the late 1950s. In other cases, trade policies are used to protest policies of other governments and to bring pressure on these governments to alter policies—for example, the Arab embargo on oil exports to the United States in 1973 and the United States trade sanctions against Rhodesia to protest racial and human rights policies.

The relationship between trade policy and international political relationships is a vast subject. Without getting into the merits of protesting another country's government, human rights policies, etc., through trade policy, the important economic consequence is that these actions generally impose costs on the country imposing the sanctions as well as the sanctioned country. Imposing an export embargo reduces aggregate demand, aggregate output, and employment in the country that imposes the embargo. Barring imports from a sanctioned country reduces the gains from trade for the country imposing the sanctions by reducing the availability of lower-priced imports—as for example, the Rhodesian sanctions eliminated United States imports of chrome from Rhodesia.

The Tokyo Round and Future Trade Policy

In April, 1979, 99 countries signed a multilateral trade agreement that culminated the Tokyo Round of Multilateral Trade Negotiations. The agreement sets the rules for foreign trade policy for at least the next decade, and perhaps for the remainder of the twentieth century. Despite growing protectionist sentiments in many of the industrialized countries, the new trade agreement sets rules that would liberalize trade considerably over a period of years.

Tariffs are to be reduced by an average of one-third in the next eight to ten years. Some "sensitive" industries—such as the steel industry in the United States—would be given the most time over which tariffs would be cut.

Lowering tariffs is a step toward freer trade, but not as important as restricting the use of nontariff barriers. In recent years, nontariff barriers to free trade—subsidizing exports, subsidizing domestic producers to exclude imports, product safety requirements designed to exclude foreign products, import quotas, "orderly marketing arrangements" that reduce imports, barring foreign bidders from government procurement contracts, etc.—have become increasingly important as methods of restricting trade. The 1979 agreement sets specific limits on the use of nontariff restrictions as well as lowering tariffs. This is the first trade agreement that has restricted nontariff barriers.

How Free Foreign Trade?

If free trade or more restrictions on trade were good for everybody, or at least made nobody worse off, there would be no controversy over trade policy. However, controversies persist because greater restriction of trade or greater liberalization of trade would make some members of the community better off, others worse off, and affect the efficiency of world production.

On the grounds of efficiency alone, the case for free trade is compelling. All trade restrictions—regardless of their professed objectives —involve some loss of efficiency. If trade restrictions were lifted everywhere in the world, the long-run trend would be toward greater efficiency of utilization of the world's resources.

Adjusting to Freer Trade

Even the strongest advocates of free trade have to recognize that lowering trade barriers won't be good for everybody, and that the liberalization of trade restrictions will create economic problems for industries that face increased competition from imports. The industries that face stiffer import competition may have to cut back on production and employment, creating obvious problems for workers employed in these industries and for the communities in which these industries are large employers. At the same time, however, lower trade barriers internationally will increase world demand for the products of industries that enjoy a comparative advantage and had been excluded from world markets by import restrictions in other countries. If resources are mobile, higher demand in the expanding export industries will attract workers from the declining import-competing industries. Of course, the reallocation of resources can't be done overnight or without costs. If trade barriers were eliminated abruptly, and no additional measures were taken to aid affected industries and communities, the long-run gains from trade may be overshadowed by short-run disruptions and costs.

This does not mean that protection and the inefficiency and costs that result from protection have to be continued indefinitely to avoid the short-run costs of liberalization of trade. It does suggest that liberalization of trade restrictions should lower barriers over a period of time to minimize the short-run disruptive effects on protected industries. It also suggests that assistance should be provided to compensate workers and communities affected adversely by imports and to facilitate the reallocation of resources to the expanding export industries.

Trade policy and legislation in the United States since the 1960s has provided assistance for industries and communities who bear economic hardships as a result of liberalization of trade. Adjustment assistance has been in the forms of retraining and relocation programs for workers and public works programs for adversely affected communities. Over the years, the requirements for adjustment assistance have been liberalized, and the assistance is more accessible now than it has been in the past.

It's impossible to compensate individuals and communities fully for the costs of adjusting to economic changes that result from liberalized trade. Communities are disrupted, and many communities lose a vital part of their population as young workers are retrained and leave the community for employment elsewhere. Community ties, friendships, and family relationships may be disrupted. Individuals leave familiar communities to take advantage of employment opportunities in unfamiliar cities and different industries. However, the only way to avoid these psychological costs would be to continue protection indefinitely, in which case society bears the costs of inefficiency, higher costs and prices, and loss of employment opportunities in exporting industries.

Close-up

"On Sudden Changes in the Channels of Trade"

Trade policy was a central issue—perhaps *the* central issue—in the development of classical economics. Adam Smith's *Wealth of Nations* is an eloquent critique of eighteenth-century British mercantilism. The issue that prodded David Ricardo to formulate the backbone of classical economics in his *Principles of Political Economy and Taxation* was the protection of British landowners by the *Corn Laws*, a tariff against imports of low-priced foreign wheat.

Ricardo was unswerving in his opposition to the Corn Laws and other forms of protection, but conceded that there would be short-run disruptions if trade barriers were eliminated abruptly. In fact, he devoted a chapter of his *Principles* to this problem—On Sudden Changes in the Channels of Trade. With uncharacteristic clarity, Ricardo recognized the need for temporary measures to minimize the disruption from liberalizing trade.

> Notwithstanding, then, that it would be more productive of wealth to the country, at whatever the sacrifice of capital it might be done, to allow the importation of cheap corn [wheat], it would, perhaps, be advisable to charge it with a duty for a few years.[1]

Of those who advocated permanent protection for domestic wheat producers, however, Ricardo remained critical.

> They do not see that the end of all commerce is to increase production, and that, by increasing production, though you may occasion partial loss, you increase the general happiness.

A more recent example of the short-term costs of "sudden changes in the channels of trade" can be seen by leaping from England in the 1820s to Greece in 1979. Greece should become a member of the European Economic Community (or *Common Market*) on January 1, 1981. This will increase import competition for some Greek industries and will expand the export opportunities for others. Some industries are attempting to minimize the short-term costs of chang-

---

1. David Ricardo, *Principles of Political Economy and Taxation,* Third Edition. London: 1821, Chapter 19.

ing trade relationships with the Common Market countries by preparing for it rather than adjusting to it after it comes.

Greek appliance producers are preparing for import competition from the more efficient producers in the Common Market by undertaking a major drive to increase efficiency: laying off workers, consolidating operations, closing down plants, and other measures. The consensus in Greece is that employment in many manufacturing industries will decline with entry into the Common Market. However, in other industries—textiles, for example—firms will enjoy a wider export market in Europe, and employment in these industries will increase as a result of Common Market membership.[2]

2. Facts on the Greek appliance industry are from Philip Revzin, "Greek Companies Try to Shape Up to Enter the Common Market in '81," *Wall Street Journal*, May 18, 1979, p. 1.

The Future of of Free Trade

It seems likely that the long-term trend will be toward freer international trade rather than more trade restrictions. Growing world population, rising expectations, and a growing realization that the planet's resources are finite make efficiency considerations increasingly important. This strengthens the case for international specialization and trade. However, in the short run, this will require efforts to minimize the costs of trade liberalization through retraining and even relocation.

It may be tempting, recognizing the limitations of monetary and fiscal policies, to look to the international sector to control domestic unemployment and inflation. This can be a dangerous course, however, and would probably create more domestic economic problems than it would solve.

Summary

1. Import restrictions generally raise the price of imports to consumers, reduce international efficiency, and reduce the gains from trade. They benefit the protected sectors of the economy.
2. The most common arguments for import restrictions are to protect domestic wages, promote full employment, and allow fair competition. Most are only partially correct and contain serious flaws. National security and infant industry arguments for import restrictions may be valid but must be examined closely.
3. Export subsidies try to increase exports by making them cheaper in international markets. The benefits go largely to the subsidized industries, and the costs of the subsidy are borne by the community.
4. Export restrictions may reduce excess demand and dampen cost-push inflationary pressures, but their effectiveness depends on many variables.
5. The persistent trade policy problems for the 1980s and beyond will be the high prices of oil imports, dumping, export subsidies, and moving toward a world with lower trade barriers.

6. Liberalization of world trade will improve efficiency in the utilization of the world's resources, but won't be beneficial to everybody, particularly in the short run. Some of the short-run disruptions and costs of liberalized trade can be reduced by assistance to industries, communities, and individuals who are injured economically as a result of lower trade barriers.

Concepts for Review

mercantilism	fair competition	cartel
tariff	infant industry	dumping
import quota	export subsidy	Tokyo Round

Questions

1. Textile workers, textile firms, and congressional representatives from textile producing states have protested imports of textiles from such countries as Hong Kong, Singapore, Korea, and Taiwan. The general complaint is that U.S. workers can't compete with the cheap foreign labor, and that textile imports contribute to domestic unemployment.
   a. To what extent is this a valid argument?
   b. Would a tariff on textile imports reduce domestic unemployment?
   c. Would you expect U.S. farmers to join in the demand for tariffs on textile imports?

2. "Self-sufficiency in energy" and "independence from foreign oil producers" were frequently stated as policy goals by the Nixon, Ford, and Carter administrations.
   a. What kinds of policies would achieve these objectives? What would be the costs and the benefits of these policies? Who would realize the benefits, and who would bear the costs?
   b. How many (if any) of the arguments for import restrictions would apply to restriction of oil imports?
   c. How would policies to ensure energy independence affect the domestic economic goals of full employment and stable prices?

3. Suppose that you are the first witness before a congressional committee to testify against a proposed program of import restrictions and export subsidies to reduce unemployment. You have been preceded by a number of witnesses testifying in favor of the proposal—union leaders, automobile producers, textile firms, the city of Detroit, etc. Construct your economic argument against the proposed program. You should point out the economic, and political consequences of the program, as well as the value judgments involved.

4. "Free trade is a joke and a myth. . . The answer is fair trade, do unto others as they do unto us—barrier for barrier—closed door for closed door." (George Meany, President AFL-CIO, December, 1977).
   a. How would you interpret the term *fair trade*?
   b. What are the implications of Mr. Meany's proposal for trade policy, for efficiency in production, for consumers, for import-competing industries, and for industries dependent on exports? Would Mr. Meany's proposed trade policy be good for the economy?

5. *Trigger prices* have been established on imports by the Treasury Department, based on the cost of production in the country that

produces the good most efficiently, plus costs of transportation. If prices of an imported good fall below its trigger price, importers are charged the difference between the import price and the trigger price.

a. What practice is the trigger price designed to discourage?

b. What are the implications of trigger prices for import-competing producers and domestic consumers?

6. "The way to achieve full employment is to promote our exports in world markets while restricting the imports that take jobs away from our workers." (Congressman I. M. Phogbound, Whig, Vermont). Evaluate the merits of this strategy for trade policy.

Problems

1. Suppose that America produces two goods, steel (S) and wheat (W). With no trade, America produces on its production-possibilities curve where $MRT = 2S/1W$, and the prices of wheat in America without trade are $50 per ton of wheat and $100 per ton of steel. In international markets, the price of wheat is $80 per ton and the price of steel is $80 per ton.

a. Would America benefit from trading at world prices? What should America export and what should she import? What would be the nature of the gains from trade?

b. Would everybody in America benefit from trade? Who would benefit and who would be hurt by free trade?

c. American steel producers argue that a $20 per ton tariff on steel is needed to protect American producers from unfair import competition. Would America benefit from trading if such a tariff were imposed? What happens to the gains from trade? What other consequences might follow the imposition of the tariff?

d. Evaluate the desirability of the tariff from the points of view of American steelworkers, wheat farmers, steel stockholders, manufacturers of fabricated steel products, and consumers.

2. Foreign governments are often accused of unfair competition by subsidizing exports to allow exporters to sell at lower prices in world markets.

a. Why would a foreign government subsidize exports?

b. How effective would export subsidies be in maintaining high levels of aggregate demand, output, and employment in the exporting country? Explain analytically.

PART SEVEN

The Economic Future

In his October 1979 speech before the General Assembly of the United Nations, Cuban Premier Fidel Castro called for a "new economic order," a redistribution of the world's wealth from the richer countries to the poorer ones. The demand for fundamental changes in the economic relationships among nations is a growing one which no responsible person can ignore. In this final section of the text, we will explore the economic outlook for the future.

We begin with the issue of **economic growth**. Much of this nation's success has stemmed from its ability to enlarge the economic "pie" faster than the increase in the number of eaters. Today, however, many people are asking some fundamental questions about the desirability of further economic growth. Have the costs begun to outweigh the benefits? Can environmental concerns be reconciled with sustained growth? Can and should growth continue? Answers to such questions depend ultimately on value judgments, but close study of the issues involved can help make your own judgments informed ones.

The second chapter of the section focuses on the problem of **world poverty**. With thousands of people the world over starving to death every day, and *billions* more barely subsisting, the problem is not one that can be easily solved. Combatting poverty through **economic development** will impose major costs on all nations, rich and poor alike, but failure to pay those costs could lead eventually to world catastrophe.

20

Economic Growth: Boon or Bane?

Preview: Living standards in the industrialized countries have changed more in the two centuries since the beginning of the industrial revolution than they had in the previous millennia since the dawn of human civilization. At the same time, the current populations of societies untouched by industrialization and growth enjoy living standards similar to those of their distant ancestors. Do the past benefits of economic growth mean that we can rely on economic growth to raise living standards and solve economic problems in the future? In this chapter, we'll explore some of the basic concepts necessary to approach intelligently the brewing controversy over economic growth.

What Is Economic Growth?

In popular terminology, economic growth means changes in GNP. All changes in GNP do not constitute economic growth in the sense that economists use the term, however. Increases in GNP during a recovery from an economic recession are quite different from those which occur as a result of expanding productive capacity.

- **Economic growth** refers to changes over time in a country's potential or full-employment GNP.

Output and Capacity

Suppose that goods are classified as consumer goods (C) and capital goods (K). The economy's production possibilities curve (PPC), labeled K^*C^* in Figure 1, defines its capacity to produce consumer and capital goods. Any combination on the PPC represents full employment of capacity, and any combination inside the PPC indicates underemployment of capacity.

Given the prices of consumer goods (P_c) and capital goods (P_k), any combination of goods will generate a GNP (Y) of

Figure 1 Growth and Production Possibilities

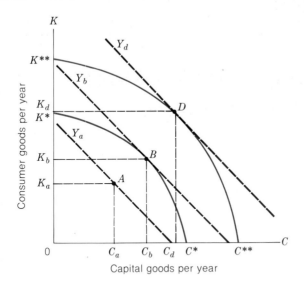

$$Y = P_cC + P_kK. \tag{1}$$

In Figure 1, combination A, with C_a units of consumer goods and K_a units of capital goods per year, yields a GNP of $Y_a = P_cC_a + P_kK_a$. Other outputs that yield the same GNP lie on the line Y_a in Figure 1. Y_a does not employ the economy's capacity fully, since combinations on the PPC lie outside Y_a.

The maximum GNP that can be produced at the given prices in Figure 1 is $Y_b = P_cC_b + P_kK_b$. Increasing GNP from Y_a to Y_b represents a rise in real GNP, but there is no change in capacity or potential GNP. This change in real GNP represents *increased utilization of capacity*, and not economic growth.

To increase GNP beyond Y_b, capacity would have to expand. Suppose that an expansion of capacity moves the PPC to $K^{**}C^{**}$, and GNP increases to $Y_d = P_cC_d + P_kK_d$. This represents an increase in the country's potential GNP at the given prices, or economic growth.

Changes in Potential and Real GNP

Distinguishing a change in productive capacity from an increased utilization of capacity is easy in the simplified example above, but actually measuring growth of potential GNP empirically is not so easy. One common measure of economic growth in the U.S. is the growth of the *estimated potential* GNP. The President's Council of Economic Advisors (CEA) estimates the U.S. potential GNP as the GNP that would be reached with a measured unemployment rate of 5.1 percent of the labor force.

Since the CEA defines *full employment* as a measured rate of 5.1 percent of the labor force, potential GNP is in fact an estimate of the country's *full-employment GNP*. Increases in the estimated potential GNP due to higher labor productivity, growth of the labor force, etc., approximate changes in capacity and economic growth.

The most common year-to-year indicators of economic growth are changes in *real GNP* and changes in *per capita real GNP*. These are more meaningful indicators of growth than changes in nominal GNP or nominal GNP per capita. For example, the nominal GNP of the United States increased by about 5 percent between 1969 and 1970 (from $930.3 billion to $977.1 billion). In constant prices, however, real GNP fell by about 0.4 percent (from $752.6 billion to $722.5 billion).

Since economic growth is promoted as a means of raising living standards, changes in per capita real GNP are important indicators of growth. If GNP rises more slowly than the rate of population growth, per capita output of goods and services and living standards will decline over time—even though real GNP is rising.

Annual changes in real GNP and per capita real GNP do not measure economic growth alone. Generally, they reflect a mixture of expansion of capacity and increased utilization of capacity.

Sources of Growth

A number of important variables determine capacity and potential GNP. These *sources of growth*, however, also define *limits* on economic growth.

Quantity and Quality of Resources

Expansion of the resource base and improvements in the quality of resources represented a major source of economic growth in the United States and in the industrialized economies of Europe through the end of the 19th century. As the American frontier pushed westward, new industrial and agricultural resources were added to the economy's resource base, and in many instances the quality of the new resources was superior to that of existing resources.

Scarcity of labor throughout the 19th century led to liberal immigration policies, which expanded productive capacity by increasing the labor force. At the same time, the new imperialism gave industrialized nations both the means (by providing an expanded base of resources) and the motive (by providing a growing market for the growing output of goods) to expand productive capacity.

As long as resources could be increased by expanding frontiers or tapping external sources, scarcities of resources were not very obvious. *Unlimited* was a term used well into the 20th century to describe supplies of vital resources. As external sources were developed and frontiers closed, however, the scarcity of resources became increasingly apparent.

Wasting resources—such as oil, metallic ores, and coal—cannot be replenished as they are used up. It takes nature millions of years to make coal, iron ore, and oil. Once the reserves of wasting resources are known and developed, sustaining growth depends heavily on improved utilization and more thorough extraction. The current energy crisis is a long-term problem that has increased awareness of the scarcity of resources to the point that some people predict that growth and even production will eventually grind to a halt as resources are depleted. However, the quantity and quality of resources are not the only sources of economic growth.

Technology

Technological change comes from new scientific discoveries that can be applied to production and from the discovery of new applications of existing knowledge to production. Technological change makes it possible to produce greater outputs from given resource inputs and has been the major source of economic growth in the industrialized countries since the early 20th century.

Although many people have a nearly unlimited faith in the ability of technology to sustain economic growth, in truth even this seeming "sure-cure" is not without its problems. First, modern agricultural and industrial technology is relatively *energy intensive*, using relatively large amounts of energy per unit of output. The replacement of human, animal, wind, and water power with machines powered by electricity, coal, gas, and oil is one of the dominant themes in the evolution of modern technology. Unless future technological changes are energy saving, however, there will be a race between energy-intensive technology and diminishing reserves of energy resources.

- To sustain economic growth, technological change must expand productive capacity more rapidly than the depletion of basic inputs contracts it.

The technological changes most likely to sustain growth in a world of finite resources are those that reduce the drain on fossil fuel reserves without imposing prohibitive environmental and social costs. New technologies that would produce a larger share of energy needs from the wind, water, and sun would reduce the depletion of resources.

Second, most technological changes that increase capacity also impose costs on the community. The costs and benefits of nuclear generation of electric power provide a good case in point. Nuclear power plants reduce the drain on fossil fuels to produce electric power. At the same time, however, they impose substantial costs on the community in the forms of the risk of accidents or environmental damage and the costs of safe and effective disposal of wastes.

Investment and Capital Formation

Expansion of the capital stock expands capacity, so investment and capital formation are important sources of economic growth.

- The greater the current level of investment, the greater will be the future growth of capacity and output.

Of course, investment requires saving, and increasing current investment for future growth thus requires reductions in current levels of consumption. If voluntary saving is insufficient to generate desired levels of investment and growth, it may be necessary to restrict consumption and force saving. The problems of generating sufficient saving and investment are most difficult in countries where current incomes and living standards are very low—as in the Soviet Union in the 1930s and in many underdeveloped countries today.

Education and Human Capital

The stock of productive skills and abilities—or the stock of *human capital*—is a determinant of capacity and potential GNP. A well educated and trained labor force will be more productive and adaptable than an illiterate and unskilled labor force of the same size.

Education and training programs that improve the quality and productivity of the labor force represent investments in human capital, and they can be an important source of economic growth. Like other types of investment and capital formation, investments in human capital require current costs to generate future growth.

Close-up

Resources, Productivity, and U.S. Economic Growth

Growth of capacity and output requires increasing inputs of productive resources or increasing the productivity of resources. Increasing resource inputs by 10 percent with no change in productivity of resources will cause a 10 percent rise in aggregate output. However, if the productivity of resources doubles—for example, due to a technological change—output will rise by 20 percent if resource inputs increase by 10 percent. As our resource base has become fully developed, increasing resource inputs have made a decreasing contribution to economic growth, while the importance of rising productivity has become increasingly important. The table below tells the story clearly.

Future economic growth will depend even more heavily on productivity than has past economic growth. A generation of steadily declining birth rates and the depletion of critical natural resources—oil and fossil fuels in particular—mean that future economic growth will depend more and more heavily on our ability to increase the output per unit of resource input. This would indicate a rising priority for research and development in such areas as energy-efficient production methods and equipment, development of energy sources that don't depend heavily on fossil fuels, more efficient forms of economic organization, and of course raising educational and training levels of the labor force.

Contributions of factor inputs and productivity to the growth of net national product, 1840–1960

Contributions of	1840–1960	1840–1900	1900–1960
Panel 1: Average Annual Rates of Growth			
(1) Labor force	1.52%	1.88%	1.12%
(2) Land supply	.21	.38	.08
(3) Capital stock	.81	1.03	.60
(4) Productivity	1.02	.69	1.32
(5) Totals (growth of NNP)	3.56%	3.98%	3.12%
Panel 2: Percentage Distributions			
(1) Labor force	42.7%	47.2%	34.8%
(2) Land supply	5.9	9.6	2.5
(3) Capital stock	22.8	25.9	18.6
(4) Productivity	28.6	17.3	44.1
(5) Totals	100.0%	100.0%	100.0%

Source: Table 2.12, p. 39, in "The Pace and Pattern of American Economic Growth," from *American Economic Growth*, by Lance E. Davis, et al. Copyright © 1972 by Harper & Row Publishers, Inc. Reprinted by permission of the publisher.

Growth and Welfare

Advocates of economic growth from Adam Smith to the present have argued that growth is essential to improve the economic welfare of the community. However, the impact of economic growth on welfare depends on both the benefits *and* the costs of growth. If the benefits and costs are unevenly distributed among members of the community, moreover, value judgements are implicit in conclusions that growth is good or bad.

Growth and Living Standards

If *everybody* is to have a larger piece of pie than he or she now has, a larger pie obviously is required. This simple fact illustrates an important point concerning growth and living standards: if everybody is to have more goods and services, capacity and output must grow.

However, the *possibility* of raising everybody's standard of living through economic growth does not mean that growth necessarily *will* raise living standards for everybody. The effect of growth on living standards depends on the types of goods that account for the growth, and the distribution of the growing output among members of the community.

If real GNP is growing due to rising output of heavy industrial equipment and military hardware, for example, the living standards of the current population may not improve at all. It is also quite possible that the segments of the community that benefit most from growth are those with relatively high incomes and living standards. Those without the necessary education, training, and employable skills may benefit relatively little—or even be worse off.

Growth, Employment, and Inflation

The relatively high unemployment rates in the U.S. in the mid 1970s have been due in part to the fact that aggregate demand and real GNP have not grown fast enough to employ a growing labor force. The labor force has been growing largely as a result of greater labor force participation by women and others who generally had low participation rates in the past.

With unemployed capacity, basically Keynesian fiscal policies and discretionary monetary policies may stimulate aggregate demand and raise real GNP and employment. However, eventually, increasing aggregate demand to employ a growing labor force requires expansion of capacity.

Growth, the Environment, and Social Costs

One of the most dramatic costs of economic growth is environmental damage. A growth-at-any-cost strategy could involve massive environmental destruction due to such things as strip mining of coal and oil-bearing shale, proliferation of nuclear power plants, greater use of chemical fertilizers and pesticides, etc.

Many environmental pressure groups tend to emphasize a number of intangible environmental costs of growth—such as loss of wildlife, aesthetic damage, and blight. These *are* important costs of growth, but in addition *the environment is a resource*. Massive destruction of the environment to foster growth in the immediate future may be self-defeating over the long haul if environmental damage reduces the potential to expand production.

Some of the means of increasing capacity and output increase the risk of physical harm to consumers of the products. Steroids, for example, made it possible to increase meat output by speeding weight gain in cattle. Insecticides, herbicides, and chemical fertilizers contributed to growing output of many field crops. Research has shown, however, that residues of some steroids, insecticides, herbicides, and other agricultural chemicals remain in food products and are related to cancer.

Simply consuming a growing output of goods also imposes environmental and social costs. The growth of automobile production and the increasing numbers of cars on the road has had a devastating effect on the quality of the air—especially in areas with heavy automobile use. Consuming more goods creates more garbage and waste as well. Growing communities often find themselves hard pressed to dispose of their wastes. Traffic jams, air pollution, litter, and garbage are just as much the products of economic growth as are higher levels of output and consumption. The unpleasant or harmful externalities of growth reduce the community's benefits from the increased output.

Distribution of Benefits and Costs

Finding the proper balance of costs and benefits of growth is complicated by the fact that these costs and benefits are unevenly distributed. Many of those who bear heavy costs of growth get few of the benefits, and many of those that benefit bear relatively little cost.

Technological change, for example, makes some products and occupations obsolete. Unless the workers who are displaced by technological change move into jobs created by growth, they will bear costs but gain no benefits from growth. Workers already employed in industries and occupations that experience rising demand due to economic growth will bear relatively little cost to enjoy the benefits of growth.

If future growth comes at the expense of current consumption and living standards, some of those who bear the current costs may not live long enough to enjoy future benefits proportional to their costs. Future generations will enjoy the benefits of growth, but none of the current costs. During the ruthless Stalinist growth strategy in the U.S.S.R. between 1928 and 1953, an entire generation bore enormous costs and reaped meager benefits from Soviet economic growth.

The uneven incidence of costs and benefits of growth requires value judgments to be made concerning the importance of the benefits to the winners and the costs to the losers from any particular growth strategy. It may also require taxation of the winners to compensate the losers for their costs.

Can Growth Continue?

A surprising number of great economists have predicted that economic growth must and will come to an end eventually. The *stationary state* (an economy with no growth) is a common theme in classical economics. Karl Marx predicted that certain features of capitalist development would bring growth to a halt. In the 20th century, similar conclusions have been reached by *secular stagnationists* and others that growth can't continue indefinitely. On the other side of the issue are those who argue that expansion of knowledge, technological change, and expanding investment opportunities will sustain growth in the future.

The Classical Prognosis: The Stationary State

The classical prediction of an eventual stationary state with no economic growth rests on three basic propositions.

1. Investment is the source of growth of employment and real output.

2. Profits are the source of investment.

3. With fixed land and given technology, goods will be produced under diminishing returns.

To understand the classical argument, suppose that real GNP (Y) is divided between wages (W) and profits (π), or

$$Y = W + \pi. \tag{2}$$

Real GNP and wages vary directly with the level of employment (N). With diminishing returns, GNP will increase at a diminishing rate as employment increases, as in Figure 2. Assuming a constant wage rate, wages rise at a constant rate with increases in employment, as shown in Figure 2.

Aggregate profits (π) are the difference between GNP and wages, or

$$\pi = Y - W. \tag{3}$$

In an initial period (1), employment is N_1, GNP is Y_1, and wages are N_1. Profits in period 1 are $\pi_1 = Y_1 - W_1$, or the vertical distance between W_1 and Y_1.

The profits in period 1 provide investment funds to expand the capital stock and raise the level of employment to N_2 in period 2. In period 2, GNP rises to Y_2, and profits are: π_2. Profits in period 2 allow employment and income to rise to N_3 and Y_3 in period 3, and so on.

Figure 2 The Classical Stationary State

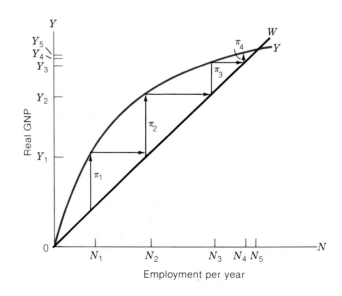

Diminishing returns eventually cause profits to fall as employment and GNP increase, as shown in Figure 2. Eventually, profits reach zero—at N_5 and Y_5 in Figure 2—and the stationary state is reached.

- In the classical **stationary state,** profits are zero, and there is no economic growth.

The Marxian Prognosis: "Fetters on Production"

Karl Marx, the great critic of capitalist society and bourgeois political economy, also predicted falling profits and an end to growth in capitalist economies. His analysis and its implications are different from those of his classical contemporaries, however. Marx argued that the drive of capitalists for profit (surplus value) encourages them to mechanize production to make labor more productive. A firm that mechanizes and thus lowers its costs, according to Marx, has an advantage over its competitors. It can sell at a lower price and earn more profit as sales increase, or it can maintain the same price as its competitors and earn greater profit as a result of lower costs. The advantage is temporary, however, and it hides another important effect of mechanization in the Marxian analysis.

Marx held that the source of surplus value is labor, not machinery. When competition drives all firms in the industry to mechanize, product prices fall and firms have lower profits than they had before mechanization. The lower rate of profit drives the weakest firms out of the market.

In the Marxian scenario, competition and the drive for profit force the remaining firms to continue mechanization of production, but competition and falling prices continue to drive the rate of profit down. As the process continues, more and more firms are driven out, and production is increasingly concentrated in a diminishing number of large firms. The monopoly power of the large firms, according to Marx, leads them to restrict output, to place "fetters on production" that cause growth to stop.

Meanwhile, displaced workers and capitalists swell the ranks of the working class (proletariat) and create a growing industrial reserve army of unemployed workers which keeps wages down. The working class becomes increasingly miserable in the Marxian model and doesn't provide expanding demand for the goods that could be produced with the growing capacity created by mechanization.

In short, according to Marx, capitalism can generate great expansion of capacity, but not a corresponding growth of demand and output. Eventually, the fetters on production by monopoly firms and the class warfare between the capitalists and the proletariat lead not only to an end to growth, but a revolutionary overthrow of the capitalist system by the proletariat.

Technological Change

The classical prediction of a stationary state assumes constant technology. Technological change may offset the effects of diminishing returns on output, profits, and growth.

Figure 3 Technological Change and the Stationary State

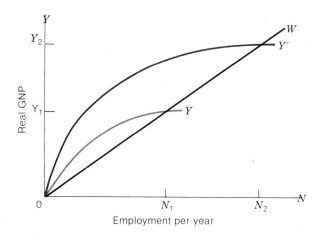

In Figure 3, the lower curve (Y) shows the relationship between employment (N) and real GNP with given technology. With no technological change, the stationary state would be reached at N_1 and Y_1 where profits are zero. Technological change shifts the curve upward to Y', and results in a higher level of output and GNP with any given level of employment. This allows employment and output to grow to N_2 and Y_2 before the stationary state is reached. Further technological changes would continue to postpone the stationary state.

The ability of technological change to sustain growth is not unlimited. Some basic resources are permanently fixed and become depleted. Also, the costs of technological change and growth may become prohibitive.

Investment Opportunities

In the 1930s, Professor Alvin Hansen of Harvard formulated a theory of **secular stagnation** that predicted declining economic growth as investment opportunities decline and the rate of return on investment falls. With no new investment opportunities, increasing investment lowers the marginal efficiency of investment (MEI), as shown by the movement along the MEI curve in Figure 4 as investment increases from I per year to I' per year. Eventually, as the rate of return on investment falls, there would be inadequate inducement to save and invest enough to sustain growth.

With the secular stagnationists' prediction of declining investment opportunities, the decline in the rate of return or the marginal efficiency of investment would be more rapid than with stable investment opportunities. In Figure 4, diminishing investment opportunities shift the marginal efficiency of investment curve to the left to MEI'. At any level of investment, the rate of return is lower on MEI' than on MEI.

Figure 4 Secular Stagnation and Investment

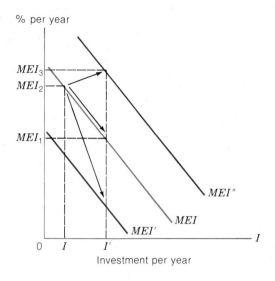

More optimistic contemporary assessments of our potential to sustain growth assert that ours is a world of expanding investment opportunities that will keep returns on investment high enough to sustain future economic growth. Expanding investment opportunities would shift the *MEI* curve to the right, as in Figure 4, and this could slow or even reverse the decline in the inducement to invest as investment increased over time. For example, if investment increased from I to I', and investment opportunities expanded at the same time and shifted *MEI* to *MEI"*, the rate of return is higher and the inducement to invest greater at I' than at I.

Changing problems and changing technology may indeed create new investment opportunities over time. The development of efficient solar energy equipment, the revitalization and reconstruction of the cities, and the improvement of public transportation technology and facilities are a few examples of areas in which investment opportunities are likely to expand in the future.

Must Growth Continue?

Simplistic growth-is-good arguments associate less or no economic growth with the end of the world. Economic growth is not an unmixed blessing, however, and a decline in growth or even zero economic growth need not be disastrous. Consider the following statement by the great classical economist, John Stuart Mill.

> I cannot . . . regard the stationary state . . . with the unaffected aversion so generally manifested by political economists of the old school. I am inclined

to believe that it would be, on the whole, a very considerable improvement on our present condition. I confess I am not charmed with the ideal of life held out by those who think that the normal state of human beings is struggling to get on. . . .[1]

The Pressure to Continue Growth

Increasing population is one source of the pressure to continue economic growth in the future. With a growing population, capacity and output must grow to keep per capita income from falling. If population growth slows down, as it has in most industrialized countries, it will exert diminishing pressure to continue economic growth.

Rising wants and expectations also exert pressure on a society to continue economic growth. As more and more people expect a rising material standard of living, economic growth becomes the only means of fulfilling the rising expectations of the poor without disappointing the rising expectations of middle and upper income groups through redistribution of wealth and income.

Declining rates of population growth, dampening material wants and expectations, and redistribution to alleviate poverty would weaken the pressures to sustain economic growth. Obviously, such goals are easier said than achieved. Population growth exerts overwhelming pressures for growth in the underdeveloped countries. Dampening expectations and changing traditional notions of the "good life" cannot be accomplished easily or quickly.

Zero Economic Growth (ZEG)

Recognition that the earth's resources are finite and that some basic resources may be depleted in a century or so at current rates of use has spawned a *zero economic growth* (ZEG) school of thought. The ZEG arguments are based on two basic propositions.

- The world's resources are insufficient to continue economic growth indefinitely, so economic growth must ultimately cease.

- The costs—pollution, environmental destruction, etc.— outweigh the benefits from continued economic growth.

The ZEG school differs from others who predict an end to economic growth in their advocacy of policies that would speed that end. Advocates of growth paint a grim picture of a world without economic growth, but the spokespersons for ZEG argue that the benefits of future growth are overwhelmed by the prohibitive costs of policies to continue economic growth and of the growth itself.

Stable real GNP with a growing population would reduce per capita GNP and eventually would depress standards of living. Therefore, the ZEG strategy is tied closely to a *zero population growth* (ZPG) strategy. If

---

1. John Stuart Mill, *Principles of Political Economy*, Book IV, Chapter VI.

population and real GNP are stable, per capita real GNP will be stable also.

ZEG and ZPG have been criticized because together they would doom the poor to poverty indefinitely. However, ZEG strategies generally include redistribution of wealth and income to raise the incomes of the poor in a world without economic growth. With adequate redistribution, ZEG need not mean abandoning efforts to alleviate poverty.

Close-up

"Bigger and Better" vs. "Small Is Beautiful"

Of the critics of modern industrial society and economic growth, none has been more critical or put forth more sweeping arguments than the late E. F. Schumacher. In a controversial book, *Small Is Beautiful*, Schumacher castigated modern industrial societies and modern economics for placing too much emphasis on the benefits from more material goods (*materialism*) and the economic advantages of large-scale production as an engine of economic progress (*giantism*). Schumacher argued that materialism and giantism lead people and society to ignore or understate the importance of social costs associated with modern industrial growth, and that they promoted forms of economic organization that are dehumanizing and lead to concentration of economic and political power.

Schumacher called for a technological revolution to improve the quality of life, but one quite different from the technological changes we have seen in our lifetimes.

> We need methods and equipment which are
> —cheap enough so that they are accessible to virtually everyone;
> —suitable for small-scale application; and
> —compatible with man's need for creativity.[1]

One of the most dramatic effects of modern technology has been the ability to produce ever greater outputs of goods and services. What if Schumacher's small-scale enterprises weren't so adept at producing as large factories are? Would this mean a decline in living standards? Schumacher admitted the possibility of producing smaller aggregate outputs of goods and services in his ideal society, but also argued that this wouldn't necessarily mean a decline in the qualitative standard of living, since the small producing units would be less destructive of the environment and would produce fewer pollutants.

Would people be happy in Schumacher's small and beautiful world with fewer goods and services than they enjoy as a result of modern large-scale production? For Schumacher, the key is to reduce the greed and envy that the modern economy has instilled in us, and to reduce and simplify our material wants—in other words, change "economic man." This is a tall order indeed!

1. E. F. Schumacher, *Small Is Beautiful: A Study of Economics as if People Mattered.* London: Blond & Briggs, 1973, pp. 29–30.

Dealing with Poverty: Growth or Redistribution?

The gap between haves and have-nots is a complex problem with serious political and social implications. Poverty tends to breed political and social instability, and these problems tend to grow with the income gap between the rich and the poor. There are two basic ways to attack poverty—by stimulating the growth of capacity and output and by redistributing wealth and income.

Growth makes it *possible* to raise the living standards of the poor and the nonpoor at the same time. However, economic growth also imposes substantial costs on the community. Many of the sources of past economic growth—such as abundant and cheap energy and unexploited sources of raw materials—are becoming exhausted. As the potential for continued growth dwindles or the costs of growth become prohibitive, dealing with poverty may require redistribution of wealth and income, and this is not accomplished easily.

Individuals tend to view their economic welfare in terms of their incomes and material standards of living. Few people would be willing to reduce their incomes voluntarily to raise the incomes and welfare of others. Contemporary hostility to welfare programs at home and foreign aid abroad, and the growing political chasm between the industrialized countries and the Third World are previews of the conflicts that might emerge with attempts to deal with poverty by large-scale redistribution of wealth and income domestically or internationally.

No effective solution to such long-range problems as poverty, unemployment, inflation, and environmental decay is easy or costless—with or without growth. Hard choices and informed and intelligent value judgements must be made on the basis of theory, facts, and political and social realities.

Summary

1. **Economic growth** refers to changes in potential, or full-employment, real GNP. Economic growth requires expansion of productive capacity.
2. Economic growth depends on increased quantity and quality of resources, technological change, and investment. These variables also impose limits on growth.
3. The effect of economic growth on economic welfare depends on the costs and benefits of growth and on the distribution of these costs and benefits among members of the community.
4. Sustaining growth in the future depends on the strength of forces that promote growth and the strength of the forces that retard growth.
5. The **zero economic growth** strategy advocates an end to policies that try to sustain growth because they see the costs of future growth as prohibitive. They also advocate a goal of **zero population growth** and redistribution to alleviate poverty in the absence of growth.

economic growth   secular stagnation   zero economic growth (ZEG)
potential GNP   fetters on production   zero population growth (ZPG)
stationary state

Questions

1. In the 1976 presidential campaign, Jimmy Carter based many of his economic policy statements and predictions on restoring and sustaining the "rates of economic growth" that had been experienced under Presidents Kennedy and Johnson between 1960 and 1968. Gerald Ford consistently referred to sustaining the trend of economic growth between 1975 and 1976.
   a. Were Carter and Ford using the term *economic growth* accurately? Explain.
   b. Do you think the candidates were realistic in predicting a continuation of the growth rate of real GNP between real GNP between 1975 and 1976 or a restoration and continuation of the rate of growth of real GNP between 1960 and 1968 in the future? Explain.

2. What are the implications of each of the following projections for the need for economic growth, the desirability of economic growth, and the potential for economic growth?
   a. a long-term decline in the birth rate and rate of population growth;
   b. aging of the population (rising average age);
   c. growing participation of women in the labor force;
   d. rising expectations of income and material standard of living.

3. Until the 1970s, most economists viewed economic growth as a major economic objective for society. During the 1970s, however, arguments critical of economic growth and even advocating a slowing or halt to economic growth became more common.

   Can you explain why historically we have tended to see economic growth as an important goal, and why attitudes have been changing on the merits of economic growth in recent years?

5. Economic growth strategies range from *growth-at-any-cost* to *zero economic growth*.
   a. Of these two extremes, which do you feel is the more appropriate? What considerations went into your answer?
   b. Combined growth strategies combine aspects of the two extremes. What do you think is the appropriate combination of strategies for growth? What considerations went into this answer?
   c. Would your answers to parts a and b be the same if you were much poorer and less educated than you are?
   d. Would your answer to parts a and b be the same if you were much richer than you are?

21

Economic Development and World Poverty

Preview: For the inhabitants of many of the world's underdeveloped countries, the problem of poverty is a matter of biological survival. The depth of poverty in these countries exerts overwhelming pressure for economic growth and development in the face of great obstacles and costs. **Economic development** involves more than the costs of growth discussed in the last chapter. Often, it requires the transformation of the entire society—economic organization and institutions, the family structure, traditional agriculture, the labor force, and the basic social and political structure. Economic analysis provides some insight into the nature of the problems and the general strategies for development, but the analysis of development is not as neat and concise as it is for most economic problems. The problems of development are complex, the solutions are seldom obvious and always difficult and painful, and most effective solutions face formidable political and social obstacles.

It is hard for most Americans to grasp the problem of world poverty because our own economic situation is so atypical.

Table 1 shows national income per capita in the various regions of the world. Per capita income in North America is high compared to Europe, let alone compared to the underdeveloped regions of Asia, Africa, and Latin America. Table 2 indicates the income gap between the underdeveloped countries and the industrialized developed countries.

The dollar figures in Tables 1 and 2 are not a completely accurate picture of the income gap between the developed and underdeveloped countries. All national income data are estimates, and there is a wide margin of error in the data for the underdeveloped countries. A great deal of production in the underdeveloped countries is by households for their own use and does not enter the national income figures.

Table 1 Per Capita Income by Region

Region	Per Capita National Income, 1975
North America	$7150
Oceania	5190
Europe	4950
Middle East	1560
Caribbean & Latin America	1160
East & Southeast Asia	590
Africa	430

Source: *United Nations Statistical Yearbook, 1977.*

Likewise the value of goods that are bartered is not included in the national income figures. The official exchange rates that express national income in the underdeveloped countries in dollars are very imperfect measures of the purchasing power of incomes earned in the underdeveloped countries. In short, the poverty in the underdeveloped countries probably is not as serious as implied by trying to live on $500 or so per year. However, the income gap is too wide to be explained away as a statistical quirk.

Table 2 Per Capita Income, Developed vs. Developing Economies

	Per Capita National Income		
	1960	1970	1975
All Market Economies	$ 520	$ 920	$1850
Developed Market Economies	1360	2670	5470
Developing Market Economies	130	210	470
Developed Economies as % of Developing Economies	1046%	1271%	1064%

Source: *United Nations Statistical Yearbook, 1972, 1977.*

The Roots of World Poverty

There is no single cause of poverty in the Third World, but a number of interrelated causes. The explanations of poverty in one country won't necessarily apply to all underdeveloped countries. The following discussion of the roots of poverty in the Third World, then, simply points out some of the general causes of poverty in these countries.

Resources

Productive capacity depends in part on the quantity and quality of resources available. Many underdeveloped countries have only modest resources, while in others the underdevelopment or underutilization of resources is a more important problem than the size of the resource base.

The quality of resources is also a problem. In many countries, the general health and literacy of the labor force is very low, so labor is not very productive. Many of the underdeveloped countries try to squeeze subsistence food output from deserts and tropical rain forests.

The underdeveloped countries have not been able to follow the pattern of countries such as Britain and Japan that developed with relatively limited resources through specialization and trade. In the first place, the resources in most underdeveloped countries are much more modest than those of Britain or Japan. The potential for specialization and trade has not been developed because many of the underdeveloped countries have been dominated economically and politically by the industrialized countries. The underdeveloped countries are developing late, and competition from the industrialized countries in export markets—and even in their domestic markets—has retarded the development of *infant industries.*

Imperialism

Imperialism—the economic and political domination of one country by another—is a frequently cited historical cause of poverty in the underdeveloped countries. The industrialized countries dominated the underdeveloped countries through the early twentieth century. Most of the European countries were colonial powers and controlled the economic development of their colonies. The economic and political interests of the United States dominated the economies of Latin America, and the United States held some "territories" (such as Hawaii, Alaska, and the Philippines) that were in fact colonies.

The imperialism of the nineteenth century was motivated by the economic interests of the industrialized countries—expanding markets for the growing output of the industrialized countries, controlling new sources of raw materials and cheap labor, and earning high rates of return on capital. The economic interests of the underdeveloped countries were seldom an important consideration.

Imperialism affected the economic development of the underdeveloped countries adversely in several ways—wastefully exploiting resources and gearing economic development to the needs of the industrialized countries. The struggles for independence following World War II retarded economic development further with great social, political, and economic disruptions. Economic problems in many of the underdeveloped countries worsened with independence, as many colonial powers simply abandoned their former colonies and left them with no effective means of ensuring sufficient political and social stability to promote economic development.

Imperialism is an emotionally charged issue, but it is not the only historical root of poverty in the underdeveloped countries. In fact, it had some positive effects on economic development that are frequently overlooked in anti-imperialist arguments. Imperialism broke down many traditional barriers to economic progress in many underdeveloped countries. Health and sanitation programs instituted by the colonial powers reduced the toll of chronic diseases and epidemics and contributed to a healthier and more productive labor force. Transportation, communication, and other types of social overhead investment promoted future development in many countries. Subsequent evidence has shown that many colonial and imperialistic ventures were unprofitable, thus contradicting the blanket explanation of the income gap in terms of the industrialized countries' earning great profits at the expense of the poorer countries in the past.

Tradition and Institutions

Traditional cultural values and institutions in many underdeveloped nations have hampered economic progress. Some traditional religions are geared more to an afterlife than to material progress and living standards, or hold basic views that hinder economic development. In many traditional societies, a person's estate is divided equally among all his heirs when he dies. This has fragmented landholdings into uneconomically small units. Extended families have hindered the mobility of labor out of the traditional agricultural sector. In some societies, traditional signs of wealth and status (such as gold jewelry or gold hoards) add nothing to productive capacity or output.

Traditional educational systems have been geared more to educating a few people for traditionally high-status positions (such as lawyers in Latin America) rather than preparing them for positions that contribute more to economic progress. Also, the traditional educational systems have not been effective in raising the level of literacy of the general population.

Population

The U.N. estimates that world population is about four billion people, and growing about two percent per year. This means that about eighty million people are added to the world's population every year, or an additional population equal to that of the United States every three years. At this rate, population grows about 219,000 persons per day, or enough additional population to populate a city about the size of Baltimore every four days.

Malthus: Population and Misery. In 1798, a British economist and clergyman named Thomas Robert Malthus wrote *An Essay on the Principle of Population*. Malthus predicted a losing race between food production and the growth of population. He asserted that the world's population grows geometrically, doubling each generation—1, 2, 4, 8, 16, . . . —while food production grows arithmetically—1, 2, 3, 4, 5, ... Thus, he predicted that food output would lag behind population growth, and that the amount of food per capita would fall over time.

According to Malthus, the growth of population would be checked only by what he called **positive checks** or **preventive checks**. Positive checks included misery, vice, war, pestilence, and famine. Preventive checks were late marriage and sexual abstinence.

Was Malthus Right? Technological change and investment in the United States and other industrialized countries have raised the output from any given labor input, offsetting the effect of population growth on living standards. As long as the effect of technological change on food output is stronger than the effect of diminishing returns with additional labor, food output may grow as fast as or faster than population.

In the underdeveloped countries, however, Malthus' grim forecast is being borne out. As shown in Table 3, birth rates, death rates, and population growth are higher in the underdeveloped countries than in the developed countries. Farming methods are primitive, farms tend to be too small to produce efficiently and are getting smaller as land is divided among a growing agricultural population. Subsistence living standards make saving for investment and technological change virtually impossible.

Table 3 Population Growth: Developed vs. Developing Countries

Country	Birth Rate per 1,000	Death Rate per 1,000	National Increase in Population per 1,000	Per Capita National Income
Kenya	48.7	16.0	32.7	$ 209
El Salvador	39.9	7.9	32.0	503
Iran	45.3	15.6	29.7	1,529
Brazil	37.1	8.8	28.3	1,239
Egypt	37.7	12.3	25.4	263
Guinea	46.6	22.9	23.7	—
India	34.5	14.4	20.1	136
Gambia	43.3	24.1	19.2	—
USSR	18.5	9.5	9.2	—
Canada	15.8	7.2	8.2	7,340
United States	14.7	8.9	5.8	6,995
Italy	14.0	9.7	4.3	2,758
France	13.6	10.5	3.1	5,860
Sweden	11.9	11.0	0.9	8,044
West Germany	9.8	11.9	−2.1	6,451

Source: *United Nations Statistical Yearbook, 1977.*

Reducing Population Growth. The faster population grows, obviously, the faster real GNP must grow to achieve a given increase in per capita income. If population grows at three percent per year, for example, real GNP would have to grow at about six percent per year to double per capita GNP in a generation (about 25 years). If population remained stable, per capita GNP would double in a generation with a three percent annual rate of growth of real GNP.

If reducing population growth is an obvious course of action, it is not easy to accomplish. Societies tend to go through several stages of transition from high birth and death rates to low birth and death rates, as sketched in Figure 1. Note that time itself is not the independent variable in Figure 1. Birth and death rates are determined by other variables that tend to vary over time—such as per capita income, education, preferences, and expected living standards.

The high death rates in Stage I are caused by epidemics, high infant mortality, local famines, and in some cases tribal warfare. Birth rates are high in this stage because people tend to have many children, expecting only a few to survive to adulthood. In agrarian societies, children are a source of farm labor and an economic asset. With extended families, a large family is a form of "social security" for the parents' old age. Traditional attitudes tend to keep birth rates high. Traditional views may see children as a sign of masculinity (*machismo*), as a source of good luck, or as gifts from heaven. With high birth and death rates, the rate of population growth (birth rate − death rate) tends to be low in Stage I, as shown by the distance between *BR* and *DR* in Figure 1.

In Stage II, the typical pattern is falling death rates and stable or rising birth rates, and an increasing rate of population growth. Note the distance between *BR* and *DR* in Stage II in Figure 1.

Reducing death rates and preserving human life are acceptable in virtually every religion and social ethic. Also, it is fairly inexpensive

Figure 1   Changes in Birth and Death Rates over Time

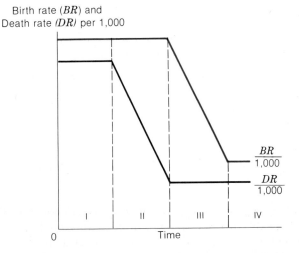

to improve public health and sanitation, and to reduce the toll of epidemic diseases by such means as mass vaccinations and spraying swamps. Economic and institutional changes also may reduce death rates in Stage II. Improvements in transportation tend to reduce the death toll from localized famines by shipping food to stricken areas or moving people out of them. Stable central governments and improvements in communication and transportation tend to reduce the toll of tribal or civil warfare.

Usually, the declining death rate is not matched by a concurrent decline in the birth rate in Stage II. Traditional views on children and family size do not change very rapidly. Preventing births is not as universally acceptable as the prevention of death and preservation of life. Many traditional religions, most notably Catholicism, are vehemently opposed to contraception and especially to abortion. Some Third World nationalists view birth-control programs in the underdeveloped countries as a subtle form of genocide by white European societies.

If the underdeveloped countries develop economically, their birth rates probably will fall—as shown by Stage III in Figure 1. In Stage III, birth rates fall as a result of education (general literacy and educational programs on the importance of population limitation), improved birth-control techniques, and the desire of people to substitute higher living standards for more children. In Stage IV—where most of the economically developed countries seem to be—population grows slowly with low birth and death rates.

Limiting population growth by simply allowing death rates to remain high in the underdeveloped countries would be unacceptable on normative grounds to many people (including the author). Limiting population with high death rates is the wrong course economically as well. High death rates in underdeveloped countries reflect high infant and child mortality. Many people live long enough to consume, but not long enough to produce anything. Many who survive chronic diseases and epidemics, which also contribute to high death rates, are left disabled and not very productive.

World Poverty: Is There a Way Out?

Economic development is a complex and difficult problem that does not lend itself to simple solutions. Economics can identify the general directions that effective development policies must take, but no set of specific policies is appropriate for all underdeveloped countries. Also, economics does not deal with the critical social and political barriers to development very well.

Investment and Capital Formation

The pressures to generate economic growth to raise living standards in the underdeveloped countries is overwhelming. Higher rates of growth, of course, require investment and capital formation to expand

Figure 2 Investment and Third World Production Possibilities

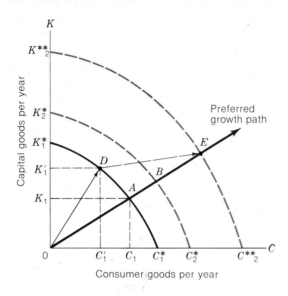

the economy's capacity to produce. The higher the rate of investment now, the greater the growth of capacity and income in the future.

To illustrate, assume that the economy's capacity to produce consumer goods (C) and capital goods (K) is given, and represented by the production possibilities curve $K^*_1 C^*_1$ in Figure 2. Suppose that the community prefers combination A on the production possibilities curve to maintain living standards. Producing K_1 capital goods per year in period 1 expands productive capacity to $K^*_2 C^*_2$ in period 2 and allows the community to move to point B on its **preferred growth path**. By increasing investment and the output of capital goods to K_1' in period 1 and moving to point D, however, it would be possible to expand capacity in period 2 to $K^{**}_2 C^{**}_2$, and to move further along the growth path to point E.

With a fully employed capacity, however, producing more capital goods to generate greater growth requires a reduction of consumer goods output—from C_1 to C_1' in Figure 2. This means even lower standards for the current generation and bodes ill for economic, social, and political stability.

Social Overhead　A substantial portion of the investment undertaken to promote economic development should be **social overhead investments**, that lay the foundations necessary for improved utilization of resources and economic growth. In most underdeveloped countries, the success of programs to foster growth will require such social overhead projects as improved and expanded transportation and communication facilities, as well as the development of power networks and other public utilities.

Most of the social overhead investment will have to come from the public sector, since social overhead projects typically pay low returns (if any) in the distant future and would not attract private capital. Also, many forms of social overhead are public goods that cannot be provided by private markets.

Land Reform and Agricultural Investment

In most underdeveloped countries, improving agricultural efficiency and output should receive the highest priority. Unless the agricultural sector can produce a surplus above the subsistence needs of the agricultural population, it will be impossible to feed a nonagricultural labor force. Also, without a surplus above subsistence, saving and investment are impossible.

Land reform and reorganization of agricultural production may make agricultural production more efficient. One possibility is to form **producer cooperatives** in which individuals would pool their land and other resources to form an economically efficient size of farm and share in the proceeds from the farm. Raising agricultural productivity also generally involves increased agricultural investment and thus conflicts with the goal of increasing investment in industry.

In many agrarian areas of underdeveloped countries, there is actually *surplus labor* where population growth and diminishing returns have led to *zero returns* from labor—i.e., the additional labor doesn't add any output. Moving surplus labor from the land would make it possible to produce other goods with the labor without reducing agricultural production. However, unless the demand for nonagricultural labor increases, there will not be any place to employ the surplus labor that leaves agriculture. One possibility is to use the surplus labor to produce the social overhead projects that would promote development.

Some of the bloodiest conflicts and worst social and economic disasters in modern times have resulted from attempts to restructure traditional agriculture. In peasant societies, traditional attachments to the land make it difficult to get people to leave the land, sell it, or share control of it with others.

Foreign Assistance

Foreign economic assistance may make the development process somewhat less painful. In Figure 3, suppose that the economy must produce C_1 consumer goods per year to maintain living standards, and a capital goods output of K_2 to produce sufficient economic growth. The production-possibilities curve makes it impossible to produce C_1 and K_2 with the country's own resources.

Figure 3 Foreign Assistance and Third World Production Possibilities

With foreign assistance—grants or loans from foreign governments, loans from private lenders in foreign countries, or direct foreign investment in the underdeveloped countries—the country in Figure 3 could purchase the capital goods it needs in excess of K_1 while maintaining living standards. It could use the assistance to purchase the consumer goods it needs in excess of C_2 while increasing capital goods output to K_2. However, foreign assistance may not be the solution of many countries' development problems.

Countries with critical resources (such as oil) or strategic international positions tend to be most successful in getting assistance from the industrialized countries. Other underdeveloped countries tend to be ignored. Even the countries that can get assistance often get it with strings attached. Underdeveloped countries that depend heavily on aid from the major military powers risk involvement in international political and military conflicts. Private investment by foreigners may give them excessive economic and political influence. These are not attractive possibilities for the underdeveloped countries that have had long and unhappy relationships with the industrialized countries in the past.

Finally, foreign assistance may not be dependable. In the United States, the favorite targets for cutting government spending are "welfare" programs at home and foreign aid abroad. In 1978, U.S. nonmilitary assistance to underdeveloped countries was about $5.2 billion —less than one-fourth of one percent of GNP, and only about one percent of federal budget expenditures. Nonetheless, opinion surveys consistently show that popular opinion views our foreign aid as excessive.

Specialization and Trade

Many underdeveloped countries have the potential to realize gains from specialization and trade which could aid in their development efforts. In many instances, however, this potential has not been realized because of competition from the industrialized countries.

Infant industry tariffs may allow underdeveloped countries to develop their potential to realize gains from specialization in the long run. There is, however, a potential danger in specialization if it involves heavy dependence on a single export. With dependence on a single export, a country's development efforts rest on fluctuations in world markets for that export.

Economic and Political Control

Most effective development policies are likely to be painful and unpopular. Leaving development to individual decisions and market forces will probably be unsuccessful, at least in the early stages of development. Economic development generally requires stringent economic and political controls.

One of the most important uses of economic control is to force the saving required for investment and capital formation. In Japan, for example, forced saving was accomplished largely through taxes. In the Soviet Union, forced saving was accomplished by such drastic efforts as collectivization of agriculture, central control over wages and prices, central control over consumer goods production, and taxes that squeezed the consumer and the agricultural sector.

Direct controls may be required to ensure that the sectors of the economy that contribute most to future growth and development receive adequate resources. This generally means allocating more resources to heavy industry and capital goods production.

While economic development may alleviate the social and political tensions in the underdeveloped countries once it has been achieved, development *efforts* tend to increase tensions and strengthen the pressure for tight political controls. The prospects for economic development with anything resembling political democracy and decentralized market decision making are remote.

Although economic controls may be necessary to promote development, there are some potential problems (in addition to all of the normative questions involved in political and economic dictatorship). First of all, effective control requires considerable technical expertise and communication facilities that many underdeveloped countries lack. Also, controls can be self-defeating if they are imposed too long. As the economy grows and develops, the task of central control becomes more complex and maintaining central controls may be a source of inefficiency. Maintaining controls may dampen incentive to the point that the development effort will be stalled.

Limiting Population Growth

The necessity of limiting population growth and the difficulties of accomplishing lower rates of population growth in the underdeveloped countries have been discussed earlier in this chapter. It is mentioned again as part of the development strategy because the effectiveness of all of the other development efforts can easily be eaten up by rapid population growth.

Economic Development: Mission Impossible?

The prospects for substantial and quick improvements in living standards in the underdeveloped countries are bleak. In the absence of dramatic technological revolutions in production and massive redistribution of income from the rich countries to the poor, it will be impossible in the near future to raise living standards in the underdeveloped countries to a level that would be minimally acceptable in most industrialized countries. The continuing population growth in the underdeveloped countries casts a further pall on their prospects for higher living standards.

It is tempting to ignore difficult problems in the hope that somebody else will take care of them or that they will simply go away. The problems of the underdeveloped nations won't go away on their own, however, and could produce disastrous consequences for all nations. Desperation, political and social instability, and tensions in the Third World may lead the poor countries to strain their resources to fight each other, and in an increasingly interdependent world with nuclear overkill lurking in the background, this is hardly a cause for complacency.

Summary

1. The income gap between the developed and underdeveloped countries is wide and has widened since the 1960s.
2. The causes of poverty in the underdeveloped countries include resources, history, institutions, traditions that are hostile to economic progress, and population growth.
3. No single set of policies will work in all underdeveloped countries, but effective development strategies must increase investment and capital formation, restructure agriculture to make it more productive, move resources from agriculture to industry, and take advantage (where possible) of potential gains from specialization and trade.
4. Effective economic development efforts generally require political and economic controls.
5. All other development efforts may fail without adequate reductions in the rate of population growth.

1. To what extent do you think each of the following explains the income gap between the rich and poor countries?
   a. Climate and geography
   b. Natural selection
   c. Traditional attitudes toward wealth
   d. Different attitudes toward work
   e. Imperialistic exploitation
   f. Resources .
   g. History and traditions
   h. Population pressure
2. How can you explain the ability of persons in the underdeveloped countries to live on incomes of $200 per year?
3. Suppose that you have the responsibility of designing a program to limit population growth in the underdeveloped countries. What would be the main features of your program? How would you convince the people of the desirability of limiting population growth? How successful do you think you'd be?
4. You have been asked to testify before Congress on the value of U.S. assistance to developing countries, and to international agencies that assist developing countries.
   a. How would you justify expenditures on foreign assistance, in light of the benefits from the funds if they were allocated to domestic programs?
   b. What would be the main features of an assistance program that would have a reasonably good chance of success in promoting economic development?
5. Outline and explain the main features of a program for economic development of an underdeveloped country. You should justify the elements of your program analytically, and in terms of their practical reality. Also, you should identify the potential problems that your program would be likely to face.

Index